CHALLENGING *CHRISTIAN ZIONISM*

Theology, Politics and the Israel–Palestine Conflict

edited by
NAIM ATEEK, CEDAR DUAYBIS AND MAURINE TOBIN

MELISENDE
LONDON

Challenging Christian Zionism
First published 2005 by Melisende
39 Chelmsford Road
London E18 2PW
England

ISBN 1 901764 42 7

Printed and bound by Cromwell Press, Trowbridge, Wiltshire

CONTENTS

Political Effects of Christian Zionism

Christian Responses to Christian Zionism

Jewish And Muslim Perspectives

Nonviolent Strategies for Peace

Religion as a Humanizing Factor

Biblical Reflections

The Archbishop of Canterbury's Message and Responses

EDITORS' NOTE

Sabeel is grateful to the many contributors to this book, all of whom presented their papers to the Conference in English even though they represent a wide array of nationalities. Included are not only Palestinians and Israelis but also internationals from across the world.

We have sought to preserve their distinctive voices and styles in this volume, maintaining differing conventions of spelling and syntax as well as of bibliographic form. Wherever footnote information was incomplete, we have presented all the data available to us.

While *Sabeel* received many of the papers in written form, several were transcribed from recordings of the Conference proceedings. We apologize to the authors for any errors that result from inaccurate transcription as well as for errors resulting from the editing process.

The content and point of view of each paper is that of the author and does not necessarily reflect the position of *Sabeel* Liberation Theology Center.

ACKNOWLEDGEMENTS

Sabeel Ecumenical Palestinian Liberation Theology Center wishes to express its deepest gratitude to all those who contributed to the success and fruitfulness of the Fifth International Conference held at The Notre Dame Center, Jerusalem, immediately after Easter 14-18 April 2004. Special thanks go to Janet Lahr Lewis, the co-ordinator of the conference, and to the many local and international volunteers who assisted us in planning and preparation, as well as to those who assisted us during the conference. We also are grateful to Catherine Nichols for organizing the pre- and post-conference trips and to those who assisted her. As always, we would not have been able to accomplish these endeavors without the faithful generosity of time and effort of many people. Our deep gratitude goes to the Board and Staff of *Sabeel* for their input and support before, during and after the conference.

A special word of thanks to Sabeel staff and volunteers who helped in transcribing many of the conference papers: Rhonda Amer, Nevart Ateek, Megan Castellan, Jeremy Clines, Martha Ferguson and Louise Gleich. We would also like to thank Joyce Wilson and Janet Lahr Lewis who assisted in the editing and proof-reading process.

We would like to acknowledge the willingness of Melisende to publish this book with its challenge and controversy. Our special thanks to Leonard Harrow and Alan Ball for their help in completing this project.

Last but not least, we would like to acknowledge with much gratitude all of our friends who generously contributed financially towards making the conference possible.

CONTRIBUTORS

The Revd Dr Naim Ateek is the Founder and Director of Sabeel Ecumenical Liberation Theology Center.

Professor Khalil 'Athamina is a professor of History at Bir Zeit University in the West Bank.

The Revd Dr Bishara Awad is the president of Bethlehem Bible College.

Dr Mubarak E Awad is the founder of Nonviolence International in Washington DC. and the Founder, President/CEO of National Youth Advocate Program Inc.

Phyllis Bennis is a Fellow at the Institute for Policy Studies in Washington D.C. She is also an author and is a co-chair of the U.S. Campaign to End Israeli Occupation.

Praful Bidwai is the former senior editor of The Times of India and a regular columnist for several newspapers in India. He is Co-founder of the Movement in India for Nuclear Disarmament (MIND) and author of several books.

The Rt. Revd Edmond L. Browning is the retired Presiding Bishop of the Episcopal Church in the USA and a long time advocate for justice and peace in the Holy Land.

Dr Gary Burge is a professor of New Testament at Wheaton College and graduate School in Chicago. He is the former president of Evangelicals for Middle East Understanding. He is also a published author.

The Revd Dr Elias Chacour is the Founder and the President of Mar Elias Educational Institution and Vice President of the executive committee of Sabeel.

The Revd Dr Peter Du Brul, SJ, is an American Jesuit, with a Ph.D. in Philosophy from the University of Lyon, France. He has been teaching Scripture, Philosophy, and Cultural Studies in Bethlehem for the past twenty-five years.

Professor Marc H Ellis is the Director of the Center for American and Jewish Studies at Baylor University, where he also teaches. He is the author of several books.

Alain Epp Weaver is currently country representative for the Mennonite Central Committee in the Occupied Palestinian Territories. Previously he served as project co-ordinator in the Gaza Strip. He is also a published author.

Gershom Gorenberg is an associate editor of *The Jerusalem Report* and senior correspondent of *The American Prospect*. He was the founder of the Israeli religious peace movement Netivot Shalom and is a published author.

The Revd Dr Göran Gunner is a Researcher with the Church of Sweden Research Department and Senior Lecturer at the Stockholm School of Theology.

Dr Jeff Halper is an anthropologist and the Director of the Israeli Committee Against House Demolitions (ICAHD). He is the author of several publications.

The Revd Dr Rafiq Khoury is a priest at the Latin Patriarchate in Jerusalem.

Jonathan Kuttab is a Palestinian lawyer and a Human Rights advocate. He is also on the Board of Sabeel.

Helen Lewis read English at Oxford and is English Adviser for Gwynned in North West Wales. She is married to John Butler, Anglican Chaplain to the University of Wales (Bangor), leader of many visits to Palestine.

The Revd Dr Michael Prior, C.M. (deceased) was a professor of the Bible and Theology at St. Mary's College, Strawberry Hill (University of Surrey, UK), and senior Research Fellow in Holy Land Studies.

The Revd Dr Mitri Raheb is currently Pastor of the Christmas Lutheran Church in Bethlehem, and Director of the International Center of Bethlehem. He is also a published author.

Professor Barbara Rossing is an ordained Pastor in the Evangelical Lutheran Church in America. She teaches New Testament at the Lutheran School of Theology in Chicago and holds a Ph.D. from Harvard University Divinity School

Rosemary Radford Ruether is the Carpenter Professor of Feminist Theology at the graduate Theological Union in Berkeley, California. She is the author or the editor of 38 books.

The Revd Dr Stephen Sizer is Vicar of Virginia Water, Surrey; Chairman of the International Bible Society UK; Vice Chairman of Highway Projects and Board Member of Friends of Sabeel UK.

Damu Smith is the director of the National Black Environmental Justice Network in Washington, D.C.

Dr Jenny Plane Te Paa is the Dean of Te Rau Kahikatea, an Anglican Theological College in Aotearoa, New Zealand. She is also Convener of the Global Anglican Peace and Justice Network, and Moderator of the World Council of Churches Working Group on Ecumenical Theological Education.

Dr Robert B Tobin holds a doctorate in Modern Irish History from Oxford and is currently studying at Westcott House, Cambridge, as a candidate for holy orders.

The Revd Dr Donald E Wagner is a Professor of Religion and Director of the Center for Middle Eastern Studies at North Park University, Chicago. He is also the author of several books.

The Most Revd and Rt Honorable Dr Rowan Williams is the 104th Archbishop of Canterbury. From 1986-1992, Dr Williams was a Professor of Theology at Oxford. He was enthroned as Bishop of Monmouth in 1992, Archbishop of Wales in 2000 and Archbishop of Canterbury in February 2003.

Jean Zaru is the presiding Clerk of the Friends (Quakers) in Ramallah and the vice-president of the Sabeel Executive Committee.

Zoughbi E. Zoughbi is the Director of Wi'am Conflict Resolution Center in Bethlehem and on the Board of Sabeel.

Dr Stephen Zunes is a Professor of Politics and Chair of the Peace and Justice Studies Program at the University of San Francisco, a Catholic Jesuit institution.

INTRODUCTION
CHALLENGING CHRISTIAN ZIONISM

Naim Ateek

In April 2004, *Sabeel* held its 5th international conference on the theme of Challenging Christian Zionism. Over 500 people representing more than 30 countries attended the conference at the Notre Dame Center in Jerusalem.

Sabeel's conference on Christian Zionism had been brewing for a number of years. Many of us were aware of the dangers of the teachings and beliefs of millions of western Christians around the world but we did not feel that sufficient scholarly research had been done to warrant a conference. By 2004, it was clear that a number of people, mostly evangelicals, had done enough important groundbreaking research to merit a public exposure of this "heresy".

But what are we talking about? Who are the Christian Zionists and what is Christian Zionism? Simply put, this is a term used to identify any Christian who, due to a particular understanding and interpretation of the Bible, supports the ingathering of all Jews to Israel and their claim to the whole land of Palestine and thereby denies Palestinian rights. In other words, such a person is a Christian who espouses the Zionist ideology, turns it into a theology and works diligently for its implementation.

The term Christian Zionism has arisen relatively recently. In fact, in its origin this concept had nothing to do with political Zionism. Surprisingly, such Christian religious thinking preceded the rise of Zionism at the end of the 19th century. Most people wrongly assume that the rise of Christian Zionism took place in the aftermath of the establishment of the state of Israel in 1948. They believe that as a result of anti-semitism and the holocaust, millions of western Christians identified with the Israeli state and the Jewish people. Such a view is not borne out by historical research. Christian Zionism, before it became known by this name, started as a religious phenomenon among certain Protestant and Evangelical circles, first in Britain and then in the United States, long before Jewish political Zionism came into existence. It was bred and nourished by a serious but literal reading of the Bible. In its inception, it had nothing to do with what Jews were thinking or doing. Sincere Evangelical Christians, on their own, were searching their Bibles for signs of the end of the world. They saw the pervasiveness of evil everywhere around them and they felt that nothing short of Christ's Return would remedy the infectious and malignant spread of sin and evil. They believed that the Bible contained all truth not only about the past but also about the present and the future. They only needed to apply themselves to serious and intelligent study, "wisely interpreting the word of truth". Since they believed that the Bible is inerrant in all of its parts, they felt free to pick and choose verses from various parts of the Bible and link them together in a way that produced a scheme and a chart for the End of Days. These Christians were fundamentalist in their approach to the Bible and in their endeavors to discover God's plan for history. Earlier schemes were continuously revised and refined or overhauled by new exegetes. Indeed, the Bible was used as a jigsaw puzzle with different pieces plucked from here and there, sometimes out of context, and placed together in order to give a composite picture of God's purpose for the End. Consequently, a road map for the Second Coming was fashioned with the number of variations depending on the person or the organization that produced it.

The central enigma revolved around one question: When will the Second Coming of Christ take place? Although Christ warned against any speculation regarding his return and the end of the world, these Biblical literalists were convinced that the Bible contained important clues that could help them discern the signs of the times. The Second Coming of Christ became the goal and the objective of their quest. One of the most important resources in this quest was the biblical prophetic material, and the central players were the Jewish people.

Since so much of the prophetic material in the Bible was written at a time in which Jews were living in exile, i.e. outside the land of Palestine, Evangelical Christians began to use these prophecies that predicted their return, not as having been fulfilled in their historical context several centuries before Christ under Persian rule, but as prophecies about to be fulfilled in their own times or in the near future. This was the central point of departure. Everything else hinged on it. They believed that in order to know the purposes of God in history, one needs to watch what is happening to the Jewish people, who are God's key players and occupy center stage in the scenario of the End. They concluded that Christ cannot physically return to earth unless the Jewish people are living in the land. Passages like Ezekiel 37 became foundational texts for the return of the Jewish people to the land. Such passages were conveniently taken out of their historical context and transposed to the 19th and 20th centuries. Around them, elaborate systems of belief were contrived and kept changing with the passage of time. Every time political and historical events rendered some aspects of their scheme untenable, modifications and revisions were readily introduced.

The real boost for Christian Zionism came in the second part of the 20th century after the establishment of the state of Israel in 1948. The immigration of hundreds of thousands of Jews from many countries of the world into Israel was, for most Evangelicals, the fulfillment of biblical prophecy and the first step towards the End of history. The real confirmation, however, came with the conquest by Israel of the West Bank, including East Jerusalem, in 1967. For these Christians, this was the beginning of the end. The Second Coming of Christ was believed to be near and Armageddon lay in sight. They were anxiously waiting for Jews in Israel to demolish the Muslim Dome of the Rock in order to build the third temple and thereby usher in the scenarios of the End.

Although some of the lectures in this book will make clear in greater detail the history, theology, and politics of Christian Zionism, I would like to lay down very briefly the reasons that led *Sabeel* to hold its conference in 2004.

1. As I have already indicated, one of the practical reasons for holding the conference then was the important research that had already been done in this field. Many of us were keenly aware of the biblical and theological problems and dangers inherent in Christian Zionism. We could detect the growing impact of this "Christian heresy" among many sincere yet misguided and misinformed western Christians but lacked sufficient research to address the issue. Once a body of research had been developed, the conference could include a number of Evangelicals who had researched and published in this field. Since the conference, more resources have been produced, including this book, in order to help people understand more thoroughly the latent dangers of this phenomenon.

2. To the chagrin of many of us Christians, the dangers of Christian Zionism have not been taken seriously by the mainline churches all over the world. To my knowledge, none of the major theological schools and denominational seminaries has been teaching any courses about it. It has been perceived largely as the view of fundamentalist groups of Christians who are simplistic in their biblical interpretation and theologically naïve and unsophisticated. They have been seen as fringe groups who reject the scholarly approach to the Bible and cling to literal interpretation, thus missing the essence of the biblical message. Then one day we woke up to discover that these supposedly fringe groups number millions of Christians and are spreading rapidly in various parts of the world. Therefore, there is a great need to help people understand who Christian Zionists are, what they believe, and how they impact the question of war and peace, especially in the Middle East today.

3. Many of us assumed that Christian Zionism exists in fundamentalist and Evangelical churches only. Upon closer observation, we discovered that in reality Christian Zionism has permeated Christians within mainline churches as well as among Catholics and the Orthodox in various levels and forms. It is an unconscious and superficial response to any Bible reading by people who have not had the benefit of theological education or have not studied the Bible carefully and so accept things uncritically simply because they are written in the Bible. This means that our problem is not only with extremist evangelicals; it is with many good hearted but ignorant Christians who need to be informed and educated.

4. Before the 1967 war, secular Zionism was the dominant and influential expression of Jewish political Zionism in Israel. After the war a gradual shift took place from secular to religious political Zionism. By 1977, the right wing coalition of political parties called Likud came to power with Menahem Begin as Prime Minister. Begin was able to forge closer links between the right wing government of Israel and the Christian Right in the United States. Most of the Christians who belong to these groups are considered Christian Zionists. This collusion between Jews and the Christian religious right served the two sides. Although Israel did not believe in their religious scenarios of the End, the close bond brought advantages to Israel. Christian Zionists provided important financial, political, and moral support to Israel. In fact, they were perceived as the best friends Israel had. They gave blind and uncritical support to Israel.

They did not question Israel's unjust policies towards the Palestinians. From their faith perspective, they believed that, in order to be faithful to God, they must stand with Israel at all times.

5. It is important to differentiate between Jewish and Christian Zionism in this regard. Whether we agree or disagree with it, the goal of Jewish Zionism has been to bring Jews from their diaspora into Israel so that they might find a safe haven and live in security and peace. Yet frankly speaking, the goal of Christian Zionism, according to their scenario of the End, is to bring the Jewish people to Israel in order to be annihilated or converted to the Christian Faith. They believe that this would fulfill God's purposes in history and usher in the Second Coming of Christ. The relationship between Jewish and Christian Zionists, therefore, reflects a tragic hypocrisy. Each is using the other for its own purposes. Perceived in this light, Christian Zionism is the worst anti-semitism one can imagine.

6. For a number of years, it has been clear that Christian Zionists are close to people of power in Washington D.C. Because they represent a sizable voting power, they wield great influence. When one combines their influence with that of the neo-conservatives and the pro-Israel lobby, AIPAC, their impact becomes formidable. In the political arena, they have been influencing American foreign policy in the Middle East, not for a just peace that takes into consideration the rights and well-being of both peoples—Israelis and Palestinians—but for whatever is in Israel's favor. In other words, they have sought to guarantee the continuation of Israel's domination and oppression of the Palestinian people.

7. Throughout the last 2000 years, the Christian Church has faced many theological heresies and controversies. Some of them were more damaging than others. Yet, the church survived with vitality and vigor. In the case of Christian Zionism, we are not up against an academic theological debate that goes on within theological schools or among scholars and bears no consequences on people's lives. We are confronted with certain false teachings based on the Bible that are a matter of life or death to fellow Christians in another part of the world. Christians living thousands of miles away engage in theological and biblical conjectures that affect the destiny of millions of people in the Middle East. This is being done in the name of God, not to better their lives but to lead millions of them to destruction.

8. As will become clearer in this book, Christian Zionists continue to

promote a violent theology of the End of history. They base this on selected passages from the Bible that are not in line with the authentic message and spirit of the Scriptures. Indeed, there are many passages in the Bible that describe war. But the biblical message is about peace, not war. Although there is much violence in some of the biblical writings, God's message for the world is about love, peace, and forgiveness and not about violence and terrorism. A theology of Armageddon with its emphasis on a violent end of the world and the massacre of millions of people does not harmonize with God's nature as revealed to us in Christ. It is, therefore, a false and untenable Christian theology of God that denies God's love for the world. That is why many Christians who oppose the theological fallacy of Christian Zionism insist that any Christian theology of the End must conform to an authentic theology of God in Christ. Any theology that promotes the massacre of millions of people cannot be of God. We must again emphasize the fact that it is a very dangerous theology because it does not take seriously God's love shown to us in the suffering, death, and resurrection of Christ.

9. The conference aimed at affirming a more authentic theology that lifts up the banner of justice and peace, a theology that calls people to act for truth and justice and to work for peace and reconciliation, a theology that resists empire and the forces of domination and calls people to a life of peace and service. Indeed, there is a great threat facing the people of Israel-Palestine. It is not, however, the threat of Palestinian terrorism. It is the threat that has its roots in the Israeli military occupation and oppression of over three million Palestinians. God cannot be pleased when the forces of empire deny God's children their basic God-given rights to life and freedom. Faithfulness to God forces us to act on behalf of our fellow human beings who are oppressed and dehumanized.

The book contains a number of papers that directly or indirectly relate to the topic of Christian Zionism. It is meant to inform and educate people. It is meant to help readers challenge their Christian Zionist neighbors with the truth and facts of what is happening in Palestine and how the Bible is being used as an instrument of oppression rather than as an instrument of liberation. This book is meant to challenge clergy to take the time to study the phenomenon of Christian Zionism and to address it through their preaching and teaching. It is also meant to challenge us all to double our endeavors in seeking and working for a just peace in Israel-Palestine.

God is not the God of Armageddon but the God of Golgotha. This is the God who continues to call us to a loving service of our fellow human beings. Ultimately, it is only by the grace of God and the toil of dedicated people throughout the world that we can address not only the heretical teachings of Christian Zionism but all the evils and myths that are preventing us from a just peace in Israel-Palestine where Palestinians and Israelis can live as neighbors in peace and security and share the land under God. We call on all people of faith to pray and work for the achievement of this goal.

Naim Ateek
Sabeel, Jerusalem
June 2005

THE HISTORICAL ROOTS OF CHRISTIAN ZIONISM FROM IRVING TO BALFOUR: CHRISTIAN ZIONISM IN THE UNITED KINGDOM (1820-1918)

Stephen Sizer

> Only one nation, Israel, stands between ... terrorist aggression and the complete decline of the United States as a democratic world power ... If Israel falls, the United States can no longer remain a democracy ... Arab money is being used to control and influence major U.S. Corporations, making it economically more and more difficult for the United States to stand against world terrorism.[1]

While many would not necessarily go as far as Mike Evans in his claims, it is nevertheless assumed by a large proportion of Christians in Britain and America that it is their biblical responsibility to support Israel. Dale Crowley, a Washington based religious broadcaster, however, describes this movement as the 'fastest growing cult in America':

> It's not composed of "crazies" so much as mainstream, middle to upper middle class Americans. They give millions of dollars each week—to the TV evangelists who expound the fundamentals of the cult. They read Hal Lindsey and Tim LaHaye. They have one goal: to facilitate God's hand to waft them up to heaven free from all the trouble, from where they will watch Armageddon and the destruction of planet earth.[2]

Christian Zionism is essentially Christian support for Zionism. Grace Halsell summarises the message of the Christian Zionist

---

1 Mike Evans, *Israel, America's Key to Survival*, (Plainfield, NJ: Haven Books), back page, p. xv.

2 Dale Crowley, 'Errors and Deceptions of Dispensational Teachings.' *Capital Hill Voice*, (1996-1997), cited in Halsell, *op. cit.*, p. 5. Grace Halsell herself defines Christian Zionism as a cult. See Halsell, *op. cit.*, p. 31.

in this way: "every act taken by Israel is orchestrated by God, and should be condoned, supported, and even praised by the rest of us."[3]

Estimates as to the size of the movement as a whole vary considerably. While critics like Crowley claim that "At least one out of every ten Americans is a devotee," advocates such as Robertson and Falwell claim the support of 100 million Americans with whom they communicate weekly.[4] Dale Crowley's own estimate is that there are between "25 to 30 million" pro-Israeli Christians in America, a number that is growing.[5] They are led by 80,000 fundamentalist pastors and their views disseminated by 1,000 Christian radio stations as well as 100 Christian TV stations.[6] Doug Kreiger lists over 250 pro-Israeli organisations founded in the 1980s alone.[7]

The National Unity Coalition for Israel, which brings together 200 different Jewish and Christian Zionist organisations including the International Christian Embassy, Christian Friends of Israel and Bridges for Peace, claims a support base of 40 million active members.[8] These organisations make up a broad coalition which is shaping not only the Christian Zionist agenda but also US foreign policy in the Middle East today. So where did Christian Zionism come from?

The British Roots of Christian Zionism

While the seeds of Christian Zionism lie within the Protestant Reformation, and several Puritan leaders spoke out in favour of the restoration of the Jews to Palestine, Christian Zionism as a movement can be dated precisely to the founding of the London Jews Society (LJS) in 1809. Lewis Way and the other early leaders were restorationists—committed to facilitating the return of the Jews to Palestine. This movement emerged out of a series of prophetic conferences held in

---

[3] Grace Halsell, "Israeli Extremists and Christian Fundamentalists: The Alliance", *Washington Report*, December (1988), p. 31.

[4] "Christians Call for a United Jerusalem", *New York Times*, 18 April (1997), http://www.cdn-friends-icej.ca/united.html

[5] Halsell, *Forcing*, *op. cit.*, p, 50.

[6] Halsell, *Forcing*, *op. cit.*, p, 50.

[7] Grace Halsell, *Prophecy and Politics*, (Westport, Connecticut, Lawrence Hill, 1986), p, 178.

[8] http://www.israelunitycoalition.com.

England from 1826. These conferences were precipitated by the traumatic events occurring across Europe and North America, including the American War of Independence (1775-1784), the French Revolution (1789-1793) and then the Napoleonic Wars (1809-1815).

In 1804, Louis Napoleon had been crowned Emperor of the Gauls in the reluctant presence of the Pope. In 1807, he plotted the division of Europe with the Czar of Russia and began a blockade of British sea trade with Europe. Two years later he arrested the Pope and annexed the Papal States. He then began the systematic destruction of the Roman Catholic Church in France, seizing its assets, executing priests and exiling the Pope from Rome. By 1815, Napoleon's armies had fought, invaded or subjugated most of Europe and the Middle East, including Italy, Austria, Germany, Poland, Russia, Palestine and Egypt.

Napoleon appointed his brothers as kings of Holland, Naples, Spain and Westphalia in what is today Germany. He even gave his own son the title "King of Rome". His plan was to create a United States of Europe, each state ruled by a compliant monarch, subject to himself as "supreme King of Kings and Sovereign of the Roman Empire".[9] Numerous preachers and commentators speculated on whether Napoleon was indeed the Antichrist.[10] Charles Finney, for example, predicted the imminent end of the world by 1838. In 1835, he speculated that "If the church will do all her duty, the Millennium may come in this country in three years."[11] Joseph Miller narrowed the return of Christ down to 21 March 1843, while Charles Russell more prudently predicted that Christ would set up his spiritual kingdom in the heavens in 1914.

This sectarian speculation came to be embraced by mainstream churches in Britain principally through the influence of two individuals— Edward Irving and J. N. Darby and those associated with a series of prophetic conferences held in England and then Ireland between 1826 and 1833.[12]

---

[9] G. H. Pember, *The Great Prophecies of the Centuries concerning Israel and the Gentiles*, (London, Hodder, 1902), pp. 236-241.

[10] J. N. Darby, 'Remarks on a tract circulated by the Irvingites', *Collected Writings,* edited by William Kelly (Kingston on Thames, Stow Hill Bible and Trust Depot, 1962), Doctrinal. IV, 15, p. 2; Andrew Drummond, *Edward Irving and His Circle* (London, James Clarke, n.d.), p. 132; Janet M. Hartley, 'Napoleon in Russia: Saviour or anti-Christ? *History Today,* 41 (1991); Richard Kyle, *The Last Days are Here Again*, (Grand Rapids, Michigan, Baker, 1998), p.71.

[11] Charles Finney, *Lectures on Revival*, (Cambridge, Harvard University Press, 1960), p306.

[12] Rowland A. Davenport, *Albury Apostles*, (London, Free Society, 1970).

On the first day of Advent in 1826, Henry Drummond (1786-1860), a city banker, politician, and High Sheriff of Surrey, England,[13] opened his home at Albury Park to a select group of some twenty invited guests to discuss matters concerning "the immediate fulfilment of prophecy".[14] Under the charismatic leadership of Edward Irving, topics included speculation on the fulfilment of biblical prophecy, premillennialism, the imminent return of the Jews to Palestine and the search for the lost tribes of Israel.

In 1826, Irving had been introduced to the views of Manuel Lacunza, a Spanish Jesuit, who, disaffected by the corruption of Rome, had written a book under the pseudonym of Juan Josafat Ben-Ezra, first published in Spanish in 1812.[15] Claiming to be the work of a converted Jew, the book was entitled, *The Coming of the Messiah in Glory and Majesty.* Irving was so excited by Lacunza's speculations about prophecy being fulfilled in their generation that he mastered Spanish in order to translate and publish the work in English.[16] Irving added a 194-page preface to the translation in which he presented, with great conviction, his own prophetic speculations about the end of the world, predicting the Last Days apostasy of Christendom, the restoration of the Jews to Palestine and the imminent return of Christ. The publication in English attracted widespread interest not least because of the association with Irving, who was becoming a very popular preacher in London.[17]

The Albury conferences continued in the early 1830s at Powerscourt in Ireland under the growing influence of John Nelson Darby. John Nelson Darby is regarded by many as the father of Dispensationalism

---

[13] Twelve elders called "angels" were appointed to pastor the congregation and administer the church in the expectation that the Lord would return to Albury in their life time. Consequently, as each elder eventually died they were not replaced until there were none to pastor the congregation.

[14] Edward Miller, *The History and Doctrines of Irvingism,* volume 1 (London, Kegan Paul, 1878), p. 36.

[15] Murray, *op. cit.*, p. 190. A four volume edition was published in English in 1816. See Flegg. *op. cit.*, p. 40.

[16] Dallimore, *op. cit.*, p. 62.

[17] Edward Irving, *The Coming of Messiah in Glory and Majesty*, by Juan Josafat Ben-Ezra a converted Jew, Translated from the Spanish, with a Preliminary Discourse, (London, L. B. Seeley & Sons, 1827), pp. 5-6. Irving's preliminary discourse was subsequently published separately and more widely than Lacunza's own work. See Flegg, *op. cit.*, p. 235, and fn 126 below.

and the most influential figure in the development of Christian Zionism.[18] He was a charismatic figure with a dominant personality. He was a persuasive speaker and zealous missionary for his dispensationalist beliefs. From 1862 onwards, Darby consequently spent more and more time in North America, making seven journeys in the next twenty years. During these visits, he came to have an increasing influence over evangelical leaders such as James H. Brookes, Dwight L. Moody, William Blackstone and C. I. Scofield. His ideas also helped shape the emerging evangelical Bible Schools and "Prophecy" conferences, which came to dominate both Evangelicalism and Fundamentalism in the United States between 1875 and 1920.[19]

Lord Shaftesbury and Restorationism

Zionism would probably have remained simply a religious ideal were it not for the intervention of a handful of influential aristocratic British Christian politicians who came to share the theological convictions of Darby and his colleagues and translated them into political reality. One in particular, Lord Shaftesbury (1801-1885) became convinced that the restoration of the Jews to Palestine was not only predicted in the Bible,[20] but also coincided with the strategic interests of the British Empire.[21] Other leading politicians who shared this perspective included Lord Palmerston, David Lloyd George and Lord Balfour. Ironically, this conviction was precipitated by the actions of Napoleon, in the spring of 1799.

During the Syrian campaign of Napoleon's Oriental expedition, in which he had sought to defeat the Ottoman rulers, cut off Britain from its empire, and recreate the empire of Alexander from France to India,[22] he became the first political leader to propose a sovereign Jewish State in Palestine:

---

[18] Donald E. Wagner, *Anxious for Armageddon,* (Waterloo, Ontario, Herald Press, 1995), pp. 81,88. This is disputed by Charles Ryrie who attempts to place the origin of Dispensationalism, some 150 years earlier, allegedly finding evidence in the writings of Pierre Poiret (1646-1719) and John Edwards (1639-1716) as well as Isaac Watts (1674-1748). See Charles Ryrie, *Dispensationalism,* (Chicago, Moody Press, 1995), pp. 65-71.

[19] Wagner, *op. cit.*, p. 89.

[20] Wagner, *op. cit.*, p. 91.

[21] Barbara Tuchman, *Bible and Sword,* (London, Macmillan, 1982), p. 115.

[22] Merkley, *op. cit.*, p. 38.

> Bonaparte, Commander-in-Chief of the Armies of the French Republic in Africa and Asia, to the Rightful Heirs of Palestine. Israelites, unique nation, whom, in thousands of years, lust of conquest and tyranny were able to deprive of the ancestral lands only, but not of name and national existence ... She [France] offers to you at this very time, and contrary to all expectations, Israel's patrimony ... Rightful heirs of Palestine ... hasten! Now is the moment which may not return for thousands of years, to claim the restoration of your rights among the population of the universe which had shamefully withheld from you for thousands of years, your political existence as a nation among the nations.[23]

Napoleon believed that with sympathetic Jews controlling Palestine, French imperial and commercial interests as far as India, Arabia and Africa could be secured.[24] Neither Napoleon nor the Jews were able to deliver. Nevertheless, his proclamation 'is a barometer of the extent to which the European atmosphere was charged with these messianic expectations.'[25] The European Powers became increasingly preoccupied with the "Eastern Question". Britain and Prussia sided with the Sultan of Turkey against Napoleon and his vassal, Mehemet Ali. The necessity of preventing French control had led not only to the battles of the Nile and Acre, but also to a British military expedition in Palestine. With the defeat of Napoleon, Britain's main concern was how to restrain Russia.[26] The race was on to control Palestine.[27]

Stirred by memories of the Napoleonic expedition, Lord Shaftesbury argued for a greater British presence in Palestine and saw that this could be achieved by the sponsorship of a Jewish homeland on both religious and political grounds.[28] British protection of the Jews, he argued, would give a colonial advantage over France for the control of

---

[23] Cited in Franz Kobler, *Napoleon and the Jews,* (New York, Schocken Books, 1976), pp. 55-57. See also: http://www.napoleonicsociety.com/english/scholarship98/c_jews98.html

[24] See Albert M. Hyamson, *Palestine: The Rebirth of an Ancient People,* (London, Sidgwick & Jackson, 1917), pp. 162-163; Salo W. Baron, *A Social and Religious History of the Jews,* (New York, Columbia University Press, 1937), 2. p. 327, cited in Sharif, *op. cit.*, p. 52.

[25] Baron, *ibid.*

[26] Sharif, *op. cit.*, p. 54.

[27] John Pollock, *Shaftesbury,* (London, Hodder, 1985), p54.

[28] Lord Shaftesbury, cited in P. C. Merkley, *The Politics of Christian Zionism 1891-1948,* (London: Frank Cass, 1998), p. 14.

the Middle East; provide better access to India via a direct land route; and open up new commercial markets for British products.[29]

In 1839, Shaftesbury wrote an anonymous 30 page article for the *Quarterly Review*, entitled "State and Restauration (sic) of the Jews". In it Shaftesbury advocated a Jewish national homeland with Jerusalem the capital, remaining under Turkish rule but with British protection.[30] Shaftesbury predicted a new era for the Jews:

> … the Jews must be encouraged to return in yet greater numbers and become once more the husbandman of Judea and Galilee ... though admittedly a stiff-necked, dark hearted people, and sunk in moral degradation, obduracy, and ignorance of the Gospel ... [They are] … not only worthy of salvation but also vital to Christianity's hope of salvation.[31]

When Lord Palmerston, the Foreign Secretary, married Shaftsbury's widowed mother-in-law, he was 'well placed' to lobby for this cause.[32] Shaftesbury's diary for 1st August 1840 reads:

> Dined with Palmerston. After dinner left alone with him. Propounded my scheme which seems to strike his fancy. He asked questions and readily promised to consider it. How singular is the order of Providence. Singular, if estimated by man's ways. Palmerston had already been chosen by God to be an instrument of good to His ancient people, to do homage to their inheritance, and to recognize their rights without believing their destiny. It seems he will yet do more. Though the motive be kind, it is not sound … he weeps not, like his Master, over Jerusalem, nor prays that now, at last, she may put on her beautiful garments.[33]

---

[29] Wagner, *op. cit.*, p. 91.

[30] Pollock, *op. cit.*, p. 54.

[31] Earl of Shaftesbury, "State and Prospects of the Jews", *Quarterly Review*, 63, London, January/March (1839), pp166-192, cited in Wagner, *op. cit.*, p91, and http://www.snunit.k12.il/heb_journals/katedra/62018.html

[32] Pollock, *op. cit.*, p. 54.

[33] Anthony Ashley, Earl of Shaftesbury. Diary entries as quoted by Edwin Hodder, *The Life and Work of the Seventh Earl of Shaftesbury,* (London, 1886), 1, pp310-311; See also Geoffrey B.A.M. Finlayson, *The Seventh Earl of Shaftesbury*, (London, Eyre Metheun, 1981), p114; The National Register Archives, London, Shaftesbury (Broadlands) MSS, SHA/PD/2, 1 August 1840.

Two weeks later, a lead article in *The London Times*, dated 17 August 1840, called for a plan "to plant the Jewish people in the land of their fathers", claiming such a plan was under "serious political consideration". Palmerston commended the efforts of Shaftesbury, the plan's author as both 'practical and statesmanlike'. Fuelling speculation about an imminent restoration, on 4 November 1840, Shaftesbury took out a paid advertisement in *The Times* to give greater visibility to his vision. The advertisement included the following:

> RESTORATION OF THE JEWS: A memorandum has been addressed to the Protestant monarchs of Europe on the subject of the restoration of the Jewish people to the land of Palestine. The document in question, dictated by a peculiar conjunction of affairs in the East, and other striking "signs of the times", reverts to the original covenant which secures that land to the descendants of Abraham.[34]

The influence of Lord Shaftesbury, therefore, in promoting the Zionist cause within the political, diplomatic, and ecclesiastical establishment in Britain was immense. Wagner claims, "He single-handedly translated the theological positions of Brightman, Henry Finch, and John Nelson Darby into a political strategy. His high political connections, matched by his uncanny instincts, combined to advance the Christian Zionist vision."[35] Indeed it was probably Shaftesbury who inspired Israel Zangwell and Theodore Herzl to coin the phrase, "A land of no people for a people with no land." Shaftesbury, a generation earlier, imagining Palestine to be empty, had come up with the slogan, "A country without a nation for a nation without a country."[36] Like Moses, Shaftesbury did not live to see his 'Promised Land' realised. However, through his lobbying, writings and public speaking he did more than any other British politician to inspire a generation of Joshuas to translate his religious vision into a political reality.

---

[34] Wagner, *op. cit.*, p. 91.

[35] Wagner, *op. cit.*, p. 92.

[36] Cited in Wagner, *op. cit.*, p92; also Albert H. Hyamson, *Palestine under the Mandate*, (London, 1950), p. 10, cited in Sharif, *op. cit.*, p. 42.

William Hechler and Theodore Herzl's Vision

By 1897, when the first World Zionist Congress met in Basle, Switzerland, Jewish leaders who favoured a Zionist State already had sympathetic support from many more senior British political figures. This was largely due to the efforts of one man, William Hechler. The son of London Jews Society missionaries in France and Germany, Hechler was an Anglican priest and became chaplain to the British Embassy in Vienna in 1885, a position of strategic significance for the Zionist movement.[37] "Imbued with evangelical millenarianism, he even formulated his own exact date for the re-establishment of the Jewish State."[38] As with Shaftesbury's slogan, so Hechler's booklet, *The Restoration of the Jews to Palestine* (1894), predated Herzl's *Der Judenstaat* by two years, and spoke of the need for "restoring the Jews to Palestine according to Old Testament prophecies."[39] Hechler became Herzl's chief Christian ally in realising his vision of a Zionist state, one of only three Christians invited to attend the World Congress of Zionists. Herzl was not religious but he was superstitious, as is evident when he records a meeting with Hechler on 10 March 1896 in his diary:

> The Reverend William Hechler, Chaplain of the English Embassy here, came to see me. A sympathetic, gentle fellow, with the long grey beard of a prophet. He is enthusiastic about my solution of the Jewish Question. He also considers my movement a "prophetic turning-point"—which he had foretold two years before. From a prophecy in the time of Omar (637CE) he had reckoned that at the end of forty-two prophetic months (total 1260 years) the Jews would get Palestine back. This figure he arrived at was 1897-98.[40]

In March 1897, the year Hechler expected the Jews to begin returning to Palestine, Herzl described their second meeting at Hechler's apartment. Herzl was amazed to find books from floor to ceiling,

---

[37] David Pileggi, 'Hechler, CMJ & Zionism' *Shalom*, 3 (1998).

[38] Sharif, *op. cit.*, p. 71.

[39] *Ibid.*

[40] Theodor Herzl, *The Diaries of Theodor Herzl,* (New York, 1956), cited in Sharif, *op. cit.*, p. 71.

"Nothing but Bibles" and a large military staff map of Palestine made up of four sheets covering the entire floor of the study:

> He showed me where, according to his calculations, our new Temple must be located: in Bethel! Because that is the centre of the country! He also showed me models of the ancient Temple. "We have prepared the ground for you!" Hechler said triumphantly ... I take him for a naive visionary ... However, there is something charming about his enthusiasm ... He gives me excellent advice, full of unmistakable genuine good will. He is at once clever and mystical, cunning and naive.[41]

Despite Herzl's initial scepticism, Hechler kept his word and gained access to the German Kaiser William II, the Grand Duke of Baden as well as the British political establishment for Herzl and his Zionist delegation. Although sympathetic to the evangelistic ministry of the LJS, Hechler's advocacy and diplomacy marked a radical shift in Christian Zionist thinking away from the views of early restorationists like Irving and Drummond who saw restoration to the land as a consequence of Jewish conversion to Christianity. Now, Hechler was insisting, instead, that it was the destiny of Christians simply to help restore the Jews to Palestine.

David Lloyd George, who became Prime Minister in 1916, was another self-confessed Zionist, sharing similar views to those of Shaftesbury. In his own words, he was Chaim Weizmann's proselyte: "Acetone converted me to Zionism."[42] This was because Weizmann had assisted the British government in the development of a new explosive using acetone and Palestine appears to have been the reward.

The Balfour Declaration and Legitimisation of Zionism

Probably the most significant British politician of all, however, was Arthur James Balfour (1848-1930), who pioneered the Balfour Declaration in 1917. Like Lloyd George, Balfour had been brought up in an evangelical home and was sympathetic to Zionism because of the influence of

[41] Merkley, *op. cit.*, pp16-17; Pileggi, *op. cit.*

[42] Weizmann had discovered how to synthesize acetone, a solvent used in the manufacture of explosives.

dispensational teaching.[43] He regarded history as "an instrument for carrying out a Divine purpose."[44] From 1905 Chaim Weizmann, then a professor of chemistry at Manchester University, began to meet regularly with Balfour to discuss the implementation of that goal. At Balfour's invitation, in July 1917, the Zionist Organisation offered a suggested draft to Balfour:

> 1. His Majesty's Government accepts the principle that Palestine should be reconstituted as the National Home of the Jewish people.
> 2. His Majesty's Government will use its best endeavours to secure the achievement of this object and will discuss the necessary methods and means with the Zionist Organization.[45]

Balfour amended this to emphasize the prerogative of the British government. On 2 November 1917, Lord Balfour made public the final draft of the letter written to Lord Rothschild on the 31 October and which became known as the Balfour Declaration:

> His Majesty's Government views with favour the establishment in Palestine of a National Home for the Jewish people, and will use their best endeavours to facilitate the achievement of that object, it being clearly understood that nothing shall be done, which may prejudice the civil and religious rights of the existing non-Jewish Communities in Palestine, or the rights and political status enjoyed by Jews in any other country.[46]

Balfour was in fact already committed to the Zionist programme out of theological conviction and had no intention of consulting the indigenous Arab population. In a letter to Lord Curzon, written in 1919, Balfour insisted somewhat cynically:

> For in Palestine we do not propose even to go through the form of consulting the wishes of the present inhabitants of the country ... the Four Great Powers are committed to Zionism.

---

[43] Wagner, *op. cit.*, p. 93.
[44] Sharif, *op. cit.*, p. 78.
[45] D. Ingrams, *Palestine Papers 1917-1922, Seeds of Conflict,* (London, John Murray, 1972), p. 9.
[46] *Ibid.*

> And Zionism, be it right or wrong, good or bad, is rooted in age-long traditions, in present needs, in future hopes, of far profounder import than the desires or prejudices of the 700,000 Arabs who now inhabit that ancient land ... I do not think that Zionism will hurt the Arabs ... in short, so far as Palestine is concerned, the Powers have made no statement of fact which is not admittedly wrong, and no declaration of policy which, at least in the letter, they have not always intended to violate.[47]

What the Balfour Declaration left intentionally ambiguous was the meaning of a "national home". Was this synonymous with sovereignty or statehood and if so what were to be the borders? Would it occupy all of Palestine or just a portion? What was to be the status of Jerusalem? Furthermore, while it stated that "the civil and religious rights of the existing population" were to be safeguarded and the territory was designated "Palestine", there was no reference to Palestinians. "They were an actual, but awkward non-identity."[48] It was clearly Balfour's opinion that "the present inhabitants' need not be consulted, either before or after."[49] That 90 percent of the population of Palestine were Arabs of whom around 10 percent were Christian seemed irrelevant to the politicians and Zionists who had another agenda.[50] So, the awkward questions were left unanswered and it is these ambiguities which have plagued Middle East peace negotiations for the last hundred years, right up to the present "Road Map to Peace".

This momentous declaration gave Zionism for the first time a measure of "political legitimacy" and provided the impetus for the colonization of Palestine.[51] From the mid-19th century, a similar marriage between religious dogmatism and political expediency in the United States was to lead theologians and politicians alike to support the Zionist cause. However, while Dispensationalism became largely marginalized in Britain, limited to the sectarianism of the Brethren, in the United States it was to become a dominant influence within mainstream Evangelicalism and Fundamentalism.

---

[47] Ingrams, *op. cit.*, p. 73.

[48] Kenneth Cragg, *The Arab Christian, A History in the Middle East,* (London, Mowbray, 1992), p. 234.

[49] Edward W. Said, *The Question of Palestine,* revised edition, (London, Vintage, 1992), p. 19.

[50] A report to the British Foreign Office in December 1918 revealed that Palestine consisted of 512,000 Muslims, 61,000 Christians and 66,000 Jews. Ingrams, *op. cit.*, p. 44.

[51] Wagner, *op. cit.*, p. 94.

FROM BLACKSTONE TO BUSH: CHRISTIAN ZIONISM IN THE UNITED STATES (1890-2004)

Donald Wagner

REWINDING THE BIBLE PROPHECY CLOCK: ISRAEL AND THE U.S. CHRISTIAN RIGHT (1890-1988)

It may come as a surprise to many that the first lobbying effort on behalf of a Jewish state in Palestine was organized and initiated by Evangelical Christians in the United States. The effort occurred in 1891, when the popular fundamentalist Christian writer and lay-preacher, William E. Blackstone organized a national campaign that appealed to President Benjamin Harrison, urging support of the establishment of a Jewish state in Palestine. Blackstone was a disciple of the noted Chicago Evangelist, Dwight L. Moody, and both had been influenced by the teachings of John Nelson Darby, the 'father' of premillennial dispensationalism. Darby's six missionary journeys to the United States in the post-Civil War era enabled him to transmit this new theology to the popular Bible and Prophecy Conference movement, where many pastors and evangelists such as Moody and Blackstone came to adopt this theology.

Blackstone gained notoriety through his national best-seller *Jesus is Coming* (1878 and 1882), which was essentially a popular summary of the end-time teachings. Blackstone was one of the first American Evangelicals to see the need for political support of the Jewish people and the establishment of a Jewish state in Palestine. His project gained a sense of urgency in light of the horrifying stories of pogroms in Russia and parts of Eastern Europe. Blackstone appealed to multi-millionaire friends such as John D. Rockefeller, the publisher Charles B. Scribner, and the industrialist J.P. Morgan to finance advertisements and a petition campaign that was subsequently carried in major newspapers from Boston to the Mississippi. Blackstone's petition (or 'Memorial' as he called it) received support from several members of the U. S. Senate and House of Representatives, the Chief Justice of the Supreme Court, and leading clergy from various Protestant denominations across the United States. In the end, Blackstone's "Memorial" was rejected by President Harrison.[1]

There is little record of significant political campaigns or public support for the Zionist cause after Blackstone's initiative, as fundamentalists began to withdraw from political activity following the Scopes' Trial and evolution battles. Many did remain active within their own communities but there is little record of any significant political activity on behalf of a Jewish state in Palestine.

However, after a fifty year hiatus, a series of significant changes began to occur after World War II. The birth of modern Israel in 1948 was viewed by many conservative Christians as the fulfillment of certain prophetic Biblical texts. This previously small and marginalized school of Biblical interpretation called "premillennial dispensationalism" suddenly began to assert itself within the larger evangelical Protestant community. Two political developments in the post-World War II era served to galvanize conservative Christians: the establishment of Israel and the Cold War.[2]

Most Evangelicals interpreted the establishment of Israel as a fulfillment of the prophetic scriptures and believed we were entering the countdown to the return of Jesus. *The Weekly Evangel*, a popular dispensationalist journal, reflected these views:

> We may wonder whether we are awake or lost in sleep merely having a very exciting dream ... Beloved, it can't be long until our blessed Lord takes us home to be forever with Him. (*The Weekly Evangel, 1948).*

However, nothing had an impact on this community like Israel's victory in the June 1967 War and the capture of Jerusalem and the West Bank (plus the Gaza Strip, Sinai, and the Golan Heights). Most conservative Christian evangelicals sensed that history had entered the latter days and the 'Clock of Bible Prophecy' was surely ticking. L. Nelson Bell, father-in-law of evangelist Billy Graham and editor of the influential journal *Christianity Today*, wrote in July, 1967: "That for the first time in more than 2000 years Jerusalem is now in the hands of the Jews gives the students of the Bible a thrill and a renewed faith in the accuracy and

---

1 See Timothy Weber, *On the Road to Armageddon.* Grand Rapids: Baker Academic Press, 2004, pp. 102-106 for a more detailed discussion of Blackstone and the Blackstone petition.

2 See Weber, *ibid.,* 9-66 for a detailed analysis of premillennial dispensationalism.

validity of the Bible."[3] The premillennialist approach gained popularity through a flurry of books, radio evangelists and television preachers. Hal Lindsay's *Late, Great Planet Earth* has sold over 35 million copies, making it one of the best selling books in history. Lindsay's message popularized the dramatic premillennialist scenario for a generation of North Americans, essentially elevating Israel to the center of the historical scenario. Lindsay's interests and impact ranged widely, including a consulting business that included several members of the United States Congress, the CIA, Israeli generals, the Pentagon, and the new Governor of California, Ronald Reagan.[4]

The Emerging Alliance

With the arrival of the American Bi-Centennial in 1976, several trends converged in Israel and the U.S. religious and political landscape, all pointing toward increased U.S. support for Israel and a higher political profile for the religious right. First, fundamentalist and evangelical churches became the fastest growing sector of American Christianity as the mainline Protestant and Roman Catholic branches were caught in a steady decline of members, budgets, and missions. Second, Jimmy Carter, an evangelical from the Bible Belt, was elected President of the United States, giving increased legitimacy to Evangelicals, as *Time Magazine* observed when they named 1976 "the year of the Evangelical". Suddenly, Evangelicals were prominent and viewed as a legitimate political and religious force.

Third, following the War of 1967, Israel gained an increased portion of the U.S. foreign and military budgets, becoming the 'western pillar' of the U.S. strategic alliance against Soviet incursion into the Middle East, particularly after 1979 when the Khomeini revolution pulled Iran from the U.S. orbit. During this period AIPAC and other pro-Israel lobby agencies began their ascent to power in shaping U.S. foreign policy. Fourth, the Roman Catholic Church and mainline Protestant denominations began to develop a more balanced approach to the Middle

[3] *Christianity Today*, Editorial, L. Nelson Bell, 16 July 1967.

[4] For a critical analysis of Lindsay, see Stephen Sizer, *Christian Zionism: Roadmap for Armageddon?*, Oxford, England: InterVarsity Press, 2005, pages 93-96, 124-136.

East, bringing them closer to the international consensus on the Palestine question. Pro-Israel organizations interpreted this shift as being anti-Israel and in turn began to court the conservative Christians. Marc Tannenbaum of the American Jewish Committee captured this sentiment when he told the *Washington Post*: "The evangelical community is the largest and fastest growing block of pro-Jewish sentiment in this country."[5]

The fifth development was the victory of Menachem Begin and the extremist Likud coalition in the Israeli election of 1977. Begin's Revisionist Zionist ideology of establishing an "Iron Wall" of domination and his policies of annexation, militarization of the conflict, and accelerated construction of Jewish settlements in the occupied territories all found ready support within the U.S. Christian right. Likud's tactic of utilizing Biblical names for the West Bank (Judea and Samaria) and Biblical arguments to defend its policies ("God gave us this land") found a resonance with the fundamentalist Christians, who held similar beliefs from their literal and predictive interpretation of the Biblical texts.

A surprising development, perhaps the linch-pin in forging the alliance, occurred in March, 1977, when President Jimmy Carter inserted the clause "Palestinians deserve a right to their homeland" into a policy address. Immediately, the Israeli lobby and the Christian right responded with a series of full-page advertisements in major U.S. newspapers. The text stated in part: "The time has come for evangelical Christians to affirm their belief in biblical prophecy and Israel's divine right to the land." The text concluded with a line that took direct aim at Carter's statement: "We affirm as Evangelicals our belief in the Promised Land to the Jewish people . . . We would view with grave concern any effort to carve out of the Jewish homeland another nation or political entity."[6] The advertising campaign was one of the first significant signs of the Likud/Israeli lobby's alliance with the Christian "right," as it redirected conservative Christian support from Carter (a Democrat) to the Republican "right". Jerry Strober, a former employee of the American Jewish Committee, co-ordinated the campaign and told *Newsweek Magazine*: "(The Evangelicals) are Carter's constituency and he (had)

---

[5] William Claibourne, "Israelis Look on US Evangelical Christians as Potent Ally," *Washington Post*, 23 March 1981.

[6] *Chicago Sun Times*, 9 November 1977.

better listen to them . . . The real source of strength the Jews have in this country is from the Evangelicals."[7]

Reagan and Begin

By the time the 1980 elections were held, the political landscape had shifted in the Middle East and the United States. Carter's support of the Shah had a domestic political price as U.S. hostages were not released by their Iranian captors until U.S. voters cast their ballots, a fact which resulted in the election of Ronald Reagan. Carter's inability to deliver the hostages was not the only factor in his defeat. An estimated 20 million fundamentalist and evangelical Christians voted for Reagan, most opposed to Carter's brand of evangelical Christianity that failed the test of unconditional support for Israel.

The power of the pro-Israel Republicans became a prominent part of the Reagan Administration with the President leading the way. On at least six public occasions, the former Hollywood actor expressed his belief in a final Battle of Armageddon. During one of his private conversations with Tom Dine (AIPAC director) Reagan said: "You know, I turn back to your ancient prophets in the Old Testament and the signs foretelling Armageddon, and I find myself wondering if—if we're the generation that is going to see that come about."[8] The conversation was leaked to the *Jerusalem Post* and picked up across the United States on the AP newswire. This stunning openness of a U.S. President with the chief lobbyist for a foreign government indicated the close co-operation that had developed between the Reagan Administration and the Israelis.

A little known feature of the Reagan White House was the series of seminars organized by the Administration and the Christian 'right' with assistance from the Israeli lobby. One example occurred at a 19 March 1984 briefing by Reagan's Middle East advisors in the State Department and AIPAC representatives. These sessions were designed to firm up the Republican Party's support from the Christian 'right' while AIPAC and Christian Zionist organizations were encouraged to advance their respective agendas. The Christian

---

[7] Claibourne, *ibid.*

[8] Larry Jones and Gerald T. Sheppard, "Ronald Reagan's Theology of Armageddon", *TSF Bulletin,* September-October, 1984, pp. 16-18.

participation, which averaged 150-200 in a series of gala dinner briefings in the White House, read like a "Who's Who" of the Christian right, including author Hal Lindsay, Jerry Falwell, Pat Robertson, Tim LeHaye (co-author of the *Left Behind* series), and Moral Majority strategist Ed McAteer. Several briefings were led by State Department official "Bud" McFarlane, one of the co-ordinators of the Iran-Contra scandal. Quietly working in the background was another Christian fundamentalist, Marine Colonel Oliver North.

Menachem Begin developed a close relationship with several leading fundamentalist clergy such as Revd Jerry Falwell, head of the Moral Majority, a favorite with Begin. Falwell received a Lear jet from the Israeli government for his personal travel and in 1981 was honored with the Jabotinsky Award in an elaborate ceremony in New York.[9] When Israel bombed the Iraqi nuclear plant in 1981, Prime Minister Begin made his initial telephone call to Jerry Falwell, asking him to "explain to the Christian public the reasons for the bombing." He called President Reagan later. Falwell also took credit for converting Senator Jesse Helms (R-NC) from a critic of Israel to one of Israel's staunchest allies in the U.S. Senate, where he went on to chair the influential Foreign Relations Committee.

Late in the Reagan era a number of sexual and financial improprieties within the fundamentalist Christian "right" (the Jim and Tammy Faye Baker scandal and the Jimmy Swaggart "confessions") began to erode its public support. In addition, Pat Robertson's ineffective run for the presidency in 1988 led to a decline in the Christian right's political fortunes. Resilient as ever, the Israeli lobby was able to reassert itself in new forms with the election of another Bible-toting Southern Baptist President, Bill Clinton, who, despite his liberal social agenda, became a 'liberal' friend of Israel.

Clinton and Bush: Decline and Rise of Christian Zionist Influence

During the Clinton era, the President increasingly inserted himself into the role of chief negotiator or personal convener of talks on the complex Israeli-Palestinian conflict. Although his background had a hint of

[9] Grace Halsell, *Prophecy and Politics*, Westport, CT: Lawrence Hill Publishers, 1986, p. 74.

Southern Baptist evangelicalism, Clinton was more inclined toward the secular Labor Party in Israel and found a close affinity with Itzhak Rabin. Meanwhile, the Likud/Christian Zionist alliance opposed the Oslo Accords and found themselves on the political sidelines.

In 1996, Benyamin Netanyahu defeated Shimon Peres and once again Likud ideology and policies dominated Israeli policy. Netanyahu had long been a favorite of the Christian Zionists, a relationship that developed during his years as Israel's representative at the United Nations. Bibi was a frequent speaker at important Christian Zionist functions, such as the Feast of Tabernacles hosted by the International Christian Embassy in Jerusalem or the annual 'National Prayer Breakfast for Israel' held in Washington, D.C. Within a few months of his election, Netanyahu convened the Israel Christian Advocacy Council, bringing seventeen American fundamentalist leaders to Israel for a political update on the situation in the Middle East. The tour concluded with a conference and statement that reflected Likud's political platform. The fundamentalist leaders signed a pledge stating "America will never, never desert Israel." Among the other pledges was a statement of support for Israeli settlements in the West Bank, Gaza Strip, and Golan Heights plus support for a united Jerusalem under Israeli sovereignty. Each statement had Biblical citations and a veneer of evangelical Christian language.[10]

The Christian Zionist leaders returned to the United States and launched a national campaign with full page advertisements in major newspapers under the banner "Christians Call for a United Jerusalem." Of little concern to the Israeli leaders and the Christian Zionists was the fact that their political positions were in conflict with U.S. policy and could undermine the fragile negotiations on the Oslo process. Signed by Pat Robertson of the Christian Broadcasting Network, Ralph Reed, then director of the Christian Coalition (a conservative Christian lobby), Revd Jerry Falwell, and Ed McAteer of the Religious Roundtable, the campaign was one of Likud's answers to the Clinton-Labor strategy.[11] The campaign was also a direct challenge to the mainline Protestant and Roman Catholic campaign led by Churches for Middle East Peace that called for a "Shared Jerusalem."

Likud also turned to the Christian Zionists for help in offsetting the dramatic decline in contributions to Israel from the American Jewish

[10] *United Methodist Review*, November, 1996.

[11] *New York Times*, 10 April 1997.

establishment during the conflict between the Orthodox and Reform-Conservative Rabbis. When the latter cut back on their generous contributions to the Jewish National Fund (JNF) in the late 1990s, several Christian Zionist-oriented churches were called upon to make up the difference. The International Fellowship of Christians and Jews, led by a former Anti-Defamation League employee and Orthodox Rabbi, Yechiel Eckstein, claimed to have raised more than $5 million from mostly fundamentalist Christian sources. Revd John Hagee, pastor of the Cornerstone Church in San Antonio, Texas, announced in February, 1997, that his church was donating more than $1 million to Israel. Hagee claimed the funds would be used to help resettle Jews from the Soviet Union in the West Bank and Jerusalem. "We feel like the coming of Soviet Jews to Israel is a fulfillment of Biblical prophecy," Hagee stated. When asked if he realized that support of Likud's policies and increasing the settlements was at cross-purposes with U.S. policy, Hagee answered: "I am a Bible scholar and a theologian and from my perspective the law of God transcends the laws of the United States government and the U.S. State Department."[12]

The Netanyahu government utilized the American Christian Zionists in yet another strategy as they sought to undermine the already faltering Oslo negotiations. A broadcast on 22 October 1997 by Kol Israel (Israel Radio) claimed that the Palestinian Authority (PA) was persecuting Christians. Two days later, the *Jerusalem Post* published an article claiming that according to classified information made known to the Government of Israel, the few remaining Palestinian Christians faced relentless and brutal persecution from the "predominantly Muslim PA." The report alleged that "Christian cemeteries have been destroyed, monasteries have had their telephone lines cut, and there have been break-ins in convents." It went on to claim that the PA had "taken control of the churches and was pressuring Christian leaders to serve as mouthpieces for Yasser Arafat and opponents of Israel." Within a month, U.S. Congressman J.C. Watts (R-OK) reiterated these charges in a *Washington Times* op-ed piece, blaming Arafat for the Christian exodus from the Holy Land and calling for a review and possible freeze on the $307 million in grants pledged to the PA from the United States. The campaign grew, thanks in part to publicity generated by the editorials of A.M.

---

[12] *Religious News Service*, 23 February 1998.

Rosenthal and William Safire in the *New York Times* and pressure exerted on Congress by Michael Horowitz, a pro-Israel lobbyist.

Palestinian Christians were quick to denounce the charges. Mayor Hanna Nasser of Bethlehem, a Palestinian Christian, stated: "Our churches have complete freedom, and I've never heard that they've been under pressure." In May, 1998, international Evangelical leader "Brother Andrew", President of the Netherlands-based organization Open Doors, and I led an investigation of the Israeli charges on behalf of Evangelicals for Middle East Understanding. We interviewed more that 60 Muslim and Christian leaders in addition to people at the grass roots throughout the West Bank and Gaza Strip as well as political leaders from the PA and government of Israel. We found no evidence of PA or Muslim persecution of Palestinian Christians, although there were three isolated cases of Christian-Muslim family disputes over intermarriage. The most telling interview came from Uri Mor, Director of the Israeli Ministry of Religious Affairs in the Department of Christian Communities, which oversees all Christian activities in Israel and the Occupied Territories. Mor noted that the charges were traceable to David Bar-Ilan, Netanyahu's chief spokesman. Mor told our EMEU team that Bar-Ilan uses shreds of information as his 'bread and butter' in the propaganda campaign against the Palestinians.

We later interviewed a staff member of the U.S. Consulate in Jerusalem that had previously interviewed Mor and investigated the problem. The U.S. Consulate had received a report on the persecution of Christian Palestinians that was a confidential internal document. Upon investigation, the Consulate determined that the basis of the report came from four Palestinians who were recent converts to Christianity. Two of the converts had criminal backgrounds and the others were suspected of collaborating with the Israeli secret police. They were converted to Christianity by a Messianic Jewish evangelist who resided in an Israeli settlement. The PA had imprisoned the converts based on their criminal activities, not because of their conversion. Apparently, Bar-Ilan's office leaked the report to the International Christian Embassy-Jerusalem, the Christian Zionist organization with a close relationship with Likud. The Christian Embassy-Jerusalem then published the stories and launched a campaign against the Palestinian Authority that eventually reached the U.S. Congress. After its investigation, Evangelicals for Middle East Understanding (EMEU) issued a statement that clarified the issues, asserting that "disturbing indications of political motivations were behind the publicity about Christian persecution" in the Holy Land. The story was published in the influential evangelical journal *Christianity Today*. The Christian Zionist campaign against the PA came to a halt but undoubtedly the tactic will be pursued again.

The Christian Right Today

In the spring of 2002, Israel responded to the Passover suicide bombing by re-invading the West Bank and conducted a devastating siege of Jenin, including the bulldozing of much of its refugee camp, following a fierce resistance. The international community brought persistent pressure on US President George W. Bush demanding that he order Ariel Sharon to withdraw the Israeli military forces at once. A stern looking President stated at a 2 April 2002 press conference: "Withdraw! Withdraw your troops now!" At that point, the Revd Jerry Falwell and other Christian Zionist leaders working closely with the pro-Israel lobby organizations responded by mobilizing tens of thousands of telephone calls, emails, and letters to the President, according to a CBS-TV "Sixty Minutes" report of 6 October 2002, demanding that the President refrain from criticizing Israel and that he allow the Israeli army to finish its job in "fighting terrorism." After this pressure, George Bush refused to ask Sharon to withdraw the Israeli troops and the Israel Defense Forces intensified its bombardment of Jenin and other West Bank cities and refugee camps. In the same "Sixty Minutes" report, long-time Christian Zionist spokesman and Israeli advocate, the Revd Jerry Falwell commented: "Evangelical Christians now know that they can count on George Bush to do the right thing for Israel every time." Falwell added: "the Bible-belt is Israel's safety net in the United States."[13]

Christian Zionist organizations and the pro-Israeli lobby are among the significant special interest groups that have converged since the election of George W. Bush to shape the new administration's policy toward the Middle East, and for that matter, much of its foreign policy. Among the other powerful forces to converge with the pro-Israel lobby

[13] "Zion's Christian Soldiers", CBS-*Sixty Minutes*, 5 October 2002.

and the Christian Zionists are the neo-conservative ideologues, the multinational construction agencies (Halliburton, Bechtel, etc.), and the military industry. In some respects, most of these organizations and political tendencies were already lined up and waiting for the proper moment to exercise their new-found power and goals. The tragic events of 11 September 2001 provided the occasion for these movements and trends to unite in such a way that they have become the primary forces that have shaped the policies of the new Bush administration.

Space permits only the most surface treatment of one of these movements, the fundamentalist Christian Zionists. Conservative Christians have been the fastest growing sector within the Christian churches of the United States since the late 1960s. Estimates of the number of evangelicals range from 90 to 100 million, out of which 20-25 percent would be classified as fundamentalist (20 to 25 million Americans). Of the fundamentalists, most but not all would be inclined to support the Christian Zionist position. A recent poll by Time/CNN noted that 59 percent of evangelicals polled believe the Battle of Armageddon, Rapture, and rise of the Antichrist are literal historical developments that will occur in the near future. The most important nation to play a role in the fulfillment of these prophetic events will be Israel, which many of the fundamentalist Christians understand to be God's favored nation. These views are the fertile ground in which the Christian Zionist movement finds its popularity and political clout.

Today, the Christian Zionists are the largest potential base of support for the militant Likud government's pro-Israeli interests in the United States. Working slowly but steadily since the late 1970s, the pro-Israel lobby has been able to mobilize both economic and political support for the state of Israel via the fundamentalist sector. For example, a relatively new organization, Stand for Israel, has emerged in the past two years to work closely with AIPAC to hold rallies and mobilize political support on behalf of Sharon's policies. On 2 April 2003, Stand for Israel held a convention and lobbying day immediately after the annual AIPAC national convention, utilizing many of the same speakers and policies that were central to the AIPAC meeting. Former US Presidential candidate Gary Bauer and a co-founder of Stand for Israel, addressed the Christian convention and urged attendees to oppose the 'Roadmap' and any exchange of land for peace. Bauer stated: "Whoever sits in the confines of Washington, and suggests to the people of Israel that they have to give up more land in exchange for peace, that's an obscenity." Others present at the Stand for Israel dinner reflected the intimate relationship the Bush Administration shares with the Christian right and the pro-Israel lobby, including former U.S. Attorney General John Ashcroft, Israeli Ambassador to the U.S. Daniel Ayalon, U.S. Senator Sam Brownback, Southern Baptist Convention leader Richard Land, and House of Representatives Minority Leader Tom DeLay. DeLay and Congressman Tom Lantos, perennial advocates of Israel's interests in the House of Representatives, received the first annual 'Friend of Israel Award' from Stand for Israel for their success in leading Congress to pass House Resolution 392, restating the strong solidarity of the United States with Israel in their joint stance against international terrorism.

Thus by combining the forces of the most powerful political lobby in Washington, D.C. (AIPAC and its various networks) with fundamentalist Christian pulpits, radio, and television, these united forces are capable of bringing significant political and economic pressure on every vote in the Senate and House, as well as on the Bush presidency. Their support of Ariel Sharon's militant Likud ideology is unquestioned and usually supported by selected Biblical footnotes. Such policies as increased Israeli settlements, pre-emptive assassination of Palestinian leaders, Israeli sovereignty over all of historic Palestine (especially Jerusalem), and more recently opposition to President Bush's 'Road Map' will bring interesting developments in the coming years. Some leaders within President Bush's rock-solid base of support in the Republican Party may in fact turn against him if he enforces his call for a Palestinian state and enforcement of the 'Road Map for Middle East Peace'. Some Christian Zionists have befriended Knesset Member Benny Elon, who advocates mass expulsion of large sectors of the Palestinian population. At the fall 2003 meeting of the powerful Christian Coalition, one of the strongest organizations of the Christian right, Elon received strong support from the organizers and audience, including his advocacy of the "transfer" option. However, Sharon's planned "Gaza withdrawal" has now caused a rift between many in the Christian Zionist camp and Israeli leaders such as Elon, who have broken with Sharon's policies.

It appears at this juncture of the Bush presidency and Sharon government that both the Christian Zionists and the Israeli settler movement are moving toward even more extreme positions than what they previously held. These forces successfully 'killed' the 'Road Map' when President Bush announced it with considerable fanfare in the summer of 2002.

Only time will tell whether they can muster the political power to block the Gaza withdrawal and definitively defeat the Road-Map or whether they will comply with the Bush-Sharon alliance. The months ahead may bring a significant split in the Christian right's love affair with George W. Bush and Ariel Sharon, or we may find the alliance gaining new strength and holding together in the years to come.

Sabeel *thanks the* Beirut Daily Star *and its editor Rami Khouri for permission to reprint the text which first appeared in a 5-part series during 9-13 September 2003.*

THEOLOGICAL AND BIBLICAL ASSUMPTIONS OF CHRISTIAN ZIONISM

Gary M Burge

The Biblical and theological assumptions of Christian Zionism were not shaped by its modern writers that we hear so much about today. To understand the key ideas that gave it shape, we have to examine Christian thinking in Britain and the U.S. over 200 years ago.

Some scholars speculate that we should begin with the 17th-century American pilgrims who saw their journey across the Atlantic as a re-creation of the Israelite pilgrimage to the Holy Land. They did not extend this metaphor to Judaism, however, but took the Biblical story as an allegory for their own exile, pilgrimage and homecoming to a North American promised land. Nevertheless this created a sympathetic understanding of the religious refugee that is seated deeply in the American psyche and likely shapes many Americans even today as they think of the modern "pilgrimage" of Judaism back to the Middle East.

THE 19TH-CENTURY ROMANCE OF PALESTINE

The more important story begins in the 19th century where we see the Bible and its narratives of land and fulfillment used in a new way. Religious interest in Ottoman Palestine grew during the Victorian era as travelers—romantic travelers in many cases—sought adventure by ship, train and horseback. And they came to Palestine in great numbers. The 1880s found a number of influential preachers there too. Revd DeWitt Talmadge, Pastor of the Brooklyn Tabernacle Church in New York, returned home from such a pilgrimage to publish his *Twenty Five Sermons from the Holy Land*. In the book, he offered an embellished picture of a Jewish renaissance in the country. He praised philanthropists such as Montifiore and Rothchild for financing the resumption of Jewish life there. Here is a sample from one of his sermons:

> Many who are large-hearted have paid the passage to Palestine for many of the Israelites, and set apart lands for their culture; and it is only a beginning of the fulfillment of Divine prophecy, when these people shall take possession of the Holy Land. The road from Joppa to Jerusalem, and all the roads leading to Nazareth and Galilee, we saw lined with processions of Jews, going to the sacred places, either on holy pilgrimage, or as settlers. All the fingers of Providence nowadays are pointing toward that resumption of Palestine by the Israelites.

In 1891 George Adam Smith wrote his popular *The Historical Geography of the Holy Land* and there portrayed an empty biblical land awaiting the return of Judaism. Such publications resonated with a growing public interest in Palestine and the Bible, especially in Britain. And during World War I with the prospect of the fall of the Ottomans, Jewish Zionist leaders influenced by men such as Theodor Herzl (1860-1904) could capitalize on these British sympathies. The "little letter" of Nov. 2, 1917, from the British foreign office—now called the Balfour Declaration—is likely the final synthesis of this religious vision and politics in Britain.

The Early Formative Dispensationalists

Among conservative Christians in Britain, this unity of political destiny and religious fulfillment was given its theological form in the hands of an Irish pastor, J.N. Darby. As Herzl was the father of Jewish Zionism, one could argue that Darby was the father of Christian Zionism, laying out many of its principal theological foundations. During his 60 year ministry, Darby fought the optimism of 19th-century liberalism (with its post-millennialism views) and called for a return to a literal biblical faith. But it was Darby's eschatology—soon to be called Dispensationalism—that taught a literal fulfillment of prophesies in the near-present age. He used the biblical books of Daniel, Ezekiel, Zechariah and Revelation to weave a consistent picture of the Last Days: the church is raptured, the anti-Christ arises, Armageddon erupts, and Christ returns to establish his thousand-year reign on earth. But above all, Darby believed, the revival of Israel would be the catalyst of the End Times.

Despite eight missionary trips to America, Darby was greeted in the U.S. with indifference. But when leading evangelists such as Dwight Moody, Billy Sunday and Harry Ironsides saw how the drama and fear and hope in this scenario influenced audiences, Darby's views caught on like wildfire. In 1881, for instance, Horatio and Anna Spafford and 16 friends opened the *American Colony* in the Muslim Quarter of the Old City to watch, as they put it, "prophesy being fulfilled".

William Blackstone (1841-1935) was a Chicago evangelist and student of Moody. In 1878 he published *Jesus is Coming,* which was America's first Dispensational best-seller. The book went through three editions and was translated into 42 languages in the late 19th century. In1890, Blackstone was visiting Jewish settlements in the Holy Land and organizing conferences in Chicago to restore Jews to Palestine. Blackstone worked closely with Jewish Zionists and in 1918 was hailed by the Zionist Conference of Philadelphia as a "Father of Zionism." In 1956 Israel memorialized him by naming a forest in his name.

In 1909 Cyrus Scofield published a popular study Bible, the Scofield Reference Bible, and in its footnotes readers throughout America inherited Darby's theological program. (To date over 2 million of them have been sold.) In 1917, five weeks after the Balfour Declaration, the Turks handed Jerusalem over to Britain to the amazement of prophesy watchers. In 1918 Dispensationalists organized their first prophesy conferences and they continued for decades. Before long—throughout the 1920s and for the next 40 years—Dispensationalism tied to Israel and prophesy became the litmus test of fundamentalist orthodoxy.

Dispensationalism had a variety of detractors over time and today we cannot think of all modern evangelicals as Dispensationalists. The theological split that came to American fundamentalism in the 1940s and gave birth to modern evangelicalism had a keen eye on this eschatology and was happy to purge a great deal of it. Pre-millennialism prevailed among many evangelicals but the Dispensationalist schema complete with wall charts slowly disappeared. But today in the U.S. it is almost impossible to give any theological definition to evangelicals since everyone from Jerry Falwell to Don Wagner uses the term.

Among fundamentalists, while formal Dispensationalism with its complex view of the covenants has lost a large following, what remains today is the skeleton of its eschatology. Technically called pre-tribulation, pre-millennialism it defends Darby's basic outline: Israel returns to the

Holy Land, the church is raptured, a seven year tribulation brings the final battle of Armageddon, and Christ returns to inaugurate judgment and set up his kingdom on earth.

Influential Dispensationalists

This eschatological framework remained prominent for American and British conservatives but throughout the 1940's, Dispensationalists began to believe that the birth of Israel was imminent. When it occurred in 1948, Dispensationalists were euphoric. The key piece was now in place. Israel's swift victory in 1967—hailed by many as a divine miracle—sparked even more zeal for prophesy. Writers such as John Walvoord and Charles Ryrie, both from Dallas Theological Seminary, and Bible colleges such as *Moody Bible Institute* in Chicago and *Philadelphia College of the Bible,* viewed modern history through this Biblical lens for a new generation. Even in Jerusalem the former *Institute of Holy Land Studies,* founded by G. Douglas Young, moved in 1967 to the historic 19th century (1853) Bishop Gobat School on Mt. Zion. It was a celebration of what was unfolding prophetically in Jerusalem. Although today's *Jerusalem University College* is far more centrist, Young's early zeal for the Holy Land was framed by pre-millennial passions.

It would be hard to underestimate the impact of 1967 for these leaders. Jerusalem had now returned to the hands of the descendants of David. The land promises to Abraham were being realized in full. Could the rebuilding of the Temple be far off?

Three years later in 1970 Hal Lindsey published *The Late Great Planet Earth* which popularized and dramatized the unfolding of political events in Israel and how the Bible had predicted them. To date, Lindsey's original book has sold 15 million copies — and this was just the beginning of his career as the "premill-prophet" of the late-20th century. *Time Magazine* called him "The Jeremiah for this Generation," and he is often hailed as the father of apocalyptic Christian Zionism. Over 27 years he has written 20 books on the subject and their titles give away his agenda: *The Everlasting Hatred: The Roots of Jihad; Planet Earth: The Final Chapter; Satan Is Alive* and *Well* on *Planet Earth; Faith for Earth's Final Hour; Apocalypse Code; The Road to Holocaust; Vanished into* Thin *Air: The Hope of Every Believer; The Liberation of Planet*

Earth.[1] Today he hosts a radio and a TV program, sends out biblical intelligence briefings, and leads prophesy trips to the Holy Land.

Lindsey continues to exert tremendous influence. And others have joined him. Throughout the 1980s and 1990s Dallas' John Walvoord offered numerous books such as *Armageddon: Oil* and *the Middle East Crisis; The Nations, Israel* and *the Church in Prophesy,* and quite recently, *Prophecy* in *the New Millennium.* These were creative writers who helped us understand—among other things—that Mikhail Gorbachev's prominent birthmark was the mark of the beast.

But today the influential voices in this movement certainly belong to Tim LaHaye and Jerry Jenkins, authors of the popular fictional *Left Behind* series, which in spring 2004 published its 12th volume and as a series has sold over 53 million copies. Do not make the mistake of thinking that these men *are* just writing fiction. "What we *are* writing is truth," LaHaye recently told the national media in the U.S. These men are not theologians of the caliber of Walvoord *or* Ryrie, but they have popularized and solidified the foundation of many laypersons' eschatology for years to come.

The remarkable publishing numbers of these books is important because they show that among countless Christians in America, there is a residual eschatology at work—and most of them have no idea where it came from. Just ask someone who goes to church in America how they think the world will end. Many will outline Lindsey or LaHaye, claiming that this is what the Bible teaches.

---

[1] Hal Lindsey, *The Late Great Planet Earth* (London, Lakeland, 1970); *Satan is Alive and Well on Planet Earth* (London, Lakeland, 1973); *There's A New World Coming, A Prophetic Odyssey* (Santa Ana, California, Vision House, 1973); *The Liberation of Planet Earth* (London, Lakeland, 1974); *The World's Final Hour: Evacuation or Extinction?* (1976); *The 1980s: Countdown to Armageddon* (New York, Bantam, 1981); *The Promise* (Eugene, Oregon, Harvest House, 1982); *The Rapture: Truth or Consequences* (New York, Bantam, 1983); *The Terminal Generation* (New York, Bantam, 1983); *A Prophetical Walk Through the Holy Land* (Eugene, Oregon, Harvest House, 1983); *Israel and the Last Days* (Eugene, Oregon, Harvest House, 1983); *Combat Faith* (1986); *The Road to Holocaust* (New York, Bantam, 1989); *Planet Earth-2000 AD.* (Palos Verdes, California, Western Front, 1994); *The Final Battle* (Palos Verdes, California, Western Front, 1995); *Planet Earth-2000 A.D. Rev. Edn.* (Palos Verdes, California, Western Front, 1996); *Amazing Grace* (Palos Verdes, California, Western Front, 1996); *Blood Moon* (Palos Verdes, California, Western Front, 1996); *The Apocalypse Code* (Palos Verdes, California, Western Front, 1997); *Planet Earth: The Final Chapter* (Beverley Hills, California, Western Front, 1998); *International Intelligence Briefing* (Palos Verdes, California, HLM), monthly journal.

Fundamental Assumptions

Today a movement called Christian Zionism has harnessed these disparate parts. While this movement is not theologically sophisticated, it is theologically passionate. Jerry Falwell, Ralph Reed, Pat Robertson, Ed McAteer, Gary Bauer, Tom Delay and Kay Arthur are not retiring personalities. Oddly, its advocates have shed much of Dispensationalism's theological program for the Bible but have kept its pre-millennial eschatology intact. Even in places such as Dallas Seminary, once 'ground zero' for this sort of thinking, classic Dispensationalism is disappearing with each generation. Rather than developing a nuanced and supple theological program for the church, this theology elevates one theme—apocalyptic eschatology—as the central defining doctrine for our generation. But more importantly, Christian Zionism weds religion with politics and interprets biblical faithfulness in terms of fidelity to Israel's future. If there is a summary criticism about its use of the Bible, it is that the movement is hermeneutically naive, using Biblical passages completely out of context and misapplying them to the present day.

Today there are few books that seem to give a thorough-going sympathetic presentation of Christian Zionism written by scholars from within the movement. However, one is notable. Published in 1998 to commemorate Israel's 50th anniversary, it is *Israel: The Land and the People. An Evangelical Affirmation* of *God's Purposes,* edited by Wayne House (Kregal, 1998). Here twelve conservative scholars try to steer a course between replacement theologians and Christian Zionists, but in the end, they defend the theological assumptions popularized by people like LaHaye and Lindsey. To understand mainstream thinking among Christian Zionists today, one need go no further than this book.

Outlining biblical and theological assumptions of Christian Zionism is only useful if we pare away those voices that live on the movement's margin, whose extreme "Israel-right-or-wrong" outlook too often defines the movement. It would be easy (and wrong) to use extreme voices to stereotype Christian Zionists in this manner. Rather, let me outline how a centrist position in the movement would develop its theology here. There are six simple steps:

1. Biblical Israel and Modern Israel

The first and perhaps most important affirmation in this system is to see that God's covenant with Biblical Israel is eternal and unconditional. And this covenant continues to be applicable to modern Judaism today. Therefore, the modern Israeli state lives in direct continuity with Abraham and is thus heir to Abraham's promises. This means that the resumption of Israel's national life today is a resumption of Israel's biblical nationhood interrupted about 1900 years ago. Theologically this means that the new covenant of Christ has not abrogated God's original covenant with Moses, that the church has not replaced Israel and that Israel's covenant privileges have never been revoked.

2. The Territory of Eretz Israel

If this historic or theological continuity is maintained, then the land promises outlined in the Bible and now realized by modern Israel are justified. And they should be defended. Since the land promise is intrinsically linked to covenant and since this covenant cannot be annulled even through disobedience—even rejection of the messiah—then the land of Israel belongs exclusively to Judaism. This is the centerpiece of God's commitment to Abraham, Isaac and Jacob, repeated numerous times in the Bible. The land is the great heritage of Israel.

This call to defend the land on behalf of Israel is revealed in contemporary events. Prime Minister Ariel Sharon has a plan to evacuate all settlers from Gaza. When he visited President Bush in the spring of 2004, the "National Unity Coalition for Israel"—an umbrella group for 200 Christian organizations—sent an "action alert" to its members calling on them to write Bush immediately, urging him to stop Sharon's plan for Gaza. Why? Because this plan would be to relinquish the Biblical promise. The letter even warns him of "the potential downside" of failing to do this and reminds him that tens of millions of Bible-believing Christians are some of his core constituency.[2]

---

[2] *Jerusalem Post Online,* April 8, 2004.

3. The Modern Application of Prophesy

The prophetic books of the Bible are describing events of today and do not exclusively refer to events in Biblical times. Therefore when we look at Daniel 7, for example, if we possess the right interpretative skills, we can see how modern history is unfolding. Above all, one key element in the Bible's prophesies stands out: the restoration of Israel to its nationhood in the land. The year 1948 is thus a watershed event that signals the beginning of fulfillment and the beginning of the "last times." The modern state of Israel is a catalyst for the prophetic countdown. And if these are the last days, then we should expect an unraveling of civilization, the rise of evil, the loss of international peace and equilibrium, a coming antichrist, and tests of faithfulness to Israel. Above all, political alignments today will determine our position on the fateful day of Armageddon.

The failings of these hermeneutically naive interpreters are most obvious here. There is no consideration of the historical context of the prophetic literature and no understanding of how it has been misused. 2500 years simply disappear in an instant and suddenly Ezekiel is talking about modern Damascus. But here is the most egregious problem: the value of the prophets in the Biblical tradition is distilled down to *predictive prophesy.* The chief message of the prophets was Israel's fidelity to the covenant, how this was lived out in a life of righteousness, and the historic judgments that will fall on the land if there is disobedience. Christian Zionists rarely discuss these themes.

4. Blessing Modern Israel

If the above three theses are correct, faithful Christians are obligated to take Genesis12:3 seriously and apply it to modern Israel: "I will bless those who bless you and curse those who curse you." Therefore Christians have a spiritual obligation to bless Israel and "pray for the peace of Jerusalem." To fail to bless Israel, to fail to support Israel's political survival today, will incur divine judgment. Now this does not mean—and here Christian Zionism is often misrepresented—that Christians are called on to blindly endorse all of Israel's political policies. Criticism of Israel is acceptable. But this possibility is secondary to our first obligation to defend against those who would question Israel's theological or historical legitimacy. And in fact, public criticisms of Israel's political policies are almost never heard.

5. *The Church*

God's plan has always been for the redemption of Israel. Yet when Israel failed to follow Jesus, the church was born as an afterthought or "parenthesis." Thus at the rapture, the church will be removed and Israel will once again become God's primary agent in the world. We now live in 'the times of the Gentiles' which will conclude soon. This means that there are *two covenants* now at work, that given through Moses and the covenant of Christ.

Perhaps the counterpoint to this position will make it clear: the great theological opponent to Christian Zionism is always seen as "replacement theology." No phrase will provoke a stronger response. I think the phrase is inadequate, too, but it gets at something important. The theology of the New Testament understands that something definitive has been fulfilled for Judaism. It is a remnant theology that sees God's ongoing faithfulness to Judaism fulfilled in the followers of Jesus. Christians are children of Abraham, Jesus is the new Moses, the 12 apostles evoke memories of the 12 tribes, etc. To neglect this vital New Testament theme is to do a genuine disservice to the New Testament itself.

6. *An Ongoing Program for Judaism*

Finally, it is critical to see that from the Christian Zionist's viewpoint, God is not finished with Judaism. Romans 9-11 becomes a critical text in which Paul outlines the mystery of Israel's rejection of Jesus and the ongoing faithfulness of God. This interest centers particularly on Romans 11 and the meaning of and timing of Israel's restoration. But here Christian Zionists are divided. Does the two-covenant idea permit the notion that Jews will be saved outside of Christ? A few say yes, but the majority will hold that although the blessings of the covenant belong to Israel—for the "promises of God are irrevocable"—Judaism's spiritual salvation will come at the end of time when Christ returns and he is embraced as Messiah.

This subject is particularly difficult and rarely discussed. Since Christian Zionists wish to embrace Israel fully, the suggestion that a two-covenant theology does not include salvation suddenly devalues Jewish identity. And at this point, interfaith support is strained. This theological decision determines why *Jews for Jesus* continues to have an evangelistic mission. And to test this further, simply ask your friends at the International Christian Embassy in West Jerusalem whether they do or do not do evangelism. Their answer will tell all.

It would not be difficult to offer fatal criticisms of this theological framework. Many biblical scholars have already done so. I would simply point you to Peter Walker at Oxford and Colin Chapman at NEST/ Beirut. For instance, the covenant's promises *are* conditional and their blessings are revoked when there is faithlessness. This is the central motif of the Book of Judges and it is simply foreshadowing for the kingdom era. The Babylonian exile is the best example of the consequences of infidelity to the covenant. In addition, the New Testament is making a stunning claim about genuine continuity between the covenants in that Christians are the children of Abraham and heirs of his promises.

While it seems clear that the biblical theology of Christian Zionism is highly debatable—some would almost call it heresy—the movement has an Achilles' heel. Two ideas, less frequently mentioned, make its theology subject to withering criticism.

First, Christian Zionism is committed to what I term a "territorial religion." It assumes that God's interests are focused on a land, a locale, a place. From a New Testament perspective, the land is holy by reference to what transpired there in history. But it no longer has an intrinsic part to play in God's program for the world. This is what Stephen pointed to in his speech in Acts 7. The land and the temple are now secondary. The fusion of national politics and religious mandate is gone. God wishes to reveal himself to the entire world. *This insight cost Stephen his life.* Such an understanding is a far cry from the views of Christian Zionists like Ed McAteer, who recently commented, "Every grain of sand, every grain of sand between the Dead Sea, the Jordan River, and the Mediterranean Sea belongs to the Jews." Stephen would be alarmed!

Second, Christian Zionism has no integrated theology of the cross. There is a Christian triumphalism here that has even been observed by culture critics in the U.S. Stephen Prothero of Boston University has recently written *American Jesus: How the Son of God Became a National Icon*. Prothero writes, "I sense a weariness among evangelicals with a friendly Jesus who doesn't stand for a lot except that he loves people. So we are seeing a shift from an effeminate Jesus to a macho Jesus."

Often history, culture and religion follow parallel trajectories and their convergence creates a religious world view that reinforces a society's interests. In the present case, Americans are living in an era of cultural triumphalism—at least this is how they view it. American language, economic influence, politics, media and music are all global. The events of 9/11 did not shake this, but added the idea that America is good and those who resist her world view are evil, that a culture war has begun and American ideals, rooted in scripture, are now to be defended.

This is the ideal context for an apocalyptic eschatology. And it can be seen in images of the new "American Jesus" which are emerging. This is a more martial, macho concept of Christ, one who defeats his foes, who no longer is silent before the shearer. Dr Tim Weber at Memphis Theological Seminary labels this the "warrior Jesus," who rescues us from the "decline of civilization and the general breakdown of order ..."[3] Boston's Prothero says, "There is a helplessness we feel, and we hope Jesus can help us. But in order to do that, he has to have a certain gravitas ..."[4]

The publication of Tim LaHaye's final *Left Behind* volume completes the picture perfectly. Entitled *His Glorious Appearing,* Jesus returns on a white horse with conviction like a "flame of fire in his eyes" and he destroys the flesh of millions of unbelievers simply by speaking. Christian Zionism unwittingly serves this apocalyptic triumphalism. America must join with Israel and in the name of God facilitate and protect all that has been prophesied.

But here is the odd thing. While Christian Zionists see tremendous religious significance to the birth of Israel, Jews do not necessarily agree. After my small book on Israel and the Palestinians was published last year, numerous critics rose up to call me blessed—and not so blessed. Perhaps the most interesting new conversation partner that came my way was a rabbi who contacted me from Chicago's Jewish Federation. After four meetings and a couple of long phone calls—which represented 10 hours of conversation and debate—I learned one thing

[3] D. Kirkpatrick, "Wrath and Mercy", *The NY Times,* Apr 4, 2004.

[4] *The Chicago Tribune,* A-13, April 11, 2004.

that I would like to pass on to my Christian Zionist friends. According to Rabbi Yehiel Poupko, 85 percent of Jews worldwide see no religious significance to Israel. And they view the Christian Zionist program with some amusement. While they enjoy their support today, they are not keen on the last chapter of the apocalyptic play when Israel either converts or gets killed at Armageddon. But here is the key: Christian Zionists must beware of projecting onto Israel a religious self-justification that may not even be there. For most Jews, the State of Israel may have less to do with God than it has to do with ethnic or cultural survival.

Religion and Politics

Today the most prominent feature of Christian Zionism in America is its political application. We are told regularly from our pulpits that we have a spiritual obligation to "bless Israel." When pastors such as John Hagee of Cornerstone Church in San Antonio, Texas, can deliver $1 million to Israel, a new definition of evangelical missions is at work. But blessing Israel is not simply a matter of giving money. It is also found in political advocacy. For instance, when Israel invaded the West Bank in April, 2002, following the reprehensible Passover bombings, President Bush urged Ariel Sharon to withdraw from Jenin. Christian Zionists mobilized an email campaign that produced 100,000 letters for Washington. And it worked. Bush never said another word.

Leaders like Jerry Falwell thus see their mission as protecting Israel politically. On American TV there is a very important program every Sunday night on CBS called "60 Minutes." On 8 June 2003, Falwell remarked, "It is my belief that the Bible Belt in America is Israel's only safety belt right now. There is nothing that would bring the wrath of the Christian public in this country down on this government like abandoning or opposing Israel in a critical matter. And when the chips are down, Ariel Sharon can trust George Bush to do the right thing every time."

These words were as much warning to Bush as anything since Bush's political analysts believe that Falwell's "Christian public" is a core constituency. According to Falwell, they're worth about 40 million voters.

Today the same strategy is at work. On 19 May 2003, twenty-three Christian Zionists sent President Bush a letter outlining what was wrong with his Roadmap to Peace and urging him to end it. Its signatories included Jerry Falwell, Gary Bauer, John Hagee, James Kennedy and others. In a similar manner Gary Bauer spoke at last year's AIPAC convention. Even Pat Robertson could rebuke Israel's foreign minister, Silvan Shalom, on his nationally syndicated "700 Club."

In recent days no one has matched House Majority leader Tom Delay (R. Texas) for his zeal to bless Israel. Delay is often sought in Washington as a spokesperson for Christian Zionism. And he is forthright in his commitment even when it contradicts the president. On 30 July of last year, he addressed the Israeli Knesset and his views were so extreme that the Labor Party leader Danny Yatom commented afterwards, "Geez, Likud is nothing compared to him!" Another legislator commented, "Until I heard him speak, I thought I was the farthest to the right in the Knesset!"

Delay announced that he was an "Israeli at heart" and then upon his return home challenged the Bush Roadmap openly. He has appeared at meetings of the influential *Christian Coalition* with Benny Elon, the leader of the pro-ethnic cleansing Moledet Party, arguing that a "transfer" of Palestinians out of Israel could be justified on Biblical authority. Recently the *Los Angeles Times* condemned Delay for using "the considerable power of his office" to "promote his personal apocalyptic views."

But in addition to blessing Israel, Christian Zionists are clear that those who fail to bless will be punished. Kay Arthur is a prominent American evangelist from Chattanooga, Tennessee. She appeared with Falwell on CBS's "60 Minutes" and there surprised her audience when she suggested that the assassination of Prime Minister Rabin was linked to his involvement in the Oslo Peace Accord.

In June CBN (The Christian Broadcasting Network which produces Pat Robertson's "700 Club") published a news item warning America about natural disasters that will be God's punishment on America. The day after Prime Minister Mahmoud Abbas was sworn in and the Roadmap was set in motion, CBN told us that the next day began the worst month of tornadoes in America's history. Their best example happened on 30 October 1991, when former President Bush (Sr.) met with Israelis and Palestinians to discuss compromises. CBN commented, "That same day, thousands of miles away, a powerful storm was brewing off the coast of Nova Scotia. On 31 October, what would be called 'the perfect storm' smashed into New England, pummeling the President's Kennebunkport, Maine, home with waves 30 feet high. It was a storm so rare that the weather patterns required to create it only happen once every 100 years."The deduction was clear: Bush had angered God in his negotiations and God had sent America punishing weather in response.

As odd as all of this may sound, it is consistent with the theological worldview embraced by Christian Zionists who believe that Christian faith and politics must be wed in Israel. To deny this synthesis is not only to contradict the Bible, but it is to stand in the way of what God is doing in history, a history foretold millennia ago by the Biblical prophets.

THE THEOLOGICAL BASIS OF CHRISTIAN ZIONISM: ON THE ROAD TO ARMAGEDDON

Stephen Sizer

> The purpose of this book is to warn about a rapidly expanding new movement in the Church that is subtly introducing the same errors that eventually and inevitably led to centuries of atrocities against the Jews and culminated in the Holocaust of the Third Reich ... They are setting up a philosophical system that will result in anti-Semitism.[1]

In his controversial book, *Road to Holocaust,* Hal Lindsey equates those who repudiate Christian Zionism with the Nazis because, from his perspective, both deny the Jews any future destiny within the purposes of God. This is somewhat ironic since in his other books, he predicts that Israel will make a 'Treaty with Hell',[2] and that two-thirds of the Jews will die in the Battle of Armageddon, when the 200 mile valley from the Sea of Galilee to Eilat will flow with irradiated blood several feet deep.[3]

The theology of Christian Zionism, espoused by Lindsey and many others, is deeply destructive, actively undermining the peace process in the Middle East. For example, in October 2000, following Ariel Sharon's provocative visit to the Temple Mount timed to bring down the government of Barak and destroy any hope of a compromise over the status of Jerusalem, an advertisement appeared in the *New York Times* entitled 'Open Letter to Evangelical Christians from Jews for Jesus'. In it they called upon evangelicals to show solidarity with the State of Israel.

> Now is the time to stand with Israel. Dear Brothers and Sisters in Christ, our hearts are heavy as we watch the images of

---

1 *The Final Battle* (Palos Verdes, California, Western Front, 1995), back page and p. 3.

2 Hal Lindsey, *The Late Great Planet Earth* (London, Lakeland, 1970), p. 151.

3 Hal Lindsey, *The Final Battle* (Palos Verdes: Western Front, 1995), pp. 250-252; *Israel and the Last Days* (Eugene, Oregon: Harvest House, 1983), pp. 20-30.

> violence and bloodshed in the Middle East ... Christian friends, "The gifts and calling of God are irrevocable" (Romans 11:29). So must our support for the survival of Israel in this dark hour be irrevocable. Now is the time for Christians to stand by Israel.[4]

Whether consciously or otherwise, Christian Zionists subscribe to a religious Jewish agenda best expressed by Rabbi Shlomo Aviner, who claims: "We should not forget ... that the supreme purpose of the ingathering of exiles and the establishment of our State is the building of the Temple. The Temple is at the very top of the pyramid."[5]

Another rabbi, Yisrael Meida, explains the link between politics and theology within Jewish Zionism: "It is all a matter of sovereignty. He who controls the Temple Mount, controls Jerusalem. And he who controls Jerusalem, controls the land of Israel."[6]

This paradigm may be illustrated by way of three concentric rings. The land represents the outer ring, Jerusalem the middle ring and the Temple is the centre ring. The three rings comprise the Zionist agenda by which the Land was claimed in 1948, the Old City of Jerusalem was occupied in 1967 and the Temple site is being contested. For the religious Zionist, Jewish or Christian, the three are inextricably linked. The Christian Zionist vision therefore is to work to see all three under exclusive Jewish control since this will lead to blessing for the entire world as nations recognise and respond to what God is seen to be doing in and through Israel.[7]

Christian Zionism can be distinguished by seven basic tenets.

1. An Ultra-Literalist Biblical Hermeneutic

Christian Zionism is constructed upon a novel hermeneutic in which all scripture is generally interpreted in an ultra-literal sense; the prophetic

---

4 Open Letter to Evangelical Christians from Jews for Jesus: 'Now is the Time to Stand with Israel', *The New York Times,* 23 October 2000.

5 Rabbi Shlomo Chaim Hacohen Aviner, cited in Grace Halsell, *Forcing God's Hand,* (Washington, Crossroads International, 1999), p. 71.

6 Yisrael Meida, cited in Halsell, *Forcing, op. cit.*, p68.

7 'Biblical Zionism, "Cutting Edge Theology for the 'Last Days'", *Word from Jerusalem,* International Christian Embassy, Jerusalem, September (2001), p. 9.

parts of scripture are seen as pre-written history; and eschatologically are believed to find their fulfilment in the interpreter's generation. This type of hermeneutic has been described as 'pesher' from the Aramaic for "interpretation".[8] This differs from a traditional Protestant hermeneutic which, while also based on literalism, nevertheless begins with the setting of the author as well as recipients and is also shaped by the historical, cultural, grammatical and theological context.[9]

The origin of this literalist hermeneutic can be traced to the early 19th century and in particular to the writings of Hatley Frere, George Faber, Lewis Way, Edward Irving and those who attended the Albury conferences from 1826.[10]

John Nelson Darby, who subsequently pioneered this hermeneutic in a more explicitly futurist and dispensational form, summed it up in one sentence when he admitted, "I prefer quoting many passages than enlarging upon them."[11] Based on his commitment to literalism, Darby formulated the doctrine of Dispensationalism and the rigid distinction between Israel and the Church which forms the basis of much contemporary Christian Zionism. Scofield explained his own literalism in this way:

> Not one instance exists of a 'spiritual' or figurative fulfilment of prophecy ... Jerusalem is always Jerusalem, Israel is always Israel, Zion is always Zion ... Prophecies may never be spiritualised, but are always literal. [12]

Dallas Theological Seminary, founded by one of Scofield's students, Lewis Sperry Chafer in 1924, has probably accomplished more for the cause of Dispensationalism and Christian Zionism than any other institution in the world. Through its faculty and students, for nearly eighty

---

8 Richard Kyle, *The Last Days are Here Again, A History of the End Times*, (Grand Rapids, Baker, 1998), p. 199.

9 *Ibid*.

10 D. W. Bebbington, *Evangelicalism in Modern Britain, A History from the 1730's to the 1980's*, (London, Unwin Hyman, 1989), p. 88; Edward Miller, *The History and Doctrines of Irvingism*, volume 1 (London, Kegan Paul, 1878), p36; Lewis Way, *The Latter Rain*, 2nd edition (London, 1821).

11 Darby, *Collected Writings*, edited by William Kelly (Kingston on Thames, Stow Hill Bible and Trust Depot, 1962) 11, p. 363.

12 C. I. Scofield, *Scofield Bible Correspondence Course*, (Chicago, Moody Bible Institute, n.d.), pp. 45-46.

years Dallas has contributed to a proliferation of dispensational thinking, from the Classical Dispensationalism of Cyrus Scofield and Lewis Chafer to the Revised Dispensationalism of Charles Ryrie[13] and John Walvoord[14]; the Apocalyptic Dispensationalism of Hal Lindsey[15] and Tim LaHaye;[16] the Messianic Dispensationalism of Moishe Rosen[17] and Arnold Fruchtenbaum;[18] and the Progressive Dispensationalism of Craig Blaising and Darrel Bock.[19]

---

[13] Charles C. Ryrie, *Dispensationalism Today*, (Chicago, Moody Press, 1965).

[14] John Walvoord, *Israel in Prophecy*, (Grand Rapids, Zondervan, 1962); *The Nations in Prophecy*, (Grand Rapids, Zondervan, 1967); *The Blessed Hope and the Tribulation*, (Grand Rapids, Zondervan, 1975); *The Rapture Question*, rev. edn. (Grand Rapids, Zondervan, 1979); *The Nations, Israel and the Church in Prophecy*, (Grand Rapids, Michigan, Zondervan, 1988); *Armageddon, Oil and the Middle East Crisis* (Grand Rapids, Michigan, Zondervan, 1990); *Major Bible Prophecies*, (New York, Harper Collins, 1991).

[15] Hal Lindsey, *The Late Great Planet Earth*, (London, Lakeland, 1970); *Satan is Alive and Well on Planet Earth*, (London, Lakeland, 1973); *There's A New World Coming, A Prophetic Odyssey*, (Santa Ana, California, Vision House, 1973); *The Liberation of Planet Earth*, (London, Lakeland, 1974); *The 1980's: Countdown to Armageddon*, (New York, Bantam, 1981); *The Promise*, (Eugene, Oregon, Harvest House, 1982); *The Rapture: Truth or Consequences*, (New York, Bantam, 1983); *The Terminal Generation*, (New York, Bantam, 1983); *A Prophetical Walk Through the Holy Land*, (Eugene, Oregon, Harvest House, 1983); *Israel and the Last Days*, (Eugene, Oregon, Harvest House, 1983); *Combat Faith*, (1986); *The Road to Holocaust*, (New York, Bantam, 1989); *Planet Earth-2000 AD*, (Palos Verdes, California, Western Front, 1994); *The Final Battle*, (Palos Verdes, California, Western Front, 1995); *Planet Earth-2000 AD*, revised edition (Palos Verdes, California, Western Front, 1996); *Amazing Grace*, (Palos Verdes, California, Western Front, 1996); *Blood Moon*, (Palos Verdes, California, Western Front, 1996); *The Apocalypse Code*, (Palos Verdes, California, Western Front, 1997); *Planet Earth: The Final Chapter*, (Beverly Hills, California, Western Front, 1998); *Where is America in Prophecy?* video (Murrieta, California, Hal Lindsey Ministries, 2001); *International Intelligence Briefing*, (Palos Verdes, California, Hal Lindsey Ministries), monthly journal.

[16] Tim LaHaye and Jerry B. Jenkins, *Are We Living in the End Times?* (Wheaton, Tyndale House, 1999); *Rapture Under Attack*, (Wheaton, Tyndale House); *Left Behind*, (Wheaton, Tyndale House, 1995); *Tribulation Force*, (Wheaton, Tyndale House, 1996); *Nicolae*, (Wheaton, Tyndale House, 1997); *Soul Harvest*, (Wheaton, Tyndale House, 1998); *Apollyon*, (Wheaton, Tyndale House, 1999); *Assassins*, (Wheaton, Tyndale House, 1999); *The Indwelling*, (Wheaton, Tyndale House, 2000); *The Mark*, (Wheaton, Tyndale House, 2001); *Desecration*, (Wheaton, Tyndale House, 2002); *The Remnant*, (Wheaton, Tyndale House, 2002).

[17] Moishe Rosen, *Jews for Jesus* (Old Tappan, New Jersey, Revell, 1974); *Y'shua* (Chicago, Moody Press, 1982); *Overture to Armageddon? Beyond the Gulf War* (San Bernardino, California, Here's Life Publishers, 1991).

[18] Arnold Fruchtenbaum, *Israelology: The Missing Link in Systematic Theology* (Tustin, Ariel Ministries, 1992).

[19] Craig A. Blaising and Darrell L. Bock, ed. *Dispensationalism, Israel and the Church*, (Grand Rapids, Michigan, Zondervan, 1992); *Progressive Dispensationalism*, (Wheaton, Victor, 1993); Robert L. Saucy, *The Case for Progressive Dispensationalism*, (Grand Rapids, Zondervan, 1993).

Patrick Goodenough of the International Christian Embassy Jerusalem (ICEJ) explains the consequence of this literalist approach: "We simply believe the Bible. And that Bible, which we understand has not been revoked, makes it quite clear that God has given this land as an eternal inheritance to the Jewish people."[20]

Rob Richards, former UK Director of the Churches Ministry Among Jewish People, (CMJ) offers a modern paraphrase of their position. "Israel is Israel is Israel."[21] The other six tenets of Christian Zionism follow from this literal and futurist reading of the Old Testament.

The fundamental error made is the refusal to acknowledge how Jesus and the Apostles reinterpreted the Old Testament. The implicit assumption made by Christian Zionists is that Old and New Testament run parallel into the future, the former speaking of Israel and the latter of the Church. This is at variance with the way the New Testament interprets, fulfils, annuls and completes the Old.

The question is not whether the promises of the old covenant are to be understood literally. It is instead a question of whether they should be understood in terms of Old Covenant shadow or in terms of New Covenant reality. This is the most basic hermeneutical error which Christian Zionists consistently repeat. This is illustrated in the way Christian Zionists continue to regard the Jews as God's "chosen people".

2. The Jews Remain God's "Chosen People"

Darby and Scofield taught that God has two separate but parallel means of working, one through the church, the other through Israel, the former being a parenthesis to the latter.[22] Thus there is, and always will remain, a distinction, "*between Israel, the Gentiles and the Church.*"[23]

Darby's Ecclesiology was indeed a form of "Replacement Theology" although he taught that Israel would replace the Church. Darby's strong and repeated condemnation of the visible church as

[20] Kathy Kern, 'Blessing Israel? Christian Embassy Responds' Christian Peacemakers Team, menno.org.cpt.news@MennoLink.org (2 November 1997).

[21] Rob Richards, *Has God Finished With Israel?* (Crowborough, Monarch, 1994), p. 23.

[22] Charles Ryrie, *Dispensationalism Today* (Chicago, Moody Press, 1965), p. 48.

[23] Ryrie, *Dispensationalism.*, p. 137.

apostate clearly influenced his innovative belief that the church era was now merely a 'parenthesis'[24] of the Last Days.

Darby regarded the church as merely one more dispensation that had failed like the previous five. Each in turn had lost its place in the divine economy and was under God's judgement. Just as Israel had been cut off, so he believed the church would also be.

In its classical form, Charles Ryrie insists the *sine qua non* of Dispensationalism to be:

> 1. A dispensationalist keeps Israel and the Church distinct ...
> 2. This distinction between Israel and the church is born out of a system of hermeneutics that is usually called literal interpretation ...[25]

Lewis Sperry Chafer, the founder of Dallas Theological Seminary, elaborates further on this dichotomy between Israel and the church:

> The dispensationalist believes that throughout the ages God is pursuing two distinct purposes: one related to the earth with earthly people and earthly objectives involved which is Judaism; while the other is related to heaven with heavenly people and heavenly objectives involved, which is Christianity.[26]

For Chafer, "Israel is an eternal nation, heir to an eternal land, with an eternal kingdom, on which David rules from an eternal throne"[27] so that in eternity, "... never the twain, Israel and church, shall meet." [28] Ryrie even concedes the conclusion of his critic Daniel Fuller in stating that the:

> ... basic promise of Dispensationalism is two purposes of God expressed in the formation of two peoples who maintain their distinction throughout eternity.[29]

---

[24] J. N. Darby, "The Dispensation of the Fulness of Times", *Collected Writings.*, Critical. Vol. I, p. 236.

[25] Ryrie, *Dispensationalism.*, pp. 39-40.

[26] Lewis Sperry Chafer, *Dispensationalism* (Dallas, Seminary Press, 1936), p. 107.

[27] Chafer, *Systematic Theology* (Dallas, Dallas Seminary Press, 1975), Vol. 4. pp. 315-323, cited in Gerstner, *Wrongly*, p. 184.

[28] Gerstner, *Wrongly*, p. 185.

[29] Ryrie, *Dispensationalism.*, pp. 44-45.

Certain implications follow the unconditional nature of the Abrahamic covenant. Based on their literal reading of the Old Testament, Christian Zionists believe that the Jews remain God's 'chosen people' enjoying a unique relationship, status and eternal purposes within their own land, separate from any promises made to the Church.

So, the promises made to Abraham remain true today for the physical descendants of Isaac, Jacob and Joseph. Based on passages like Genesis 15, Christian Friends of Israel, for example, insist that:

> The Bible teaches that Israel (people, land, nation) has a Divinely ordained and glorious future, and that God has neither rejected nor replaced His Jewish people.[30]

Similarly, Jews for Jesus perpetuate the dispensational distinction between God's purposes for Israel and that of the Church:

> We believe that Israel exists as a covenant people through whom God continues to accomplish His purposes and that the Church is an elect people in accordance with the New Covenant, comprising both Jews and Gentiles who acknowledge Jesus as Messiah and Redeemer.[31]

David Brickner affirms the position first propounded by Darby, that the Jews remain 'God's chosen people' while the church is merely "a parenthesis"[32] to God's future plans for the Jews. The implicit assumption is that the Jews continue to enjoy a special covenant relationship with God apart from Jesus Christ.

In the New Testament, the term "chosen" however, is never used of the Jewish people. It is therefore no longer appropriate to designate the Jews as God's "chosen people". The term has been redefined to describe all those who trust in Jesus Christ.

---

[30] Christian Friends of Israel, *Standing with Israel*, information leaflet, n.d.

[31] Jews for Jesus,, *Our Doctrinal Statement*, www.jews-for-jesus.org

[32] David Brickner, *Future Hope, A Jewish Christian Look at the End of the World*, 2nd edn. (San Francisco, Purple Pomegranate, 1999), p. 18.

3. The Restoration to and Occupation of Eretz Israel

Since Christian Zionists argue that the Jews remain God's chosen people, they also insist the promises concerning the land made to Abraham, Isaac and Jacob still apply unconditionally and in perpetuity to their physical descendants. On the basis of such promises they actively encourage Jews to 'return' to Zion. The contemporary State of Israel is seen as evidence of God's continuing protection and favour toward the Jews. However, they insist that the present borders of Israel are only a fraction of those God intends for the Jews. The geographical extent of "Eretz Israel", as Arnold Fruchtenbaum explains, is non-negotiable and covers everything from Egypt to Iraq:

> At no point in Jewish history have the Jews ever possessed all of the land from the Euphrates in the north to the River of Egypt in the south. Since God cannot lie, these things must yet come to pass.[33]

Fruchtenbaum makes this deduction from his literalist reading of Genesis 15:18. "On that day the Lord made a covenant with Abram and said, 'To your descendants I give this land, from the river of Egypt to the great river, the Euphrates.'"

Scofield, like many dispensationalists since,[34] bases his belief in a third final restoration on Ezekiel 37 and the vision of the valley of the dry bones.[35] Following the publication of the Balfour Declaration, for example, a CMJ editorial of 1918 was one of the first to assert that a Jewish State would be the fulfilment of Ezekiel's vision.[36]

It is difficult to conceive how such an entirely futuristic interpretation would have brought comfort to the Jewish exiles in Babylon to whom Ezekiel was sent to minister, yet this and similar passages provide the motivation for the restorationist movement today.

The Third International Christian Zionist Congress held in Jerusalem in February 1996 under the auspices of ICEJ, some 1,500

---

[33] Arnold G. Fruchtenbaum, 'This Land is Mine', *Issues*, 2. 4. www.jewsforjesus.org.

[34] Lindsey, *Late*, *op. cit.*, p. 51.

[35] Scofield, *Scofield*, *op. cit.*, fn. 1, p. 881.

[36] Kelvin Crombie, "CMJ and the Restoration of Israel", *Shalom*, 1, (1998). See also Anne Dexter, "The Eternal Covenant, Part 3, Exile and Restoration", *Shalom*, June (1989), pp. 10-11.

delegates from over 40 countries unanimously affirmed a proclamation and affirmation of Christian Zionism including the following beliefs:

> The Lord in His zealous love for Israel and the Jewish People blesses and curses peoples and judges nations based upon their treatment of the Chosen People of Israel ... According to God's distribution of nations, the Land of Israel has been given to the Jewish People by God as an everlasting possession by an eternal covenant. The Jewish People have the absolute right to possess and dwell in the Land, including Judea, Samaria, Gaza and the Golan.[37]

The tension between Christians who call for the implementation of international law and Zionists is no where more clearly polarized than on the issue of the status of Jerusalem.

4. Jerusalem, Eternal and Exclusive Jewish Capital

The place and purpose of Jerusalem, or "Zion" as it is sometimes called,[38] is deeply felt within Christian Zionism. Margaret Brearley insists, 'Jerusalem is the place where the Lord has 'chosen to place his name'. Lindsey also points out that:

> Jerusalem's importance in history is infinitely beyond its size and economic significance. From ages past, Jerusalem has been the most important city on this planet ... More prophecies have been made concerning Jerusalem than any other place on earth.[39]

In 1992, the ICEJ sponsored various receptions marking the 25th anniversary of what they referred to as the "Reunification of Jerusalem".[40] In 1996, at the International Christian Zionist Congress,

---

[37] *International Christian Zionist Congress Proclamation*, International Christian Embassy, Jerusalem. 25-29 February 1996.

[38] Zion more specifically refers to the hill on the western edge of the Old City of Jerusalem.

[39] Lindsey, Israel, *op. cit.*, p. 20.

[40] International Christian Embassy Jerusalem (Jerusalem, ICEJ, 1993), p. 24.

this position was reiterated when the 1,500 participants signed a declaration insisting:

> Because of the sovereign purposes of God for the City, Jerusalem must remain undivided, under Israeli sovereignty, open to all peoples, the capital of Israel only, and all nations should so concur and place their embassies here ... the truths of God are sovereign and it is written that the Land which He promised to His People is not to be partitioned.[41]

In 1997 the ICEJ also gave support to a full page advertisement placed in the *New York Times* entitled, "Christians Call for a United Jerusalem". It was signed by 10 evangelical leaders including Pat Robertson, chairman of Christian Broadcasting Network and President of the Christian Coalition; Oral Roberts, founder and chancellor of Oral Roberts University; Jerry Falwell, founder of Moral Majority; Ed McAteer, President of the Religious Roundtable; and David Allen Lewis, President of Christians United for Israel:

> We, the undersigned Christian spiritual leaders, communicating weekly to more than 100 million Christian Americans, are proud to join together in supporting the continued sovereignty of the State of Israel over the holy city of Jerusalem. We support Israel's efforts to reach reconciliation with its Arab neighbors, but we believe that Jerusalem, or any portion of it, shall not be negotiable in the peace process. Jerusalem must remain undivided as the eternal capital of the Jewish people.[42]

Readers were invited to "Join us in our holy mission to ensure that Jerusalem will remain the undivided, eternal capital of Israel." They claimed, "The battle for Jerusalem has begun, and it is time for believers in Christ to support our Jewish brethren and the State of Israel. The time for unity with the Jewish people is now."[43]

---

[41] "International Christian Zionist Congress Proclamation", International Christian Embassy, Jerusalem. 25-29 February (1996).

[42] "Christians Call for a United Jerusalem", *New York Times*, 18 April (1997), http://www.cdn-friends-icej.ca/united.html.

[43] *Ibid*.

The contradiction between the flow of biblical revelation in the New Testament and the Zionist agenda is no where more clearly seen than in the question of the Jewish Temple. This is also the most controversial issue uniting Christian Zionists with the more extreme Jewish Zionists.

5. The Rebuilding of the Jewish Temple

Just 500 metres by 300 metres it is according to Hal Lindsey, 'the most disputed 35 acres on the Planet.'[44] "I believe the fate of the world will be determined by an ancient feud over 35 acres of land."[45] Lindsey is representative of many Christian Zionists who are convinced that the Jewish Temple will be rebuilt very soon:

> Obstacle or no obstacle, it is certain that the Temple will be rebuilt. Prophecy demands it ... With the Jewish nation reborn in the land of Palestine, ancient Jerusalem once again under total Jewish control for the first time in 2600 years, and talk of rebuilding the great Temple, the most important sign of Jesus Christ's soon coming is before us ... It is like the key piece of a jigsaw puzzle being found ... For all those who trust in Jesus Christ, it is a time of electrifying excitement.[46]

David Brickner bases his belief on a futurist reading of Daniel 9:

> Obviously the Temple has been rebuilt because Daniel tells us this ruler puts an end to sacrifice and sets up some kind of abomination (a loathsome horror that would be anathema to Jewish worship) right inside the Temple in Jerusalem. Ultimately this ruler is destroyed in a final conflagration of enormous proportion.[47]

The conviction that the Jewish Temple must be rebuilt is, ironically, the Achilles' heel of Christian Zionism for it is inevitably also associated with the reintroduction of the Mosaic sacrificial system.

---

[44] Hal Lindsey, *Planet Earth 2000 AD* (Palos Verde, California, Western Front, 1994), p. 156.

[45] Hal Lindsey, "World's fate hangs on 35 acres", FreeRepublic.com 21 February 2001.

[46] Hal Lindsey, *The Late Great Planet Earth* (London, Lakeland, 1970), pp. 56-58.

[47] Brickner, *Future*.

The immediate context for Ezekiel's vision of a rebuilt Temple is the promised return of the Jews from Babylonian exile, not some long distant eschatological event. This would have been utterly meaningless to the exiles longing to return to Israel. How could Ezekiel be referring to some future millennial age, when Jesus Christ fulfilled the role of the sacrificial system, once for all, by the shedding his own blood?[48] To suggest that animal sacrifices must be reintroduced undermines the New Testament insistence that the work of Christ is sufficient, final and complete.[49]

It is not surprising however that Christian support for Jewish sovereignty over the Land, Jerusalem and the Temple Mount, inflames tensions between Jews and Arabs. This is further exacerbated by the language used to describe Arabs and Palestinians who oppose Zionism.

6. Antipathy Toward Arabs and Palestinians

Christian Zionists, while lovers of Israel, rarely show the same feelings toward Arabs and Palestinians. Anti-Arab prejudices and Orientalist stereotypes are common in their writings.[50] Comparisons between Hitler and the Arabs are common.[51] Hal Lindsey, the most prolific Christian Zionist writer, declares:

> Long ago the psalmist predicted the final mad attempt of the confederated Arab armies to destroy the nation of Israel ... The Palestinians are determined to trouble the world until they repossess what they feel is their land. The Arab nations consider it a matter of racial honour to destroy the State of Israel.[52]

Rob Richards justifies Israel's apartheid regime on the grounds that Palestinians are the biblical equivalent of the "alien" residents in Eretz Israel, to be respected but not entitled to the same status or equal

---

[48] Gary DeMar, *Last Days Madness* (Atlanta, American Vision, 1997), p. 85.

[49] Hebrews 2:17; Romans 3:25.

[50] Edward Said, *Orientalism* (New York, Vintage, 1978).

[51] Jan Willem van der Hoeven, *Babylon or Jerusalem?* (Shippensburg, Pasadena, Destiny Image Publishers, 1993), pp. 132-133.

[52] Lindsey, *Israel and the Last Days* (Eugene, Oregon, Harvest House, 1983), pp. 38-39.

rights as the Jews. "Palestinians and Arabs who have made Israel their home come under that biblical word 'alien'."[53]

Richards ignores the fact that most Palestinians did not choose to "make their home in Israel." Those over the age of 55 were living in their own land of Palestine long before the State of Israel was unilaterally imposed upon them in 1948. While the United Nations is invariably viewed with mistrust, America and Israel, like Siamese twins, are perceived to be pitted against an evil world dominated by Islam,[54] in which people like Yasser Arafat or Saddam Hussein are manifestations of the Anti-Christ.[55]

Regrettably such instances of racism which demonise Arabs and deny Palestinians the basic right to self determination are difficult to square with the New Testament ethic. The followers of Jesus Christ are called to be peace makers (Matthew 5:9), to love their enemies (Matthew 5:44) and to no longer regard others from a worldly point of view but instead to reach out to the widow and orphan, the poor, the sick and the stranger, through a ministry of reconciliation (2 Corinthians 5:16-20). Tragically, many Christian Zionists, it seems, are more concerned with heralding Armageddon than building peace.

7. Anxious for Armageddon

In the history of Christian theology, speculation concerning the interpretation of Revelation 20:1-10 and the meaning of the millennium have led theologians to suggest four alternatives:[56] Preterism teaches that the prophecies concerning the return of Christ were fulfilled in AD 70. (David Chilton and Max King). Amillennialism teaches that the millennium is symbolic, or already 'realised'[57] and refers to heaven where

[53] Rob Richards, *Has God Finished with Israel?* (Crowborough, Monarch/Olive Press, 1994), p. 159.

[54] Merrill Simon, *Jerry Falwell and the Jews* (Middle Village, New York, Jonathan David, 1984), pp. 63-64, 71-72.

[55] Charles Dyer, *The Rise of Babylon* (Wheaton: Tyndale, 1991).

[56] Stanley J. Grenz, *The Millennial Maze, Sorting out Evangelical Options*, (Downers Grove, InterVarsity Press, 1992); Robert G. Clouse, ed., *The Meaning of the Millennium*, (Downers Grove, InterVarsity, 1977); Cornelis P. Venema, *The Promise of the Future*, (Edinburgh, Banner of Truth, 2000), pp. 189-362.

[57] *Ibid.*, p. 235.

departed souls reign with Christ (Augustine, Luther, Calvin, Berkhof). Postmillennialism teaches a literal or symbolic period of a thousand years in which the Church triumphs over evil before Christ returns (George Whitefield, Jonathan Edwards). Premillennialism teaches that Christ will return to save the Church from evil and then reign for a literal thousand years on earth (Darby, Scofield, Chafer, Ryrie).

The 1967 "Six Day War" marked a significant watershed for Christian interest in Israel and Zionism. Most Christian Zionists, like Lindsey, Robertson and Falwell subscribe to a pessimistic and deterministic premillennial view of the future.

Charles Ryrie first described the Bible as "history prewritten",[58] while Charles Dyer views the dispensations as 'providing us with a chronological map to guide us.[59] Derek Prince amplifies this further by claiming, "The central theme of biblical prophecy … revolves around the land and the people of Israel."[60] Lindsey has popularised this idea that biblical prophecy is essentially futuristic and predictive, revealing God's future plans on earth and specifically concerning the future of Israel. So he claims, 'The center of the entire prophetic forecast is the State of Israel. Certain events in that nation's recent history prove the accuracy of the prophets. They also force us to accept the fact that the "countdown" has begun.'[61]

For example, without any hesitation or doubt Lindsey insists:

> And look what's happening in the Middle East—ground zero in the end-times events ... This phony peace deal in the Middle East thus only ensures that eventually there will be a thermonuclear holocaust in the Middle East ... This seems to parallel predictions in Revelation ... Mark my words. It will happen.[62]

> Let's talk about World War III ... We can almost see the handwriting on the wall ... Does this sound like a scenario that

[58] Charles Ryrie, *The Living End*, (Old Tappan, Revell, 1976), p. 80.

[59] Charles Dyer, *The Rise of Babylon, Signs of the End Times*, (Wheaton, Illinois, Tyndale House, 1991), p. 189.

[60] Prince, *Last*, *op. cit.*, p. 54.

[61] Lindsey, *1980's*, *op. cit.*, p. 11.

[62] Lindsey, *Planet.*, pp. 243-244.

> could happen in the very near future? Perhaps at almost any minute? You bet it does.[63]

The titles of Lindsey's books are typical of many other Christian Zionist writers in showing an increasingly exaggerated and almost pathological emphasis on the apocalyptic, on death and suffering, especially as the year 2000 approached.[64] Lindsey's last but one book, *The Final Battle*, includes the following:

> Never before, in one book, has there been such a complete and detailed look at the events leading up to "The Battle of Armageddon".[65]

At times Lindsey's description of the suffering inherent in this most terrible scenario of a nuclear holocaust is tasteless if not repulsive.

> Man has pretty much exhausted his arsenal. There are few popguns left, but not very much left to pop them. At least four billion people have perished in the first 14 Judgments alone. Now it's God's turn.[66]

Lindsey, along with people like Jack Van Impe offer graphic maps showing future military movements of American, Russian, Chinese and African armies and naval convoys which they claim will contend with one another in the battle of Armageddon.[67]

In viewing prophecy in this way, Lindsey and Van Impe detach predictions concerning the future from the covenantal context within which the prophecies were originally given. Lindsey's view is at variance with the Hebrew prophets themselves who consistently stress that their

---

[63] Lindsey, *Planet.*, p. 255.

[64] *Satan is Alive and Well on Planet Earth* (London, Lakeland, 1973); *The Terminal Generation* (New York, Bantam,); *The 1980's: Countdown to Armageddon* (New York, Bantam, 1981); *Combat Faith* (1986); *The Road to Holocaust* (New York, Bantam, 1989); *Planet Earth-2000, Will Man Survive?* (Palos Verdes, California, Western Front, 1994); *The Final Battle* (Palos Verdes, California, Western Front, 1995); *The Apocalypse Code* (Palos Verdes, California, Western Front, 1997);

[65] Hal Lindsey, *The Final Battle* (Palos Verdes, California, Western Front, 1995), front cover.

[66] Lindsey, *Planet Earth: The Final Chapter*, p. 254.

[67] Hal Lindsey, *The Late Great Planet Earth* (London, Lakeland, 1970), p. 155; Louis Goldberg, *Turbulence Over the Middle East* (Neptune, New Jersey, Loizeaux Brothers, 1982), p. 172.

intention was to call God's people back to the terms of their covenant relationship, not reveal arbitrary and otherwise hidden facts about predestined future events. Authentic biblical prophecy is always conditional rather than fatalistic. The promises and warnings are conditional upon how people respond to God's instructions.

Such literalist assumptions preclude any possibility of an alternative reading of the Bible, history or a just and lasting outcome to the search for peace in the Middle East.

A Theological Critique of Christian Zionism

Satirically, Kenneth Cragg summarises the implications of Christian Zionism's ethnic exclusivity:

> It is so; God chose the Jews; the land is theirs by divine gift. These dicta cannot be questioned or resisted. They are final. Such verdicts come infallibly from Christian biblicists for whom Israel can do no wrong, thus fortified. But can such positivism, this unquestioning finality, be compatible with the integrity of the Prophets themselves? It certainly cannot square with the open peoplehood under God which is the crux of New Testament faith. Nor can it well be reconciled with the ethical demands central to law and election alike.[68]

Christian Zionism only thrives on a futurist and literal hermeneutic when Old Testament promises made to the ancient Jewish people are transposed on to the contemporary State of Israel. To do so it is necessary to ignore, marginalise or by-pass the New Testament which reinterprets, annuls and fulfils those promises in and through Jesus Christ and his followers.

The fundamental question Christian Zionists must therefore answer is this: What difference did the coming of Jesus Christ make to the traditional Jewish hopes and expectations about the land? We may not interpret the Old Covenant as if the coming of Jesus made little or no difference to the nationalistic and territorial aspirations of 1st-century

[68] Kenneth Cragg, *The Arab Christian A History in the Middle East* (London, Mowbray, 1992), p. 238.

Judaism. In the process of redemptive history a dramatic movement has been made from type to reality, from shadow to substance.

Christian Zionism is an exclusive theology that focuses on the Jews in the land rather than an inclusive theology that centres on Jesus Christ, the Saviour of the world. Christian Zionism provides a theological endorsement for apartheid and human rights abuses, rather than a theology of justice, peace and reconciliation which lies at the heart of the New Covenant.

Like Isaac's children Jacob and Esau, it is time to stop fighting over the birthright and start sharing the blessings.[69] Garth Hewitt has written many songs about the plight of the Christian community in Israel and Palestine. One of them, based on some verses from the Jewish Talmud, is called "Ten measures of beauty God gave to the world" and serves as a prayer for all the peoples of the land:

> May the justice of God fall down like fire
> and bring a home for the Palestinian.
> May the mercy of God pour down like rain
> and protect the Jewish people.
> And may the beautiful eyes of a Holy God
> who weeps for His children
> Bring the healing hope for His wounded ones
> For the Jew and the Palestinian.

---

[69] Yehezkel Landau, An illustration given at St George's, Jerusalem, December 1998.

KEYS FOR UNDERSTANDING THE CHRISTIAN ZIONISTS' INTERPRETATION OF THE BIBLE

Göran Gunner

A survey of 230 books and pamphlets published over the past one hundred years by Swedish writers and by British, American, and international writers available in Swedish translation reveals a broad array of writers with a Christian Zionist Biblical perspective. Although many would not describe themselves as Christian Zionists, they share several basic keys to Biblical interpretation.

The *first key* for a Christian Zionist interpretation is the use of a particular Canon within the Biblical material. There is an overall assumption about the Biblical textual material to be used. The Second Coming of Christ is the determining factor, not just as one among others but as the most important prophetic message. The next major step in human history, according to the plan of God in these selected texts, is to be the Second Coming of Christ. The popular "Left Behind" series of books by Tim LaHaye and Jerry Jenkins has sold at least 40 million copies and concentrates on events around the Second Coming of Christ.[1]

A *second key* used by Christian Zionists is that Biblical interpretation and Israel are closely interrelated. The idea is that if people read the Bible without giving Israel its right position, they will be lost and talk nonsense. And, of course, this has been increasingly accentuated after the establishment of the State of Israel. The finger of God is viewed as directly related to the special privileges of Israel. At the same time, Israel is the center of destiny for all humanity.

The *third key* is that Biblical prophecies are expected to be fulfilled in the human world according to the plan of God. Surprisingly, quotations from the Bible are relatively few and the authors use a set of small text-units in a certain pattern in which often one text is used to comment

---

[1] See www.leftbehind.com

upon another text, as though the author is building a puzzle. The following texts relate to the specific questions of Israel and not to other events in the overall end-time scenario.

Very few of the Christian Zionist authors take quotations from the New Testament in their argument for Israel or the role of Israel and the Jewish people in their speculations about the end time. The following list indicates which New Testament books provide frequently used quotations:

Matthew: 21 verses (19: 28; 23: 37-38; 24: 32-34; 25: 31-46)
Luke: 9 verses (1: 31-32; 21: 24, 29-33)
Mark: none
John: none
Acts: 8 verses (1: 6-7; 3: 19-21; 15: 15-17)
Romans: 23 verses (8: 17-23; 9: 4-6, 27-29; 11: 1-2, 5-7, 11, 15, 25-27)
2 Thessalonians: 2 verses (2: 3-4)

It is easy to conclude that this is not a major issue in the New Testament. From Matthew only 21 verses are used at all and from Luke only 9 verses, whereas none are used from Mark and John. The most commonly used verses are Luke 21: 24 and 29-33 and Romans 11: 25-27. Luke 21: 24 is about Jerusalem trampled underfoot by the Gentiles until the day of the Gentiles has run its course. Luke 21: 29-33 is the lesson from the fig tree and all other trees. Romans 11: 25-27 is about a divine secret concerning Israel and the Gentiles when God is granting the gracious gift of a covenant with Israel and taking away Israel's sins.

Thus, we must turn to the Old Testament and the prophets for analysis of frequently cited texts. Christian Zionists seldom quote the Minor Prophets either. The quotations in use are Hosea 1: 11, 2: 14-23 3: 4-5 and 11: 11; Obadiah verses 15 and 17-21; Micah 2: 12, 4: 1-8, 5: 2-3 and 7-8, 7: 11; Malachi 3: 3-6; Amos 9: 11-15; Joel 2: 23, 26-32 and 3: 1-2, 17-18; and Zechariah 2: 4-12, 8: 7-8 and 10: 6 and 10. The 230 books surveyed produced a pattern that divides prophetic statements as having already happened in history, as going on just now, or as still to come in the future. By far the largest number of authors view the prophecies as not yet having happened but coming in the future.

Whether using Major or Minor Prophets, however, Christian Zionist authors disagree among themselves as to how to interpret the time of the fulfillment of the prophecies. Authors of every decade reflect this disagreement. The Christian Zionist authors mainly use these texts to describe the blessings of the Messianic kingdom even though some assume the fulfillment is occurring in the Middle East today in the lifetime of the author.

The books of Jeremiah and of Isaiah are used more frequently in referring to the return of the Jews, a flourishing land and the establishment of the State of Israel. In spite of that, out of 52 chapters in the book of Jeremiah, only 54 verses are quoted: 3: 14-18; 16: 14-18; 23: 3-8; 29: 14; 30: 3-7, 10-11; 31: 1, 3, 7-12, 15-17, 31-40; 32: 36-44; 33: 14 and 50: 4-5.

For Isaiah, the same pattern may be seen: 2: 1-4; 9: 1-7 and11; 19: 23-25; 32: 15-18; 33: 17-24 and 35; 41: 18-19; 43: 1-6; 49: 11-23; 55: 12-14; 60; 61; 65 and 66. These frequently used verses also are divided by various authors as to whether prophecies will occur in the future, are now occurring, or have already occurred. Again, the expectation of future fulfillment outweighs fulfillment in the present or past but various authors disagree about when completion of the prophecies will occur.

The quotations from chapters 7 and 11 are the texts that the Gospel of Matthew says have been fulfilled with the birth of Christ.

Some verses from the Book of Revelations are cited to give the pattern for the Second Coming of Christ and the campaign of Armageddon. The book of Daniel, especially 9: 24-27, gives the pattern of dispensations and the idea of one dispensation for the church to be replaced after the Second Coming of Christ by a dispensation of Israel. A few verses from Genesis (12: 1-7; 13: 14-15; 15: 13-18; and 17: 7-8) give the geopolitical framework believed to describe the future borders of the Promised Land. A greater Israel is predicted, sometimes including Lebanon, Jordan, Syria, northern Saudi Arabia, Kuwait, and parts of Iraq. Thus, to ask what will happen to the West Bank is of no interest at all. It is much more interesting to predict how Israel will get the East Bank. The prophet Ezekiel (chapters 36-39) provides the pattern of all coming invasions of Israel and equates nuclear Armageddon theology with the final catastrophe.

It is obvious that the Christian Zionist authors do not read the Bible in totality but use the hermeneutical principles of the Second Coming of Christ and the priority of Israel as keys. They often tell their readers there is a fulfillment of prophecies according to the Bible or according to the word of God, but only to a small degree do they use the Bible itself.

The *fourth key* to Christian Zionist Biblical interpretation is based on the assumption that the prophetic understanding is to be revealed in our time. It is never enough to read the Biblical texts or even the few selected verses from the Bible alone. Readers always need an interpretation made through preaching or in a written commentary. The prophetic message always requires an accurate interpretation. Nancy Ammerman has concluded that the people of one Zionist congregation prefer reading about the prophecies to reading the Bible itself.[2]

A typical statement from the Christian Zionists runs like this:

> In light of all that's going on in our world today, I love to read the newspaper every morning and tune in the cable news channels ... God's prophecies in the Bible serve as the guide, master plan, or picture on the box by which we can evaluate the many current events in our world today to see how they fit together in God's program for this world.[3]

The present time always directs the interpretation for each author. A survey of book covers gives an idea of some of the priorities of Christian Zionist interpretation over the past several decades.

In the 1920s and 1930s, the dispensational model was used to introduce the Second Coming of Christ and was shown on book covers of the time. The covers show Christ in the sky or an angel on the threshold of heaven with titles like *Look, He is Coming* or *Jesus is Coming.* But the authors also found current signs in Palestine by using Isaiah 19: 23 as describing the new railroad to Baghdad or Haggai 2: 19-23 as being fulfilled by the entry of General Allenby into Jerusalem. Of course, the greatest sign of fulfillment of prophecy was the establishment of Jewish communities in Palestine during this era.

During the 1940s, Adolph Hitler finds a place in the apocalyptic scenario. He was looked upon as part of a divine plan for salvation and his historic mission was being the hunter in Jeremiah 16: 16 who forced the Jews to go to Palestine as preparation for the Second Coming of

---

[2] Nancy Ammerman, *Bible Believers: Fundamentalists in the Modern World*, Rutgers Universeity Press, New Brunswick, N. J., 1987.

[3] Mark Hitchcock, *The Coming Islamic Invasion of Israel*, Multnoma Publishers, Sisters, Or., 2002.

Christ. In the time after the Second World War, the titles on book covers asked questions like *Is There One More War to Come?* with pictures from the ruined Europe. Later the mushroom cloud put the focus on the nuclear bomb in Biblical light. The continuing immigration of Jews and the flourishing *kibbutzim* were among the signs of the time. It was easy to see the geopolitical questions of the day as prophetic issues.

In the 1960s and 1970s, Russia entered the agenda along with the authors' fears of the threat of Communism and the anticipated Russian invasion of Israel. Book covers from the period show the Cossacks under the Red banner or Soviet tanks entering Israel. Book titles proclaim *Gog and his War against Israel* and *The Coming Russian Invasion of Israel.* They represent Christian Zionism in the shadow of an Armageddon theology anticipating a nuclear catastrophe.

The establishment of the State of Israel in 1948 was a complete surprise to the Christian Zionists, at least in Scandinavia. They did not expect a state created by the people themselves but had been longing for the Millennium inaugurated by Christ's coming again. Thus, they developed new interpretations. First, at the end of the 1950s, the State of Israel became a sign of the end time. In the 1960s, it developed as an alternative version of Christian Zionism compared to Armageddon theology. The stress was put on the State of Israel and the Christian support for the state while Armageddon theology was reduced. Book covers of the time proclaimed *Zionism, a Liberation Movement, Israel—The Destiny for the Entire Humanity* and *For or Against Zionism* with the obvious right answer being FOR.

In the 1980s, the focus was on the coming evil ruler of Islam in the figures of Ayatollah Khomeini in Iran and President Saddam Hussein in Iraq, with book covers stating *The West at the Crossroad* and *The New Babylon.*

At this time, Swedish material practically disappears, along with American translations into Swedish, although recently the *Left Behind* series has appeared in Scandinavian languages. However, much more has occurred in the American area. After 9/11, the question asked is about the role of the United States in prophecy. The authors agree that there is no major role but say that the United States has a duty to protect the world against terror and to support freedom and democracy.[4]

[4] I have discussed this in an article: "9.11 and Armageddon. The Christian Right and George W. Bush" in *Holy Land Studies* No. 1, September 2003.

What will happen after the Second Coming of Christ when all born-again Christians in the U.S. are together with Christ in the sky? Included will be all responsible persons in the U.S. government, military, business sector, and so on, so one must look at Europe for the future. Maybe the European Union is the future major actor, according to some interpreters, and perhaps Prince Charles of Great Britain is the coming Antichrist!

In the Armageddon theology of today, the future of the Middle East is spelled WAR and TERROR. Within this type of Christian Zionist interpretation, there is no place for negotiation between Israelis and Palestinians and no place for peace. The next major catastrophe for the Middle East is expected to happen very soon.

According to Armageddon theology of today, Islam will play a decisive role. It is important to see that the coming war focuses on the Dome of the Rock as a symbol of Jerusalem. And, of course, the Dome will be replaced by the Jewish Temple.

The Christian Zionist interpreters more or less use the same Biblical texts as proofs for the events currently in progress in the Middle as being foretold by God. The intention is to provide evidence that God is in control and is actually directing the force of history even when the military powers of nations are in use.

All the books cited in the paper are playing on this same field. They count on people reading the books but not the Bible itself and not comparing one book to another. Every author claims to reveal the truth but obviously each one cannot tell the truth since the "truth" differs all the time. Still, the authors assure the reader that they know the truth.

The *fifth and last key* to understanding the Christian Zionist perspective is that the author is retelling the Biblical text, or—we may say—is manipulating the text. Some examples reveal the authors' recognition of Islam as the enemy of Israel. Under the heading "ISLAM'S JIHAD FOR JERUSALEM", one text begins: "Let us first have a look at a text from Zechariah 12: 2-3" and then follows:

> "Zechariah predicted: Behold, I am going to make Jerusalem a cup that causes intoxication to all the surrounding peoples, and when the siege is against Jerusalem, it will also be against Judea (the Jews). And it will come about in that day that I will make Jerusalem a burdensome stone for all the peoples; all

> who attempt to lift it will be severely injured. And all the nations of the earth will be gathered (for war) because of it."[5]

The author, Hal Lindsey, assures the reader that this is a literal translation directly from Hebrew. That is to say, they should forget all other translations because his is the correct one. Inserted into the translation, however, are the words "the Jews" and "for war". This manipulation of the text presents the author's interpretation as if it were within the actual Biblical text. Of course, the heading has already told the reader how to view the passage: it is about "Islam's Jihad for Jerusalem". Then there are sentences of explanation describing the neighboring states to Israel as being Muslim today so that "Just as a drunken person acts emotionally without reason, so it was predicted the neighboring states would be intoxicated with religiously driven passion and hate." According to the author, this is major evidence that God has predicted everlasting hatred against the State of Israel and the coming Armageddon as the climax of hatred.

It is obvious that the intention is to say that when readers grasp the meaning (or the manipulated meaning) of the text, they will understand the real intent of the passage. So far, no one during history, not even the prophet himself, has, according to the authors, understood the actual meaning of these Biblical prophecies.

Under the heading "The Final Jihad," the author Mark Hitchcock believes that Ezekiel 38-39 describes the final Jihad. Although the word Jihad is not mentioned by Ezekiel, the author argues that the reasons for Jihad are given there:[6]

> ... Notice the reasons God gives for why this horde of nations invades Israel: "You will go up, you will come like a storm; you will be like a cloud covering the land, you and all your troops, and many people with you."

The interpreter continues:

> They will be motivated by a Satanic hatred for the Jewish people to completely cover their land and wipe them out of

---

[5] Hal Lindsey, *The Everlasting Hatred: The Roots of Jihad*, Oracle House, Murrieta, CA., 2002.

[6] Hitchcock, *op. cit.*

> the face of the earth. Of course, this is nothing new today. This is the stated goal of almost every Islamic nation.

Then the next quotation from Ezekiel follows: "... go up against those who are at rest, that live securely, all of them living without walls and having no bars or gates ..."

The interpretation is that militant Islamic regimes would love nothing more than to invade Israel and if they can, to bring about a blow against the West at the same time. The author claims, "...well, that would just be icing on the cake." The book was published in 2002 and it would be interesting to listen to the literal interpretation of the text in 2005. Israel living without walls is seen as a prerequisite for the Islamic Jihad. The Ezekiel message about the Wall in the West Bank seems to be clear—if we dare to use the literal interpretation when we face the Israeli-built Wall!

Then the author excludes half a verse before continuing with: "Have you come to capture spoil? Have you assembled your company to seize plunder to carry away silver and gold, to take away cattle and goods to capture great spoil?" Part of the Islamic Jihad against Israel is assumed to be to plunder. But the missing Biblical text tells us that the question is put by "Sheba and Dedan and the merchants of Tarshish." In another part of his book, the author identifies Sheba and Dedan with Saudi Arabia. However, by excluding that part from his quotation, Hitchcock makes it appear as if Israel is putting the question to the Islamic invaders, while according to the same literal interpretation, it should have been Saudi Arabia putting the question to Israel. Talk about manipulating the Biblical text!

Here is another example from the same author. Under the heading of "The Islamic Legion," he combines Ezekiel 38: 10 with 38: 5:[7]

> "Thus says the Lord God: 'It will come about on that day that thoughts will come into your mind and you will devise an evil plan.'
>
> "Persia, Ethiopia and Put with them, all of them with shield and helmet."

[7] Hitchcock, *op. cit.*

The reason for this combination is that Hitchcock wants to give the message that "God says that the end-time invaders of Israel have an "evil plan" since "God doesn't hesitate at all to use the word 'evil'." Now follows an interesting statement: "Just as President Bush had his list of three nations he identified as the axis of evil, in Ezekiel 38: 5, God lists three nations that we might call the 'end-time axis of evil'." He does not even put God first, but President Bush. God, by this interpretation, is following Bush. Interestingly, the author finds one of the nations on the presidential list also included in the list of God—Persia/Iran. The author goes on to identify Ezekiel's axis of evil with "Persia, Ethiopia and Put." These nations are named as part of the Islamic legion even though we know that Ethiopia has a majority of Christians.

Under the title *The War against Babylon: The First Prophetic War*, Grant Jeffrey, the author, finds in the book of Jeremiah a prophetic description of the future war:[8]

> "For, lo, I will raise and cause to come up against Babylon an assembly of great nations from the north country: and they shall set themselves in array against her; from thence she shall be taken: their arrows shall be as of mighty expert men; none shall return in vain." (Jeremiah 50: 9)

When the explanation is added, the "arrows" have become "missiles." A rhetorical question asks furthermore if Jeremiah in his vision saw the Tomahawk cruise missiles. The answer must be "yes" and the obvious conclusion to be drawn by the reader is that the U.S. war against Iraq was predicted by Jeremiah in the Bible.

One more example reveals this use of ancient texts as proof of current events. Under the title "*The Key Terrorist-Supporting Nations*" with a sub-title *The Ten Lost Tribes and the Pashtun Tribe*", Jeffrey argues that "Since God's promises are unbreakable, we must conclude that He has preserved the ten tribes until He will restore them to the Holy Land in the final days."[9] He goes on to quote Ezekiel 37: 21:

> "Thus saith the Lord God: 'Behold, I will take the children of Israel from among the heathen, whither they be gone, and

[8] Grant R. Jeffrey, *War on Terror: Unfolding Bible Prophecy*, Frontier Research Publications, Toronto, On., 2002.

[9] Jeffrey, *op. cit.*

> will gather them on every side, and bring them into their own land.'"

The author of the book argues that the Afghan Pashtun tribe may be the remnant of the ten lost tribes of Israel. The president of Afghanistan, Mr Karzai, is Pashtun as well as the U.S. ambassador to Kabul, so this tribe may be considered to be on the "right" side in the War against Terrorism. But the Taliban also belong to the Pashtun tribe. The author is aware of the contradiction and declares it "one of the greatest historical ironies if it turns out that the Taliban, a Jewish-hating group and supporter of terrorism against Israel, who belong to the Pashtun tribe are actually descendants of the ancient Lost Tribes of Israel." The conclusion is not that the U.S.has tried to wipe out the rest of the lost tribe but that the "Good Shepherd knows the sheep of his pasture and will fulfill the word of His prophecy."

Theology and the sacred texts have been applied and adjusted to the development of the modern Israeli state. The Christian Zionist authors claim to be friends and supporters of Israel, yet they predict a catastrophe for the Jews. They urge activism even though there is no choice. According to the divine plan, everything is predicted and unavoidable. This is a type of "power theology" that creates friends and enemies while putting up fences around a small group of Christian Zionists. Jewish nationalism has been viewed as an answer to the divine call to the Holy Land and should be defended, encouraged, and, if necessary, corrected in order to fulfill the geography and structural goals of the divine plan. On the contrary, Arab and Palestinian nationalism as well as Islamic movements are conceived as demonic forces to be defeated at all costs.

The Christian Zionist authors are prisoners of their own preconceived notions which consist of a fixed set of expectations, hermeneutical rules, and deliberate strategies. In this "power theology," people of the Middle East become pawns in a game. A politicized interpretation does not object to adjusting geographical borders in favor of Israel or to Israeli land grabbing and occupation. It is about legitimizing an Israeli military expansionist policy in the name of Christian theology.

ISRAEL AS AN EXTENSION OF AMERICAN EMPIRE

Jeff Halper

There are many tragic and self-destructive features of the Occupation for Israel itself. Although the country was founded on the "original sin" of exclusivity and the expulsion of the refugees, it nevertheless had (has?) the potential to develop into a normal, even progressive society. Many of the socialist principles that accompanied the Zionist program led in those directions. Israel always talked of democracy, even extending citizenship to its Arab population in 1948, even though the underlying concept of a "Jewish democracy," coupled with a deep-based fear of demographics only exacerbated by the Occupation, has emptied that of much of its content. It constituted itself as a welfare state, only to see that largely dismantled as the Israel-Palestine conflict gave dominance to the right, whose agenda, together with expansion, was anti-socialist and pro-privatization. Israel became a member of the Socialist International and engaged in constructive development work in Africa, Asia and Latin America, but its need for military strength, coupled with a self-serving "alliance" with the US, has led it to become a major arms dealer on a global scale, a subverter of progressive civil society elements throughout the developing world.

One of the tragic developments related to this rightward shift of Israeli politics and social policies—even defining Israel's view of itself in the world—is its emergence as a center for the global right-wing, a constellation of nefarious ideologies, groups and forces that seek nothing less than American-Christian hegemony over the entire world. In a unique and, again, tragic confluence of historical processes, the rise of an aggressive neo-con ideology and militaristic foreign policy, centered in the US but not limited to it, coincides with the emergence of the Israeli right and an expansionist Israel. 'Coincides' might understate the case: in fact, the rise of a religious right in the West owes much of its impetus to Zionism and Israel, while Israel is able to pursue its Occupation only because of its willingness to serve Western (mainly US) imperial interests—including acting as a galvanizing center for global neo-con forces. What follows is a brief survey of those forces and their interplay with Israel.

Israel as a center of neo-con ideology and mobilization

Many of the founders of neo-conservatism in the 1970s and most of its prominent advocates today are Jewish. This is not an irrelevant fact, nor is it "anti-Semitic" to say so. Neo-conservatism emerged not of traditional anti-New Deal Republican conservatism, which was largely WASP and Middle Western in its roots, but out of Roosevelt's New Deal itself, which resonated with Eastern European Jewish immigrants, many of whom were working class and attracted to socialism and communism. From there they and their children gravitated to the New Left and then to liberalism (Irving Kristol has described a neo-con as "a liberal mugged by reality.") The Jewish magazine *Commentary*, a publication of Jewish liberals who were indeed mugged by the Sixties, became the fountain and mouthpiece of neo-conservatism as it emerged and entered into power politics during the Reagan Administration (when Jeanne Kirkpatrick became the leading non-Jewish luminary).

Just a glance at some of the most prominent neo-cons—*Commentary* founder and editor Norman Podhoretz; Irving Kristol, former *Commentary* editor and founder of The Public Interest; Elliot Abrams, head of the Middle East Desk of the National Security Council and Podhoretz's son-in-law; Douglas Feith, Undersecretary of Defense and one of the architects of the occupation of Iraq; Paul Wolfowitz, former Deputy Secretary of Defense now heading the World Bank; Richard Perle, former Chairman of the Pentagon's Defense Policy Board; William Kristol, son of Irving, co-founder of the Project for a New American Century; Daniel Pipes, Middle East Studies professor and founder of the notorious Campus Watch; Charles Krauthammer, *Washington Post* columnist; Dov Zakheim, former Comptroller of the Department of Defense; David Wurmser, Cheney's chief Middle East advisor; Kenneth Adelman, a hawkish arms control expert and senior Pentagon official, just to name a few—points up a Jewish connection that is hard to understate.

Israel, of course, has long been of prime concern to these pillars of the American Jewish community, who now enjoy the political clout to integrate that issue seamlessly into the neo-con doctrine—and thereby into the very fabric of American foreign policy and military strategy. It is a measure of how Jews have assimilated into American life, how they identify completely with the United States—of which they see Israel as an extension, the "only democracy in the Middle East." In the "clash of civilizations" paradigm that defines the neo-con approach, the United States has embarked on a pre-emptive crusade to generate a "global democratic revolution"—regime change to usher in governments more reflective of US values and thus more in tune with American interests—all under American (corporate) tutelage: American Empire in a truly New American Century. Israel, then, fits neatly into the equation in three ways. First, it represents just that kind of American underling the U.S. holds up as its model (and how Israel benefits from American largesse should help persuade other regimes); second, it possesses the military capacity and political readiness to further American interests; and third, it is located in the Middle East, the primary "theater" of the Crusade, where it is engaged with America's declared arch-enemy, "radical Islam." A strong Israel, then, represents a strong America.

The centrality of Israel to Christian fundamentalists

All this dovetails neatly with yet another powerful strand of right-wing ideology, that of Christian Zionism. According to Stephen Sizer, the author of *Christian Zionism* (2003), modern Christian fundamentalism is largely defined by a notion of dispensationalism, the idea that humanity will go through seven periods of Divine testing, culminating in Armageddon and the Second Coming of Christ. In this eschatology, the Jews and the modern state of Israel play such a key role that fundamentalism, dispensationalism and Christian Zionism are virtually interchangeable. As explained by Sizer, Christian Zionism claims not only that every act taken by Israel is orchestrated by God and should be condoned, supported, and even praised by everyone else, but that the Jews will lead the process since, in the fundamentalist view, this will lead to blessing for the entire world as nations recognise and respond to what God is seen to be doing in and through Israel …

While Christian Zionism also has pockets of strength elsewhere—in Holland and Scandinavia, for example, as well as among many fundamentalists in the developing world—its center is certainly the United States, where it was brought from England in the middle 19th century by John Nelson Darby, whom Sizer describes as "the father of Dispensationalism," for whom a revived Israel became a cornerstone of his apocalyptic theology ... While Christians enjoy the Second Coming and the salvation of the Millennium, Jews, their supposed allies, suffer a much different fate: at Armageddon two-thirds of the Jews die and the final third convert to Christianity, a precondition of the Second Coming. Dispensationalism is hardly a Jewish-friendly theology. The three major types of dispensationalism, however—*Apocalyptic* (pre-occupied with the End of Time; *Messianic* (busy evangelising Jews for Jesus); and *Political* (using political means to defend and 'bless' Israel)—share the same basic tenets: a commitment to biblical literalism; a futurist eschatology; and the restoration of the Jews to Palestine.

Israel's independence in 1948 and its stunning victory in the 1967 'Six Day War'—foreshadowing Armageddon—galvanized Christian Zionists, but only with the election in 1976 of President Jimmy Carter, a 'born again' Christian, which coincided with Menachem Begin's 1977 election as Prime Minister of Israel, did they truly begin coalescing as an organized political force within American politics—a trend consolidated by the subsequent election of Reagan and the emergence of Jerry Falwell's 'Moral Majority'. Not only did the Zionist Jewish lobby in the US have a champion in the White House, but Christian Zionists—including Attorney General Ed Meese, Secretary of Defense Casper Weinberger, Secretary of the Interior James Watt and, indeed, Reagan himself—achieved political power for the first time. Hal Lindsey, Pat Robertson and Falwell, who in 1982 was invited by Reagan to give a briefing to the National Security Council, gained formal access to American political leaders and policy-makers.

Mobilizing the global extreme right

Just as it has benefited from the rise of the Right in the U.S. and elsewhere in Europe, Israel under the Likud (though not exclusively under the Likud) has become a center for mobilizing right-wing ideological and political forces on a global scale. Most visible in this regard is the annual Jerusalem Summit (actually held in the Israeli city of Herzliya), where the neo-con tribe gathers and galvanizes its plans for world domination around their concern for Israel. We are not speaking of marginal 'kooks', but of top right-wing political leaders from Israel, the U.S., Europe and other parts of the world, high military officers and leading academics. Its leading lights include: Baroness Caroline Cox, Deputy Speaker of the U.K. House of Lords and the non-executive director of the Andrei Sakharov Foundation (I wonder what Sakharov, who spent his whole life upholding human rights, would think of that!); Sam Brownback, Republican U.S. Senator from Kansas; Prof. Moshe Kaveh, President of Bar-Ilan University; Prof. Daniel Pipes, Board Member, United States Institute of Peace, Director of the Middle East Forum and Initiator of CampusWatch; and Dr. Yuri Shtern, Knesset Member, National Union and a leader of the Russian community and a member of the extreme right.

Their worldview and agenda is summed up in what is called the 'Jerusalem Declaration'. It covers a range of issues of concern to the global right. But it also brings Israel into the center of the global right-wing agenda, suffusing it with Israeli claims and terms. Thus, Israel and its exclusive 'right' to the entire Land of Israel is inserted into the very center of the neo-con agenda. The Jerusalem Declaration asserts:

> ISRAEL AS THE KEY TO THE HARMONY OF CIVILIZATIONS
>
> Billions of people believe that Jerusalem's spiritual and historical importance endows it with a special authority to become a center of world unity.
>
> Israel's unique geographic and historic position at the crossroads of civilizations enables it to reconcile their conflicts. Israel's unique spiritual experience enables it to find a golden mean between the fault lines dividing civilizations: between tradition and modernity, religion and science, authority and democracy.
>
> We call upon all nations to choose Jerusalem, the eternal and indivisible capital of Israel, as a center for this evolving new unity. We believe that one of the objectives of Israel's divinely-inspired rebirth is to make it the center of the new unity of the nations, which will lead to an era of peace and prosperity, foretold by the Prophets.

> Most Islamic countries, regrettably, have sworn to destroy Israel. We call on the countries of the Free World to realize the following: if the people of Israel can live in peace in their Promised Land, peace will have a chance to reign in the whole world. If radical Islam succeeds in destroying Israel, there will never be peace, and Western civilization will fall to Jihad as well.
>
> For the sake of the entire world and those therein, the land of Israel must belong to the people of Israel …

And what of the Palestinians? They are disposed of neatly, almost matter-of-factly, in the Jerusalem Declaration:

> PLO STATE AS A THREAT TO PEACE
>
> Supporting the creation of a PLO state in Judea and Samaria is a historical injustice of colossal proportion.
>
> A tiny democracy is urged to concede the only thing it lacks—territory—to totalitarian regimes in exchange for the promises of the only thing they cannot provide—peace.
>
> In pressuring to attain this suicidal arrangement, the "free world" betrays the very principles on which it is based. Anti-Israel and anti-Zionist attitudes, which disguise primordial anti-Semitism, constitute one area where hypocrisy in international politics is most visible.
>
> The genesis of a totalitarian PLO state would represent an act of surrender to radical Islam's false rhetoric and a capitulation to terror.
>
> The totalitarian PLO state would become a safe haven for international terrorism, a new Taliban-esque refuge, replete with plots to destroy both Israel and the West. Thus the future generations of the Free World will pay in blood for their fathers' moral blindness.
>
> We call on the government of Israel to provide moral leadership to the world in the struggle against terror:

> —Cease negotiating with terrorists and proffering mass releases of captured murderers.
>
> —Eliminate the terror-sponsoring capabilities of the Palestinian Authority.
>
> —Liberate Arabs residing in Judea, Samaria and Gaza from the Jihad propaganda machine, which has turned them into a morally depraved people who worship murder and terror.
>
> —Promote a viable humanistic alternative for just and secure peace instead of creating a terrorist PLO state.
>
> We call on all free nations to:
>
> —Unite in order to remove from power despotic Islamic regimes and re-educate an entire generation of Muslim children to embrace the democratic traditions of normative Islam.
>
> —Recognize the PLO/ PA as the terrorist organization which it is.
>
> —Cease forcing Israel to negotiate with terrorists.
>
> —Encourage Israel to establish full sovereignty throughout the land of Israel.
>
> We must reject moral relativism and confront creeping 'anti-Zionism' on Western campuses.

A favorite target of global neo-cons, Christian fundamentalists and the Israeli right is 'radical Islam'—convenient for Israel if it can succeed in depicting the Palestinians at part of that nefarious but mystifying conspiracy/population. Says a statement issued by the Jerusalem Summit:

> The front line in the war we are fighting rests in the birthplace of Judeo-Christian civilization. The stakes are high: if Israel and Jerusalem are fortified, they will become the center where mankind will gather to usher in an era of peace and prosperity.

> But the West's failure to save them may well spell doom for civilization itself.
>
> Just as in the past the Free World stood together against Fascism and Communism, so it today must do to combat the third challenge: radical Islam. We prevailed then, and we shall prevail now. United around Jerusalem and armed with our eternal values, we cannot fail.

But a second target—a favorite with the neo-cons of the Bush Administration as well—are NGOs, the very body and soul of civil society. Well, that is not exactly true. After all, some of the favored neo-con organizations—fundamentalist churches, right-wing think tanks, The Project for a New American Century, the Zionist Organization of America and others—are also of civil society. Let's rephrase: a favorite target of neo-cons are *progressive* NGOs. These are blamed for being undemocratic (!) organizations whose main *raison d'être* is to constrain American power. The prominent Australian neo-con Gary Johns in his well-known article "The NGO Challenge: Whose Democracy is it Anyway?" writes:

> The work of the state is as much to counter the tyranny of the minorities, including individuals, as well as to [sic] counter the tyranny of the majority. The task is to limit the claims on the commons, to depoliticize much of life, to make it less amenable to public dispute ... In the most egalitarian and peaceful of nations, there is the invention of a permanent litany of human rights abuses.

None other than the venerable American Enterprise Institute, (NGO) home to some of the major neo-cons, runs a website called 'NGO Watch', which keeps an eye on other 'undemocratic' NGOs. Since NGOs constitute a serious threat to American Empire by exposing its workings, countering its dis-information, and mobilizing civil society opposition (European NGOs are particularly suspect), it is not surprising that Israel, too, has its own anti-NGO website, 'NGO Monitor', an off-shoot of the NGO Watch whose declared objective is "to end the practice used by certain self-declared 'humanitarian NGOs' of exploiting the label 'universal human rights' to promote politically and ideologically motivated anti-Israel agendas." Operated by an 'approved' NGO headed by Dore Gold, Netanyahu's Ambassador to the UN, NGO Monitor targets such organizations as the Ford Foundation (who, according to the Monitor, "provided funding to a number of human-rights based NGOs that engaged in demonization and anti-Israel activities"), Christian Aid, ICAHD, B'tselem, Human Rights Watch and Amnesty, together with all Israeli NGOs favoring 'peace' (including the mild New Israel Fund) and, virtually by definition, all Palestinian NGOs. By intimidating funders of NGOs whose views are unacceptable to them, the 'monitors', the neo-cons and their Israeli clones hope to limit the effectiveness of progressive civil society groups, thus strengthening the hand of governments in which such 'democratic' elements as themselves, religious fundamentalists, corporations and the military have the upper hand.

Bringing the Israeli right into the global neo-con alliance

Although hardly a fan of Christians, Menachem Begin and his Likud colleagues appreciated their ideological similarities and the dovetailing of their political worldviews, especially since a militarily strong Israel able to use its Occupation for expansion was at the common center of their concerns. In order not only to strengthen the right-wing position at home but to influence policy towards Israel deriving from the U.S.-led international community, Israel's right wing has worked diligently to insert itself into the global right alliance.

The Likud has long courted the Christian Right. In 1980, Falwell became the first non-Jew to be awarded the Vladimir Ze'ev Jabotinsky medal for Zionist excellence by Begin. It was well known that Benjamin Netanyahu, when visiting Washington as prime minister, used to meet first with Falwell and The National Unity Coalition for Israel, a gathering of more than 500 fundamentalist Christian leaders, and only then with the President and Congressional leaders. That continues: Pat Robertson received Israel's Freedom Award in 2004, and both Netanyahu and Benny Elon, the leader of the extreme right National Union Party, conduct extensive and ongoing contacts with them. It is a case of strange bed-fellows of great use to each other: Elon and other xenophobic orthodox rabbis who hold Christianity in contempt embracing dispensationalists who look forward to the End of Days and the end of the Jews. Yet each has its own interest in using Israel as a vehicle for its political program—and of course the Jewish neo-cons lend a legitimacy to the relationship. All use the others.

Another interesting wrinkle is provided by another xenophobic and in principle anti-Christian community in Israel, the leaders of the Russian immigrants in Israel such as Nathan Sharansky and Avigdor Lieberman, Netanyahu's former office chief. United by their fierce anti-communism and similar neo-con views of the world (Sharansky, who has been called 'Bush's guru', was instrumental in getting the U.S. to isolate Arafat), the Russian immigrant leaders carry on an intimate relationship with Washington through both the neo-cons and the Christian Right, while ensuring through their mobilization of the one million-strong Russian community in Israel the continued rule of the Likud (even though they actually stand to the right of it).

Through their control of the organized Jewish community in the US and elsewhere, demonstrated most openly in the work of the American-Israel Public Affairs Committee (AIPAC), the Likud and Russian elements in Israel have even succeeded in turning what was historically a liberal Jewish establishment into another uncritical arm of Israeli policy, and thus of the extreme right.

Operational conclusion: Israel against progressive civil society

The operational upshot of all this is not merely a well-organized, well-financed and well-articulated global cabal of neo-cons, religious fundamentalists, and academics who will legitimize their positions and political leaders, but the integration of Israel into a global military system—again, led by the U.S. but involving the elites of almost every country, including Arab and Muslim ones—whose purpose is to subvert progressive civil society elements and create an 'environment' conducive to American empire and the well-being of those compliant international elites. Israel's leading position in this military alliance, then, has global implications, but it also serves to give Israel the military strength and political umbrella needed to transform its occupation into annexation while advancing a *Pax Americana* over the Middle East.

Israel's military influence as a point-country for American empire stems from four main sources:

(1) Israel has inserted itself into the center of the U.S. military industry. This, at least, is how AIPAC is able to sell Israel to members of Congress. According to its website in 2001 (www.aipac.org):

> The United States and Israel have formed a unique strategic partnership [a formal "strategic alliance" was signed in 1985] … Perhaps more than any two countries, the US and Israel share vital intelligence on terrorism, weapons proliferation and other threats. With US help, Israel is able to maintain its qualitative military edge for deterring aggression by its potential enemies. By collaborating with Israel, the US has a reliable, democratic and technologically-advanced partner *in securing American strategic interests*. This partnership includes: bilateral strategic agreements on military planning, ballistic missile defense and counter-terrorism; joint development of weapons and technologies; intelligence sharing; and combined military exercises … By working closely with the Israeli Defense Forces, and by pre-positioning equipment in Israel, the United States military enhances the readiness of its own forces responding to future crises in the Middle East. The US pre-positions hundreds of millions of dollars worth of military equipment, including spare parts, trucks, ammunition and armor in Israel. This equipment can be used by Israel as emergency supplies in times of crisis and is available to US forces for military contingencies in the region … Israeli defense companies have become a significant provider of military equipment to the US Armed Forces. Israel represents one of the top five suppliers of high-tech military hardware to the United States, and is first on a per capita basis. An average of 300 US Department of Defense and military personnel travel to Israel every month, more per capita than to any other US ally.

Needless to say, Israel provided key support for the U.S. in Iraq, including the construction of mock Iraqi neighborhoods and villages in the Negev where American troops could train. The American military government in Iraq, the 'Civil Administration', was patterned after the Israeli Civil Administration that rules the Occupied Territories. Israeli involvement in the defense-related economies in the districts of most members of Congress explains to a great degree why Israel enjoys the uncritical support it does. The Israeli astronaut who died in the Challenger accident testifies to the intimate involvement of Israel in the most guarded parts of the American military, where even European countries are excluded. In fact, Israel has just taken delivery of advanced F-16s and helicopter gunships that have been denied Europe.

(2) Israel also serves as the major arms subcontractor for American arms. It recently signed two agreements, worth $1.5 billion each, to train and equip both the Chinese and Indian armies with Israeli-tinkered U.S. weaponry. The U.S. uses Israel as a conduit when it wishes to avoid Congressional bans, embodied in the Arms Export Control Act, on selling arms to countries with serious human rights violations or, as in the case of India and Pakistan, when it wishes to avoid taking sides.

(3) Because of access to American technology and financial support, Israel has become the third largest arms producer in the world, making more weapons than China, Britain or France. In fact, Israel produces 12 percent of the world's arms. And it sells to countries few other want to associate with: Apartheid-era South Africa (where it trained the notorious security forces and helped develop the regime's nuclear program), Mobutu's Zaire, Liberia under Charles Taylor, the Burmese generals, Argentina, Brazil, Chile, Honduras and Guatemala under their military dictatorships, the corrupt and brutal regimes of Central Asia—and Rwanda, where it sold small arms to the Hutu before *and during* the genocide, then, without interruption, to the Tutsis immediately afterwards.

(4) Israel has become a military superpower in its own right. Its army and air force rival those of the major European countries, and it has become the world's fourth largest nuclear power, despite never signing the Nuclear Non-Proliferation Treaty. It works closely with the US military. For example, Seymour Hersh wrote in *The New Yorker* (January 24-31, 2005) that "The next strategic target [is] Iran ... The [Bush] Administration has been conducting secret reconnaissance missions inside Iran at least since last summer ... Defense Department civilians, under the leadership of Douglas Feith, have been working with Israeli planners and consultants to develop and refine potential nuclear, chemical-weapons,

and missile targets inside Iran." And it pursues an aggressive military policy of its own, although with tacit or explicit American 'permission'. Israel has become a leading subverter of human rights and progressive change throughout the world. It has military advisors and mercenaries in Columbia (both on the side of the government and of the drug cartels). Its mercenaries (all of whom operate under the supervision of the Ministry of Defense) are active in West Africa, where they broke the UN's boycott on 'blood diamonds', as in many other conflictual locales. Israeli advisors completely built Singapore's army, today the strongest in Southeast Asia. Israel also has major weapons development programs with *every* country in the European Union.

As an Israeli (and an immigrant to the country to boot), I write all this with sadness and concern. For all the violence and injustice that accompanied its birth, this is not the country it was intended to be. The slogan of the Israeli peace movement, "occupation corrupts," has proven to be true with a vengeance. Israel has become a Sparta, an aggressive country with no moral brakes that endangers its neighbors, peoples of far-away land and, in the end, its own population. The fact is that Israel has become a handmaiden (to choose a nice word) to American empire and that it has compounded the sins of occupation by joining forces with chauvinistic neo-cons, corporations pursuing war profits, anti-Semitic fundamentalists and other dubious forces subverting progressive civil society elements around the world. This is the greatest betrayal, not only of what Israel might have been had it sought accommodation and peace with the Palestinians and its other neighbors but of the Jewish people as a whole, who have been disproportionately represented among the progressive forces seeking to spread universal human and civil rights, and who themselves have a fundamental stake in such principles prevailing. The purpose of this paper is not to 'knock' Israel, but to shake it, to yell at its leaders and citizens: "What are you doing? What have you become? Save yourselves!" If not that, then at least to constrain it, as we must constrain American empire, for the sake of us all.

THE SECOND SUPERPOWER: ORGANIZING IN OPPOSITION TO THE NEW EMPIRE

Phyllis Bennis

Knowing a lot about Christian Zionism doesn't mean anything unless we do something. What we can do comes from a long time favorite of mine, a union organizer in the mines called Mary Jones, known to the miners as Mother Jones, who said "Don't moan; organize." I am not going to talk anymore about how terrible everything is except to say that we are facing very terrible times. Certainly here in Palestine things have rarely been worse. On a global level, Iraq is in flames. The U.S. drive for empire in Afghanistan, Haiti and elsewhere is proceeding apace. The United States is the most powerful country not only in the world today, but the most powerful center of empire that has ever existed. Think back to the Ottoman empire, the British, the French, the Roman empires: no Roman legionary ever would have imagined that there could be a global empire whose influence could reach to the skies and to the bottom of the oceans and could circle the globe, an empire whose economic clout and military strength and cultural influence, unfortunately, were unequalled by what the U.S. commands today. That is a very dangerous reality. But if we compare that reality today in the ongoing time of the U.S. invasion of Iraq, we see some very important advances in the global scene of the response to empirical power. At the beginning of the Iraq war, governments around the world were clambering to get onboard against the wishes of their own populations. Now, they are scrambling to get out, because they have seen how dangerous it is for them to be there. The American population is turning against this war and turning towards peace in numbers greater than ever before because we have seen the lies that this war was based on. The lies are no longer exposed by a lone voice in the wilderness. Cynthia McKinney, the brave Congresswoman in Georgia, lost her seat in Congress partly for asking embarrassing questions.

We are not any longer facing a world where global public opinion does not matter. We celebrated in March 2004 the first anniversary of the "Second Superpower", so named by the *New York Times*, which acknowledged at the outset of the war that there were once again two global superpowers: the United States, and global public opinion, and those two superpowers were again going head to head. And that is very important. A million people in the streets of London marched to say 'No' to war. In Rome, a million and a half people draped the Eternal City in the Rainbow Flag of peace. With people carrying the Rainbow Flag, Palestine emerged as the other issue. Palestine is no longer marginal to the global peace movement, and that is a huge accomplishment. That was not true even quite recently. This is a huge advance we have made.

But we have to be very sober about what it is going to take to recreate the energy of the anti-war protests. We were not able, ultimately, to stop the war. The second superpower was new-born. It wasn't strong enough yet to stop the war. But we did stop the war from being something that anyone could call legitimate and legal. We stopped the United Nations from endorsing it; we supported the 6 uncommitted countries that used to say yes to the Bush administration, and you know what? At the end of the day, despite all the pressure that was brought to bear, despite the threats to Cameroon and New Guinea that they would lose the small pittance of aid that they get from the United States if they didn't vote to support the war, despite the threats to Chile that it would lose its much touted free-trade agreement with the U.S., despite the threats to Mexico that there would be no more negotiations over immigration, we all got away with it, and none of those things happened.

Three months later at Cancun at the meeting of the World Trade Organization, the bigger and stronger countries of the global south, countries like South Africa, India, China, Brazil, and Argentina got together and said, "No, we know now we can fight back. We have the people of the world on our side." So they created something that came to be called the Group of Twenty-One to say no to the United States and Europe, putting pressure on them to expand the powers of trade in the WTO. They said "no" and they got away with it too.

And this is the lesson. When you organize, Mother Jones is proven right. When you organize, you get away with it. Rosemary Reuther expressed her concern for Jews who are speaking out against the occupation because they are being demonized. Yes, that happens. A few people have had problems, problems getting a job or similar difficulties, but do you know what? Jews all over the United States are now organizing, and they are not being demonized any more. When we Jews speak out, we are not the ones being targeted anymore. The community at risk today in the United States is not the Jews against the occupation. And it is not the Christians that are against the occupation. It is the Muslim community, and the immigrant community and the Arab community. We need to be very clear about that when we talk about whom we need to defend in the context of our work of peace and justice. Do not worry about the Jews. Don't worry about the Christians. Do worry about the Muslims, worry about the immigrants, worry about the Arabs. Because right now, they are the ones at risk. They are at risk of what we see in Palestine today. They are at risk of being arrested arbitrarily; they are at risk of being held without trial; they are at great risk. So when we talk about who is at risk for speaking out, we need to be very clear about who is at risk, and who has a greater responsibility to speak out for those at risk.

When we look at the question of how U.S. policy is built, the issue of the Middle East is very fundamental. Remember the context of 1967. You remember 1967! 1967, aside from the Israeli occupation that resulted from that war, was also in the middle of the Cold War. The U.S. embrace of Israel which followed Israel's occupation of Palestinian land, of Jordanian land, for a time of Lebanese land, of Syrian land, of the entire Sinai of Egypt, had everything to do with the Cold War. Because the U.S. strategic thinkers, such as they were, looked around after the Six Day War, after the military of this apparently small country had trounced the militaries of six Arab countries in six days and said, "You know, these guys aren't bad. We could use them. These guys could be very useful." It was not just because they liked militarism for its own sake; they liked militarism in defense of their policies around the world. And their polices were shaped by the Cold War. When the Israeli triumph of occupation happened in 1967 within the embrace of the Cold War, Israel was set to become the key Middle East actor in the Cold War. That led to a tightening of the strategic embrace and a coalescing of the domestic political pressure with the strategic international role that Israel was willing and more than able to play.

It was in that context that the intersection between the role of political pressure and the role of the various lobbies, initially primarily the Jewish lobby and now the parallel lobbies, one Jewish, one fundamentalist Christian, arose. The goals of the lobbies, on the one hand, merged with the strategic needs of the U.S. government on the other: the needs around the expansion of the U.S. military might, Israel as a cat's paw of U.S. power, Israel as the intersection of the arms industry for both countries. But in that context of 1967, Israel was only one pillar of U.S. strategy in the Middle East. One pillar was Israel. The second pillar was oil. The third pillar was market friendly stability. The U.S. was watching all of those.

But like most things, when you want all of them, you usually cannot have them all, even when you are the only superpower left in the world. So at different times and with different administrations, different ones of those three pillars have become primary. During the Clinton years, there is no doubt that Israel was the primary of those three. And that was domestically driven. In the post-Cold War era, the U.S. military was functioning in a very different way, using the claim, although it was a false claim, of multilateralism towards interventions around the world. But the political pressure to support Israel was very, very strong. Clinton was extremely accountable to this pressure, so Israel was at the top of the agenda. His commitment to Israel was evident in his micromanaging of the so-called peace process. When Bush II came into office, there was a lot of thought that things were going to be different because these were oil guys. Israel was not their thing. Very clearly, when they first came into power, when the Supreme Court anointed the un-elected George Bush, the immediate pull back from engagement in Middle East diplomacy was very clear. Oil was the name of the game and secondary to it was the question of stability of markets and expanding economic interests in the region.

But then came September 11th and with September 11th, there were some very fundamental changes. The drive of this administration towards empire had been visible from the moment they took power. It was not something that happened after September 11th. September 11th did not change what this administration wanted to do. What changed was their ability to do it. And the reason is summed up in one word: *Fear*. The fear of the American people has been a very useful tool for the Bush administration. They have not hesitated to use the country's fear and abuse it endlessly. That fear is what made it possible for them to take a strategy that had first been identified in 1992, when they were not in office, in a paper that was called "The Project for the New American Century". It called for a remilitarization of U.S. foreign policy that privileged the Pentagon above the State

Department, putting greater resources and money in the Defense budget, taking it out of the budget of diplomacy and foreign aid, and telling the world in no uncertain terms that never would any country or group of countries be allowed to match, let alone surpass, U.S. military capacity. The leadership of the Republican Party took one look at this paper and said, "You guys have to be nuts, we'd never get away with this." And they put it on a shelf and there it sat, until the year 2000, when the Bush II Administration suddenly got the idea that they were going to come into office. In 2001, when they did come into office, they took that paper off the shelf and began to implement it, with a vengeance. However, something had happened in between.

In 1996, that same group of ideologues, that same group of neoconservative types got together with a new plan. This group actually has three heads: a third of them are from the Christian right, a third of them are conservative Jews, and the rest aren't any particular religion but are just neoconservative in their own right. They got together and they went off to Israel and they met with Netanyahu and they said to him, "We're going to draft for you an election strategy." Their strategy paper for Netanyahu, when he was running for prime minister, was a paper called "Making a Clean Break: Defending the Realm." They even talk in the language of empire! What they proposed for Benjamin Netanyahu was an Israeli version of what they had drafted for the United States: the same policy on a regional level that they had wanted to impose on a global level for the United States.

The Clean Break paper talked about the remilitarization of Israel's relationship with all of its neighbors; Israel should make clear, in no uncertain terms, that its relationship with Iran, with Iraq, with Syria, with Lebanon, with all of the countries of the Arab world would be based on military might and not diplomacy. The Palestinians should be told in no uncertain terms that they were not going to get a state made up of all of the land occupied in the 1967 War, of all of the West Bank, Gaza, and East Jerusalem, and that they better just get used to it. Most important, the military role of Israel would remain primary. Thus, it was very much the same policy that was created for the U.S. and for Israel.

So Christian Zionism is only one part of the strategic direction that the United States has been taking for a long time. What our American government does is very dangerous to the rest of the world. We cannot change this government; we cannot achieve regime change alone. We need a global movement, a global peace movement to be part of in order to say no to the Bush doctrine as the world is saying no to the Bush War. That is what is going to make it possible for those of us working within the United States to make those changes.

We have to reject the fear that has been such a crucial part of the American psyche since September 11th. We have to say "Fear is not going to prevent another terrorist attack" because terror doesn't grow out of the sky. It does not arise because people hate freedom. People commit terrorism when they are denied freedom. And what is even more important is that most of us simply cannot put ourselves in the mindset of someone who would take a planeload of ordinary people and use it as a weapon against a building of ordinary people. I cannot conceive of that, I cannot comprehend that, anymore than I can comprehend being the pilot of a B-52 dropping bombs on people I cannot see 50,000 feet below. I can't conceive of either one.

But what I can conceive is why some people languishing in a Gaza refugee camp might see on television the blowing up of the World Trade Center and think to themselves, even as they mourn the victims, "You know, they kind of had it coming." We Americans are paying the price for the propaganda of our government, the propaganda that says that the U.S. is the biggest democracy, the strongest democracy, the best democracy that money can buy, and the rest of you better model yourselves after our democracy. The message is that Americans control their government, and if we did not like their policies, we could change them. And if we do not change them, it must be because we like them. Among other things, it makes those of us ordinary Americans walking the streets of Ramallah or walking the streets of Kabul or walking the streets of London a much greater target than we ever were before. Before, people always understood that the American government was not the same as the American people. Our government is making that distinction go away. We are going to pay the price for it, not our government. The question of U.S. policy becomes the key. So what do we do about it?

In the U.S., we have created the U.S. Campaign to End Israeli Occupation, focusing on the occupation, not because that is the only aspect of injustice in Palestine, but because that is the central theme of U.S. policy in the region. We may have to put the question of the right of return equal to the occupation of the West Bank, Gaza and East Jerusalem because that has now become a key component of U.S. foreign policy in a much more explicit way than ever before. Sabeel was a founding member of the U.S. campaign, I am glad to say. When Sabeel and the others got together, we were 40 organizations. Now there are 120 organizations—church organizations, Islamic organizations, African American organizations, secular organizations. We constantly worry that we have too many Jews and too many Arabs on the steering committee and that we need more varied representation speaking for Palestine! This is where the churches come in; the churches are very, very important. When we say we have to organize, we realize that it will not be easy. Indeed, this is going to be very difficult work, but we have a model to go by.

When we talk about empire, when we talk about the drive towards empire of which our country is the centerpiece, we can look back at empires of old, and see how they were brought down with blood and fire and great violence. That is one way to bring down an empire, and it's a terrible way, with a terrible human price. But there is another way, because as citizens of the empire, although our rights are being systematically stripped from us, we still have some rights that other subjects of the empire around the world do not have. We still have the vote, maybe for the moment, but we still have the vote. For the moment, there are still elections planned. For the moment, we can still do voter education, voter registration, voter mobilization. And that is very, very important.

The key is education. When we talk about changing U.S. policy on Palestine, part of our work in the U.S. campaign has a Congressional focus. We now have Congressional district co-ordinators in 130 Congressional districts in the United States. That is huge. That has never existed before in the United States. That does not mean that we can change their minds or change the policy in the Congress over night. But it is part of the process of education and mobilization that we teach people how to go and talk to their Congress-people and demand a change. And we are not going to worry about being called anti-Semitic. If we are called anti-Semitic, we shall fight them on it, because it is not anti-Semitic to oppose injustice. It is not anti-Semitism to oppose occupation, and anyone who says so is lying, and has to be exposed as a liar. And that is our job. That is not a hard job; that is truth telling. Churches are good for that, right? This is what churches do.

We need to look at the worker example of the network, the network of Jewish anti-occupation organizations. When they met in

Chicago at the Jewish Unity conference, there were over a thousand people there. In every major city in America, there are groups like Jews against the Occupation, Jewish Voices for Peace, Jews for Peace in Palestine and Israel. Christian churches need the same types of organizations: Churches against the Occupation, Churches for Middle East Peace, Evangelicals Against the Occupation. It is not enough to know that your denomination has a good position on the issue at the highest level of the hierarchy. Ironically enough, most of them do. Even the Pope has spoken. These high level statements are not enough; they do not do much good.

Statements do not change policy until their meaning comes down to the level of the parish priest, the minister, the rabbi, the imam. That is where people hear them. It is the people in the pews that do the work to go out and mobilize voters and change minds and educate people, change the curriculum in the high schools. I do not know if the curriculum in faith-based private schools is as bad on this issue as the public schools but if it is, then we all need a lot of work. These are jobs that we all need to take more seriously than ever before. The support for Israel in the United States is both strategic and political and we need to attack it from both levels. We oppose it strategically because we are on the wrong side of history when we support occupation, when we support colonialism. That is over, that is history, that is so last year. It is time we got over it. It is time we put ourselves on the right side of history. That means standing against occupation, standing for liberation. That means standing against occupation in Iraq, against occupation in Palestine. If occupation is wrong in Palestine, why are we supporting it in Iraq? Why is the U.S. military relying on the model of the Israeli military? The Pentagon is taking lessons from the IDF, beginning with Jenin, about how to occupy an Arab country. Now how sick is that? How sick is that? The American people have no idea.

The American people have no idea what occupation looks like. We have not been under military rule in our country. When someone says 'checkpoint' in our country, people think it means that we hold up an ID and drive on past. They do not know about the humiliation. When people hear curfew, they think it is what keeps the 12 year olds from staying too late at the mall. They do not know about what it means to be under a 24-hour shoot-to-kill curfew where people are shot and killed for setting foot on their own balcony because they were desperate for a breath of fresh air. Americans do not know about that. We have to teach them about these realities. This is a teaching moment since it is now our soldiers who are occupying Iraq, and we are seeing on television just how horrific occupation is. That means we can point to it and say, "You know what, that is what has been going on in Palestine since 1967 when this occupation began." That becomes our obligation.

How do we fight occupation? We fight it on the basis of human rights and international law and the United Nations. We do not have to say, "You have to come down on the side of the Palestinians because the Palestinians are right and the Israelis are wrong." That is not what it is about. It's not about "I like the Palestinians better." It is not about "My friends are Palestinians and I don't like the Israelis." It is about being on the side of law, and holding our government accountable to international law. There are laws in the U.S. even if the U.S. is saying that our government is not accountable even to our own laws. There are laws in the world, and the U.S. is saying, "We are not accountable to those laws; we will withdraw from those treaties as we choose, and we will operate on the basis of the law of empire."

The Melian Dialogues date from the time when the Athenians created democracy; they went to the island of Melos because they needed land and their democracy was little and fragile and weak. They went to the island of Melos and said, "We need your land." When they met resistance, the Athenians said, "We're bigger and stronger than you; we're taking your land." Melos said, "What about the democracy that you Athenians are so big on anyway?" And the Athenians said, "For us, there is democracy. For you, there is the law of empire." That is the basis on which the Bush Administration today is violating international law and making us into a nation of outlaws—a rogue state. Many of us Americans do not like living in a rogue state. We want to live under the rule of law. We do not want people thinking when we travel around the world that we somehow represent the kind of lawlessness that this government has come to represent all around the world. We have a huge job to do. The United States is carrying out attacks of unprecedented character and calling them peace.

A famous Roman once wrote about that too, Tacitus, the Roman historian who followed the legions as they laid waste across the land. He once climbed a hill after a battle in Scotland and looked out over the devastation of the valley at the dead bodies that had been left behind. And he wrote, "The Romans left devastation, but they called it peace." It is our job to make sure the United States does not get away with doing the same thing.

THE INFLUENCE OF THE CHRISTIAN RIGHT IN U.S. MIDDLE EAST POLICY

Stephen Zunes

Recent years have seen the emergence of a politicized and right-wing Protestant fundamentalism as a major factor behind U.S. support for the policies of the rightist Likud government in Israel. Indeed, given that a willingness by the U.S. government to pressure Israel to make the necessary compromises is crucial if there is to be a permanent Israeli-Palestinian peace settlement, there may be no greater threat to the revived peace process than the influence of the American Christian Right.

To understand this influence, it is important to recognize that the rise of the religious right as a political force in the United States is a relatively recent phenomenon that emerged as part of a calculated strategy by leading conservatives in the Republican Party who—while not fundamentalist Christians themselves—recognized the need to enlist the support of this key segment of the American population in order to come to power.

Traditionally, American fundamentalist Protestants were not particularly active in national politics, long seen as worldly and corrupt. This changed in the late 1970s as part of a calculated effort by conservative Republican operatives who recognized that as long as the Republican Party was primarily identified with militaristic foreign policies and with economic policies that favored the wealthy, they would remain a minority party. Over the previous five decades, the Republicans had won only four out of the twelve presidential elections and controlled Congress for only two of its twenty-four sessions.

By mobilizing rightist religious leaders and adopting conservative positions on a number of such highly-charged social issues as women's rights, abortion, sex education, and homosexuality, they were able to bring millions of fundamentalist Christians who—as a result of their lower-than-average income were not otherwise inclined to vote Republican—into their party. Through such organizations as the Moral Majority and the Christian Coalition, they promoted a right-wing political agenda through radio and television broadcasts as well as from the pulpit. Since that time, Republicans have won five out of seven presidential races, have controlled the Senate for eight out of thirteen sessions and have controlled the House of Representatives for the past six.

Those who identify with the religious right are now more likely than the average American to vote and to be politically active. They constitute nearly one out of seven American voters. The Christian Right firmly controls the agenda of the Republican Party in about half of the states, particularly in the South and Midwest. A top Republican staffer noted: "Christian conservatives have proved to be the political base for most Republicans. Many of these guys, especially the leadership, are real believers in this stuff, and so are their constituents"[1]

Revd Barry Lynn of Americans United for Separation of Church and State noted: "The good news is that the Christian Coalition is fundamentally collapsing. The bad news is that the people who ran it are all in the government." He noted, for example, that whenever he goes to the Justice Department, he keeps seeing former lawyers of the prominent right-wing fundamentalist preacher Pat Robertson. [2]

As the *Washington Post* observed, "For the first time since religious conservatives became a modern political movement, the president of the United States has become the movement's de facto leader." Former Christian Coalition leader Ralph Reed noted his movement's triumph this way: "You're no longer throwing rocks at the building; you're in the building." He added that God "knew George Bush had the ability to lead in this compelling way." [3]

The Rightward Shift of Republican Policy Toward Israel

Due to the longstanding support for Israel as a refuge for a persecuted

---

1 Ken Silverstein and Michael Scherer, "Born-Again Zionists", *Mother Jones*, September/October 2002.

2 Matthew Engel, "Meet the New Zionists", *The Guardian*, 28 October 2002.

3 Dana Milbank, "Religious Right Finds Its Center in Oval Office: Bush Emerges as Movement's Leader After Robertson Leaves Christian Coalition", *Washington Post*, 24 December 2001.

people and respect for the country's democratic institutions (for its Jewish citizens) by American liberals, as well as the disproportionate political influence of Zionist Jews within the party, the Democrats traditionally took a harder line toward the Palestinians and other Arabs than did the Republicans. By contrast, Republicans—who generally tended to be more hawkish on most foreign policy issues—traditionally took a somewhat more moderate stance due to the party's ties to the oil industry and concern that too much support for Israel could lead Arab nationalists toward a pro-Soviet or—in more recent years—a pro-Islamist orientation.

This is no longer the case, thanks to the influence of the Christian Right. Though Christian fundamentalist support for Israel dates back many years, only recently has it become one of the movement's major issues. As a result, in recognition of their political influence, there has been a notable decrease in the reluctance among many American Jews to team up with the Christian Right. Fundamentalist leader Gary Bauer, for example, now receives frequent invitations to address mainstream Jewish organizations, something which would not have occurred prior to the Bush presidency. This is partly a phenomenon of demographics: Jews constitute only 3 percent of the U.S. population and less than half support the policies of the current Israeli government.

The Israelis also recognize the power of the Christian Right: Since 2001, Bauer has met with a number of Israeli cabinet members and with Prime Minister Ariel Sharon. Former Prime Minister Benyamin Netanyahu noted that "We have no greater friends and allies" than right-wing American Christians.[4]

It used to be that Republican administrations had the ability to overcome pressure from AIPAC and other Jewish Zionist lobbying groups when it was deemed important for American interests, such as the Eisenhower Administration's pressure on Israel during the Suez Crisis of 1956, the Reagan Administration's 1981 sale of AWACS planes to Saudi Arabia, and the first Bush Administration's delay of the $10 billion loan guarantee until after the pivotal 1992 Israeli election. Furthermore, since a sizable majority of Jewish Americans tended to vote Democratic, there was a sense that Republicans had little to lose for occasionally challenging Israel.

---

[4] Timothy P. Weber, "How Evangelicals Became Israel's Best Friend", *Christianity Today*, 5 October 1998.

Thanks to the rise in influence of the Christian Right, however, this is no longer the case. For the first time, the Republican Party has a significant pro-Israel constituency of its own that it cannot ignore. Top White House officials, including National Security Council Near East and North African Affairs director Elliot Abrams, have regular and often lengthy meetings with representatives of the Christian Right. As one leading Republican put it, "They are very vocal and have shifted the center of gravity toward Israel and against concessions. It colors the environment in which decisions are being made."[5] Indeed, the degree of the Bush administration's support for Sharon has surprised even the most hard-line Zionist Jews.

It appears, then, that rightwing Christian Zionists are, at this point, more significant in the formulation of U.S. policy toward Israel than are Jewish Zionists.

To cite a couple of examples of their influence under the administration of President George W. Bush:

> —After the Bush Administration's initial condemnation of the attempted assassination of militant Palestinian Islamist Abdel Aziz Rantisi in June 2003, the Christian Right mobilized their constituents to send thousands of emails to the White House protesting the criticism. A key element in these emails was the threat that if such pressure continued to be placed upon Israel, they would stay home on Election Day. Observers noted that within twenty-four hours, there was notable change in tone by the president. Indeed, when Rantisi fell victim to a successful Israeli assassination in April 2004, the administration—as it had done with the assassination of Hamas leader Sheik Ahmed Yassin the previous month—largely defended the Israeli action.

> —When the Bush Administration insisted that Israel stop its April 2002 military offensive in the West Bank, the White House received over 100,000 emails from Christian conservatives in protest of its criticism. Almost immediately, President Bush came to Israel's defense. Over the objections of the State Department, the Republican-led Congress adopted resolutions supporting Israel's actions and blaming the violence exclusively on the Palestinians.

---

[5] Silverstein and Scherer, *op. cit.*

—When President Bush announced his support for the Road Map for Middle East peace, the White House received more than 50,000 postcards over the next two weeks from Christian conservatives opposing any plan which called for the establishment of a Palestinian state. The administration quickly backpedaled and the once highly-touted Road Map essentially died.

The U.S., Israel and Manichaeism

Christian Zionism is based in large part on the belief that a hegemonic Israel is a necessary precursor of the second coming of Christ. Ironically, this theology also assumes that upon Christ's return, "unrepentant" Jews would be subjected to eternal damnation, essentially seeing the Jews in a crucial supporting role but absenting them from the final act.

Yet while this millennialist theology is certainly an important part of the Christian Right's support of a militaristic and expansionist Jewish state, fundamentalist Christian Zionism in America may be largely a subset of an even more dangerous heresy: that of Manichaeism, the belief that reality is divided into Absolute Good and Absolute Evil.

The day after the terrorist attacks of 11 September 2001, President Bush declared "This will be a monumental struggle of good versus evil, but good will prevail."[6] The reason America was targeted—according to President Bush—was not U.S. support for Arab dictatorships, the large U.S. military presence in the Middle East, U.S. backing of the Israeli occupation, or the humanitarian consequences of U.S. policy toward Iraq, but simply that they "hate our freedoms."[7]

Ignoring that the Gospels make clear that the line separating good and evil does not run between nations, but within each person, President Bush cited Christological texts to support his war aims in the Middle East, declaring, "And the light [America] has shone in the darkness [the enemies of America] and the darkness will not overcome it." [America shall conquer its enemies.][8]

---

6 President George W. Bush, "The Deliberate and Deadly Attacks ...Were Acts of War", White House Press Office, President's Address from Cabinet Room following Cabinet Meeting, 12 September 2001.

7 President Bush, White House Press Office, Address before Joint Session of Congress, 20 September 2001.

8 Juan Stam, "Bush's Religious Language", *The Nation*, 22 Dec. 2003.

Even more disturbingly, Bush has stated repeatedly that he had been "called" by God to run for president. Veteran journalist Bob Woodward noted, "The President was casting his mission and that of the country in the grand vision of God's Master Plan," wherein he promised, in his own words, "to export death and violence to the four corners of the earth in defense of this great country and to rid the world of evil."[9] President Bush believes that he has accepted the responsibility of leading the free world as part of God's plan. He even told then-Palestinian Prime Minister Mahmoud Abbas that "God told me to strike Al-Qaeda and I struck them, and then he instructed me to strike at Saddam, which I did."[10] Iraq has become the new Babylon, and the "war on terrorism" has succeeded the Cold War with the Soviet Union as the quintessential battle between good and evil.

The identification which so many Americans feel with Israel may be based in part upon the fact that both countries share the contradiction of—on the one hand—being settled in part by those fleeing religious persecution who then established a new nation rooted in high ideals and a political system based upon relatively progressive and democratic institutions and—on the other hand—establishing their new nation through the oppression, massacre and dislocation of the indigenous population. Like many Israelis and their supporters, Americans often confuse genuine religious faith with nationalist ideology.

John Winthrop, the influential 17th-century Puritan theologian, saw America as the "City on the Hill" and "a light unto the nations". In effect, there is a kind of American Zionism that assumes a divinely-inspired singularity which excuses what would otherwise be considered unacceptable behavior. Just as Winthrop defended the slaughter of the indigenous Pequot peoples of colonial Massachusetts as part of a divine plan, 19th-century theologians defended America's westward expansion as "manifest destiny" and the will of God. Such theologically-rooted aggrandizement did not stop at the Pacific Ocean: the invasion of the Philippines at the turn of the previous century was justified by President William McKinley and others as part of an effort to "uplift" and "Christianize" the natives, ignoring the fact that the Filipinos (who by that time had nearly rid the country of the Spanish colonialists and had

---

9 Bob Woodward, *Bush at War*, New York: Simon & Schuster, 2002.

10 Cited in Al Kamen, "Road Map in the Back Seat," *Washington Post*, 27 June 2003.

established the first democratic constitution in Asia) were already over 90 percent Christian.

Similarly, today, in the eyes of the Christian Right, the Bush Doctrine and the expansion of American military and economic power is all part of a divine plan. For example, in their 2003 Christmas card, Vice-President Dick Cheney and his wife Lynne included the quote, "And if a sparrow cannot fall to the ground without His notice, is it probable that an empire can rise without His aid?"[11]

It is noteworthy that polls show that the ideological gap between Christian conservatives and other Americans regarding the U.S. invasion of Iraq and related Bush Administration policies in the "war on terrorism" is even higher than the ideological gap between Christian conservatives and other Americans on Israel and Palestine.

In many respects, much of the American right may be at least as concerned about how Israel can help the United States as how the United States can help Israel. Due to the anti-Semitism inherent in much of Christian Zionist theology, it has long been recognized that their support for Israel does not stem out of a concern for the Jewish people *per se*, but from a desire to use the Jews to hasten the Second Coming of Christ. This is also true of those who—for theological or other reasons—seek to advance the American empire in the Middle East.

And while a strong case can be made that U.S. support for Israeli policies ultimately hurts U.S. interests, there remains a widely-held perception that Israel is an important asset to American strategic objectives in the Middle East and beyond. The Christian Right is, in effect, willing to fight the Muslims to the last Jew.

How Israel Helps American Hegemonic Ambitions

In a region where radical nationalism could threaten U.S. control of oil and other strategic interests, Israel successfully has prevented victories by radical nationalist movements, not just in Palestine but in Lebanon and Jordan as well. They have kept Syria, with a nationalist regime once

---

[11] Associated Press, "Cheney says despite Christmas card, U.S. does not see itself as an empire", *San Francisco Chronicle*, 24 January 2004.

allied with the Soviet Union, in check. Israel's air force is predominant throughout the region.

Another function Israel provides is that its frequent wars have allowed for battlefield testing of American arms. In addition, Israel's own arms industry has provided weapons and munitions for governments and opposition movements supported by the United States. Moreover, Israel has been a conduit for U.S. arms to regimes and movements too unpopular in the United States for the government to openly grant direct military assistance. Regimes receiving arms via Israel include South Africa under the apartheid regime, Iran's Islamic republic, Guatemala's rightist military juntas, and the Nicaraguan Contras. Israeli military advisors have also assisted the Contras, the Salvadoran junta, and other movements and governments backed by the United States. The Israeli intelligence agency Mossad has cooperated with the CIA and other U.S. agencies in intelligence gathering and covert operations. Israel has missiles capable of reaching thousands of kilometers and has co-operated with the U.S. military-industrial complex in the research and development of new jet fighters and anti-missile defense systems, a relationship that is growing every year.[12] As one Israeli analyst described it during the Iran-Contra scandal, where Israel played a crucial intermediary rule, "It's like Israel has become just another federal agency, one that's convenient to use when you want something done quietly."[13]

The pattern of U.S. aid to Israel reveals striking attention to the utility of Israel for U.S. interests. The stronger, more aggressive, and more willing to co-operate with U.S. interests that Israel has become, the higher the level of aid and strategic co-operation. An Israel in a constant state of war—technologically sophisticated and militarily advanced, yet lacking an independent economy and dependent on the United States—is far more willing to perform tasks that might be unacceptable to other allies than would be an Israel at peace with its neighbors. As former Secretary of State Henry Kissinger once put it, in reference to Israel's reluctance to make peace with its Arab neighbors, "Israel's obstinacy ... serves the purposes of both our countries best."[14]

---

[12] Karen L. Puschel, *U.S.-Israeli Strategic Cooperation in the Post-Cold War Era: An American Perspective*, Boulder: Westview Press, 1993, p. 150.

[13] Glenn Frankel, *Washington Post*, 19 November 1986.

[14] Henry Kissinger, *Years of Upheaval*, Boston: Little, Brown, Company, 1982, p. 621.

Throughout Europe in past centuries, the ruling class of a given country would, in return for granting limited religious and cultural autonomy, set up certain individuals in the Jewish community to become the visible agents of the oppressive social order, such as tax collectors and money lenders. When the population would threaten to rise up against the ruling elites, the rulers could then blame the Jews, sending the wrath of an exploited people against convenient scapegoats and resulting in the pogroms and other notorious waves of repression that have taken place throughout the Jewish Diaspora over the centuries. Unfortunately, one of the more unsettling aspects of U.S. policy today is how closely it corresponds with this historic anti-Semitism.

The idea behind Zionism was to break this cycle of the centuries through the creation of a Jewish nation-state where Jews would no longer be dependent on the ruling class of a given country. But in a tragic irony, as a result of Israel's unwillingness to make peace, Israel's role over the decades has been to perpetuate this cycle on a global scale. Israel has been used by Western powers—initially Great Britain and France[15] and more recently the United States—to maintain their interests in the Middle East. In a horrible echo of the past, autocratic Arab governments, Islamic extremists, and others are blaming Israel, Zionism, or the Jews for their problems, leaving largely untouched the broader exploitative global economic system and their own elites who benefit from and help perpetuate such a system.

The ramifications of U.S. policy are quite apparent when it comes to the suffering of Palestinians. But it also has a negative impact on Israel. The late respected Israeli intellectual Yishayahu Leibowitz observed, "The existence of the Jewish people of 60 to 80 generations. ... was a heroic situation. We never got from the goyish world a cent. We supported ourselves. We maintained our own institutions. Now we have taken three million Jews, gathered them here and turned them over to be parasites—parasites of America. And in some sense we are even the mercenaries of America to fight the wars of what the ruling persons in America consider to be American interests."[16]

---

15 For example, when Great Britain and France sought to oust nationalist president Gamal Abdul-Nasser in 1956 to protect their commercial interests, they sent in the Israeli army to invade the Sinai Peninsula.

16 Interview, Film "Israel Faces the Future", Public Broadcasting System, 1987.

Zionism, like other nationalist movements, consists of a variety of currents, including those who seek justice and peace with the Palestinians. As a result, it could be argued that Israel's flagrant violations of international law and other abuses are less a matter of Zionist ideology *per se* than of those taking such actions simply because they can. No other country could get away with the kinds of policies that Israel has pursued for more than a half century without serious consequences. Israel, however, has the unconditional military, economic and diplomatic support of the world's one remaining superpower

None of this absolves Israel or the Zionist movement of its moral responsibly for its actions. Nor does this analysis deny the existence of a politically powerful pro-Israel lobby in the United States. It would be a mistake to over-emphasize the power of Jewish Zionists in the development of U.S. policy, however.

One reason for caution in attributing U.S. policy to AIPAC and allied groups is that the influence of the Zionist lobby is often exaggerated by American officials in order to shift responsibility for their actions onto others. For example, members of Congress and their aides, in discussions with human rights activists, will often claim—always off the record—that they or their boss has to take pro-militarist and anti-human rights positions towards the Israeli-Palestinian conflict because of the need for Jewish campaign contributions.[17] Similarly, as a means of diverting Arab criticism from U.S. policy makers, American diplomats routinely tell representatives of Arab governments that wealthy Jews essentially dictate U.S. Middle East policy.[18]

However, ultimately, the primary purpose for U.S. backing of Israel—like the backing of other repressive governments—is part of strategic calculation rather than simply the result of ethnic politics. To give just one example, for nearly a quarter of century, the United States supported the brutal occupation of East Timor by Indonesia and to this day supports the Moroccan occupation of Western Sahara, despite the absence of a powerful Indonesian-American or Moroccan-American lobby. (Interestingly, even though the former case involved a

---

[17] This is based on the author's periodic experience lobbying for arms control and human rights on Capitol Hill since 1973 as well as anecdotes from colleagues who have had similar experiences.

[18] Based on this author's interviews with a half dozen Arab foreign ministers and deputy foreign ministers between 1990 and 1994.

predominantly Muslim country conquering, occupying, and terrorizing a predominantly Christian country, there were virtually no protests coming from the Islamaphobic Christian Right.)

The difference between these other occupations and that of Palestine by Israel is that the United States was able to get away with its support for Indonesia and Morocco due to their relative obscurity. This is certainly not the case with Israel and Palestine. As a result, those who support justice for the Palestinians—or even simply the enforcement of basic international humanitarian law—must go beyond simply raising awareness of the issue to directly confronting those who make such policies possible.

The Silence of the Liberals

The Christian Right has long been a favorite target for the Democratic Party, particularly its liberal wing, since most Americans are profoundly disturbed by fundamentalists of any kind influencing policies of a government with a centuries-old tradition of separating church and state. Yet we find most liberal Democrats in Congress taking positions on the Israeli-Palestinian conflict that are far closer to the reactionary Christian Coalition than to the moderate National Council of Churches, far closer to the rightist Rev. Pat Robertson than to the late leftist Rev. William Sloan Coffin, far closer to the ultra-conservative Moral Majority than to the liberal Churches for Middle East Peace, and far closer to the fundamentalist Southern Baptist Convention than to any of the mainline Protestant churches. Rather than accuse these erstwhile liberals of being captives of the "Jewish lobby"—a charge which inevitably leads to the counter-charge of anti-Semitism—those who support justice for the Palestinians could just as accurately accuse them of being captives of the Christian Right. Turning the focus away from ethnic politics and toward the dangerous fundamentalist ideology which is currently at least as influential in shaping U.S. foreign policy toward the region would more likely advance the ability of those who support peace, justice, and the rule of law to highlight the profound immorality of their support for the Israeli occupation.

It will not be possible to counter the influence of the Christian Right in shaping American policies in the Middle East, however, as long as otherwise progressive-minded elected officials continue to support the same policies.

Ironically, the Orthodox churches, the Roman Catholic Church, the historic peace churches, and the mainline Protestant churches—while firmly supporting Israel's right to exist in peace and security—oppose the occupation and colonization of the West Bank and Gaza Strip as well as support Palestinian independence and call for a shared Jerusalem. Despite the fact that both the Republican and Democratic parties reject such a moderate position and instead back the policies of the right-wing Israeli government, these churches—which collectively represent the majority of elected officials and the majority of Americans overall—have rarely challenged U.S. Middle East policy with the same intensity with which they have challenged government policies in regard to such issues as poverty, racial justice, and the nuclear arms race.

It is unlikely, therefore, that Democrats and moderate Republicans will be willing to challenge the Christian Right over Middle East Policy until the liberal-to-mainline churches mobilize their resources in support of peace and justice for Israel and Palestine as strongly as the right-wing fundamentalists mobilize their resources in support for occupation and repression.

ISRAEL AND INDIA: DISTURBING PARALLELS

Praful Bidwai

I come from the only other part of the world, apart from Israel and Palestine, which has been in constant turmoil for 50 years or longer. We've had a continuous hot Cold War going on in the Indian sub-continent for longer than 50 years. Palestine-Israel is probably the only other region in the world which is comparable in terms of the emotional, political, and social turmoil; the traumas this has produced; the potential for catastrophe and—in my part of the world — the potential for nuclear war. I will talk about the kinds of turmoil that this constant, continuous hot Cold War, driven by religion and politics, has produced in South Asia, the Indian sub-continent.

In 1947, we had a partition of the country when the British rulers left, and India and Pakistan became two independent states. One and a half *million* people died in the bloodshed that took place. In 1971, Pakistan, itself, split into two. In Bangladesh, which is geographically separated and lies east of what remained as Pakistan on the western side of India, there was butchery during the Bangladeshi freedom struggle when something like half a million people died. You all know about the Taliban and the developments in Afghanistan, which again combine this weirdly adverse relationship between religion and politics and represent a continuing struggle despite U.S. occupation.

What we have now in India, which, with one billion people, is the largest country in that part of the world, is a party in power which seeks to shift the old forces of politics itself by mixing religion into politics, into the State, in a fundamental way. And this party came into power, just as the Nazis came to power, through elections. The party won elections although it only had about a quarter of the popular vote—and it has led a coalition for the last six years which has brought serious trouble upon our part of the world. It has inflamed passions of the basest variety, of the most violent variety.

Everyone knows about the Gujarat-Godhra incident only a few years ago. More than 2,000 Muslims, in one of the most culturally-integrated states in India, were butchered in actions that were planned by the BJP (*Bharatiya Janata Party*) and which were executed by the government of Vajpayee. Not one person has, so far, been brought to court for this terrible massacre, which actually fits the definition of genocide according to the International Convention on Genocide of 1948. On the contrary, Muslims are still being arrested for the incident that was cited as the provocation for this savagery. In fact, there is no logical connection between the two—between this massacre and the Godhra killing of 59 Hindus in a train coach.

This party has also launched a systematic campaign to politically silence and disenfranchise the religious minorities, which number something like 180 million people—the size of a population larger than, for example, Russia today or more than half the European Union. These vast numbers belonging to minorities have increasingly over the last few years experienced being second-class citizens who must abide by the will of the Hindu majority, which makes up 82 percent of the population. More precisely, they must abide by the will of the Hindus as defined by the sectarian, fundamentalist party of the BJP. Otherwise, they have no role in public life at all. It is this party now which has begun to practise what you might call Hindu Zionism. This is not at a theological nor theoretical level at all, but rather it is a political practice that sees the fate of what is regarded as Hindu India as being closely tied up with Likudnic Zionist Israel, with the kinds of Zionist practices which are visible right here in Palestine-Israel.

Before I come to this new axis that has been forged, it is very important to indicate that the Indian people have been the strongest supporters of Palestinian nationhood for the past 50 to 60 years. In fact, the government of India, until 1992, did not seek to have full-scale diplomatic relations with Israel. It considered itself a strong supporter of the cause of Arab nationalism, and, in particular, of the two-state solution to the Palestinian question. People like Arafat were extremely popular. I remember the PLO being able to organize, in cities like Calcutta, rallies of 40 million people—so popular was it in the 70s and 80s. This is the country which actually led one of the greatest movements for decolonization in the world and, therefore, had a political culture which identified with the decolonization, freedom, and liberation of Third World peoples and supported their potential for emancipation and the construction of modern secular societies. It is on this foundation that solidarity existed. It is this foundation which the BJP itself now seeks to destroy.

What you have now is the formation of a strategic triad, a strategic three-way partnership among the neo-conservatives of the United States, the most extreme Zionists of Israel, and the Hindu fundamentalists and Islamaphobes of India. This relationship is reinforced at the level of politics, diplomacy and strategic relations. In fact, India is one of the three biggest buyers of armaments and is probably Israel's single largest market. There is increasing military co-operation among these three governments—they have joint exercises and training for each other's countries' insurgency forces. They have top policemen and secret service agents being trained in one another's countries, and they have huge numbers of arms purchase agreements. At the end of 2003, the U.S. approved the sale of a high technology early warning and control system made in Israel with U.S. technical collaboration. This system, called the *Falcon,* involves detecting some three dozen aircraft on a 360 degree axis in order to attempt to intercept them. Because much of this system was actually developed via collaboration between the United States and Israel, the sale needed and received U.S. approval.

Moreover, India is also in the market for all manner of things including tanks, submarines, high speed attack boats, un-manned Israeli-made carrier vehicles, surge-acquisition and fire-control radar, upgrades of various kinds of aviation systems, all kinds of sensors to monitor the boundary border with Pakistan, and so forth. This list indicates only some of the privileged strategic collaboration that has taken place between India and Israel, among other countries of the world. Thus, Israel has apparently emerged as India's single biggest military collaborator.

So in September 2003, Sharon was invited, to our government's disgrace, to make an official visit to New Delhi, something which would have been *inconceivable* even a year before! In fact, what set the stage for this visit was 9/11 and the drum-beating rhetoric of fighting terrorism. Because India, the United States and Israel have been considered the greatest victims of terrorism, a new axis to fight terrorism has produced this strategic triad. There were strong protests in India against Sharon's visit, as a third of Sharon's delegation consisted of representatives of the armaments industry, including Israeli Military Industries Ltd, Israeli

Aircraft Industries Ltd., the Armaments Developments Authority, and so on. These contracts with India are some of the biggest deals Israel has ever signed.

But the India-Israel relationship is not limited just to arms purchases or mutual training or even to sharing of intelligence. It extends to political co-operation in international forums such as the Commission on Human Rights, where Israel and India both come under frequent attack and, I think, receive well-deserved criticism. They now form joint lobbies to resist and deflect that criticism. Similarly, within the United States where the Zionist lobby is very powerful, the Indian non-resident community, a very ambitious group of almost two million people, is the United States' single richest ethnic minority. These are professionals who left India to settle in the United States after having benefited a great deal from the Indian education system. They practice what we call long-distance nationalism, which is even more toxic and more chauvinist than the nationalism back home. They are actually lobbying for the most conservative and right-wing policies in India, and they are in collaboration, increasingly, with the Zionist lobby. There are several examples in which the elections of candidates to U.S. State Senates were actually determined by these two lobbies (the Indian right-wing lobby and the Zionist lobby) getting together to seek the defeat, for instance, of black candidates or those who were progressive and who wanted the kinds of policies most of us would support. Similarly, this particular alliance is likely to grow in response to many other international forums.

The essential point is that this new alliance was founded by a party whose ideological roots, ironically, lie in an organization called the RSS (The National Volunteer Corps), which is like a secret male society, founded in 1925, that follows the ideology of the classic European fascism of the 1930s and the 1940s. In fact, it had active contacts with Mussolini in Italy, and its representatives were strong supporters of Hitler. The RSS continues to be the ideological mentor, political master and organizational gatekeeper of the BJP. Party members like Prime Minister Vajpayee have all been life-long members of the RSS. The RSS deals with military training and its ideal is fundamentally to establish a Hindu nation that would exclude religious minorities from true first-class citizenship, from the decision-making core of society. The RSS says in a direct quote from the 1940s: "For us, the true path to racial purity and to strong militarized nation-hood is demonstrated above all by Hitler and his Nazi

Party." The defense of the Aryan race is seen, in fact, as something very close to the old core agenda of the RSS, which views the Aryans themselves as Hindus, the original inhabitants of India. The irony and the most perverse thing about such ideologies is that the same people who defended and supported Hitler's Holocaust now want to support the worst of Zionist practices and ideologies. In fact, the Zionists should be deeply embarrassed about receiving support or offers of collaboration from them, whether domestically, bi-laterally, or internationally. But they are not.

What is it about the power of certain exclusivist ideologies and exclusivist nationalism that attracts these two political currents to each other? One is the idea of defining the land of origin, of birth, as sacred land and something that gives one special claim to be a nationalist. In other words, as the most important ideologue of this position has said, it is not enough for people, in order to be true Indians, to be born in India, but they must also regard India as their sacred land, their Holy land; otherwise they are not truly Indian. So that excludes people like Muslims, who are supposed to have their loyalties with Mecca and Medina. That excludes Jews, who came to my country 2, 000 years ago. That excludes Christians, 30 million of whom live in India, because they are supposed to have come from the other side, and so on. So the only true Indians are Hindus and they, by virtue of being Hindu, have a special right to Indianness and they are authentically Indian. This closely parallels Zionist propositions, that Jews by virtue of being Jews constitute a nation, that they are an authentic community. But I think the parallels go much deeper.

I will take up two fundamental propositions just to simplify matters a bit. One is the idea that there was a Golden Age in India's history and culture. This has been variably defined as extending from the period of 300 to 500 A.D. until the tenth century A.D. It was seen as a period in India which was quintessentially Hindu and then allowed itself to become so docile and servile to the world that it was invaded repeatedly, conquered, subjugated, dominated by outsiders. So the first proposition was that India was quintessentially a Hindu country and that the invaders were various kinds of people: Turks, Afghans, Central Asian people like Uzbeks, Greeks and the lot. Thus, this is the land of honey and treacle that allowed itself to be pillaged by these invaders until Hindus became gradually subdued and all other kinds of people began shaping India. Historians, however, tell us that India was never a quintessentially Hindu country.

There have always been Buddhists as well as indigenous peoples practicing different faiths such as ancestor worship, and there continue to be a variety of beliefs and practices. There are nature worshippers. There are Jews. There are Christians. St Thomas the Apostle came in 56 A.D. Christianity in India is older than Christianity in Europe. Islam in India goes back to 640 A.D., the time of the building of first mosques. It is impossible to distinguish between the people from some of the Gulf States—Qatar, Bahrain—and the people of Kerala. They have a common language. Even today something like 10 percent of the population of Kerala, on the west coast, know Arabic and historically have had more to do with people living across the Arabian Sea than with any other parts of India. These are indigenous people; they are our people; they did not come from the outside. They were part of India. Islam in India is older than Protestantism in Western Europe, and yet Hindu fundamentalists of the BJP mentality, *deny* this central fact about Indian society—that it has always been plural, multilingual, multi-ethnic and multi-religious. At no point in time did more than 60 or 70 percent of India define itself in religiously and ethnically uniform terms. For instance, India has something like 18 major languages, 300 other languages which have actual written scripts, and something like 4,000 minor languages or dialects. That is the kind of plurality and diversity that India has.

The second idea is a myth of Hindu tolerance, the idea that Hinduism is uniquely tolerant and thus can be easily subverted and subjugated. This is simply not true! In fact, this is the same faith that ordains untouchability, which excludes people on the grounds of caste. And yet, I think that the whole notion of victimhood and demonology that is shared with the Zionists is very central to this particular ideology of the BJP. Both have the idea that Israel and India are surrounded by hostile forces, in particular by Muslims, who do not want us to live happily, who want to destroy our identity, our self-respect, our genuine ethnic character, and who then must be punished, who must be held at bay. They cannot be trusted and we cannot have friendships with these political forces.

The whole idea of the demonizing and de-humanizing of non-Hindus, in particular Muslims, is central to this ideology, and so Hindu fundamentalists have a special fascination with Israel. They admire it because it has been so successful in subjugating its enemies, the Arabs, the Palestinian people. They admire it because they see it as a highly militarized society. That is exactly the ideal they want to emulate. They admire Israelis because they have made revenge into a virtue and define success itself in terms of revenge against history. Now this is very important. We all talk about al-Haram al-Sharif and so on. What some of the worst Zionists would like to do by destroying it and building a temple is what the BJP actually did! In 1992, in Ayhodya, a 16th century mosque was razed in the most barbaric fashion, based on the belief that the mosque had been built on historical ground where a Hindu temple had been destroyed. In fact, there is no archaeological, historical, or contextual evidence that a temple had existed where that mosque was built at the order of the first Moghul Emperor. This is not just an act of vandalism; it actually led to tremendous violence with something like 2,000 people being killed in different cities after the demolition of the mosque in December of 1992. So in many respects, I think their agendas are driven by common beliefs and both having similar ideals and objectives.

The purpose of sharing all this is not just to reveal the collusion that is taking place between these horrible forces. Their shared world view leads to a destruction of social cohesion, multiculturalism, morality and diversity in our society. For us in India, the struggle for democracy, for secularism, for human dignity, for peace, for social cohesion of the family, is very closely tied up with the struggle to see our own objectives, our own perspective within the historic envelope of broader people's movements. Just as we take a great deal of pride in the fact that India was the first of the great anti-colonial mass movements, we ought to see the efforts of the Palestinian people as the last of the struggles against colonialism, the last of the great struggles, especially after the defeat of the Apartheid regime in South Africa. Unless we are able to grasp this relationship, we will not be able to build a bond of international solidarity. We must recognize that India's struggle to regain our secular space and to separate religion from politics, especially when that religion is tied up in ethnicity and nationalism, is part of the larger struggle internationally and, very powerfully, is part of the Palestinian people's struggle. That is why for us it is very important to establish close bonds and to take them forward. It is in this spirit that I have emphasized the importance of the universal bond of solidarity among us all.

VIOLENCE AND THE BIBLICAL LAND TRADITIONS

Michael Prior (1942 - 2004)

We at Sabeel give thanks to God for the life and witness of our brother and friend Michael Prior and we commend him to the love and mercy of God. Michael devoted the better part of his life in the service of justice and liberation for the Palestinians. His strong prophetic message will reverberate until justice for the Palestinians is done and peace and reconciliation are achieved in the Holy Land for all its people.

The Revd Dr Naim Ateek

Editor's Note: Because of Dr Prior's untimely death on 23 July 2004, Sabeel was unable to secure the text of the talk he delivered at the Sabeel Conference of April 2004. However, his remarks on that occasion were quite similar to those delivered in March 2004 to The Society for Biblical Studies in Belmont Massachusetts. With the kind permission of The Revd Peter J. Miano, Executive Director of The Society for Biblical Studies, we provide below a somewhat abridged version of that address. To read it in its entirety, please visit www.sbsedu.org.

Since I am by training a biblical scholar, I will focus on what the biblical narrative contributes to the theme of "The Clash of Civilisations". Permit me to make an observation, a *caveat* concerning the remarks that follow. I have hard things to say about some of the traditions of the Bible. Someone from an Islamic tradition, in particular, might see in this merely an illustration of what Muslims believe anyway, namely, that the earlier revelations were imperfect, or even corrupt, and reached perfection only in the revelation to the Prophet. My concern is not about particular traditions within one specific faith community, but about the general moral question that arises from the realisation that religion and violence have never been strangers. Religious zeal has frequently fuelled violence in the past, and is clearly doing so in our own day. If, as I contend below, religious motivation is invoked as part of the justification for colonialism and imperialism from so-called Christian cultures, other religious cultures also have their cases to answer.[1]

Political scientists, anthropologists, historians and sociologists, and other specialists also will issue their own clamour for attention. However, even in our current secularised phase in the West one simply has to acknowledge that there is no single cultural artefact that has had as much influence in framing Western culture as has the Bible, with its continuous impact in virtually every facet of life for close on two thousand years. Let me say right away that I think the Bible, at least in certain key areas, contributes enormously to the acceptance of whatever bifurcation one might detect in human society, and in life in general.

The Western self-perception of having arrived at the highest level of evolutionary progress so far, I contend, has much to do with the biblical narrative in which God's very own "Chosen People", having taken possession of the Promised Land, are to so comport themselves as to be models of a utopian civilisation springing from conformity with a legal code of no less than divine provenance. There is a certain moral problem, however, right below the surface. It appears from the biblical narrative itself, or certain traditions thereof, that the establishment of the utopian society which is at the very core of the *Torah* must be preceded by the divinely-mandated extermination of the indigenous people of Canaan. It is part of the uniqueness of some religious discourse that that kind of violence which would otherwise be dismissed as barbarism is sanctioned in the name of a higher value. Religions, of course, are not alone in such evaluations. History is replete with examples of the justification of the unjustifiable in the name of some or other higher ideology.

The biblical narrative in several places demands a strict wall of separation between the clean and the unclean, the sacred and the profane, the ways of the godly and those of the heathen. The division is expressed

---

1 See my "The Bible and the Redeeming Idea of Colonialism", in Marcella Althaus-Reid and Jack Thompson (eds), *Studies in World Christianity*, 5(1999, 2, *Postcolonialism and Religion* (Edinburgh: Edinburgh University Press and Maryknoll, NY: Orbis), pp. 129-55.

ritualistically in the cult of the Israelites, and in the whole range of activities commanded or forbidden by their legal codes. Worse still, as I demonstrate extensively in my book, *The Bible and Colonialism: A Moral Critique,* certain traditions of the foundational documents of Jews and Christians—whether one calls them the Hebrew Scriptures or the Old Testament does not remove the embarrassment—promote violence. The most focused conclusion I derived from simply reading the biblical narrative of the promise of land to Abraham and his descendants, and the conquest of that land under Joshua, was that the bounty of the divine land regulator was tied inextricably to the religious requirement to exterminate the indigenous people of Canaan. The process of taking possession of the Promised Land, a land flowing with milk and honey, required that it flow also with the blood of its indigenous population. But even yet worse: the genocide of the indigenous population was *mandated* as an act of pious conformity to the directives of God. Thus, the divinely-mandated shedding of the blood of the natives would be redemptive. Through this 'ethnic' massacre the land would be cleansed of the defilement with which the native population had polluted it. Let just one example from the biblical narrative suffice to illustrate the imperative to ethnically cleanse the land of Canaan.

In the rules for the conduct of war, when a besieged town surrenders, all its inhabitants shall do forced labour; if not, the Israelites shall kill all its males, and take as booty the women, children, livestock, and everything else in the town (Deuteronomy 20.11-14). The narrative presents 'ethnic cleansing', then, as not only legitimate, but as required by the divinity:

> "But as for the towns of these peoples that Yahweh your God is giving you as an inheritance, you must not let anything that breathes remain alive. You shall annihilate them—the Hittites and the Amorites, the Canaanites and the Perizzites, the Hivites and the Jebusites—just as Yahweh your God has commanded, so that they may not teach you to do all the abhorrent things that they do for their gods, and you thus sin against Yahweh your God" (Deuteronomy 20.16-18).[2]

---

[2] I discuss all the relevant texts from each of the books of the Bible in my *The Bible and Colonialism,* pp. 16-33.

Indeed, the term 'ethnic cleansing' itself, I suggest, is related to a conflation of the biblical notions of "unclean"/"profane" with the command to "drive out" the inhabitants of Canaan (Exodus 23-24; Numbers 33; Deuteronomy 33 and Joshua), because, according to the biblical legend, they had defiled themselves by their evil practices (Leviticus 18.24). Uniquely in ancient literature, the biblical legend projects the extermination of the defiled and defiling indigenes as a divine mandate. With the authority of its religious provenance the biblical value system of disdain for the indigenous people has entered, as we shall see, into various European imperialist ideologies, "legitimising" the destruction, displacement, or at least the subjugation of indigenous peoples.

It needs to be acknowledged that the biblical text is problematic not only because of the history of its reception as an agent of oppression of colonised peoples, but also in virtue of its very content. G.E.M. de Ste. Croix, an expert on class politics in the ancient world, asserted that the Israelites were the one people who felt able to claim that they had a divine command to exterminate whole populations among those it conquered. There is no text in ancient culture, he added, that matches the Bible in terms of ferocity, a detail seldom dwelt on today by either Christians or Jews, despite the fact that such incomparable ferocity is revealed not by hostile sources but by the very literature they themselves regard as sacred.[3] This conceptual moral problem of the relevant biblical narratives is exacerbated by the fact that their value system, with all the authority their religious provenance confers, has been incorporated as a "legitimising" agent in the ideologies of virtually all European imperialist enterprises, the consequences of which have been the irreversible suffering of entire indigenous communities and, in some cases, their virtual annihilation as a people.[4]

While it may be plain to modern readers of the Bible that some of its narratives have played a huge part in Europe's imperialising impulse, it appears not to bother biblical scholars to the point of critical opposition. The Book of Deuteronomy, for example, despite its requirement of the genocide of the indigenous population of Canaan, is held in the highest esteem in the biblical academy. Commentators conventionally assess it to be a theological book *par excellence*, and the focal point of the religious

---

[3] G.E.M. de Ste. Croix, *The Class Struggle in the Ancient Greek World from the Archaic Age to the Arab Conquest* (London: Duckworth, 1981), pp. 331-32.

[4] See my *The Bible and Colonialism.*

history of the Old Testament. In the 1995 Lattey Lecture in Cambridge University Professor Norbert Lohfink interpreted the laws of Deuteronomy in terms of defining a utopian society in which there would be no poor.[5] Naturally one found the prospect inviting, and was pleased to reflect upon "Mount Zion as the place where they (the nations) can learn how a better society functions." Moreover, Lohfink dealt with the Book of Exodus only in terms of the delivery from Egypt of a marginalised and exploited group, without any reference to what was to follow. In my role as the formal proposer of a vote of thanks I invited Professor Lohfink to consider whether, in the light of the Book of Deuteronomy's insistence on a mandate to commit genocide, the utopian society predicated in that book would be possible only after the invading Israelites had wiped out the indigenous inhabitants. The protocol left the last word with me, and subsequently I was given a second word, being invited to deliver the 1997 Lattey Lecture, for which I chose the title, *A Land flowing with Milk, Honey, and People.*[6]

Study of the Bible has customarily been in the hands of people of religious affiliations, in whom one might not unreasonably expect to find concern for upright moral behaviour. One would not immediately, for example, count on finding support for ethnic cleansing within a religious culture committed to the worship of God and the love of the universal neighbour. But yet, such support has never been lacking, whether in the past or even in our own day. Toleration and even admiration of ethnic-cleansing is to be found within the biblical academy itself.

Even the Book of Joshua, that chronicle of divinely-mandated serial genocides, if one were to imagine it to belong to the literary classification of history, rather than, what I take it to be, legend, has no shortage of admirers. Only a decade after the full horrors of Nazi "ethnic cleansing" had been revealed, William Foxwell Albright, the doyen of biblical archaeologists, had no qualms about the plunder attendant upon Joshua's enterprise, a project he understood in a largely historically reliable way:

---

5 'The Laws of Deuteronomy. A Utopian Project for a World without any Poor?' (St Edmund's College, Cambridge: Von Hügel Institute, 1996), published also as, 'The Laws of Deuteronomy. A Utopian Project for a World without any Poor' , in *Scripture Bulletin* 26 (1996): 2-19.

6 Michael Prior, *A Land flowing with Milk, Honey, and People* (Cambridge: Von Hügel Institute, 1997), and in *Scripture Bulletin* 28(1998): 2-17.

> From the impartial standpoint of a philosopher of history, it often seems necessary that a people of markedly inferior type should vanish before a people of superior potentialities, since there is a point beyond which racial mixture cannot go without disaster ... Thus the Canaanites, with their orgiastic nature worship, their cult of fertility in the form of serpent symbols and sensuous nudity, and their gross mythology, were replaced by Israel, with its pastoral simplicity and purity of life, its lofty monotheism, and its severe code of ethics.[7]

Prior to Keith Whitelam's critique, no commentator had drawn attention to Albright's undisguised racist attitudes, which were typical of virtually every Western colonial enterprise which predicated that the "superior" peoples of the West had the right to exploit, and in some cases exterminate, the "natives".[8] Reflecting these conventional values, Albright also judged that through Zionism Jews would bring to the Near East all the benefits of European civilisation.[9]

---

[7] William F. Albright, *From the Stone Age to Christianity: Monotheism and the Historical Process* (New York: Doubleday, 1957), pp. 280-81. In a similar vein, George E. Wright, another distinguished American biblical scholar, justified the genocide of the narrative of Joshua in terms of the inferiority of the indigenous culture (in G.E. Wright and R.H. Fuller, eds. *The Book of the Acts of God: Christian Scholarship Interprets the Bible*, London: Duckworth, 1960, p. 109). In the previous century, Heinrich Ewald, who in his five-volume history of Israel (1843–1855) was determined to demonstrate the Israelites' unique, tireless efforts to achieve true and perfect religion, wrote: 'It is an eternal necessity that a nation such as the majority of the Canaanites then were, sinking deeper and deeper into a slough of discord and moral perversity, must fall before a people roused to a higher life by the newly awakened energy of unanimous trust in Divine Power'. Similarly, G.F. MacLear in his commentary on Joshua (1880) could write: 'When ... God entrusted the sword of vengeance to Joshua, was ever campaign waged in such an unearthly manner as that now inaugurated by the leader of the armies of Israel?' He ends by quoting a sermon of Thomas Arnold: 'The Israelites' sword in its bloodiest executions, wrought a work of mercy for all the countries of the earth...they preserved unhurt the seed of eternal life' (quoted in A. Graeme Auld, *Joshua Retold: Synoptic Perspectives*, Edinburgh: T.& T. Clark, 1998, p. 133).

[8] Keith W. Whitelam, *The Invention of Ancient Israel. The Silencing of Palestinian History* (London and New York: Routledge, 1996), p. 88.

[9] William F. Albright. 'Why the Near East needs the Jews', *New Palestine* 32(1942, 9): 12-13. For an attempt to account for Albright's ethnocratism see note 43 below.

From 'The Chosen People' to 'We Chosen People'

The problematic character of the land traditions of the Bible is not merely rhetorical. History witnesses to their deployment in ideological support of colonial and imperial projects, many of which have caused devastation in several regions in the past. My *The Bible and Colonialism* demonstrates this thesis by reference to three different regions, periods and religious provenances: the pre-Reformation Christian Iberian conquest of Latin America in the 15th century; the Calvin-inspired support for Afrikaner domination of southern Africa, which began with the Dutch incursion into the Cape Colony of southern Africa in 1652, and continued throughout the 19th and 20th centuries up to our own day; and the Zionist settler-colonialism of Palestine in the 20th century.[10]

These colonialist enterprises, of course, were propelled by other compelling factors, invariably those related to greed and power, and it would be facile to point to the biblical narrative as the primary motivation in each case. Nevertheless, the biblical paradigm was at hand to "legitimise" the displacement of indigenous societies and their cultures, and, as I have demonstrated, were deployed in fact. Colonial enterprises were elevated to a new mode of justification when they could appeal to religious motivation of no less than (allegedly) divine provenance.

Although I do not consider that the relevant biblical traditions depict the past as it actually happened—their literary form falls broadly into the category of myths, or legends of origin, rather than history—they have in fact been utilised in support of a range of European colonialist enterprises which promote the appropriateness of planting outposts of European progress in the heart of Oriental or African darkness, to adapt the metaphors of Joseph Conrad. All too frequently the higher values of religion—the worship of God and the love of others—were eclipsed by the imperatives of exclusivist colonial or nationalist enterprises of expansion, leading frequently to a desecration of God's name as well as to the destruction of peoples. Yet, such matters seldom seem to bother biblical scholars to the point of engaged opposition.

---

[10] See Michael Prior, *The Bible and Colonialism. A Moral Critique* (Sheffield: Sheffield Academic Press, 1997). In my forthcoming *An Bíobla agus an Leatrom. Staidéir Comparáideach ar Úsáid an Bhíobla sa Pholaitíocht* ('The Bible and Oppression. A Comparative Study of the Use of the Bible in Politics', Maigh Nuad: An Sagart, 2003) I extend the discussion to include the deployment of the Bible as an instrument of oppression in Ireland.

Zionism in Palestine: 'The Bible is our mandate'

In the case of Zionism, the role of the Bible is of particular interest, since whatever justification the European settlers in South America, South Africa or Ulster had for deploying it as a legitimating charter for their settler colonisation, Jews appear to require less defence. The claim that the Bible legitimates the implementation of the Zionist political programme is widespread. Although Zionism was a secular ideology and enterprise from the beginning, and was bitterly opposed by the Jewish religious establishment, its supporters, when it suited their purposes, could look to the Bible for support, particularly the narratives of the promise of land to Abraham and his descendants, and the execution of the promise in the narrative of Joshua's conquest. Even for secular or atheist nationalists uninterested in it as the repository of a theological claim, the biblical narrative could function as the "historical account" of Jews' title to the land. Thus, for David Ben-Gurion, Israel's first Prime Minister, the Bible was the "Jews' sacrosanct title-deed to Palestine ... with a genealogy of 3,500 years."[11] For Theodor Herzl (1860–1904), the founder of Political Zionism, too, the biblical narrative was available to provide legitimising support whenever called upon.

Like other Westerners of his day who found it difficult to conceive of the possibility of any other civilisation, Herzl had no doubt about the superiority of Europeans over the other peoples of the globe. His Political Zionism was replete with typical Western attitudes of superiority, and his diaries and writings reveal such racist attitudes. He, too, saw colonialism as the bestowal of civilisation and good order upon inferior peoples.

---

[11] David Ben-Gurion, *The Rebirth and Destiny of Israel* (New York: Philosophical Library, 1954), p. 100. Ben-Gurion regularly convened the 'Prime Minster's Bible Study Circle', which included President Zalman -Shazar. His lecture, 'The Bible and the Jewish People' (Nahalal, 20 July 1964) makes abundant use of biblical texts, especially those dealing with the promise of restoration. While he alludes to the Hebrew prophets and their concern for justice, Ben-Gurion does not deal with the injunctions to disinherit the Canaanites, the Joshua legend, nor with the biblical traditions that reflect racist, ethnicist, xenophobic and militaristic tendencies. His sole oblique reference to the indigenous Palestinians is that while the whole world regarded Israel with respect and admiration, 'Our Arab neighbours have as yet not made peace with our existence, and their leaders are declaring their desire to destroy us' (*Ben-Gurion Looks at the Bible* (trans. from the Hebrew by Jonathan Kolatch, London & New York: W.H. Allen.1972, p. 294). See also Moshe Dayan's *Living with the Bible* (Philadelphia: Jewish Publication Society; New York: William Morrow, 1978).

Rather than its precipitating a clash of civilisations, his proposed state for Jews would be "a portion of the rampart of Europe against Asia, an outpost of civilisation *[Kultur]* opposed to barbarism" (p. 30).[12] In addition to providing "a house to shelter the Jewish nation", his project would "advance the interests of civilisation, by establishing a cultural station, on the shortest road to Asia, a task Jews were ready to undertake as the bearers of culture."[13] Herzl reflected elsewhere also the typical world-view of European racist superiority. He assured the Grand Duke of Baden that Jews returning to their "historic fatherland" would do so as representatives of Western civilisation, bringing "cleanliness, order and the well-established customs of the Occident to this plague-ridden, blighted corner of the Orient".[14] To adapt the language of Joseph Conrad, Herzl's Jewish State would be an 'outpost of progress' in "the heart of darkness".

But Herzl's Zionism went beyond the customary colonial pattern of disdain for the natives. He knew what was needed to establish a state for Jews in a land already inhabited. The project required the removal, rather than merely the subjugation of the indigenous population, irrespective of whether or not the indigenes constituted a civilisation. An item in his diary entry for 12 June 1895 signals his plans. Having

---

[12] The German original reads, 'Für Europa würden wir dort ein Stück des Walles gegen Asien bilden, wir würden den Vorpostendienst der Kultur gegen die Barbarei besorgen' (*Der Judenstaat. Versuch einer Modernen Lösung der Judenfrage*, Leipzig und Wien: M. Breitenstein's Verlags-Buchhandlung, 1896). *Der Judenstaat* was translated into English by Sylvie d'Avigdor as *A Jewish State*, and in 1946 as *The Jewish State*, and published by the American Zionist Emergency Council. *Der Judenstaat* would more accurately be translated by 'The State for Jews', to distinguish it from the implications of a Jewish state (*Jüdischer Staat*). The seventh edition, *The Jewish State. An Attempt at a Modern Solution of the Jewish Question*, revised with a foreword by Israel Cohen was published in London (Henry Pordes) in 1993. Quotations and page references here are from the seventh edition.

[13] *Protokoll des I. Zionistenkongresses in Basel vom 29. bis 31. August 1897* (Prag: Selbstverlag — Druck von Richard Brandeis, 1911), p. 15.

[14] *The Complete Diaries of Theodore Herzl* (translated by Harry Zohn, and edited by Raphael Patai in five volumes, New York: Herzl Press, 1960), Vol. I, p. 343. Herzl began his Diaries in 1895, and continued until shortly before his death. The project of publishing all Herzl's writings was completed in 1996: Vol. I, 1983, *Briefe und Autobiographische Notizen. 1886-1895*; Vol. II: 1983, *Zionistiches Tagebuch 1895-1899*; Vol. III, 1985: *Zionistiches Tagebuch 1899-1904* (Vols I-III, ed. Johannes Wachten, *et al.*); Vol. IV, 1990, *Briefe 1895-1898*; Vol. V, 1993, *Briefe 1898-1900*; Vol. VI, 1993, *Briefe Ende August 1900-ende Dezember 1902*; Vol. VII, 1996, *Briefe 1903-1904* (Vols. IV-VII, ed. Barbara Schäfer, *et al.*) (Berlin: Propylaen Verlag).

occupied the land and expropriated the private property, "We shall endeavour to expel the poor population across the border unnoticed, procuring employment for it in the transit countries, but denying it any employment in our own country."[15] He added that both 'the process of expropriation and the removal of the poor must be carried out discreetly and circumspectly.'

In public, however, Herzl showed a different face. In one of the earliest recorded Palestinian reactions to Zionism, Yusuf Diya' al-Din Pasha al-Khalidi, former mayor of Jerusalem and deputy for the city in the Ottoman Parliament (first elected in 1868, he served until its suspension in 1878), wrote to Herzl, via Zadok Kahn, Grand Rabbin of France. He warned him that while Zionism was 'in theory a completely natural and just idea' as a solution to the Jewish problem and might work elsewhere, Palestine was a part of the Ottoman Empire, was heavily populated by non-Jews, and was venerated by 390 million Christians and 300 million Muslims. He asked, "By what right do the Jews demand it for themselves?" Wealth cannot purchase Palestine, "which can only be taken over by the force of cannons and warships." He warned that Zionists would never become masters of the country, and concluded, "For the sake of God, leave Palestine in peace." In his response of 19 March 1899, referring to al-Khalidi's fear of Arab expulsions, Herzl assured him: "But who would think of sending them away? It is their well-being, their individual wealth, which we will increase by bringing in our own."[16] As Herzl wrote in his diary on 23 October 1902, "Not everything in politics is disclosed to the public—but only results of what can be serviceable in a controversy." This kind of duplicity was a characteristic of Zionist discourse, producing "a not-undeserved reputation in the world for chronic mendacity".[17] Moreover, after his death in 1904, Herzl's diaries were held by the Zionist movement, and until 1960 only edited versions were released, carefully omitting his 'population transfer' plans.

---

[15] 'Die arme Bevölkerung trachten wir unbemerkt über die Grenze zu schaffen, indem wir in den Durchzugsländern Arbeit verschaffen aber in unserem eigenen Lande jederlei Arbeit verweigern' (Theodor Herzl, *Briefe und Autobiographische Notizen. 1886-1895.* Vol. II, ed. by Johannes Wachten *et al.*, Berlin: Propylaen Verlag, 1983, pp. 117-18).

[16] See the discussion in Rashid Khalidi, *Palestinian Identity. The Construction of Modern National Consciousness* (New York: Columbia University Press, 1997), pp. 24 (n 44, p. 219), 74-76 (n 55, p. 235).

[17] Christopher Sykes, *Crossroads to Israel. Palestine from Balfour to Bevin* (London: Collins, 1965), p. 26.

Herzl was not alone among the Zionist ideologues in promoting "population transfer". Privately, the majority of Zionists were in no doubt that the realisation of the Jewish dream would require a nightmare for the indigenous population. Despite public protestations to the contrary, Zionist leaders from the beginning were aware of the demographic reality in Palestine, and as early as November 1882 the use of arms was envisioned by some Jews in Palestine.[18]

Moreover, we now know what was hidden in the Zionist archives until recently. Nur Masalha demonstrates that the imperative to "transfer" the indigenous Arab population was at the core of the Zionist enterprise from the beginning. His studies, based on primary research in various Zionist archives, fundamentally undermine the hegemonic Zionist narrative that its intentions were altogether innocent, if not indeed altruistic. The "mountain" of evidence in these archives traces the consistency of the 'transfer' mode of thinking within the Jewish leadership in Palestine. It demonstrates that the expulsion of the indigenous Arabs was foreseen as necessary, was systematically planned and was executed at the first opportunity in 1948. From it we learn in detail how prominent was the necessity of "transfer" in the collective thinking of the Zionist leadership from the middle 1930s in particular, although there is a substantial *catena* of quotations from prominent Zionists well before then.

By uncovering such evidence, Masalha demonstrates that the imperative to "transfer" the indigenous Arab population was at the core of the Zionist enterprise from the beginning, was pursued with determination at the levels of both planning and execution, and, in particular since the *intifada* which began in September 2000, has again moved towards centre-stage in Zionist intentions to this day. Masalha's

---

[18] One of the *Biluim*—the *Biluim* (the plural of an acronym of the opening words of Isaiah 2.5), an offshoot of the *Lovers of Zion*, were a group of early Jewish settlers in Palestine—said, 'The Jews, if necessary with arms in their hands, will publicly proclaim themselves masters of their own, ancient fatherland' (in Walter Lehn, in association with Uri Davis, *The Jewish National Fund*, London and New York: Kegan Paul International, 1988, p. 10). In Moshe Smilansky's dialogue between two Zionist pioneers (1891), the revolutionaries would expel the Arabs to Transjordan, and further,. Nahman Syrkin, the ideological founder of Socialist Zionism, too, insisted in 1898 that Palestine must be evacuated for the Jews. Chaim Weizmann, later to become the first President of Israel, spoke of the necessity of fitting the gem (the Jewish people without a country) into the ring (the country without a people)—see Simha Flapan, *Zionism and the Palestinians 1917-1947* (London: Croom Helm, 1979), p. 56, and Doreen Ingrams, *Palestine Papers 1917-1922: Seeds of Conflict* (London: John Murray, 1972), pp. 31-32.

contribution to the discourse on 1948 is more complete than that of the Israeli "New Historians". He not only lets the Zionist evidence concerning 1948 speak for itself, but also shows how prominent was the necessity of "transfer" in the thinking of the Zionist leadership from the middle 1930s, at least. We read in the Zionist archives of the establishment and comportment of the two "Population Transfer Committees" (1937 through 1944) and the third Population Transfer Committee established by the Israeli cabinet in August 1948.[19] Masalha's most recent book is a comprehensive treatment of the imperial imperative within Zionism.[20] The catastrophe (*Nakba*) visited upon the indigenous population, then, was neither accidental nor due to the unique pressures of war, but was at the heart of the Zionist enterprise from the beginning.

Despite the fact that Herzl himself had no sense of Jewish national culture, and no inward relationship to Judaism or to his own Jewishness[21]—indeed, while in Vienna in 1881-82, he had considered even mass Jewish conversion to Catholicism as a solution to the problem of being a Jew in Europe—he was well aware of the potential of appeal to religious sentiment. Herzl acknowledged that the notions of "Chosen People" and "return" to the "Promised Land" would mobilise Jewish opinion, despite the fact that the leading Zionists were either non-religious, atheists or agnostics. He appealed for the support of the rabbis (p. 54), and asserted, "Our community of race is peculiar and unique, for we are bound together only by the faith of our fathers" (p. 71). Nevertheless, the Jewish State would not be a theocracy: "We shall keep our priests within the confines of their temples in the same way as we keep our professional army within the confines of their barracks" (p. 71). However, despite such references to religious matters, Herzl's enterprise was an altogether secular one.

---

19 See Nur Masalha, *Expulsion of the Palestinians: the Concept of 'Transfer' in Zionist Political Thought, 1882-1948* (Washington, D.C: Institute for Palestine Studies, 1992). See also Nur Masalha, *A Land without a People. Israel, Transfer and the Palestinians 1949-96* (London: Faber and Faber, 1997).

20 *Imperial Israel and the Palestinians: The Politics of Expansion, 1967-2000* (London: Pluto, 2000).

21 So Martin Buber at Herzl's graveside (1904)—see Robert Wistrich, 'Theodor Herzl: Zionist Icon, Myth-Maker and Social Utopian', in Robert Wistrich and David Ohana (eds), *The Shaping of Israeli Identity: Myth, Memory and Trauma* (London: Frank Cass, 1995: 1-37), pp. 30-31. Although Herzl's motivation was utterly secular, at various times people referred to him as the Messiah, or King of Israel, and as the fulfilment of the prophecies of the Jewish Scriptures.

Zionism was not merely a variant on the Jewish faith, but a very substitute for it. That the Zionist movement would arrogate to itself the agency for the restoration of the Jewish people to its ancestral land—a task uniquely for accomplishment by the Messiah—was, for Orthodox Jews, nothing short of blasphemy. Thus, rabbis representing all shades of opinion denounced Zionism as a fanaticism, and contrary to the Jewish scriptures. Herzl and his Zionism were anathema to the most influential eastern European rabbis almost as a matter of course.[22] Even within the small circle of the Orthodox supporters of Zionism there was the widespread recognition that Zionism was not merely a variant on the Jewish faith, but a very substitute for it

The Zionist movement, then, was considered to be a rebellion against classical Judaism, and with good reason. For political Zionists in general, religion was irrational, and a repressive and regressive force. For them, salvation lay in escaping from the prison of the sacred, and the hypnotic spell of the Bible. Judaism was a weight of lead attached to the feet of Jews, and was a symptom of Jewry's sickness in exile. For such people, Zionist Palestine would be new, secular, and qualitatively different from the past of the diaspora.

Understandably, therefore, the Jewish religious establishment was vehemently opposed to the Zionist programme. For Orthodox Jews the diaspora was a condition ordained by God, who alone would bring it to an end. Reform Judaism, for its part, viewing Jewish history as evolutionary and dynamic, and according no essential significance to any one period, rejected the notion that Jews outside of Palestine were 'in exile', and insisted that Jews constituted a religious community, and not a nation, and had made their homes in and had become citizens of many states.[23]

Yet today, and since 1967 in particular, no body is more supportive of Zionism's achievement than the religious establishment, both inside and outside Israel, and many religious Jews accord the state redemptive

---

[22] David Vital, *A People Apart. The Jews in Europe 1789-1939* (Oxford: Oxford University Press, 1999), p. 625.

[23] I trace the metamorphosis in both Orthodox and Reform Jewry on the question of Political Zionism in Michael Prior, *Zionism and the State of Israel: A Moral Inquiry* (London: Routledge, 1999), pp. 67-102.

and even messianic significance.[24] Indeed, most of the religious establishment in Israel and outside is at the forefront of the opposition to political 'compromise' with the Palestinians. Thus, the hitherto secular enterprise of Zionism has been metamorphosed into an ideology which the majority of religious Jews regard as of divine origin: according to a former Chief Rabbi of the British Commonwealth, Lord Sir Immanuel Jakobivits, the state has "its religious significance as an extraordinary manifestation of Divine favour."[25] Moreover, despite the anti-religious stridency of Political Zionism, the late Chief Rabbi could say,

> The origins of the Zionist idea are of course entirely religious. The slogan, "The Bible is our mandate" is a credo hardly less insistently pleaded by many secularists than by religious believers as the principal basis of our legal and historical claim to the Land of Israel...Modern Political Zionism itself could never have struck root if it had not planted its seeds in soil ploughed up and fertilised by the millennial conditioning of religious memories, hopes, prayers and visions of our eventual return to Zion ... No rabbinical authority disputes that our claim to a Divine mandate (and we have no other which cannot be invalidated) extends over the entire Holy Land within its historic borders and that halachically we have no right to surrender this claim.[26]

---

[24] For many religious Jews in Israel and elsewhere, *Eretz Yisrael* is the normative context for the observance of the *Torah*. The land, therefore, has fundamental *halakhic* significance. Not only are certain laws (e.g., the sabbatical year and the tithes) applicable only in *Eretz Yisrael*, but the entire *Torah* is designed for the people in *Eretz Yisrael*. For such people, observing *halakhah* in the *galut* (exile) is only preparing one to do so in *Eretz Yisrael* (see Nahmanides, Commentary on Lev 18.25). For other religious Jews in Israel and elsewhere, the Zionist movement is seen as an expression of God taking his people out of the house of bondage, and with fire and cloud leading them to the promised land. *Aliyah* and the determination to build a just society, then, are religious ideals. The *Shoah* (Holocaust) itself can be interpreted within this matrix as promoting redemption: it constitutes 'the birth pangs of the Messiah'. The War of Independence and the 1967 war, for their part, are moments of salvation: acts of God's intervention (adapted from Michael Rosenak, 'State of Israel', in Arthur A. Cohen and Paul Mendes-Flohr [eds], *Contemporary Jewish Religious Thought. Original Essays on Critical Concepts, Movements and Beliefs* New York: The Free Press/ London: Collier Macmillan, 1987, pp. 909-16). Despite such rhetoric, however, 'working the land' has seldom been high on the list of priorities of religious, or even secular Jews in Israel, who invariably employ non-Jews to do such redemptive work.

[25] Jakobivits, *The Attitude to Zionism* ..., p. 20.

[26] *The Attitude to Zionism* ... Jakobivits goes on: "But what is questionable is whether we must, or indeed may, assert it at the risk of thousands of lives, if not the life of the State

Political Zionism, then, has undergone a process of sacralisation, whereby irreligious, secular, nationalist salvation has been endowed with the mythology of traditional Jewish soteriology. Thus, the religious dimension has entered the national narrative in a fundamental fashion, bringing with it the guarantee of divine approval.

Conclusion

Clearly, the land traditions of the Bible pose fundamental moral questions, relating both to their content and to the ways they have been deployed in favour of oppressive ideologies. In the light of the double problematic of the land traditions of the Bible—their projection of genocide as being divinely *mandated*, and their deleterious use in favour of oppressive colonialism—perhaps every copy of the Bible should contain a health warning: "Reading this Book may Damage Somebody Else's Health." It is possible to insist that the relevant land traditions are historical in the sense that they approximate to what actually happened—and many evangelicals do so. To do so, however, leaves one with a god who is a xenophobic nationalist and a militaristic ethnic-cleanser. Reliance on the authority of the gift of land from such a god, then, should be problematic for any reader who might presume that the divinity would entertain the values of the Fourth Geneva Convention and the Universal Declaration of Human Rights, at least. On moral grounds, therefore, one is forced to question whether the *Torah* in fact provides divine legitimacy for the occupation of other people's land, and the virtual annihilation of the indigenous peoples.

While traditional biblical commentators search out whatever can be ascertained about the social, religious, and political context of the biblical writings, they are invariably oblivious to their own contexts, and the impact that these might have on their interpretations of the

---

itself. ... We are halachically compelled to leave the judgment on what provides the optimum security for Jewish life in Israel to the verdict of military and political experts, not rabbis. Included as a major factor in this difficult judgment must also be the overriding concern to preserve the Jewish character of Israel which may clearly depend on the proportion of Jews within the State" (pp. 20-21). Jakobivits asserts the unique Jewish title to Jerusalem, and accepts the need for an eventual withdrawal 'on Israeli terms' from territories occupied (p. 21).

texts.[27] Moreover, few see it as necessary to evaluate the more morally problematic biblical texts in terms of general ethical criteria, or display any inclination to involve their scholarship in social transformation. Biblical scholars, any more than other academics, do not see themselves as called to become critical transformative intellectuals with a responsibility for criticising systems of oppression on the world scale.[28] Fascination with the unrecoverable past satisfies their intellectual appetites.

The biblical discourse in the West is in the control of the university departments of biblical studies—as it was in Church/Synagogue circles previously—and it is they who decide upon which questions are important. Virtually all Western biblical scholars, who live in comfort and in guaranteed security, and are respected members of prestigious academic institutions—I cannot pretend that I myself live otherwise—customarily interpret the Bible from their positions of power. A different dynamic operates in liberation theology circles, where authentic theological endeavour incorporates three elements: reflection, ethical option and action (praxis). Because it arises from being immersed in the concrete situation of people, such a theology introduces a fundamental ethical option, one which properly leads to implementation.[29]

---

[27] In reflecting upon an aspect of the discipline which is scarcely ever taken into account, namely the "ideological baggage" of the individual researcher, Burke O. Long situates W.F. Albright's concerns in the apologetic context of protecting Western values from the threat of Communism and totalitarianism. Christianity and "the Jewish-Christian tradition" were the pinnacle of all religious reflection, and, of course, were enshrined within the American way of life. Albright's efforts had much to do with maintaining social stability and ideological conformity against those movements which threatened the American way of life as he knew it (Burke O Long, "Historical Imaginings, Ideological Gestures: W.F. Albright and the 'Reasoning Faculties of Man'", in Neil Asher Silberman and David B. Small (eds.), *The Archaeology of Israel: Constructing the Past, Interpreting the Present* (JSOTSS, 237; Sheffield: Sheffield Academic Press), pp. 82-94.

[28] In Elisabeth Schüssler Fiorenza's estimation, the biblical academy distinguishes itself by detachment from issues of contemporary ferment, operating as if in a political vacuum, and being accountable only to its 'in-house' fraternity of scholars, who pay no attention to their own social locations, or to how the discipline serves political functions. Thus, in a forty-year period no president of the prestigious Society of Biblical Literature used his presidential address to consider the political context of his scholarship: since 1947 no presidential address alluded to any aspect of world or national politics, such as the civil rights movement, liberation struggles, Martin Luther King, the *Shoah*, etc. (Elisabeth Schüssler Fiorenza, *Rhetoric and Ethic: The Politics of Biblical Studies*, Minneapolis: Fortress Press, 1999, p. 23).

[29] On the richness of the historical context of reflection, see Ignacio Ellacuría, *Filosofia de la realidad histórica* (Madrid: Editorial Trotta, 1990).

My own "exegetical place" in Jerusalem, a city under military occupation, where I undertook some of my postgraduate biblical studies, provided a unique context for developing a hermeneutic which involved an ethical and theological evaluation of my own context as a *reader* of the Bible—the prevailing Historical-Critical Method of biblical studies focused virtually exclusively on the place and circumstances of the biblical *authors*—and pointed to the necessity of a reassessment of the nature of the discipline of Biblical Studies itself. It was one thing to learn that 80 percent of the indigenous Arab population of 77 percent of Palestine (some 750,000 people) had been expelled in 1948, and that a further 300,000 had been expelled in 1967, since which year the remaining 23 percent of Palestine had been under Israeli military occupation. It was quite another to realise that Religious Zionists, in particular, were claiming that the Bible provided the ideological legitimisation and support not only for the establishment of the state, but for Israel's ongoing occupation of the West Bank, Gaza and the Golan Heights.

Even if such concerns appeared to be of little import to the biblical academy, either that *in situ* in the land of the Bible, or anywhere else, they provided a unique context for me. Being sensitive to the victims of various colonial enterprises in recent times, one was led into reading the biblical text "with the eyes of the Canaanites". While struggling to make sense of my context and my task, of course, I had no sense of establishing a novel methodology, such as might later be classified as a political, or public paradigm for biblical interpretation. In 1984 I had no sense of embarking upon what subsequently would be called a 'post-colonial' study—or, to use a not altogether elegant term "Contemporising Interpretation"[30]—of the biblical narrative. Nor had I a sense of engaging in a discourse that might later be designated a Moral Exegesis of the Bible. Over the last twenty years, I have confronted some of the morally problematic traditions of the Old Testament/Hebrew Scriptures. This engagement has brought about changes not only in my own judgements, but in my perception of the task of the discipline of Biblical Studies and the public responsibilities of its practitioners.[31]

---

[30] See Heikki Räisänen, *Beyond New Testament Theology. A Story and a Programme* (London: SCM, 2000), pp. 203-209.

[31] In 'Studying the Bible in the Holy Land' I have laid out the genesis and the different stages of the development of my views in the light of my experience in the Holy Land (in Michael Prior, [ed.], *They Came and They Saw. Western Christian Experiences of the*

The claim in our own age that the biblical narrative, however repulsive its deployment as part of the ideological support for colonialism in the past, legitimises the "ethnic cleansing" of the Palestinian Arabs, should not remain unchallenged within the biblical academy. Biblical scholars, at least, might be expected to protest against outrages perpetrated in the name of fidelity to the biblical covenant. Biblical exegesis, in addition to probing into the circumstances of the composition of the biblical narratives, should concern itself also with the moral quality of these traditions, particularly in the light of the impact they have in promoting the clash of civilisations.[32] In the light of my remarks, perhaps you may agree that Biblical Studies as we practise it in the universities and seminaries needs to be reformed, so that it takes seriously the problematic traditions within the Bible, and uses the biblical narrative in a way which deals with the real issues of people's lives.

Holy Land [London, Melisende, 2000, pp. 104-27]—see also my 'Confronting the Bible's Ethnic Cleansing in Palestine', in *The Link* [Americans for Middle East Understanding] 33[2000, December]: 1-12). I have produced a more discursive account in my "A Moral Reading of the Bible in Jerusalem", in Thomas L. Thompson and Salma Khadra Jayyusi (eds), *Jerusalem History and Tradition* (Sheffield: Sheffield Academic Press, and Nexus/Prota [in Arabic], 2003 [in press]).

[32] I offer a systematic critique of establishment Biblical scholarship, and urge its practitioners to assume moral responsibility for improving the world, in my forthcoming 'The State of the Art: Biblical Scholarship and the Holy Land', in *Holy Land Studies. A Multidisciplinary Journal* 2 (March 2003).

THE EFFECTS OF CHRISTIAN ZIONISM ON PALESTINIAN CHRISTIANS

Rafiq Khoury

Christian Zionism is a mixture of religious fundamentalism, apocalyptic visions, messianic interpretations, political ideology and societal projects which have always existed in history in different forms, religious or secular, carrying with them blind fanaticism and resulting often in horrible massacres and human sufferings. The roots of Christian Zionism reach far back in history to the 16th century, where we find the first elements of such a trend, as many scholars have already pointed out, but the phenomenon was partly marginal and espoused only by a minority. This is no more the case today. What characterizes Christian Zionism today is:

—*First,* that it has become an effective force, not perhaps in itself, but because of its alliance with similar political and ideological forces.
—*Second,* these political ideologies are not only intellectual trends, but they are in a position of power and active, mainly in the United States of America.
—*Third,* and because of that alliance, it is in possession of huge means of action (economic, political, media and even military) which makes it a real danger today.
—*Fourth,* it presents itself in a Western style, that is, with alleged rationality and ethical grounds, which make it acceptable and attractive.

All these elements make Christian Zionism very dangerous and, at the same time, very difficult to confront. This conference can contribute to deconstructing and dismantling this ideology in order to reveal its contradictions and fallacious interpretations.

Christian Zionism has effects on several different levels. These levels include the three monotheistic religions, the Christians of the Arab

World and the search for peace in the Middle East in general and in the Holy Land in particular. I am sorry for presenting this analysis in a rather polemical and, therefore, perhaps a reductive way. The Palestinian Christians are under such psychological pressure that a certain distance from what is happening on the ground in the Holy Land is quite difficult, if not impossible.

Effects on the three monotheistic religions

We know that similar religious ideologies, which can be found and identified in all existing religions, have played a negative role in human history, carrying with them fanaticism, blindness, massacres, injustices, etc. ... The path of human history is filled with innocent victims caused by such ideologies in their different forms. That is the dark side of the history of religions.

Actually, at this turning point of our history, the different religions try to overcome these sad side effects by developing a concept of religion which truly honors God. They try to put the transcendent principles at the service of humankind and formulate aspirations for reconciliation, peace, togetherness, development and comprehensive progress (material, human, ethical, and spiritual). The different religions are trying to get back to their very deep and positive roots in order to offer to humankind an alternative to destruction and death.

Christian Zionism and all connected and allied religious and secular ideologies endanger this religious effort, presenting religion as an ideology working against the human being and contributing in presenting religion as a disastrous element in human history. Instead of doing the will of God, these ideologies tend to implement their own will. As a French intellectual puts it, with some irony: *les fondamentalistes veulent faire la volonté de Dieu, que Dieu le veuille ou pas* ("Fundamentalists want to do the will of God whether God wants it or not"). Fundamentalism, and Christian Zionism as a form of it, deform the very essence of religion.

We cannot discuss Jewish Zionism as a whole because we know that many trends exist within Jewish Zionism, both secular and religious, in Israel and in the Diaspora. We deal here with that form of Jewish Zionism, both secular and religious, which is extremist and which is actually in power in the Jewish state. Because of its narrow minded religious interpretations and its alliances with the fundamentalist trends in the religious arena of Judaism and with the most extremist trends among the political ideologies in Israel and in the Diaspora, Christian Zionism is harming Judaism. Christian Zionism presents Judaism as an oppressive power and as a cause of injustices and violence. Many enlightened Jews are confused, deeply worried and dismayed about this corruption of the true tradition of the Jewish people and of Judaism. Many prominent religious figures since the '67 war, such as Leibowitz and Marc Ellis among others, have warned about this seduction of power. The Judaism of the Torah and of the Prophets does not deserve such an unfortunate service. By connecting Judaism with political power, with all its ambiguities and injustices, Christian Zionism is endangering Judaism, the Jewish people and the highly spiritual Jewish heritage.

Here must be emphasized the deep ambiguities of this alliance of Christian Zionism with extremist elements of Jewish society. Each has in the background contradictory and even excluding positions, and they know it. But all this can be portrayed as useful for the good of the cause. Each party is profiting from the other for different and contradictory purposes. Christian Zionism finds indirect support for its apocalyptic views, and Jewish extremism profits for its own political purposes.

While contributing to the corruption of Judaism, Christian Zionism is mainly corrupting Christianity. In the last centuries, Christian theologians and the Christian Churches have undertaken many efforts to liberate Christianity from the different political ideologies which have harmed it so much in the past. Christianity is not a political ideology at the service of a political power, especially one which happens to be mostly oppressive power. Christianity is not even an ideology at all, but Good News for humanity.

Christian Zionism brings us back to the starting point by transforming Christian faith into a political ideology based on badly digested messianic and apocalyptic ideas. In that case, Christianity becomes a blind ideology which confines realities to narrow religious categories in a mythological way. This ideology is founded on an interpretation of the Word of God considered as letter more than spirit and separated from any textual and historical criticism. Like any form of fundamentalism, it considers salvation history as static without the dynamism and the vitality that characterize the Word of God. Zealots have always been and still are a blight in the Christian body, one which the Church has often condemned after having suffered from it.

One of the constants of Christian Zionism and its allies is their fierce and rancorous attack on Islam. According to an apocalyptic mentality, this sort of ideology always needs an enemy, an Antichrist. It is an essential part of their mental categories. At a certain time, this Antichrist was Judaism; at other times it was Communism. Now the Antichrist is Islam and the Muslims.

It has to be emphasized, that this visceral animosity against Islam is a sort of anti-Semitism. In the past, this anti-Semitism was directed against the Jews and Judaism. Today, the target is Islam. It would be very interesting to review the literature of anti-Semitism directed against the Jews in the last centuries with what is said about Islam today and to discover a strange parallelism between these two discourses. In fact, it is not strange because we are facing the same pathological system. The anti-Muslims of today can very well be the anti-Jews of tomorrow.

It could also be investigated to what extent the repeated slogan in the West today concerning "our Jewish-Christian origins" has to be put in that framework. In the past, the slogan was "our Greek-Roman origins" (and we know to what disasters that led); today it is this new slogan. The background is to exclude Islam from the human heritage, preparing the ground for "clashes" between the cultures, religions and peoples (as is the case actually in some parts of the world). It is strange and even very amusing to know that this slogan is actually common, even among many secular intellectuals. History is sometimes comic.

Effects on the Christians of the Arab world

As we know, Christian minorities live in the Arab world. These Christians have a long tradition and a rich heritage with their Churches, theology, spirituality, liturgy, way of life, and social organizations. These Christians are integrated in their societies and constitute a part of them, sharing their difficulties, their problems and their aspirations, contributing to the welfare of their societies and trying to witness to the values of the Gospel despite all difficulties. These Churches are not only *among* Muslims, but also *for* Muslims, in the sense that they are witnessing before God their sufferings and aspirations and asking God to embrace them in His mercy and love.

Christian Zionism has tragic effects on these Christians and their Churches. The common people are not always able to distinguish between these sectarian groups and Christianity. At the very least, they are embarrassing the Christian Churches, especially in the Holy Land. It is known that these people organize arrogant, triumphalistic and provocative manifestations in the Old City of Jerusalem on the occasion of Succot (Feast of Tabernacles) and other Jewish festivities under the protection of the Israeli police and soldiers. They march before the powerless, revolted eyes of the Arab population, Christians and Muslims alike. It is true that the Christian Churches have condemned Christian Zionism and revealed its sectarian and perverted Christian character. But who hears the voices of the Palestinian Christians, who are included by these sects as targets in their attack on Islam and the Muslims?

Christian Zionism has a strong proselytizing movement within the Christian community in the Holy Land and elsewhere in the Arab world through different sects coming mostly from the United States of America to win converts to their mentality and ideology. These sects, in addition to their huge financial and material means, enjoy the protection of certain influential American organizations under the pretext of religious freedom and human rights. In this way, they are further fragmenting the Christian community, which is already very fragmented, and thus limiting the credibility of its witness. Christian Zionism, through these sects, is also approaching Muslims in an arrogant and aggressive way, without any respect for their sensibilities. This provokes the dismay and the anger of the Muslims, has a negative effect on their attitude toward the local Christians, and has a negative effect on the Christian witness of the Christians in their milieu.

This proselytizing discourse is also directed at the Arab Christians of the Diaspora. The limited success they have is enough to win some people who are then presented to the mass-media as representatives of the Christian communities in the Arab world, provoking intentional confusion and embarrassment.

Effects on the search for a just peace

I avoid the common terminology of "peace process" and "peace negotiations" as they are actually conducted. Despite our initial enthusiasm for a peace process and for peace negotiations, it is clear to us now that such language has become a farce, a low level comedy, which convinces nobody anymore. It is a process in which the stronger partner dictates the terms to a weaker one. When this weak partner does not accept these terms, he is labeled a terrorist, and consequently a candidate to be killed. I prefer to use the term "search for peace" because this search remains a noble priority of many people of good will in the world.

As far as Christian Zionism is concerned, we have to say that this ideology is not merely an ideology of a limited sector in the world. It has become indeed a major force in the contemporary international arena. In addition to their growing number (they count, according to the letter of invitation to this conference, one hundred million people in the United States of America—not a small number), Christian Zionism benefits from an alliance with many large groups, such as the Evangelicals, the new right wing in the United States and many extremist Zionist organizations. These groups are not only lobbying groups, but they are in a position of political power. They are a fundamental part of the American administration actually in power in the White House, a fact which makes these groups a danger to peace in the world in general and in the Holy Land in particular. It has to be said that all these groups have a large, sophisticated and hermetic net of mass-media, which are on watch to counterattack in a fierce and sometimes immoral way the different views that are presented to public opinion. Edward Said told us in one of his last books, *The End of the Peace Process*, about all the troubles he encountered in this propaganda net, which tried to silence his courageous voice.

On the international level, Christian Zionism and its allies are endangering peace in the world. This ideology exaggerates certain issues, such as international terrorism, and with a mixture of lies and military force, they confront very important and real problems in our world according to their own agenda. On the other hand, in their confrontation with terrorism, they often use its same mentality and even its same terminology and discourse. In that way, the opposing ideologies find themselves at two extremes of the same phenomenon. They are enemies who, in reality, are brothers. Here also, a parallelism should be investigated between these two ideologies to reveal that they are similarly extreme. In the meantime, the tenets of this ideology involve conducting wars here and there and disseminating confusion and death in different parts of the world. In this way, two wars have already taken place since the beginning of this new millennium, and we do not know where we are going with this system.

On the local level in the Holy Land, Christian Zionism, in the logic of its system, is a strong ally of the most extremist wings in the Israeli society, thereby making peace impossible to achieve. To this extremist voice in Israel, they are offering strong media support with their powerful propaganda, obstructing any way to peace. This propaganda machine is represented in the Holy Land by the so called "Christian Embassy" in Jerusalem, which is neither Christian nor an embassy, and which organizes regular provocative manifestations, mainly in the Old City of Jerusalem.

To this propaganda and political support, they add their financial support to building new settlements in the Palestinian Territories, as is the case, to give only one example, with a settlement south of Jerusalem that has been built with the financing of Christian Zionists in Holland.

How are we to deal with Christian Zionism? Christian Zionism is a real challenge to us all. We have to co-ordinate all efforts to deal with this ideology at many levels, international, regional and local:

At the international level, before all else, an intellectual effort has to be undertaken in order to unveil the theological, biblical, political, ideological background and interpretations of Christian Zionism through conferences, forums, meetings, and research. However, this intellectual effort is not enough. It has to be sustained by a plan of action to counter this ideology on its own turf. This plan of action can take a form like the campaign against the Vietnam War in the seventies or the form of the campaign against the apartheid regime in South Africa. Both campaigns were very successful in winning over public opinion to their views. Edward Said, in the above-mentioned book, calls on readers to address public opinion in the United States, especially the common people who are well intentioned but badly informed and who are truly sensible to the human rights issues. This campaign should be undertaken by specially trained people who understand the language of the American public.

On the regional level, the different Churches in the Arab world and its various organizations (such as the Middle East Council of Churches) have a special task. Every Church has its own international connection which represents a field of action. Also common action by these Churches is needed to address the different churches of the world and to share with them their concerns and fears.

On the *local* level, we have to say that the different Christian Churches in the Holy Land are the most directly implicated in that action. I fully agree with the five suggestions presented by Fr David Neuhaus, SJ, in preparation for this conference, which are:

> —Presentation of the common Christian experience in the Holy Land (Christian identity, Christian life, and Christian witness) as an antidote to Christian Zionist ideology.
> —Common work on the integral reading and interpretation of the Bible with the wealth of methods of reading the Bible, both traditional and modern.
> —Common promotion of a real and fruitful dialogue among the three monotheistic religions of the Holy Land. This dialogue among the three religious traditions of the Holy Land is a response to the partial dialogue undertaken in different parts of the world within a political perspective.
> —Collaboration of the different Churches with forces within the three religions which are concerned with a real, lasting and just peace in the Holy Land.
> —Renewal of the Churches of the Holy Land, intellectually, theologically, spiritually, pastorally and ecumenically to deal with the different challenges they are facing, Christian Zionism being one of them.

These strategies are of extreme importance. The challenge we are facing invites us to be truly Christians and to be Christians together. It is the special task awaiting the theologians of the different Churches of the Holy Land. They have to work together in order to take part in this effort of the Churches of the Holy Land. This task is not only an individual one but a common effort undertaken through different centers such as Al-Sabeel Center, Al-Liqa Center, the International Forum and other similar organizations, as well as in collaboration with other Palestinian organizations such as Passia and others. This work has to be conducted with as little emotion as possible. I know from my own experience that it is not easy because of the frustrations and humiliations that we experience. In Arabic we say: "Those who are being beaten by sticks are not like those who are counting them." But this distance from our emotions is necessary in order to develop an objective and fruitful work.

I am grateful to Sabeel for organizing this international

conference to confront the ideology of Christian Zionism and its practices. It is true that this ideology is in possession of huge means of action, but that does not mean that we must remain inactive and powerless and give up our efforts. We have to act, but more importantly to develop and present an alternative to this ideology. Otherwise, these ideologies will lead us to hell. The challenge is great; greater should be our determination.

CHRISTIAN ZIONISM AND MAIN LINE WESTERN CHRISTIAN CHURCHES

Rosemary Radford Ruether

There is a danger in discussing Christian Zionism as if it were only a phenomenon of a particular kind of Christian fundamentalism and therefore a viewpoint that mainline churches can dismiss as literalist and fanatical, holding themselves to be innocent of its distortions. Equally problematic is a more subtle and unnamed Christian Zionism in mainline churches which also functions to deliver the whole of the Holy Land to the State of Israel as a nation at the expense of Palestinian historic existence as a people of this land. In the message of Archbishop Rowan Williams, "Holy Land and Holy People", included in this collection, we see an example of this more sophisticated and unconscious Christian Zionism in the established churches.

The foundational defect in the Archbishop's message is his assumption that he is doing a "liberation theology" in relationship to the idea of Israel as a land and people. Unfortunately, in his message he lacks the basic methodology of a liberation theology; namely, a theology done from the perspective of the oppressed or, in this context, from the perspective of the conquered people of this land. Williams focuses his talk exclusively on Israel as a Jewish people whose modern state is somehow in continuity with Biblical concepts of election and divine promise of the land. He ignores the Palestinian people as a people of this land. Hence his talk remains oblivious to the basic issues of linking ancient concepts of election and Promised Land with the modern State of Israel.

Most importantly, Williams never asks the question of what kind of God is posited as one that gives an invading people a land by mandating the taking away of the land from those already resident there. In effect, he creates a theology of people and land from the perspective of the conquerors, while rendering the conquered invisible. Canaanites in antiquity, and Palestinians today, are "ethnically cleansed" from the "Holy Land," which is assumed to have been "given" and to belong exclusively to Israel, by not even noticing that they were and are there.

Any treatment of the claims of the State of Israel to land and peoplehood must begin by acknowledging the reality of the existing population. It cannot be presumed to be some "other" topic that one can get around to apart from discussion of Israel's claims on this land. The treatment of the Palestinian people by the State of Israel has been an endlessly worsening crime that has unfolded over more than a half century. This crime has taken place with either the active or the passive collaboration of Western Christianity. How has it happened that Western Christianity has played such an evil role in this historical crime and tragedy?

Christians of Western Europe and North America fall into two major lines of thought toward Israeli-Palestinian relations, or more appropriately, toward Israel, since Palestinians are seldom thought about at all in either view. A small but militant and influential group, associated with more fundamentalist forms of Protestant Christianity, are Christian Zionists. A larger but more diffuse group of Western Christians share some Christian Zionist views, but their main perspective is shaped by a desire to compensate for past Christian anti-Semitism by affirming positive ecumenical relations with Jews. The latter group is the focus of this paper.

While the sentiment that Christians should repent of past anti-Semitism and cultivate a positive relation with Jews and Judaism are appropriate in themselves, unfortunately they have been construed primarily as a Christian duty of uncritical adulation for the State of Israel. This means that mention of the Palestinian plight is ignored altogether as such Christians avoid learning anything about the Palestinians. It is implicitly assumed that any concern for injustice to Palestinians, indeed any discussion of Palestinians at all, is to be construed as anti-Semitic. Such Christians evade knowing and hence having to speak about them in order not to be denounced as anti-Semitic by those Jews with whom they wish to cultivate 'ecumenical relations.'

Christian repentance for the Holocaust and anti-Semitism have been effectively distorted into a silencing of Western Christians in regard to Palestinian human and civil rights, a view carefully nurtured and reinforced by the Jewish establishment, especially in North America. Any effort to break through this wall of self-censorship of Western

Christians in regard to injustices to Palestinians by those seeking to communicate an alternative reality encounters built-in walls of ignorance and self-silencing among Christians. It is difficult to communicate to them that concern about justice for Palestinians can also be an expression of positive regard for Jews, including Israeli Jews. The notion that Christians can only have good relations to Jews by turning a blind eye to the plight of Palestinians seems unshakable. Palestinians are made to pay for the sins of Western Christians against the Jews.

Western Christians need to understand what is happening to Palestinians in Israel and the Occupied Territories, but we also need to understand our own role as well in the promotion of the ethnocide of the Palestinian people. In effect it is Western Christians, especially British and American Christians, who created and continue to create the historical framework in which this process of ethnocide goes on. We have done it and continue to do it in the name of reconciliation with 'the Jews.' It is Americans particularly who provide the money and arms through our government to allow this to happen. But it is Western Christians who have created the historical ideology that legitimizes this process. We legitimize it as something that is 'due' to the Jews, both from Biblical land claims, and also as compensation for our past guilt. This legitimization is then reinforced by the wall of silence around the resulting injustice to the Palestinians that prevents this from being seen, heard and understood. Thus, we seek to salve our bad conscience for our past genocide of European Jews.

Christians in the West need to critically examine four theological themes that have been used effectively to silence Western Christians in regard to justice for the Palestinians. These are the beliefs that: 1) Jewish election by God includes a promise of the land of Palestine (Israel) to the Jews in a total, exclusive and permanent sense; 2) Jewish restoration to Palestine is part of a messianic, redemptive process by which God is bringing redemption to the world; 3) Zionism is identical with Judaism and so any critique of Zionism or the State of Israel is necessarily anti-Jewish or anti-Semitic; and 4) uncritical support of Israel is due from Christians as payment of their guilt for the Holocaust.

God's Promise of the Land of Israel to the Jews

Western Christians are often led to a one-sided assumption that Jews have an exclusive "right" to Palestine by an ignorance of the actual history of the area. This land has never been a land of one people, but a land of many peoples. Many peoples lived there before the period of Hebrew political hegemony in antiquity. Many peoples continued to live side by side with the Hebrews during that period of Hebrew hegemony. Many peoples have come to this area, in migrations and amalgamations of peoples and cultures, for the last 2500 years. These people became predominantly Christian in the 4th century and became predominantly Muslim after the 7th century, with a significant Christian minority and a tiny Jewish minority. All three communities became Arabized in language and culture.

The descendants of all those people are Palestinians. As residents, these people had the primary right to the land of Palestine in the mid-20th century. These people were still the majority, some 70 percent of the population, when the land was partitioned in 1947. Thus, whatever rights must now be given to the Israeli Jewish population, largely descended from people who immigrated to this land in the 20th century, can only be on the basis of a recent construction of a national community in the region, not on the basis of ancient religious claims. This national community has shaped its occupation of the land through a continual process of conquest and displacement of the earlier people that is fundamentally unjust. These unjust "facts" of history must be adjusted to make place for at least an equal claim to the land of those who were present as the majority population until their forced and cruel displacement over the last fifty-five years.

What then of the claim that God gave this land to the Jews in ancient times and thus they have a prior claim to it? This claim makes essentially ethnocentric assumptions about God which are unacceptable to Christian theology. However much Christians need to honor the Jewish people and Judaism as our religious ancestors, Christians cannot accept an ethnocentric notion of God and of God's election of one people at the expense of others. Fundamental to Christian theology is a belief that God is a God of all nations, all peoples. In Christ there is no more Jew or Greek (Gal. 3: 28). No one people is especially favored by God against others.

There is no doubt that Jews have a deep emotional symbolic identification with the land that is rooted in ancient experience and has been carried through their religious tradition. But Palestinians also have a deep identification with the land rooted in their family and communal memories. Many Palestinians who have been refugees for more than fifty years still keep a vivid identification with their ancestral village and home. Ancient memories from two thousand years ago cannot be used to expel people from their homes who have been resident continually to recent times.

Christians have often misconstrued their own universalism to deny Jewish particularity and to turn Christian universalism into imperialism. Authentic universalism must reject both a reversion to tribal ethnocentrism and also universalist imperialism. This means that Christians should affirm a multi-particularist vision of the co-humanity of many peoples and cultures. One should not use Jewish particularity to deny the rights of Palestinians nor the reverse. One should affirm a co-humanity of Jews and Palestinians, actualized, as far as possible, in a just co-existence of both national communities in the land of Israel/Palestine.

Archbishop Rowan Williams's paper fails to address this problem by failing to include the Palestinians in his purview. He seeks to address the tensions between particularism and universalism in Christian thought by affirming the ongoing validity of the particularism of the Jewish people and then seeking to add on Christianity or the Church as a universal extension of Judaism, but without supersessionism. As long as one continues to address these two terms in this way, the tension between them remains unresolved, stuck, as it were, between two stools. Only when one brings in the reality of two peoples (Israelis and Palestinians) and three religions (Judaism, Christrianity and Islam) in this land can one transform the duality of Judaism and Christianity *qua* particularism and universalism into a multi-particularity of peoples and religious communities called to mutual recognition.

The Founding of Israel as the Fulfillment of Prophecy and the Beginning of Redemption

In the Jewish Scriptures and traditions the idea of a messianic return to the land as part of redemption was premised on an ethical vision of what redemption means. For both Jewish and Christian traditions the future fulfillment of redemptive hope includes the healing of enmity between nations. Swords are beaten into plowshares. The weapons of destruction and death are transformed into the tools of cultivation of new life. Justice and peace flourish between nations. But Christian and Jewish militant fundamentalists ignore these ethical criteria for what is redemptive. They ignore the obvious fact that the foundation of the State of Israel has not been a means of healing between nations, but the source of an enormous outbreak of new enmity between nations in the Middle East and across the Christian and Muslim worlds.

The foundation of the State of Israel has been for Palestinians what they call the *nakbah* (the catastrophe), destroying their old way of life and continually evicting them from their land, destroying their society, killing or exiling their people. In no way is this redemptive history. It expresses utterly unredeemed modes of behavior between peoples. To call such history "redemptive" and the beginning of messianic times is a blasphemous distortion of those terms. This is false messianism, garbing evil-producing political projects with divine blessing. This does not mean that the State of Israel is any worse than any number of other conquest and colonizing projects which have brought disaster upon other people and often upon one's own people. It means that these evil realities cannot be covered up by the trapping of special divinely ordained sanctity.

Rowan Williams, in his talk, did recognize that there are injustices in Israel which contradict its covenantal and redemptive claims. But he presumed that these could be resolved by calling Israel to "live up" to its calling to justice, as though this calling could be addressed solely within Israel's own identity. Because Palestinians are never named as a people of this land, the basic problems of what the injustices are from which Israel "suffers" remained unnamed.

Palestinians remain anonymous, as "resident aliens" or as "neighbors" (like Syrians, Lebanese and Jordanians?). But Palestinians are neither "resident aliens" (people from some other land temporarily resident in this land) or "neighbors," like these other people outside Israel's borders. They are the people of this land who have been displaced from their own land in order to create a land for Israel. This is the root of the injustice from which all other injustices flow in this history of the modern State of Israel. Without recognizing it, one cannot address the structural violence of Israel's existence in this land, a structural violence which is not merely a "failure" to "live up" to its calling, but endemic to its self-definition.

Zionism as Integral to Judaism

In fact, when Zionism first arose in the late 19th and the first half of the 20th century, it was generally rejected by both Orthodox and Reform Judaism. For Orthodox Jews the return to the land of Israel could only be carried out by the Messiah. For them Zionism was an unholy project carried out by non-observant Jews and thus fundamentally contradicted their understanding of the conditions for restoring Israel to the Land. Reform Jews also rejected Zionism because it denied their political universalism. Reform Judaism sought to detach Judaism as a religion from secular political identity and to make Jews a religious community that could exist in any land as full and equal citizens.

It is not correct to claim that Judaism is unique in having a communal identity that unites religious and collective political identity. In their classical forms, Judaism, Christianity, Islam, and even Buddhism and Confucianism, had collective forms that sought to create religio-political states. Today fundamentalist movements within all these religions are seeking to reestablish religious states. But such religious states are by nature exclusivist. They claim that only those of the established religion can be full citizens. The unjust treatment of the Palestinians is rooted in the effort to create an ethnically and religiously exclusive state or "Jewish state" where, ideally, Jews are the absolute majority.

In Israel as a Jewish state, only those defined as Jews in an ethno-religious sense can enjoy full citizen benefits. Palestinians are denied equal citizenship within Israel. This also makes it unacceptable to many Israelis to consider giving the Palestinians in the occupied territories citizenship in Israel since this would mean Jews would become a bare majority and perhaps eventually a minority. This is seen as a "demographic problem." But continued numbers of Palestinians are a demographic problem only if one continues to define Israel as a Jewish state, rather than accepting the reality that there are two national communities and three religions in this land. For justice and peace to be possible in Israel/ Palestine any state or states in this land have to accommodate and give equal citizenship to all people across this ethnic and religious diversity.

Christian Guilt for the Holocaust and Demands for Uncritical Support for Israel

Western Christians (although not Palestinian Christians) surely bear a burden of guilt because of the way their long standing traditions of anti-Semitism were used to persecute Jews in western Christendom. These traditions were used by the Nazis to gain passive and active support of Christians for their project of genocide. But what is appropriate repentance among Christians for this guilt? It would seem that Christians must seek to purge anti-Semitism from Christian teachings and work to see that Jews are no longer burdened by this heritage in areas where Christians predominate. It is not appropriate to construe such repentance as collaboration with another injustice toward another people who are victims of the State of Israel.

On both the Jewish and the Christian sides there must be a distinction between the question of the Holocaust and its theological and ethical consequences for each religion and the questions about the State of Israel and its ethical deficiencies. One must stop using the Holocaust as if it mandated a "compensation" that includes the right to create a state based on the expulsion of another people from their homeland. Although there are certainly emotional connections between these two events, they need to be delinked symbolically. Quite simply, one evil does not justify another.

One cannot continue to argue that the State of Israel is necessary because it provides a secure haven for Jews against the possibility of another anti-Semitic outbreak by Christians. Rowan Williams still harbors this myth of Israel as a "safe haven" for Jews, both necessary and deserved as compensation for past anti-Semitism of the gentiles. But in fact in the last fifty years there is no place more insecure for Jews than Israel. This is not because there is some "cosmic hate" against Jews by gentiles, but because Israel has been built on an antagonistic relationship to the Palestinians in particular and the Arab world in general that generates a cycle of violence. There is certainly a desire of many on all sides, Jewish Israelis and Palestinian Arabs, Muslims and Christians, and in the larger Arab world to end this cycle of violence. But this can only happen if there is real movement on the part of Israel and the West to recognize the historical injustice to the Palestinians and to grant some sharing of land and political self-rule that would bring some ability of Palestinians to live normal human lives in which they can cultivate their land, go to school and work and get medical care without threat of injury and death.

My experience suggests that Western Christians cannot break out of the myopia created by arguments on behalf of Israel that ignore or dismiss the Palestinians. These contradictions remain invisible to them. It is only through corrective experiences, especially personal contact with Palestinian people in their own homeland, that Western Christians can come face-to-face with the realities that can shatter their self-enclosed framework and open them up to a different approach. Palestinian Christians are key mediators here both to introduce Western Christians to the Palestinian reality, and to correct the misuse of Christian concepts, such as repentance, the promised land and Jewish-Christian ecumenical relations that have been misconstrued in Western Christian perspective.

It is here that Palestinian liberation and contextual theologies, as these are being developed by Palestinian Christian theologians such as Naim Ateek and Mitri Raheb, can play a key role to shatter this distorted use of Christianity that justifies Israeli colonialism and also to enunciate a positive theology of just co-existence of Jewish and Palestinian people in the homeland they both love. Central to these theologies is an affirmation of a God of justice for all people who calls us into mutually affirming co-existence. This is incompatible with exclusivist views that identify the oneness of God with the unique election of one religious group against others. Only a vision of God that loves and commands justice for all peoples equally can create the framework for just co-existence of the two people, Israelis and Palestinians, and the three religions, Judaism, Christianity and Islam, calling them to be equal partners, brothers and sisters, in sharing the land together in justice and peace. This is authentic ecumenism.

JUSTICE AND MERCY: THE MISSING INGREDIENTS IN CHRISTIAN ZIONISM

Jonathan Kuttab

The group attending this conference is comprised of quite a number of new faces, as well as a large number of old familiar faces of those who have stayed in this struggle, who have committed their time, their energy, and their resources for a very long time. Some of you have suffered and struggled with us for many years and know quite a lot about this situation. To you it comes as no surprise that no matter how bad the situation appears on the outside, it is even worse for those of us who have to live under it day in and day out. No matter how bad it gets, just when we think it can't get any worse, it does. It is worse and worse. During the last two or three years, we have seen on a weekly basis a worsening of the daily sufferings, humiliations, restrictions, and deprivations of the Palestinian people. We have seen a continuing erosion of the few remaining restraints that we believed stood in the way of unbridled violence and oppression. We saw the Israeli government moving further and further to the right and getting more and more direct support and approval from the United States government. The events of 9/11 as used by this US administration have opened the flood gates to a total all-out attack on values, principles, freedoms, laws, and structures that we always felt had some restraining effects but which now appear to be no longer effective in restraining the evil under which we exist.

As Palestinians and Palestinian Christians who feel the need to respond to this situation, the tasks set before this conference appear to be very, very important because it is true that the moral, theological, legal, and political underpinnings for the present state of affairs ultimately rest on people in the United States, ordinary citizens, and therefore on Christians. We cannot simply blame it all on Jewish influence. Yes, there are very powerful, well funded, well connected, well organized, pro-active, pro-Israeli and pro-Zionist lobbies in the United States; yes, there is no question about that. They do exercise a lot of power and influence, but a lot of it utilizes the support, stated or implicit, of many Christians in the United States. Therefore it is important that we respond to Christian Zionism. It is an imperative that we have to take up.

Palestinian Christians, who have suffered so much at the hands of theologies and interpretations of scriptures which provide a mantle of divine legitimatisation for the ideology of Zionism, are looking for something different from a theology that justifies our suffering at the hands of the "chosen people" to whom the "promised land" belongs. One of our constant complaints has been that Christian Zionism ignores, sidesteps the Palestinian people on whose land the State of Israel was created.

I believe that as we engage in discussion with Christian Zionists, there is one important central theme that cannot be ignored. This is the whole issue of justice and mercy. In Luke there is a story of a long disputation between Jesus and the Sadducees in which they were trying to trick him with all sorts of different theological issues about the resurrection from the dead, about this, that and the other. At one point, they thought they had him because there was a man with a paralyzed arm. It was Jesus' turn to ask them a question: Is it proper, is it kosher, is it theologically correct, is it 'biblically' permissible to heal him on the Sabbath? They were silent. The gospel tells us that Jesus was saddened by their silence.

Yes, we need to address Christian Zionism theologically. Those of us who are more conservative perhaps and who hold a more literal view of the scriptures feel they have to trade text for text and Bible verse for Bible verse and make sure that they read the Bible correctly within its context and do not abuse it and misinterpret it and misapply it. Those of us who are of a more liberal tradition need to point out the inaccuracies and misinterpretations in applying certain verses of scripture to the current situation. This is an important task which needs to be handled just as Jesus handled those discussions with the Pharisees and the Sadducees of his day. But at some point, the centrality of Jesus' love, caring, mercy and justice needs to come through. At some point, Christians need to look at Christian Zionism not only through quoting scriptures but through what it is doing to the children of God living today in the Holy Land, whether they are Jews or Arabs.

Christian Zionism needs to be challenged specifically on the human, moral costs and consequences of their theology: if you want to set up a Jewish state in Palestine, fine, but what does that mean to the original inhabitants? Are you going to endorse their exile, permanent exile, making them refugees forever? Are you going to tolerate the wholesale theft of their land, of their shops, of their farms because of some theological covenant given to Abraham? We are talking about my home: the bedroom, the bathroom, the garden, the trees that are being uprooted by these bulldozers. Are we willing to endorse that? We need to ask the Christian Zionists.

And for the Jews, how compassionate are you Christian Zionists who condemn them to a situation of eternal strife and enmity, of being required to set up a militaristic culture that needs to live constantly by the sword and in fear and in struggle with Palestinians. Stop for a minute and think of what creating this theological paradigm, this paradigm state that you want to set up for Jews, means in concrete human terms. Where is your compassion? Where is justice? Are you willing to totally throw outside the door all international law, all human rights covenants, all international organizations, all ethical requirements, all restraints and restrictions on weapons of mass destruction, nuclear, biological and chemical? Part of your price as Christian Zionists would seem to be a profound silence on Israel's acquisition and perhaps use of these weapons of mass destruction. This is a central challenge that needs to be made to Christian Zionism, and one way to bring that challenge is to convey reality directly to Christians, particularly in the West. This truth telling and challenge is the operative part of this conference. A friend of mine told me that this Wall that is going up may in fact bring about a major turn-around because it is concrete and visible, unlike the horrendous humiliations and daily indignities and restrictions and sufferings accumulating upon the Palestinian people. The Wall is very concrete, high, visible, ugly, oppressive—its message is very clear.

The father of a friend of mine who grew up with Christian Zionist theology and accepted it hook, line and sinker came and visited this land. After ten days, he started shaking his head and saying, "I don't care what the Bible says; this is wrong; this is evil." The Bible does not say that this is correct, that this should be tolerated. But perhaps this is what we need to do—to create and communicate the concrete image of human suffering on both sides—not just the Palestinian. The Israelis, too, are traumatized and oppressed because this Christian theology encloses them within a racist paradigm. It enforces upon them a supremacist, exclusionary system. It reinforces in their own minds a ghetto mentality, a garrison mentality of us against the rest of the world; and they need to be liberated from that as well. However, Christian Zionism would like very much to imprison and enclose them within that particular worldview.

So this is the challenge that we face, and I think it is a challenge that we can live up to. Sometimes I think that a conference like this which brings to our attention so many depressing facts leaves us almost hopeless, breathless. One time I saw a power-point presentation about the Wall and the effect it is going to have on the communities, and I felt helpless and hopeless. When we think about US power under such an administration and its crusading mentality of projecting that power militarily throughout the world, of going out to punish and kill, to discipline everyone into complying with its dictates, then we think, "Who are we? What resources do we have, what candidate can we support, what influence can we have against this tremendous power that is marshalled against us?" In times like these, I go back to my faith, to our faith, and I am glad I did not throw out the Bible at that point because there I see the affirmation and confirmation first and foremost of the sovereignty of God. God continues to be sovereign in the affairs of people—not George Bush, not Washington, not the tanks, and the guns, and the fleets, and the bulldozers, and the police, and the Apache helicopters and the Wall and the money. God continues to be sovereign. Any time you are tempted to feel helpless and hopeless, to read the world map through worldly eyes, to count how many tanks, how many planes, how much ammunition, how much power, how much influence, then you need to go back to the Bible, maybe to the Old Testament, to Elijah, who said, "I am the only one who is left worshipping you!" Looking outside at all the armies that are surrounding his city, we need the angel of God to open our eyes to see that God is with us, and he is stronger than all the forces of evil, of war, of violence, of oppression, of racism, of control that are marshalled against us. We need to go back to the Resurrection, to see that Christ has conquered death itself.

It is very interesting that one of the first messages that the angels told the disciples is "Fear not!" We need to conquer fear. We know our fear is being used now as a weapon to convince people to give up their freedoms, their liberties, to accept new taxes, more armies, more oppression of others. Fear not! Jesus has conquered death itself. And there are signs of hope, and indications in history, many indications, some very recent, of powerful regimes and movements that were at one time thought to have been totally dominant and all powerful, which have been overthrown. The apartheid regime in South Africa is a very recent example. There is no question that the white minority that was ruling there had the weapons, had the arms industry, had the technology, the modernization; they could defeat not just the blacks of that country, but the entire African continent—easily! Yet many of you who were in the struggle against apartheid, while you could not tell exactly how it was going to happen, knew that that regime was doomed because it was built on injustice and could not prevail. We need the faith, the knowledge that evil and oppression in this part of the world also cannot continue to prevail forever.

How is change going to come about? When is change going to come about? I don't know, I can not tell you, but that faith is there. And you will be surprised to know that that faith is also shared by many Palestinian Muslims! And that the cry of "Allahu Akhbar," translated into English as God is Greatest, really is God is *greater*—*greater* than the powerful oppressor, *greater* than the tank, *greater* than Bush and Washington. This deep abiding faith in the sovereignty of God continues to give the Palestinian people today faith and hope against all hope that ultimately justice will prevail.

I can let you in on a little secret. One of the dynamics that will ensure that justice prevails is that evil carries within itself the seeds of its own destruction. Whether we are talking about the Zionist movement or the American Empire—it cannot continue to be both evil and successful at the same time. There is now an American campaign to push for democracy and reform throughout the Arab world—American style, of course. But that democracy, to the extent that it comes, necessarily turns against the empire. Did we not think what a great coincidence it was that the single country of those Arab Muslim countries surrounding Iraq which refused the American forces entry was Turkey! Would you believe it? And all because the democratic parliament of that country insisted that American soldiers would not use their soil to enter Iraq. The army was all for it—the government was all for it. There were strategic reasons and alliances why Turkey would love to have been in Iraq, but to the extent that there was a parliament, that there was a democracy to some degree in Turkey—people spoke, people made their wishes known. We know that in Europe today democracy is strong and people are coming out in their millions against the war in Iraq, against the recent declarations of Bush and Sharon, saying no, they are not right.

I want to end on this positive point. We cannot leave feeling hopeless, helpless or defeated. The one who is with us is greater than these forces that are marshalled against us. As long as we keep this in mind, it is not a matter of partisanship, of being pro-Israeli or pro-Palestinian. This is God's love and justice and caring for all his children, and that justice must prevail. Without mercy, without justice our theologies are really worthless.

HOLOCAUST, CHRISTIAN ZIONISM AND BEYOND A JEWISH THEOLOGY OF LIBERATION *AFTER*

Marc H Ellis

After my second visit to Israel—some twenty years ago—the idea of a Jewish theology of liberation began to resonate within me. During my first visit in 1973 that began before and continued during the 1973 Arab-Israeli war, I witnessed a fundamental disparity between Jews and "Arabs," as I then called them. The Jewish Israelis I met were European in background and were clearly transplanted from other geographic areas of the world. They were also dominant in politics and economics. The Arabs I met were Palestinian, clearly indigenous to the land, and on the margins of this newly created Jewish state.

It is remarkable how little I knew of the history of the State of Israel, let alone the history of Palestine and the Palestinians. Growing up in 1950s America, we were taught little of contemporary Jewish history; even the Holocaust was yet to be named and had yet to become central to Jewish identity. In retrospect, those days of innocence were halcyon in their quality. At that time Jews were involved in the great African-American civil rights struggles. Could it be possible that elsewhere Jews were depriving others of their human and political rights?

Like most Jews in America, I was unaware of the divide in Jewish life, a divide that has deepened considerably in the past decades. But with that growing awareness, I was faced with a conundrum: how do I as a Jew speak about a contradiction in Jewish life that is unspoken, buried and seen as threatening to Jewish continuity and empowerment? This is especially difficult in light of Jewish suffering in Europe, an event that would wait until the 1960s to be named as "Holocaust".

The difficulty is compounded when one thinks of the enormity of the Holocaust and the pressures it places on contemporary Jews for empowerment. Could I criticize our new-found power when so recently and tragically we were without power? And since as a community Jews were grappling with a language requisite to the Holocaust, a landscape so terrible and unprecedented that words could hardly describe the suffering, could I, with other Jews, fashion a language that illustrated our own complicity in the suffering of others?

This difficulty has not changed over the years. In many ways it has worsened. Knowledge about the Holocaust has exploded in scope and detail; it has become the most studied event in world history. The situation in Israel and Palestine has become the most media-covered situation in the world. In the 1950s and 1960s neither Holocaust nor Israel was central to Jewish identity; today they form the core of our Jewishness. Without them, one wonders what Jewish identity would look like. With them, Jewish identity is becoming more and more fractured, almost schizophrenic. For if at the heart of the covenant is justice and compassion, what do Jews do with our suffering and the suffering we are causing?

It was in 1984 that I was determined to meet Palestinian Arabs and to see first-hand their plight. After this visit, which confirmed and deepened the intuitive understandings I had formed in 1973, I had to find my voice and words to articulate this division in Jewish life, which also was somehow a division in the covenant. Or perhaps better stated, I could sense that the division in Jewish activity on behalf of justice—in America for justice, in Israel against justice—was also a division within the Jewish covenant; Jewish history was at war with itself and thus inevitably Jews were at war with one another. Could Jews remain united when the entire history of Jews and Judaism was at stake, not only in the Holocaust but now in Israel and Palestine?

Constantinian Judaism/Jews of Conscience

These questions form the center of *Toward a Jewish Theology of Liberation*, a book I originally published in 1987. I extended these reflections in the second edition published in response to the Palestinian uprising that began shortly after the first edition was published. The final chapter of the second edition is aptly titled "The Palestinian Uprising and the Future of the Jewish People", for I ask in those pages whether, now completely aware of what I had only dimly perceived fifteen years earlier, we as Jews could continue on as if we are only victims of the Holocaust. In a short period, a little more than four decades, we had embarked on a project of empowerment that yielded new victims, the Palestinian people, and that victimization continued to increase after the emergency years of the Holocaust were p*ast.* I noted then a fact which is even truer today: we as Jews come after the Holocaust *and* after Israel. After Israel means after what we as Jews have done and are doing to the Palestinian people.

After is an understanding in Jewish life that denotes tragedy and possibility. To Jews and others, the tragedy of the Holocaust needs little explanation. *After* is obvious: what can we say about God after the Holocaust; what can we say about humanity? After Israel, the gaze is turned inward toward us, our history, leadership and future. In the Holocaust, Jews were innocent. In the displacement of Palestinians in 1948 and beyond, Jews are culpable. With the Holocaust, Jews remember as a people; memory is not only for those who directly experienced death and destruction. We are called upon to remember collectively. So, too, in regard to Israel. Israel is a collective work hardly restricted to Jews in Israel. The entire Jewish world has been mobilized on behalf of Israel and therefore is culpable in the plight of the Palestinians. Lobbying for Israel and attempting to define and control the debate on Israeli policies has been the central work of the Jewish establishment in America over the last decades. Are they not as well responsible for Israeli policies toward the Palestinians?

This responsibility has increased as the situation in Israel/Palestine continues to worsen. It is not only the expulsion of the Palestinians in 1948 to make room for the creation of the state of Israel or even the conquering of the West Bank and Gaza in the 1967 war. Today the Jewish settlements in Jerusalem and the West Bank, settlements that threaten the very viability of a Palestinian state, have become permanent. Indeed, their expansion is taken for granted. A ghetto wall is being constructed in the West Bank to protect Israeli expansion; it will enclose a million or more Palestinians. A recent interview with Prime Minister Sharon calls attention to the possibility of the transfer of "tens of thousands" Palestinians within Israel proper once the wall is completed. Targeted assassinations continue apace. The Jewish establishment in America is silent and punishing of dissent.

For me the journey from 1984 to 2004 is immense and, though the seeds of my understanding were already there two decades ago, the reality is much starker today. Thus the need for a third and expanded edition of *Toward a Jewish Theology of Liberation*, published in the fall of 2004. It carries the subtitle *Into the 21st Century*. This expanded edition continues the narrative into the 21st century with a more formidable question: the path of power has already been taken by the Jewish community in Israel and America: the conquering of Palestine is virtually complete; Jewish political and economic ascendancy is unparalleled in Jewish history.

As the new edition indicates, the Jewish community is divided between those who support Jewish power without question and those who resist the use of that power to oppress and silence. A Constantinian Judaism has come into being, mirroring the empire-oriented Christianity that emerged in the 4th century and beyond. At the same time, Jews of conscience confront Constantinian Judaism and its collusion with power and the state. There is a civil war in the Jewish world that crosses geographic and cultural differences. There are Constantinian Jews in Israel and America; there are Jews of conscience all over the Jewish world. The civil war was already in evidence in 1987; in 2004 it is everywhere and, I think, permanent.

Constantinian Judaism is an assimilationist Judaism, an assimilation to power and the state. Jews of conscience resist that assimilation and in so doing are exiled from the Jewish community. Constantinian Judaism is becoming more and more powerful; however, the exilic community of Jews of conscience is growing. In terms of power the struggle is unequal; witness—a witness without power or reward—is the only avenue left for Jews of conscience.

Blaming the Jews and Christian Zionism

The struggle is difficult. The assault from the Jewish establishment continues and accelerates, impugning the very character of Jews of conscience: Are these Jews self-haters, and in their critique of power, creating a context for another holocaust? There are other assaults, including attacks from those who impugn Jewish empowerment as a cover for impugning Jews themselves or even the Jewish witness in history.

Included here are those Christians who see colonialism as the essence of the Hebrew bible and Christianity in error only when it adopts these Judaic elements. Included as well are those Christians who fight Christian Zionism as if somehow that form of Zionism is an import from Judaism. There is no question that Israel and Jews in general are culpable in the disaster that has befallen the Palestinian people. However, the culpability of Jews pales in comparison to that of Christianity, especially in its Western variant, in the creation of global violence. Perhaps this is simply a feature of the differential in size and power over the centuries. As it turns out, Jews may be as violent and empire-hungry as their Christian counterparts, but the historical record is clear. Christians should pay attention to their own misuse of power and, from that vantage point, enter into a critique and solidarity with Jews who critique Jewish power.

Is this also the case for Islam? After all, there has been historically and is today a Constantinian Islam. There are also Muslims of conscience. Like Judaism and Christianity, Islam contains elements of both beauty and violence. The continuum is shared as is the struggle. One wonders if Constantinian Jews, Christians and Muslims should be seen as a community bent on power and exploitation while Jews, Christian and Muslims of conscience are gathered together as seekers of justice and compassion. Then the critique of all three religious perspectives can be internal and across boundaries. Aren't all people of conscience fighting the same battles within their communities and outside of them? All people of conscience are to some extent losing; they are involved in a witness that raises the possibility of an alternative path. Pitting one against the other is counterproductive: it is also false and self-serving, protecting the innocence of a "true" faith belied by its own history.

So why blame the Jews? There is no question that the Jewish narrative of innocence and redemption found in Holocaust theology and identity is the driving force behind the displacement of Palestinians. Since the 1967 war, that narrative has been joined by a Jewish messianism concretely embodied in the settler movement and a Christian Zionism that resides primarily in the United Kingdom and the United States. At the same time, a Christian Holocaust theology—one that emphasizes the need for Christian repentance in the face of historic Christian anti-Semitism which eventuated in the Holocaust—has flourished. It is a repentance whose vehicle is Israel. Coupled with the weakness of the Arab world and the Palestinians themselves and the power of Israel and the United States, these Jewish and Christian narratives have been important, perhaps even decisive for the empowerment of Israel and instrumental in the Palestinian catastrophe.

September 11th has raised the stakes here; the narrative linking the terror visited on American soil with the "terror" visited upon Israel has been strong. Most critical thought on the issue in the Islamic world, especially relating to Israel and the Palestinians, has dissipated. The Jewish establishment has increased its call for unity and the punishment of dissenters, and the Sharon government has used September 11th as a green light to re-invade Palestinian territory and begin construction of the Wall of Separation in the West Bank. On the one hand, this wall simply demarcates territory Israel already controls. On the other hand, the construction of the wall further limits Palestinian life and possibility. Symbolically and concretely, the wall being constructed on both sides of the West Bank is a ghetto wall, similar to the ghetto walls that at different points in history have been constructed to enclose Jews.

Christian Zionism is part of this narrative and real-time ghettoization and is now being called to task, and rightly so. By privileging Jews in their eschatological drama, and thereby making Palestinians invisible or demonic, Christian Zionists are participants in this crime against the Palestinian people. Yet seeing this as a Judaization of Christianity is wrong; seeking to distance Christianity from Judaism is also wrong. When a distance is created between the two faiths, we return to previous struggles within Christian history about the role of the Hebrew scriptures in Christian theology.

To return to that issue is to raise again the question of the influence of Jews in Christian texts and theology, even the Jewishness of Jesus. We re-enter here the terrain of heresy, declarations which throughout Christian history have led to anti-Semitism and intra-Christian wars. The internal struggle to define Christian heresy has often led to an anti-Semitism that eventuates in the murder of Christians by other Christians. The controversies surrounding Marcion come to mind, but also the Crusades. Who can forget the role Jews played in Luther's imagination and the status of the Jews in Christian theology in the Reformation and Counter Reformation?

Declaring Christian Zionism a heresy is the easy path. It has no political clout; it simply draws a line between authentic Christians and those in error. But after this long history of defining heresy and thus orthodoxy, can one really declare what is and is not Christian? Christian Zionism is a way of being Christian just as those who oppose this sensibility represent a way of being Christian. Like the struggle between Constantinian Judaism and Jews of conscience, the battle is joined. The attempt to define Constantinian Judaism as not being Jewish—as being heretical—is foolish. Jews of conscience oppose this form of Judaism because, in conscience and in context, these Jews choose a certain path within Judaism and Jewish life. To struggle for definition is different from declaring the other side as being "not" Jewish or Christian in the proper way; it is to argue that the practice of faith always needs correction and vision.

There is little doubt that Constantinian Judaism is in debt to that which went before it, Constantinian Christianity. Does this mean that the Christian influence on Judaism needs to be excised or that Jews can blame Christians for this dangerous and "inauthentic" import? Would Jews return to innocence if this "Christian" influence was isolated and denied? Or should we say that the evolution of Constantinian Judaism has many sources, including complex and various interactions in history, and that those influences are part of Jewish history and in this sense are Jewish, whether we oppose elements of these borrowings or not?

Perhaps it is best to understand that Judaism and Christianity are not innocent, are not formed in purity and then distorted, and cannot be purified. Therefore there is no heresy *per se*, only a constant struggle within an impure, always evolving and constantly contested tradition we call Jewish or Christian. In the end, the standard cannot be belief, or how that is judged and it is difficult to see how it is important or even proper to change people's belief as a project. The challenge is to modify political practice that comes from certain beliefs so that conscience and justice are at least considered, if not at the center.

So, yes, it is possible for Jews to believe that Israel is promised to Jews by God: the Hebrew bible certainly has this as a major theme. And, yes, it is possible for Christians to believe that Jews are chosen by God and that their "return" is an eschatological sign. Do Christians have to see Jews only as a fossil replaced by the church at the time of Jesus? What we can say to these beliefs is that the movement of faith and theology into the public realm must be limited by the question of justice. Belief cannot be turned into action without restraint and the dislocation of peoples must be prevented. Belief must await another kind of power beyond the present and the human.

Perhaps better stated, belief must work within history with limitations and restraint. If belief oversteps these boundaries, it must be restrained, theologically yes but also politically. In politics the use of force is inherent and contested. Theological force, including the declaration of heresy, is counterproductive. It represents violence against the internal life of the person and of communities. It also represents a simplification of history and tradition, itself a form of violence to diversity and culpability.

An Alternative Path

So the alternative path is clear: Jews, Christians and Muslims of conscience must come together, pooling the resources from their own now-fragmented traditions into a broader tradition of faith and struggle. The broader tradition is a witness found throughout history but is as yet unnamed. Naming it in our time at least clarifies the stakes involved; it also can become a gathering place for all people of conscience, regardless of religious affiliation or non-affiliation. The exilic community grows until a new diaspora comes into being, a diaspora that honors particularity in the service of the universal.

A Jewish theology of liberation enters the 21st century humbled by the failures of the Jewish world. It is also buoyed by the emergence of Jews of conscience and people of conscience everywhere. The losses are clear; the end of Palestine means the end of Jewish history as we have known and inherited it. The end of Palestine is a tragedy that is already at hand, yet at the same time Palestinian identity and consciousness is stronger than ever. At this end, Jews of conscience are in solidarity with the Palestinian struggle as a way of testifying to a new beginning. In the Jewish and Palestinian diaspora, creative and deep relationships continue to be forged; the situation on the ground in the Middle East is so terrible that more and more Jews and Palestinians recognize that their fate is common, interconnected, bound together in place and time. One wonders if the ghetto walls can contain this solidarity forever.

A Jewish theology of liberation is a prophetic theology, a return to the roots of the Jewish experience, a re-embracing of our most lasting contribution to the world. For if Jews do not practice the prophetic, who, then, will? It is true that the greatest gift is the one given to others, freely and without expectation of reward or attribution. And truly the prophetic is now everywhere in the world. Jews, especially those of the Constantinian variety, often have difficulty recognizing the prophetic, especially as it is now firmly pointed toward us, as a critique of unjust power.

It is of little solace to remember that the prophetic, our great gift to the world, our indigenous practice, has always been heard and rejected by the Jewish community. The prophets have always been persecuted within the Jewish world and one hears through the ages the cries of Aaron and Moses, Jeremiah and Isaiah, Amos and Jesus. They have always and everywhere been surrounded by darkness and violence. Is this the same darkness and violence that surrounded Archbishop Romero of El Salvador and Rachel Corrie of the United States, both of whom gave their lives in service to others?

One remembers the cry of Romero, who said that after death he would be resurrected in the history of the Salvadoran people. Is this not our common hope, to live as a witness for and within our own peoples and the peoples of the world? As a Jew, I think also of Edward Said, the late Palestinian intellectual, who embraced Jews as he embraced his own people. As a Jew I cannot withhold my embrace of him and therefore of his own people. That embrace must be given freely as a sign of justice and compassion.

I cannot embrace my own history or religion without embracing the Palestinian people. I cannot affirm the prophetic without practicing it in my own lifetime. The prophetic is not for the few or for someone else or for another time. It is the now deeply grasped, even in loss and at a cost.

In the end, a Jewish theology of liberation is simply an expression of that prophetic voice in the 20th and now 21st century. May there be a time when the different editions of this book will only be a historical curiosity of the time *before* justice, *before* a reconciliation of Jews and Palestinians, *before* the broader tradition of faith and struggle became the norm rather than the exception. Then the *after* can take on a new meaning and substance: a time when misfortune and injustice come to an end.

Yet in the meantime, the radical questions posed by a Jewish theology of liberation must be moderated by the political realities of our time. Justice would be extra-ordinary in our context and certainly in the Middle East. For the foreseeable future Israel will dominate and the Palestinians will be a subject people, not only in relation to Israel but also the Arab world. To survive, even the Palestinians will participate in their own subjugation: at the lower levels Palestinian workers will, as they have for years, help build settlements; as even today they are workers in construction of the Wall of Separation. Palestinian elites will sell land to Jews and also, on a corporate level, bid for settlement and wall construction contracts. Betrayal is everywhere, as is the simple need to feed one's family.

At the same time as the very survival of the Palestinian people in Palestine is at stake, a renewed call for the implementation of the right of return is being voiced. While understandable, even principled, the right has become part of a rhetoric that seeks a war unto death. Wars unto death sometimes materialize and those who speak in this ideological way are free to do so; perhaps they are being faithful to their history and people. However, it is wrong to involve the collective, perhaps even force the collective, into a situation where all or nothing is the result. So often the nothing is the result, and no one remains to pick up the pieces of shattered lives and communities.

Of course it is the oppressor who is first and foremost to blame for the situation. One must never lose sight of this. Still the oppressed have a responsibility to think through and survive the disaster in order to struggle another day. Like religions, the history of a people is complex and the pretense to innocence, even when a people is being oppressed, is superficial and dangerous. The subversive is not suicidal and martyrdom becomes the seed of a future beyond injustice rather than a call for a war unto the end. Martyrdom is the sign of a resistance that will be carried on over time; without compassion and the hope for a new world for the oppressed and oppressor, martyrdom becomes a form of suicide and violence. It fuels the cycle of violence that may engulf all.

The moderate course in Israel/Palestine is one where the hurts, complaints and hopes of both peoples are expressed and where a political framework of peace and stability is constructed within the parameters that are possible. Today is not forever and the psychological and physical borders and boundaries of one generation are not those of the next. The relentless land-grab of the Israeli government must be stopped and the Wall of Separation must be dismantled, with force if necessary. Still, the immediate goal of this force is to re-establish the possibility of a future for Jews and Palestinians, not the radical implementation of a justice that will not come to fruition or a justice that to come to fruition would mean the dislocation of millions or even their murder.

ESCHATOLOGY AND APOCALYPTIC LITERATURE IN EARLY ISLAM

Khalil 'Athamina

The End of Days has been a topic of special interest in Muslim religious literature. Many tens of verses of the Qur'an relate to the theme of the end of this world, using a wide range of expressions, concepts and phrases to denote the Day of Judgment. In the various compendia of *hadith*, special chapters have been devoted to this subject. Moreover, individual collections of apocalyptic predictions attributed to the prophet have been dedicated to the same issue.[1]

The *hadith* literature discussed in greatest detail all the questions related to the theme of the End of Days, providing clear explanations for the obscure matters that the verses of the Qur'an fail to clarify. It also deals with other predicted strange occurrences that possibly happen simultaneously with the event itself, or very shortly before. It refers to them as preceding signs, *asrat al-sa'a,* which will herald its coming.[2] Furthermore *hadith* literature refers to the historical and apocalyptic characters involved therein. It reveals the role that these characters are expected to fill when the time comes. It provides review of the chain of events and references to the place in which these events will occur, giving

[1] Ibn Kathir (747/1346) has listed these names and phrases under the title "The names of the Day of Resurrection according to its appearances in the Qur'an; see Ibn Kathir (1398/1969: I, 255-56). For further details on the Day of Resurrection see Gardet (1986), Rubin (1995).

[2] The great bulk of traditions about the End of Days are recorded in those chapters in *hadith* collections entitled *fitan* or *malahim*, i.e. tribulations, war and civil strife, and may be sought in the following: Ibn Abi Shayba (1396/1967: XV, 5-247); al-Bukhari (1380/1960: *kitab* no. 39); 'Abd al-Razzâq (1390-92/1970-72: nos. 20769-20846; al-Muttaqî al-Hindî (1400/1979: XI, 107f.); Ibn Maja (n.d.: *kitab* no. 39), etc. Among the individual collections: Ibn Tawus (1409/1988); Nu'aym b. Hammad (1414/1993).

the name of the city, province or the country. A description of the human behavior is included in the eschatological literature.[3]

Day of Judgment is not merely an event which will take place independently at a certain point in time and in a defined territory; it is rather a compound event involving a number of factors, human and superhuman, apocryphal and historical. It should be preceded with unusual natural phenomena, especially natural disaster, and drastic changes in the social structure and the cultural order. Religious and moral degeneration will become the most characteristic symptoms of the time. Some Arab sectors will revert to idolatry in the fashion of the Jahiliyya times; pilgrimage to the Ka'ba will be renounced. On the social level nomads will construct high buildings, masters will be born to slave-girls, lower ranks and the wicked will become the leaders of the community in the Muslim countries.[4]

The eschatological literature does not clearly distinguish between two elements whose fusion created this literary genre: the historical and the legendary prophetic elements. The authors of this genre seem not disconnected from the impact of the historical occurrences and some specific events which actually took place in the political arena, nor could they ignore the character of the personages involved in those events. It was those personages and those historical events that were envisioned when attempting to imagine the predicted occurrences that would precede the Day of Judgment. Thus, legend merged with and was nurtured by reality to the point where we can sometimes learn from the eschatological material a great deal with regard to historical characters and events not sufficiently reported on by the historical sources. On the same basis, the *hadith* of the *Mahdi,* the Expected Restorer, thus became associated with the revolt of Ibn al-Zubayr against the Umayyads. Ibn al-Zubayr was never referred to as the *Mahdi* in its messianic significance. However, the chain of events

---

[3] A detailed survey of events, which will occur after the emergence of the *mahdi* (the rightly guided one who will restore the faith of Islam and fill the earth with justice), is reported by Nu'aym b. Hammad (1414/1993: 235-307).

[4] The Day of Judgment according to the Qur'an and *hadith* will be preceded by a chain of natural disasters and the spread of both social and human degeneration and miracles, which were defined as *ashrat al-sa'a* (the porters of the Hour) which are usually traced back to the apocalyptic utterances of the Prophet (see Nu'aym b. Hammad 1414/1993: 385-98; al-Bukhari 1380/1960: no. 61, *manaqib*; Ibn Hajar 1310: XIII, 72f.; 'Abd al-Razzaq 1390-92/1970-72: nos. 20791, 20821; al-Maqdisi 1899-1919: II, 158-209; Ibn Abî Shayba 1396/1976: XV, 163f.; Muslim 1349: XVIII, 2-46). For further details see Madelung (1981: 291-305; 1986a); Tottoli (1999: 193-210); Cook (1993: 25-31).

which occurred during his revolt were to become the prototype for events at the time of the appearance of the *Mahdi* from *ahl al-bayt,* the family of the prophet.[5] The political experience undergone by Muslim society in the 1st and 2nd centuries of its existence had a significant effect on the formation of the theory concerning the End of Days. The political positions of the parties who fought for rule in that period were reflected in Muslim eschatological literature. Their unfulfilled political desires, against the background of the prevailing reality, were expressed through apocalyptic traditions which predicted their success in the End of Days.[6]

Dynasties that actually ruled by means of force and did not enjoy legal recognition by their political rivals, sought the longed-for legality through the integration of real or fictional characters into that literature, and ascribed to themselves imaginary roles in occurrences likely to happen at some future time.[7] Moreover failed political movements viewed the eschatological literatures as a life preserver to grab hold of in order to save their movements from extinction and keep them alive until more suitable moments for sudden resurgence. This trend was repeatedly experienced by the Shi'ite movement all along the Umayyad period and during the early period of the Abbasids in the aftermath of the collapse of al-Mukhtar movement in Iraq in the last quarter if the 7th century CE. The disappointed supporters of the 'Alid family who fled from Kufa to Basra had referred to a certain person called Musa ibn Talha as to their expected *Mahdi*.[8] Later on, and after the tragic murder of al-Husayn ibn 'Ali, the Shi'a propaganda claimed his half brother Muhammad ibn 'Ali, who was known by his nickname Ibn al-Hanafiyya, as the Shi'ite *Mahdi*, as the verses of the pro-Shi'ite poet Kutayyir 'Azza confirm.[9] Less than a century later, the member of the 'Alid family, Muhammad ibn 'Abdallah ibn al-Hasan ibn al-Hasan, the Shi'ite rebel

---

5 The case of the revolt of 'Abdallah b. al-Zubayr is typical in this regard. A great deal of information concerning his revolt after the death of Mu'awiya, and the fate of the Syrian army which the Umayyad Caliph sent against him, is included in the eschatological literature while not mentioned in historical sources (see: Nu'aym b. Hammad 1414/1993: 103-7, 199-204).

6 Madelung 1981: 293-294 Van Vloten, 1934: 107-118.

7 In the case of the Umayyad dynasty see al-Farazdaq (1386-1966); Maqdidi (1899-1919: II, 176), In the case of the Abbasids see Ibn Kathir (1402/1981: I, 50-51); al-Duri (1391-1971: 245, 247, 286, 288).

8 Ibn Manzur 1989: xxv, 290.

9 Abu al-Faraj al-Asfahani, VIII, 32-33.

in the reign of the 'Abbasid al-Mansur, who bore during his life time the title *Mahdi ahl al-bayt,* the expected restorer of the family of the Prophet, was given another title after his death. His new title *al-nafs al-zakiyya,* the pure and righteous soul, came to convince his adherents that the expected *Mahdi* was not the murdered leader, but another member of the family whose emergence they should expect in the future.[10]

The use of eschatological material was not restricted to political affairs. Rather, it covers a wide range of subjects boldly connected with the essential field of life in Muslim society. Social strata or tribal groups suffering from discrimination and ill-treatment by the ruling dynasties and by the administrative or the legal institutions, found in this kind of literature their last hope for a better future for themselves and for their descendants. According to this belief, the *mawali,* had also adopted the idea of the *Mahdi,* but their *Mahdi* was to be a descendant of non-Arab origin, who was supposed to emerge in Jerusalem on the eve of the End of Days. Here he would dispatch the Arabs and restore the longed-for justice which the *mawali* had sought for long time.[11]

The historical tribal dispute between the Southern and the Northern Arab tribes, known by the term *'asabiyya,* was manifested in the eschatological literature. It was restricted now to one specific issue and focused on the tribal identity of the *Mahdi.* The Northern or the Qaysi version, on the other hand, traces the origin of the *Mahdi* back to the Northern race, more precisely to a Qurayshi origin. The Southern version asserts that the *Mahdi* should emerge from the ranks of the Yemeni race. In order to emphasize its Southern origin, he was referred to as the *Qahtani.* The notion of *al-Qahtani* was developed simultaneously with the idea of the *Mahdi* in Medina during the 7th to 13th centuries CE by a *hadith.* It was transmitted on the authority of Abu Hurayra on the eve of the revolt of Ibn al-Ash'ath against al-Hajjaj in the Eastern Muslim province during the reign of the 'Abd al-Malik. The southern tribes had pinned their hopes on the rebel Ibn al-Ash'ath and referred to him as *al-Qahtani,* their expected *Mahdi.* He was called also by the synonymous epithet *al-mansur,* the victorious.[12] The suppression of the rebellion led by

---

[10] Abu al-Faraj 1390/1970b: 233, 239, 246; al-Duri, 1391/1971: 394; al-Mubarrad n.d.: IV, 114-120; al-Duri 191: 123-32.

[11] Nu'aym b. Hammad 1414/1993: 243.

[12] Al-Mas'udi 1893: 314; Maqdisi 1899-1919: II, 184; al-Baladhuri 1883: IX, 334; Van Vloten 1934: 120; Madelung 1986a; al-Duri 1981: 124.

Ibn al-Ash'ath did not eliminate the hopes of the Southern Arabs in their own Qahtani. They, as many *hadiths* of the eschatological literature attest, continued to believe that the Expected Restorer from Himyar would come in the future. He was to restore the lost leadership of the Yemen from the hands of Quraysh before the End of Days.[13]

Poor and needy people in Muslim society played with the idea of getting rid of suffering on the eve of the End of Days. During this period of time, unparalleled prosperity would replace poverty, which would totally vanish from the face of the earth.[14]

Those military missions for the conquest of bordering countries and cities which failed during the height of Muslim power became an issue dealt by the eschatological *hadith*. Some prophetic traditions had predicted the conquest of these lands by later Muslim generations before the coming of the End of Days. Fearsome enemies who had ever threatened the Muslim frontier and the Muslim rule in the East and the North provinces were not forgotten by the authors of eschatological literature, especially the Turkish tribal elements and the Byzantine imperial troops. It was predicted that the joint forces of the Turks and the Byzantines would invade the Syrian territory, *bilad al-Sham*. The invaders would succeed in occupying its land from Antioch in the North to the Carmel Mountains in Palestine. *This* event would take place in the period of time which antedates the emergence of the *Mahdi,* whose first mission would be to re-conquer the occupied territories and annihilate the invaders.[15]

The Muslim's perpetual attempts to propagate and spread the Islamic faith among the peoples of the world so that Islam would become the sole existing faith on earth, the final goal of Islamic mission, was also dealt with. This strategic goal thus became an issue on the agenda of the End of Days. The prophetic tradition predicts that Islamic faith will spread all over the world. Jesus, after descending from heaven, in his role as the Expected Restorer, will appear in Jerusalem. He will break the cross and pray after the expected *Mahdi* of Islam, who will lead the prayer in Jerusalem. Monotheistic believers, including the great majority of Jewish people, will convert to Islam. Those whom the *dajjal,*

---

13 Nu'aym b. Hammad 1414/1993: 243.

14 'Abd al-Razzaq 1390-92/1970-72: XI, 371-372; Ibn Kathir 1389/1969: I, 30.

15 Nu'aym b. Hammad 1414/1993: 243.

the false Messiah or the Antichrist, leads astray, will find their death together with him.[16]

Secular aspects which contributed to the development of the messianic literature in Islam did not succeed in concealing the Judeo-Christian influence on the Islamic theory of the *Mahdi*. The Judeo-Christian influence is denoted by the fact that the Muslim eschatological literature puts Jerusalem in the centre of its concern. The Holy City, according to this literature, will be the appropriate theatre on which the main occurrences and events related to the End of Days will take place. Jerusalem is seen as the most favorable city and the most holy site among other holy cities in the Muslim world. It is more favorable than both Mecca and Medina, the traditional holy cities in Islam.[17] Moreover, End of Days literature praises the value and the role of Jerusalem, which in the period prior to the Day of Judgment will become the only safe asylum for the true believers on earth. From the four corners of the universe, true believers are commanded to immigrate to Jerusalem. It will play the same role as a *Dar Hijra* as it was the destination of Abraham, the forefather of believers and the first Muslim who preached the monotheistic faith.[18]

As the Day of Judgment approaches, the Holy Land will not tolerate the presence of the wicked and of evil doers within its border. They will be expelled from it and will meet their doom outside its confines, struck down by the consuming fire that seeks and burns those who follow the path of evil.[19]

Jerusalem then becomes the shield, which in that future time will protect believers from evil. The army of the false Messiah, *al-dajjal,* will halt outside its walls, after having overcome all other countries.[20] Only Medina, the city of the Prophet, like Jerusalem, will be saved from

---

[16] Ibn Kathir, 1402/1981: 1, 27; Ibn Abi Shayba 1396/1976: XV, 144-45, 159; Nu'aym b. Hammad 1414/1993: 223, 346; 'Abd al-Razzaq 1390-92/1970-72: XI, 339; Ibn al-Murajja 1995: 216, 217, 222; al-Wasiti 1979: 63; al-Qunduzi 1385/1965: 506; Ibn Qutayba 1392/1972: 188; al-Haythami 1385/1965: 164.

[17] Ibn Manzur 1410/1989: 1, 56, 60; al-Hanbali 1393/1973: 1, 228.

[18] Ibn Manzur 1410/1989: 70, 72; Nu'aym b. Hammad 1414/1993: 383; Ibn Kathir 1389/1969: 1, 229-230; 'Abd al-Razzaq 1390-92/1970-72: nos. 20778, 20790; Ibn al-Murajja 1995: 160.

[19] Ibn Abi Shayba 1396/1976: XV, 245; Ibn Manzur 1410/1989: 1, 120; Nu'aym b. Hammad 1414/1993: 383.

[20] Ibn Abi Shayba 1396/1976: 1, 146-48; Nu'aym b. Hammad 1414/1993: 346; al-Hanbali 1393/1973: 1, 234.

its might.[21] But the siege imposed by *al-dajjal* on Jerusalem will not last long, and salvation will come with the arrival of Jesus, the true Messiah who will annihilate the Antichrist near the Lydda Gate, close to King David's Tower.[22]

Jerusalem will flourish and prosper while death and destruction overtake all other cities; even Medina will not be saved from ruin. Construction and development in Jerusalem at the End of Days, however, will be unprecedented.[23] All the treasures of Jerusalem which adorned the city and of which it had been robbed after its destruction will be returned to it after the *Mahdi* succeeds in rescuing them from ships which sank into the depths of the sea.[24] In that day, the Muslims will have their revenge over Constantinople, conquering it and taking its treasures as the spoils of war, in fulfillment of the vow by which God swore to lay the city waste in revenge for the destruction of His city and His temple by the Romans. Thus, the *Mahdi* will close a circle which had remained open for hundreds and thousands of years.[25]

The sacred rock on the Temple Mount will be transformed into shining pearl; its size will increase to fill the area of Heaven and Earth, so that there will be room for all creatures to stand before God, the Greater Judge, who will give them judgment. Above the Rock, an angel will arise and blow the ram's horn as a signal for the resurrection of the dead, *al-hashr;* thus Jerusalem will be called *al-mahshar,* the place where all of humankind will be assembled in preparation for the Day of Judgment.[26]

Al-Ka'ba will not remain in Mecca, but will be brought to Jerusalem in a ceremony similar to that by which a bride is brought into her husband's house. The building of al-Ka'ba will be fastened with chains of gold and pearls which will be grasped by all of the former generations who made pilgrimage to Mecca, who visited al-Ka'ba or admired it.[27] The holy mountains, referred to as the mountains of the Day of Judgment, will also be moved to the holy territory of Jerusalem and set up at its four

---

[21] Ibn Abi Shayba 1396/1976: XV, 152; Nu'aym b. Hammad 1414/1993: 343; Ibn Kathir 1389/1969: 1, 59.

[22] Nu'aym b. Hammad 1414/1993: 334.

[23] Nu'aym. Hammad 1414/1993: 380; Hanbali 1393/1973: I, 240.

[24] Al-Qunduzi 1385/1965: 522.

[25] Ibn Kathir 1389/1969: I, 58-59.

[26] Al- Nuwayri n.d.: I, 334-35; Ibn Kathir 1389/1969: I 251; Ibn al-Murajja 1995: 104.

[27] Nu'aym b. Hammad 1414/1993: 381; Ibn al-Murajja 1995: 211-13; al-Wasiti 1979: 92-93; al-Nuwayri n.d.: I 339; Ibn Abd Rabbihi 1385/1965: VI, 265.

corners, and will be transformed into shining pearls to light up the place where the judgment will be handed down.[28]

The bones of the Prophet Muhammad, which according to tradition will play a central role in the ceremony of *shafa'a,* the pleading before God to forgive and pardon those worthy few of His servants, will be transferred from his grave in Medina to Jerusalem, so that the Prophet can be present on that day.[29] A balance scale will be set up on the Holy Rock for God to weigh the deeds of every person and determine his fate, Heaven or Hell. Also the path, the *sirat,* will be erected on the rock to lead the faithful to Heaven and the heretics to Hell. Both of these destinations will be at opposite sides of Jerusalem so that the survivors will walk through the western gate to Paradise and the condemned through the eastern gate to Gehenna, *wadi jahannam*, or *wadi Hannum*.[30]

These are the changes in Jerusalem as part of the preparation process for the Day of Judgment. But the city has another role at the End of Days. It also becomes the focus of political activity by the forces struggling for control of the Muslim nation during the period prior to the Day of Judgment. The struggle is determined by two factors. The first is that control of Jerusalem and Mecca constitutes a prerequisite for any Muslim ruler claiming moral and religious legitimacy, without which he cannot be deemed a legitimate ruler, irrespective of his strength and power. The second is derived from the belief, common in the mid-7th through the mid-13th centuries CE, that the Prophet foresaw that as the end of the world approached, a representative of the Muslim nation would arise who would lead the Muslims in justice and integrity. This leader would defeat tyranny and oppression throughout the nations. In view of this prophecy, it was obvious that anyone who would rule Jerusalem would be the one indicated by the Prophet and would accordingly be the one intended to lead the nation with no rivals.

Prophetic traditions set no date for the appearance of the *Mahdi,* the restorer of justice who would become the legitimate ruler who would deserve the blessing of the Prophet himself.[31] This gave rise to the trend of contradictions inherent in the eschatological traditions with regard to the identity of the *Mahdi*. In fact each of the political groups considered

---

[28] Al-Wasiti 1979: 56.

[29] Al-Wasiti 1979: 102.

[30] Ibn 'Abd Rabbihi 1385/1965: VI, 265; Hanbali 1393/1973: I, 266-67.

[31] Madelung 1986a.

itself a legitimate candidate from whose ranks the *Mahdi* could arise. It is no wonder that the *Mahdi* could be from the Umayyad dynasty, from the Banu 'Abd Shams, and in view of the internal struggles within the dynasty, from the Marwand or the Sufyanid branch.[32] Or he could be from the house of 'Abbas, and given the internal struggle within the dynasty, he could be the first Abbasid, caliph called al-Saffah, or the second, al-Mansur, or his son, the third 'Abbasid caliph, who inherited his father's place and was, in fact, called al-Mahdi.[33]

Al-Mahdi could rise from the 'Alid dynasty, and according to the widely circulated tradition among the adherents of Ali, the fourth righteous Caliph, he was foreseen as the expected *Mahdi*.[34] But in light of the competence required for the right of leadership forwarded by the rival branches of the dynasty, the eschatological traditions were accordingly contradictory. The pro-Fatimid line of propaganda had claimed that the Mahdi should come from the children of Fatima, the daughter of the Prophet and 'Ali's first wife.[35] Meanwhile, the rival branch of Muhammad b. Hannafiyya, the son of 'Ali from Hawla, his concubine,

---

[32] According to the traditions which deal with the identity of the expected *Mahdi*, he was traced back to the lineage of Banu 'Abd Shams, of whose ranks came the Umayyad Caliphs (Nu'aym b. Hammad 1414/1993: 229, 231). He could be a descendant of the Sufyanid branch of Banu 'Abd Shams clan. In one version he was identified as Mu'awiya, the first Umayyad Caliph himself (*ibid*: 224). In order to assert this version it was reported that the *Mahdi* is he who will be recognized as caliph in Jerusalem (ibid: 218), following the fact that Mu'awiya was given thè pledge of allegiance, *bay'a* in Jerusalem. About this *bay'a* see al-Tabari (1879-1901: II, 4); al-Mas'udi (1861:V, 14); Maqdisi (1899-1919: IV, 87); Ibn Qutayba (1381/1961: 211); Ibn al-Jawzi (1412/1992:V, 167); Ibn Manzur (1410/1989: XXV, 43); Ibn Kathir (1402/1981:VIII, 130, 131). In another version the Sufyanid candidate for this position was not other than the expected Sufyani, whom the eschatological tradition identified as Abu Muhammad 'Abdallah b. Khalid b. Yazid b. Mu'awiya who died in Medina during the reign of the Abbasid Caliph al-Mansur (Ibn Kathir 1402/1981: X, 52-53; see also Madelung 1986b). On 'Umar II, of the Marwanid branch of the clan of 'Abd Shama, as the *Mahdi*, see Nu'aym b. Hammad (1414/1993: 230-31); Maqdisi (1899-1919: II, XXX); Ibn Kathir (1389/1969:VI, 189).

[33] For the same reason and against the rival claim of the 'Alid clan, pro-Abbasid tradition claimed that the *Mahdi* could rise from the ranks of this clan (see Nu'aym b. Hammad 1414/1993: 228, 230; Ibn Khaldun n.d.: 573-74). Sometimes the 'Abbasid tradition identifies him as al-Saffah, the first caliph of the dynasty (Nu'aym b. Hammad 1414/1993: 213; Ibn Kathir 1402/1981: X, 50). And sometimes he was third caliph, the son of al-Mansur whose real name was al-Mahdi (Nu'aym b. Hammad 1414/1993: 209; al-Haythami 1385/1965: 165-66).

[34] Ibn Kathir 1402/1981: II, 182-183.

[35] Nu'aym b. Hammad 1414/1993: 228-31; Ibn Kathir 1389/1969: I, 27; al-Haythami 13885/1965: 163; Ibn Khaldun n.d.: 556.

had insisted that the *Mahdi,* should be Ibn al-Hanafiyya himself. His adherents have maintained, through a widespread *hadith,* that the name of the expected *Mahdi,* should be identical with the Prophet's name, *Yuwati ismuhu ismi.*[36]

The dispute about the identity of the *Mahdi* also emerged within the Fatimid branch itself; one set of eschatological traditions refer to al-Hasan as the expected *Mahdi*, while another set of traditions identify him with al-Husayn.[37] According to another tradition, the Mahdi ought to be from the Quraysh, the men of Mecca; any clan of that tribe could produce the Mahdi.[38]

The *Mahdi,* in fact, could be any Muslim personage, *al-Mahdi min hadhihi al-umma,* irrespective of his lineage or ethnic origin, according to yet another tradition. This gave various rebels, Arabs and non-Arabs, the opportunity to claim legitimacy for themselves and for their rebellions by claiming that their respective leader was the *Mahdi.*[39] The above mentioned *hadith* could serve as evidence to support the Kharijite's notion of the Caliph's identity, which states that candidates are assessed on merit, irrespective of race and color.

Against these contradictions, and against the Shi'ite obstinacy which insisted that the *Mahdi* must come from the house of 'Ali, arose a kind of consensus among Sunnite circles, stating that the *Mahdi* to whom the Prophet had referred was solely and exclusively the Mahdi who would appear at the End of Days and to whom fealty would be sworn in Jerusalem.[40]

Muslim eschatological tradition set the rules according to which the real *Mahdi* would operate. The historical background and the chain of events prior to his appearance were taken into consideration. As the prerequisite for the coming of the *Mahdi*, al-Sufyani would appear in the Hims area of Syria. Thus he would send his armies into Iraq and the eastern province, where he would achieve military victories, eliminate the Abbasid rule, and destroy the cities of Iraq. In the eastern province, a

---

[36] Maqdisi 1899-1919: II, 180-81; Nu'aym b. Hammad 1414/1993: 227; al-Haythami 1385/1965: 168.

[37] Nu'aym b. Hammad 1414/1993: 230-31; Ibn Kathir 1389/1969: I, 25; al-Qunduzi 1385/1965: 512-13, 597.

[38] Nu'aym b. Hammad 1414/1993: 231-37, 244.

[39] Nu'aym b. Hammad 1414/1993: 230; 'Abd al-Razzâq 1390-92/1970-72: no. 20771; Goldziher 1982: 219.

[40] Van Vloten 1934: 121.

man of the Prophet's dynasty, the Banu Hashim, would arise, rally his supporters and fight al-Sufyani's army. The commander of the Hashimite forces, a man of the Tamim tribe, would lead his army to victory over al-Sufyani. After nine months, Al-Sufyani would be totally defeated and would be executed. At that point, the *Mahdi* would appear in the city and rule there for 14 years, although according to other traditions, his rule would be limited to 7 to 9 years.[41] After the death of *Mahdi*, Jerusalem would be ruled by a Southern man, a certain descendant of the ancient Yemenite royal dynasty, the kings of Himyar, who would call himself the *Mansur* of Jerusalem. His rule would last for 21 years. In the first 15 of those years, he would rule in justice according to the laws of the Qur'an. In the last six years, however, he would become a tyrant and show hostility to the northern Arabs, the *Mudar*, and the non-Arab Muslims, the *Mawali*. The Mawali, in response, would unite and appoint a leader from among their midst, who would attack the Southern ruler, kill him, and become the ruler of Jerusalem, but within a short time, he would behave like his predecessor and oppress the Arabs, Northern and Southern alike.[42]

In the days of the *Mawali* rule, the Turks and the Byzantines would join forces against the Muslims and conquer Syria and Northern Palestine to the foothills of Mount Carmel.[43] The *Mawali* ruler would not succeed in coping with the threat posed by the allies and would die of sorrow at his own impotence in the face of that threat. After his death, the true *mahdi* would appear and deal with the threat of the Turkish-Byzantine allies. It would be he who would conquer Constantinople and even Rome, the capital of the Roman Empire. It would be he who would withstand the threat of the Antichrist; it would be he whom Jesus would help in preventing *al-dajjal* from entering Jerusalem.[44]

After the killing of *al-dajjal*, Islam would become the faith of humankind. The *Mahdi*, who would find the original copy of both the Torah and the New Testament in a cave in the mountains of Palestine, would succeed, by virtue of these discoveries, in bringing the Christians and the Jews to the conclusion that there is no other religion but Islam,

---

[41] Nu'aym b. Hammad 1414/1993: Maqdisi 1899-1919: II, 162; al-Qunduzi 1385/1965: 512; Ibn al-Murajja 1995: 221.

[42] Nu'aym b. Hammad 1995: 235-43.

[43] Nu'aym b. Hammad 1995: 243.

[44] Ibn Kathir 1389/1969: I, 58-59, 128-29; Nu'aym b. Hammad 1414/1993: 241-43, 246; Ibn al-Murajja 1995: 219.

whereupon they would convert.[45] In order to overcome the reluctance of certain stubborn Jewish circles, he would enlist the aid of the Ark of Immanence, which would be revealed on the surface of the Sea of Galilee, leaving them no choice but to adopt Islam.[46]

The reign of the real *Mahdi*, according to the eschatological tradition, would last five, seven or nine years.[47] At the end of his reign would come the moment suitable for the End of this World and the beginning of the process to prepare this world for the Day of Judgment.

References

'Abd al-Razzaq (1390-92/1970-72) *Al-Musannaf*, ed. al-A'zami, 12 vols. Beirut.

Abu l-Faraj al-Asfahani (1390/1970a) *Kitab al-Aghani*, ed. Bulaq, 21 vols. Repr. Beirut. (1390/1970b) Maqatil al-talibiyyin, ed. A. Saqr. repr. Beirut.

Al-Baladhuri (1883) *Ansab al-ashraf*, ed. W. Ahlwardt. Greifswald.

Al-Bukhari (1380/1960), *Sahih*, 9 vols. Cairo.

Cook, M. (1993) "An Early Islamic Apocalyptic Chronicle". *Journal of Near Eastern Studies* 52, 25-31. Chicago.

al-Duri, ed. (1391/1971){Anonymous} *Akhbar al-dawla al-'abbasiyya*. Beirut.

(1981) *Al-Fikra al-mahdiyya bayna al-da'wa al-'abbasiyya wa-l-'asr al-'abbasi al-awwal*, in W. al-Qadi (ed), *Dirasat 'arabiyya islamiyya*, 123-32. Beirut.

Al-Farazdaq (13986/1966) *Diwan*, 2 vols. Beirut.

Gradet, L. (1986) "Kiyama". *Encyclopaedia of Islam* 5, 235-38. Leiden.

Goldziher, I, (1982) *Introduction to Islamic Theology and Law* (trans. A. and R. Hamori). Princeton.

Al-Hanbali, Mujir al-Din (1393/1973) *Al-Uns al-Jalil*, 2 vols. Beirut.

Al-Haythami, Ahmad b. Hajar (1385/1965) *Al-Sawa'iq al-muhriqa*. Cairo.

Ibn 'Abd Rabbihi (1385/1965) *Al-'Iqd al-Farid*, ed. Ahmad Amin *et al.*, vols. Cairo.

Ibn Abi Shayba (1396/1976) *Al-Musannaf fi'l-ahadith wa'l-athar*, 15 vols. Bombay.

Ibn al-Jawzi(1412/1992) *Al-Muntazam*, ed. Muhammad and Mustafa Ata, 19 vols. Beirut.

Ibn Hajar al-Asqalani (1310/1892) *Fath al-bari, sarh sahih al-Bukhari*, 10 vols. Cairo repr. Beirut n.d.

Ibn Khaldun (n.d) *al-Muqaddima*. Beirut.

Ibn Kathir (1389/1969) *Kitab al-nihaya al-fitan wa l-malahim*, ed. Taha al-Zayni, 2 vols. Cairo.

---

45 Nu'aym b. Hammad 1414/1993:221; 'Abd al-Razzaq 1390-92/1970-72: XI, 399.

46 Nu'aym b. Hammad 1414/1993: 233; Ibn al-Murajja 1995: 222; al-Hanbali 1393/1973: I, 268.

47 Maqdisi 1899-1919: II, 182-83; Ibn Kathir 1389/1969: I, 31; 'Abd al-Razzaq 1390-92/1970-72: XI, 371-72; al-Haythami 1385/1965: 164; Nu'aym b. Hammad 1414/1993: 233-34.

(1402/1981) *Al-Bidaya wa'l-nihaya*, 14 vols. Beirut.
Ibn Maja (n.d.) *Sunan*, 4 vols Cairo.
Ibn Manzur (1410/1989) *Mukhtasar ta'rikh madinat Dimasq*, ed. M. Sagargi, 29 vols. Damascus.
Ibn al-Murajja (1995) *Fada'il bayt al-maqdis*, ed. O. Livne-Kafri. Shfaram.
Ibn Qutayba (1381/1961) *Al-Ma'arif*, ed. Tarwat Ukasa. Cairo.
(1392/1972) *Ta'wil mukhtalif al-hadith*, ed. Muhammad al-Naggar. Beirut.
Ibn Tawus, 'Ali b. Musa (1409/1988) *Al-Malahim wa-l-fitan*. Beirut.
Madelung, W. (1981) "'Abd Allah b. al-Zubayr and the Mahdi", *Journal of Near Eastern Studies* 40, 291-305. Chicago.
(1986a) "Al-Mahdi". *Encyclopaedia of Islam*, 1230-38 Leiden.
(1986b) "The Sufyani between Tradition and History". *Studia Islamica* 63, 5-48. Paris.
Al-Maqdisi, Ibn Tahir (1899-1919) al-Bad'wal-ta'rih, ed. C. Huart, 6 vols. Paris.
Al-Masudi (1861) *Muruj al-dhahab*, ed. Barbier De Meynard, 9 vols. Paris.
(1893) *Al-Tanbih wa-l-ishraf*, ed. M.J. De Goeje. Leiden.
Al-Mubarrad (n.d) *Al-Kamil*, ed. Abu al-Fadl Ibrahim, 4 vols. Cairo.
Muslim (1349/1930) *Sahih*, 18 vols. Cairo.
Al-Muttaqi al-Hindi (1400/1979) *Kanz al-ummal*, I I vols. Beirut.
Nu'aym b. Hammad (1414/1993) *Kitab al-fitan*, ed. Suhayl Zakkar. Beirut.
Al-Nuwayri (n.d.) *Nihayat al-'arab*, 32 vols. Cairo.
Al-Qunduzi (1385/1965) *Yanabi' al-mawadda*. al-Najaf.
Rubin, U. (1995) "al-Sa'a" *Encyclopaedia of Islam* 8, 656-57. Leiden.
Al-Tabari (1879-1901) *Ta'rikh al-rusul wa'l-muluk*, ed. M. J. De Goeje et al., 3 vols. Leiden.
Tottoli, R. (1999) "Origin and Use of the Term Isra'iliyyat in Muslim Literature". *Arabica* 46, 193-210. Leiden.
Van Vloten, G. (1934) *La domination arabe, le Chi'itisme et les croyances messianiques sous le Khalifat des Omayades*. Cairo (In Arabic).
Al-Wasiti (1979) *Fada'il al-bayt al-muqaddas*, ed. I. Hasson. Jerusalem.

THE DANGER OF MILLENNIAL POLITICS

Gershom Gorenberg

For the sake of clarity, I must begin by announcing myself as a religious Jew, as an advocate of many years for a two-state solution and for the right to self-determination, and as an Israeli by choice. My argument is that Christian Zionism is not in fact a Zionist theology, but is a classic anti-Jewish ideology. It is because of my fascination with the paradox of this situation that I have come to write on this subject, looking at the strange partnership between the Israeli right and those calling themselves Christian Zionists. In order to understand this relationship, we need first to look at the phenomena of millennialism in Christianity and Messianism in Judaism: the belief that history as we know it will end, to be followed by the divine kingdom, and the belief that it's about to happen *now*.

There are two major aspects of this belief. One is that it is a form of theodicy, a form of justification of God. A classic problem in all religions is that if the creator is good, why is the world so flawed? This is a basic question of faith, and we all know the catalogue of answers. Perhaps the most radical answer of all is millennialism. It admits that the world is in fact flawed, and that God will come to fix his world and establish a reign of justice because he is good. In this sense, millennialism expresses the finest ethical sense of religion, because it emphasizes that there is something wrong with the world we are living in and we should not be satisfied with it. However, one should note that in history different millennialist movements disagree strongly with what exactly is wrong with the world as it is. If a millennialist movement suggests that nation should not take up arms against nation, it has one meaning about what is wrong with today's world as it is, but if it stresses the unbelief of nations, it has a different meaning.

The second aspect is that millennialism is also a form of literature. It looks at history as a novel, written by God. It so happens today that Christian fundamentalists have discovered that the novel is a particularly useful method of conveying dogma, because the medium fits the message. Millennialism says that history is written by a divine author. The creation and the end are captured by the same narrative. History has a plot, centred around a divine conflict with heroes and villains. And as in every good novel, everything has meaning. The gun on the wall that we see in the first act must go off by the third act. This means that every detail we see today foreshadows the coming events. Another point is that characters are not what they seem to be; they have not worked out exactly what the other characters are about. Today's events, for those who have eyes to see, conform to the outcome, so millenialists say that the leader of the millennialism group is a detective—one who is in tune with the author, who knows how to read the clues, who knows what is coming. Everybody else is clueless. In millennial history, the good events are foreshadowing the outcome, the last chapter, where villains get their comeuppance, and the heroes win. The evils in history are the signs of the rising tension before the end. As in any good story, the heroes appear to be in the greatest danger just before the end. The chase scene has to come before the end. That is when the heroes seem to be in the greatest danger. And that is why a cataclysmic event can be interpreted to be the dark chapter that precedes the light chapter at the end of the story.

This view of history fosters a view of the people in the story not as people, not as God's created human beings, but as characters in a drama that they do not understand themselves. They become actors in the midst of a drama. And here is a great contradiction: millennialism may begin with the ethical sense that the world is not as it should be, but it ends up looking at history in a mythic sense, where characters are not really people you have to have respect for as individuals; they' re just actors in a drama.

Now, like any story, this story has a setting. The story of history ends, as we know, what began in Judaism, was rewritten in Christianity, and written again, in Islam. In all three monotheistic traditions, the story ends right in Jerusalem. The Holy Land, especially Mt. Zion, the Mt. of Olives, for Christians, Megiddo, or as it is called in the New Testament, Armageddon, Mt. Carmel, all these places are part of the stage of the end. Now there have been many millennial movements throughout history that have interpreted these names. There were the Branch Davidians with Mt. Carmel in Texas, and there have been many in Nigeria. However, when momentous events take place on the stage of the Holy Land, as in fact they have in the tragic events between Jews and Arabs, it is inevitable that some people will interpret those events as those of prophecy. After all, they are taking place on the stage of prophecy; this must be the last chapter of the story. And that is particularly likely to take place in an age such as ours that is afflicted with biblical literalism. So in Judaism, in Christianity, in Islam, there have been movements, there have been writers that have interpreted events of recent years as having been events sympathetic to the end times. To some extent they also influence each other and borrow from each other's works, if the information is not clear enough.

Millennialism can also have contradictory trends; it can cause a move away from politics. God will come and fix things and asks his people only to wait. But in many cases, millennialism combines with a political movement, and in that case, it provides a non-conventional motivation for change because the activist in a politicized millennialist movement expects not incremental improvement to this world, but a perfected world. The end to be achieved is an end that is so much better than current visions that any means can be used to achieve it. The believer in a politicized millennial movement is likely willing to risk more, to give more and to break the normal ethical rules. One example is indicative. An early-80s Jewish underground group, among other things, stole explosives from the Israeli army in a plot to blow up the Haram Al-Sharif. Luckily the plot was foiled and the leader arrested. He said in his confession to police, "It was a problematic act on the face of it—theft, pure and simple. But we cultivated the operation in the belief that if we succeeded, and the whole process of redemption also succeeded, then this act would also become legitimate." If an action is to bring about the redemption of the world, anything done to that end is acceptable. Some of the statements of Osama bin Laden suggest that some of the same ideas are taking place in al-Qa'ida. If you are going to achieve the millennial end, then you can do almost anything to get there. This is the danger of millennial politics; the participants are people acting in terms of a great narrative, not in terms of practical or ethical consequences.

In that context, we must look at the relationship between Zionism and Jewish messianism and also look at "Christian Zionism." The relationship between political Zionism and messianism is a complex one, but to express it in the simplest terms, perhaps even over-simplification,

Zionism is a turning away from messianism. Zionism was a secular movement, and it rejected the expectation that God was going to solve such problems as the Jewish exile and the need for the repatriation of the people to the homeland. In political Zionism, Jews move away from a backdrop of a drama that takes place primarily between God and the Jewish people. Jews and the Jewish people enter the political arena, and actions are measured by their political, pragmatic, and ethical worth and scale, not their historical worth and scale. Secular Zionism therefore created a challenge to traditional Judaism and there are a series of potential responses. We've seen many of them over the course of the past 150 years.

One of them is the response of rejection. There is a strong stream in Judaism that Zionism should be rejected because human beings are taking into their hands what should be God's role. Another response is a kind of acceptance on a pragmatic level. It is a religious response which regards Jews acting politically in this world to be the equivalent of going to the doctor. In other words, why pray to get better when you can go to the doctor? There are some people who claim that going to the doctor is taking matters out of God's hands, but most religious people accept that as a legitimate thing to do. Then the religious question ceases to become only whether your prayer is effective at bringing healing and becomes whether what the doctor does is ethical. In the same way, it is fine to engage in politics; the question then becomes the pragmatic outcome: does it work? And the ethical question: are the means acceptable?

There's one more approach which is perhaps the best recognized, but is by no means the only one, and that is the problematic, to say the least, synthesis between revision and modern nationalism. This is one strand of Jewish nationalism and one form of religious Zionism. It is not the only one, but it is one that has been very influential in recent years. In this view, the Zionism movement is regarded as God acting in history. The Jews' return to their land heralds the approach of silent redemption. The secular Zionists are regarded as acting without being aware of the significance of their own actions. They become actors in a drama they do not understand. The hope is that eventually they will understand the meaning of their own faith. This view is associated very strongly with the Rabbi Abraham Isaac Cook and especially with his son Rabbi Steven Cook.

Until 1967, the messianic strand in religious Zionism was relatively marginalized. This may be because the creation of the State of

Israel seemed so far from the messianic vision. The Jews did not rule Jerusalem, except for a small part here and there. Who could regard that as the final gathering in of the exile? At best it was, as one prayer put it, "the first running of redemption". Something might be happening, but it was very broad and in the future. And Rabbi Cook was a very marginal rabbi at that time. The National Religious party, which was his party, was known at that time as a very dovish party. The surprise and shock of the Israeli victory in 1967 changed that because Cook's supporters had a ready explanation for something that most people could not understand. Israel's victory was the next step in the redemptive cycle. The state and the army were carrying out God's will. These were events foretold in prophecy, they argued. Believers were those who merit the prophets, who believe in them. They could also draw in and become partners to God and participate in the divine plan by settling the newly occupied territories, which they would never refer to in those terms. They saw themselves as a vanguard and looked down upon the secularists who did not understand what was really happening.

In 1974, Cook, by then an old man, asserted in a speech to his students that "We are not just in the entry hall of redemption; we are in the living room." That is to say, we are already in the midst of redemption. Wars came to be interpreted as the battle of Gog and Magog. In that sense, the decisions by secular leaders to give up land to Egypt in 1979 or in 1993 in the Oslo process were not just political defeats in the eyes of Messianic Zionists, but theological crises. Daniel Barries, another member of the 1980s Jewish Underground and advocate of what would be called redemptive Zionism, said about the Oslo process several months after the signing of the agreement, "Visionaries have seen their vision ripped asunder before their eyes." This is a classic expression of what, in the business of millennial studies, we call millennial disappointment. This did not fit the script. Something was not working the way it was supposed to. Following such disappointments, there arises an impulse to put history back on the right track, which is a very dangerous impulse.

This kind of philosophy provides an intense motivation and a mythic reading of history. It contradicts the original Zionist impulse to engage in pragmatic politics, and it is, I would stress, only *one* Jewish response to Middle East politics. However, it is one that bears some uncanny resemblances to Christian Zionism as well as carrying the seeds of a collision with Christian Zionism. Christian Zionism is a product mainly of a theology known as pre-millennial dispensationalism. Since the 19th century, this philosophy has had its own version of how the millennium will come to be, how the end will come. In contrast to many earlier Christian theologies, it dropped the aspect of trying to predict when the end would come by using such sources as the Book of Daniel because it argues that we are now living in what is known as the mature age, which defies biblical predictions because it was not supposed to happen. Why was it not supposed to happen? Because history was supposed to end at the time of the first coming but the Jews did not accept Jesus. So says pre-millennial dispensationalism. So the entire idea that we have not yet reached the end is blamed upon the Jews. At the same time, rather interestingly, the theology asserts that God is still in covenant with the physical Jewish people, and therefore, at the end of days, as the Bible says, the Jews must return to their land, create their kingdom and build their temple on the Temple Mount. The Jews become what the dispensationalists often refer to as God's timepiece, and this creates an incredible fascination with what Jews are doing.

The Balfour declaration, the establishment of Israel, the war in 1967—each increased the expectation that the Second Coming was near because prophecy was coming true. However, the desire to see Jews fulfil these prophecies—to hold on to the land of Israel, to build the temple—are all seen as vehicles in a Christian drama. The stage is the same, the characters are the same, but the script is different. We can see the same thing going on in popular Islamic writings of recent years; just switch to the third side of the stage, and identify the same characters and events which are important for the end time. The person who is labelled the Jewish anti-christ in one drama is the messiah in another and the false messiah in Islam in a third script.

Christian Zionism asserts that it is pro-Judaism and pro-Israel, but at the end of the script, Jews must die or convert. Popular promoters, people who insist that Christians support Israel more than the Jews do, tell me in the same breath that the Second Coming will be worse for the Jews than the Holocaust. This is a strange attitude to take for someone who claims to be an ally of the Jews, and an even stranger attitude for someone embraced by some Jews as being their ally. The Jews become actors and characters in the Christian myth, not people with their own beliefs, not people who are making their own choices. Christian Zionism therefore, becomes a rejection of Jews as normal people in history. It supports hard-line policies of the Israeli government, not for the benefit of Israel or the Jews, but to realize the scenario of Armageddon in which blood will flow as high as a horse's bridle in the Holy Land, and the Jews will be destroyed. Arabs and Palestinians, by the way, tend to become little more than stage props in this round. Actions and politics themselves are measured neither by their pragmatic outcomes nor by their ethical outcomes, but by their mythic outcomes.

Therefore, how does an alliance take place in this situation? There are two bases for the alliance between some parts of the Israeli right and the Christian Zionists. One is that particularly among the religious, on the Jewish side as well as on the Christian, there is a certain resonance, a certain similarity between the ways of looking at the world, even though the details are different. More importantly, though, this is a classically instrumental relationship. It is a relationship in which each side is involved with the goal of gaining something to the detriment of the other side. It is a relationship that is seen to be necessarily short-term. Each is pleased by what the other does but assumes that the other is acting mistakenly. There is a combination of a proclamation of friendship and a profound disrespect running through this alliance.

On the basis of this analysis, and to sum up, we can make at least some preliminary statements. First of all, I would reject the idea of Christian millennialists being Zionists. Second of all, I would reject the view that these people are supporting Israel in a deep sense. They are not interested in the welfare of the Jews. They are certainly not interested in the welfare of the Jews in the most pragmatic sense. I would argue that the thing that is most in the interest of Israel is reaching a peace agreement, but such considerations simply do not figure in the schemes of Christian Zionists because their goal is not peace in a pragmatic, political sense. It is to bring the end. The assertion that Christian Zionists very often make is that there can be no real peace until the second coming takes place, and therefore, we wait until then and simply serve a holy purpose. I do not believe that is a perspective which is interested in serving the State of Israel. I would argue further that any real Jewish-Christian dialogue must begin with both sides taking off the lenses of myth, the spectacles of myth and looking at the others as real people, as creatures of God. The Jews must cease to be actors in a Christian drama; they must become believers in a different religion, not as mere rejecters of Jesus, not as vehicles toward the end, not as re-enacting the crucifixion.

To turn away from the sad history of interfaith relations, each side needs to look at the other people as people, not as mere pawns. And finally, I would argue that we must reject the seductive power of millennial politics. We must drop the stirring drama of the end for the immediate issues of today by facing their practical and, particularly, their ethical costs and benefits. To quote the American Jewish political philosopher, Michael Walter, "We must seek not to get to a perfect place, but to get to a better place."

BREAKING DOWN THE IRON WALL: REFLECTIONS ON NONVIOLENCE IN PALESTINE/ISRAEL

Alain Epp Weaver

To discuss "strategies of nonviolence" requires that one tackle an interrelated set of questions.[1] First, what is the goal to which nonviolent action is to be directed? Nonviolent direct action, after all, can be employed by a wide variety of people—including Israeli settlers—for a wide variety of ends. Second, what sustains our commitment to nonviolent methods of action? Third, what is the context in which we seek to be nonviolent actors? As a non-Palestinian, I am very reluctant to preach about or hold forth on the "strategies of nonviolence" that Palestinians should adopt. Nonviolence, if it is to be effective and powerful, should emerge from the energies and creativities of those in the conflict, and Palestine has been blessed with several creative and visionary practitioners of nonviolence, many of whom are based in the Bethlehem area and are present today. The only justification I can venture as to why Sabeel asked me to address the topic of "strategies of nonviolence" is that the Mennonite Central Committee, the organization for which I work, has been privileged to accompany many of these groups and individuals in their work. Recognizing the limits of my ability to speak to questions of strategy, I'll confine my remarks to the questions with which I began: first, by briefly noting the theological and Christological foundation of nonviolence as a practice and vision of reconciliation; second, by contrasting this practice and vision with the "iron wall" strategy of

---

[1] This paper was originally presented as part of a panel discussion on "strategies of nonviolence." The panel was held the day after the targeted killing of Hamas leader Abdel-Aziz Rantisi by the Israeli army. More than one person suggested to me that, given the violence of the previous day, I would undoubtedly have to rewrite my presentation. To my mind these suggestions were misguided, failing to grasp that the struggle for justice, peace, and reconciliation is a long-term struggle, and that the nonviolent struggle must therefore be informed by a theological vision and by historical knowledge that endure beyond the daily violence.

Zionism from Ze'ev Jabotinsky through to Ariel Sharon; and finally, by discussing the challenges and promises involved in confronting the iron wall.

I shall begin with the good news, the proclamation to the church at Ephesus of the peace and reconciliation made possible in Christ Jesus: "For he is our peace; in his flesh he has made both groups into one and has broken down the dividing wall, that is, the hostility between us" (Ephesians 2:14, NRSV). Here we have one of the great peacemaking texts of Scripture, speaking of a practice and vision of reconciliation between two peoples, Jews and Gentiles, with the stories and histories of those once divided by hostility but now reconciled in one body. The difference between the two is not erased by this reconciliation: peace is not about homogenizing or obliterating difference, but rather about breaking down dividing walls of hostility and about the formation of bridges and bonds between those who remain different.[2] The Ephesian vision is incarnated whenever the dividing walls of injustice, oppression and violence that fuel hostility are brought down, and opportunities for a shared existence made possible. For those of us here who confess Christ as Lord, I believe it is hard to find a more compelling image for the peace and reconciliation toward which nonviolent action should be directed. For Muslims, Jews, and others, different images will, of course, be more compelling.

Now contrast the Ephesian vision with the political program outlined by Ze'ev Jabotinsky, the leader of Revisionist Zionism in the early decades of the 20th century and the spiritual ancestor of the Israeli Likud party. In a 1923 article entitled "The Iron Wall," Jabotinsky wrote that "We must either suspend our settlement efforts or continue them without paying attention to the mood of the natives. Settlement can thus develop under the protection of a force that is not dependent on the local population, behind an iron wall which they will be powerless to break down." The colonization of Palestine, Jabotinsky understood, was a unilateral action, one that would have to be imposed on the indigenous population. Until the native Palestinian Arab population accepted the Zionist goal of creating a state with a Jewish demographic majority in

---

[2] For a perceptive study of Ephesians that complements my reading of how the Epistle addresses peace and reconciliation, see Thomas R. Yoder Neufeld, *Ephesians* (Scottdale, Pa: Herald Press, 2002).

most or all of Mandate Palestine, the Zionist movement would have to depend on unilateral actions.[3]

The construction of the "separation wall" and Ariel Sharon's "disengagement plan" should be understood as late developments in a Jabotinsky-style iron wall strategy that Israel has been implementing for over 55 years. The nine-meter concrete walls and zones of patrol roads, razor wire, and electrified fences did not simply emerge from nowhere. Rather, they function as a blunt continuation of a long line of legal and physical walls that Israel has erected against the Palestinian population. Consider the legal barriers erected by Israel to prevent the return of property and proper restitution to Palestinian refugees and internally displaced persons (or "present absentees").[4] Or consider the legal and planning barriers Israel erects to deny Palestinian citizens of Israel land for urban expansion.[5]

Following its conquest of the West Bank, East Jerusalem, and the Gaza Strip in 1967, Israel has been erecting legal and physical walls aimed at trying to solve its dilemma of wanting control over all of the occupied territories while simultaneously excluding Palestinians in those territories from political life, a dilemma of wanting territorial control without jeopardizing demographic control. The left and the right of the Israeli political spectrum (not counting the far left) have favored Israeli control over all of the "land of Israel," with the religious right viewing "Judea and Samaria" as the biblical heartland and with the secular left and right considering control of the Jordan Valley, the aquifers of the northern West Bank, and large areas around Jerusalem and the western

---

[3] Ze'ev Jabotinsky, *Writings: On the Road to Statehood* (Hebrew) (Jerusalem, 1959), 251-260, quoted in Avi Shlaim, *The Iron Wall: Israel and the Arab World* (New York: W.W. Norton & Company, 2000), 13-14. Jabotinsky advised that "the only way to achieve a settlement in the future is total avoidance of all attempts to arrive at a settlement in the present" (quoted in Shlaim, 14)—the insistence of contemporary Israeli politicians that "there is no partner" can be understood as a way of avoiding a settlement based on international law in order to impose a settlement more to Israel's liking upon the Palestinians.

[4] For a useful overview of Israel's policies and attitudes towards Palestinian refugees, see Nur Masalha, *The Politics of Denial: Israel and the Palestinian Refugee Problem* (London: Pluto Press, 2004). The Badil Resource Center for Refugee and Residency Rights in Bethlehem has produced an impressive body of research on how incorporating refugee rights of return and property restitution into peace agreements makes them more durable.

[5] For a study of Israeli restrictions on Palestinian land use inside Israel, see Hussein Abu Hussein and Fiona McKay, *Access Denied: Palestinian Access to Land in Israel* (London: Zed Books, 2003).

edge of the West Bank to be strategic military assets. Outright annexation of the West Bank (not to mention the Gaza Strip), however, has not been an option for the major Israeli parties, as annexation would mean that the Palestinians in the conquered territories would become Israeli citizens, endangering the Jewish demographic majority in the state.

The Israeli dilemma since 1967, then, can be understood as a struggle about how to maximize control over all of Mandate Palestine while minimizing the number of Palestinians under its direct control. Israeli military and political leaders have forwarded various plans that would minimize Israeli responsibility for Palestinians in the occupied territories by granting some form of "autonomy" to those Palestinians in specific enclaves: the Allon Plan, which would have created northern and southern enclaves in the West Bank, separated by Israeli-annexed territory from Jerusalem to Jericho and up and down the Jordan Valley; the "Village Leagues" plan of the late 1970s that would have granted semi-autonomous status to Palestinian cities in the West Bank; and, most recently, the Oslo Accords, in which the newly created "Palestinian Authority" was given semi-autonomous control over portions of the West Bank and the Gaza Strip.

To repeat: the separation wall now being built throughout the occupied territories, and the accompanying disengagement plan, are best understood in this historical perspective. The wall will allow Israel to maximize its control over the occupied territories while avoiding any responsibility for the Palestinian population from which it separates itself by walls and fences: enjoying the fruits of occupation without any of occupation's responsibilities. The wall will function as a means of demographic control.[6] Ehud Olmert, former mayor of Jerusalem and a

---

[6] Israeli political scientist Yossi Alpher observes that, for many Israelis, the wall appears "to offer a means of at least mitigating" what Alpher calls "the demographic threat." Arnon Soffer, a professor at Haifa University, argues that, counting foreign workers inside Israel and non-Jewish Israeli citizens, Jews are already a minority in the land from the Jordan River to the Mediterranean Sea, and believes that the wall is a key tool in creating and maintaining a space where there is Jewish hegemony. It is difficult not to describe a situation in which Israel rules over all of this land while denying citizenship rights to nearly 3.5 million Palestinians as one of apartheid (a "separation," an exclusion, of Palestinians from political life). In such a reality, some Israeli Jews have voiced fears of a binational reality emerging. Avraham Burg, a leader in Israel's Labor party, states "I am not afraid of weapons and terrorism. I am afraid of the day that all of them [the Palestinians] will put their weapons down and say, 'one man, one vote.' " Israeli public opinion researchers Ephraim Yaar and Tamar Hermann found that "The strong desire for a separation, even a unilateral

leader of the Likud party, outlines the goals of this "unilateral solution" with characteristic bluntness: "To maximize the number of Jews; to minimize the number of Palestinians; not to withdraw to the 1967 border and not to divide Jerusalem."[7] This formula, which apparently now has received US approval, means the *de facto* annexation of large settlement blocs around Jerusalem (Gush Etzion, Ma'ale Adumim, Givat Ze'ev), in the northern West Bank (the Ariel bloc) and the Jordan Valley. Palestinians will be left with discontiguous cantons, cut off from key water resources, cut off from Jerusalem, cut off from each other.

That Ariel Sharon and George W. Bush can talk about these pieces of land being a future Palestinian "state" should underscore that statehood is not an end in itself, that a Palestinian "state" in and of itself is not a solution to the conflict. It's not that we as Christians should be for or against a Palestinian state, or an Israeli state, but rather for a politics of justice, peace and reconciliation in which Palestinian and Israeli alike might sit under his or her own fig trees, real and metaphorical, without fear (Micah 4: 4). For many years now, a majority of the proponents of peace—Palestinian, Israeli, and international—have thought that a two-state solution, with a Palestinian state in all of the West Bank, East Jerusalem, and the Gaza Strip, could meet the demands of justice and make peace and reconciliation possible. But what if it becomes increasingly clear, in the face of the walls being erected and in the face of official US approval of the *de facto* (if not *de jure*) annexation of settlement blocks, that a two-state solution is being or has been eclipsed?[8]

---

one, is connected to a fear among the overwhelming majority of the Jewish public regarding the emergence of a de facto binational state." The separation wall, in this context, can be viewed as an attempt to keep such a binational state from emerging. See Yossi Alper, "The Fence Affects Demography, Too," *Bitter Lemons* (12 Jan. 2004), distributed electronically; Arnon Soffer, "Time is in the Palestinians' Favor," *Bitter Lemons* (12 Jan. 2004), distributed electronically; Avraham Burg, quoted in interview with Ari Shavit, "On the Eve of Destruction," *Haaretz*, 14 Nov. 2003; Ephraim Yaar and Tamar Hermann, "Peace Index/Demographic Fears Favor Unilateral Separation," *Haaretz*, 7 Jan. 2004.

[7] Quoted in David Landau interview with Ehud Olmert, "'Maximum Jews, Minimum Palestinians," *Haaretz,* 14 Nov. 2003.

[8] The recent United States' backing for Sharon's disengagement plan is but the most recent example of how the United States has served as a "dishonest broker" when addressing the Israeli-Palestinian conflict. For key studies of U.S. policy towards Israel and the Palestinians, see Naseer H. Aruri, *Dishonest Broker: The U.S. Role in Israel and Palestine* (Cambridge, MA: South End Press, 2003); Donald Neff, *Fallen Pillars: U.S. Policy Toward Palestine and Israel since 1945* (Washington, D.C.: Institute for Palestine Studies, 1995); and Kathleen Christison, *Perceptions of Palestine: Their Influence on Middle East Policy* (Berkeley, Ca.: University of California Press, 1999).

The Ephesian vision versus the iron wall, or, as Pope John Paul II phrased it, bridges instead of walls: that is the alternative facing the Holy Land today. The iron wall has, strangely enough, produced a distorted version of the Ephesian vision: the walls and fences meant to divide Israeli from Palestinian are, by solidifying Israeli territorial control over all of Mandate Palestine, binding Palestinians and Israelis more tightly into one body. There is, after all, only one sovereign power between the Jordan River and the Mediterranean Sea, Israel, a sovereign power that denies rights of citizenship and other basic human rights to 3.7 million Palestinians. Thus, there is one political body, but with walls and fences of hostility dissecting it; one body, but without reciprocity and reconciliation between equals. The alternative suggests itself: one political body for two peoples, or the binational state. But how to get there?

Ariel Sharon has boasted, "The Palestinians understand that [the disengagement] plan is, to a great extent, the end of their dreams, a very heavy blow to them."[9] For those Palestinians who refuse to quit dreaming, and for those Israelis and internationals who dream with Palestinians of a future in which Palestinians and Israelis will live in justice and equality in the land, the question is how best to counter the ideology and practice of the iron wall. An increasing number of Palestinians, I believe, are answering, "Nonviolence."

Ayid Murar from the village of Budrus near Ramallah, a village that has been at the forefront of nonviolent protest against the separation wall, perceptively observes that nonviolent action can empower a broader segment of the population than can violence. "We have to bring the entire Palestinian people into the struggle against the occupation," says Murar, "women, children, the aged—and they cannot take part in a violent struggle. But they can take part in this kind of struggle, which also contributes to the unity of our nation. We also know that a nonviolent struggle puts more pressure on the Israelis," he continues, noting that, while soldiers know how to respond to armed attacks, they are caught off guard by nonviolent protest.[10]

The daily protests in Biddu, Budrus, Beit Surik, and many other villages have been inspiring and galvanizing, even though the predictable Israeli stigmatizing of nonviolent protest as "terrorism" has been

---

[9] Quoted in Aluf Benn interview with Ariel Sharon, "Down in the polls—but not down in the dumps," *Haaretz*, 7 April 2004.

[10] Quoted in Aviv Lavie, "Back to the Grassroots", *Haaretz Friday Magazine* (16 April 2004), 7.

depressing. That after years of roadblocks, curfews, economic siege, and daily violence, Palestinian communities are finding the resources to organize to try to stop bulldozers from uprooting trees and clearing the path for the wall is truly a testament to God's Spirit at work to bring blessing and hope in the midst of destruction, apathy, and hopelessness.

When speaking about nonviolent direct action in Palestine, it is important not to minimize the challenges before those communities who gather to face the bulldozers. In the summer of 2002, residents of villages such as Jayyous and Falamiyeh in the Qalqilyah district were organizing to try to stop the uprooting of their trees and the construction of the separation barrier on their lands. Now the wall has been in place for nearly a year. In October 2003, the Israeli civil administration of the military government announced that non-Israelis would require a permit, issued by the civil administration, in order to enter the "seam area" between the wall and the 1949 Armistice Line or the Green Line. This meant, for example, that villagers in Jayyous would have to obtain a permit if they want to work land on the other side of the wall. Vigorous discussions ensued within communities whose lands had been segregated by the wall. Should people try to negotiate the hostile, Kafkaesque bureaucracy of the civil administration in order to try to get a permit to pass through the gates in the wall? Or should they refuse on principle? The idea of refusing to apply for a permit in order to access one's own land has a moral purity and power about it that is undeniably attractive. But I would certainly hesitate before criticizing a farmer whose entire livelihood depends on accessing his land for applying for a permit. As it is, only a small percentage of farmers in Jayyous and other affected communities have managed to obtain the required permits, and most fear that it is only a matter of time before Israel begins confiscating land behind the wall on the pretext that it is not cultivated.

Were the nonviolent protests in Jayyous two years ago then for naught? Will the protests in villages around Ramallah and Jerusalem be for naught? Aziz Armani from Khirbata, one village near Ramallah where the wall is going up now, suggests not. "The main thing," he says, "is that we feel we are doing something—if not for ourselves then for the coming generations. Even if we are able to get the fence moved two meters and save a few meters of our land, that will be something."[11]

---

[11] Quoted in Aviv Lavie, "Back to the Grassroots", 7.

Armani's words might seem to provide little comfort and hope, measuring success in the nonviolent struggle in getting the walls and fences moved a couple of meters, saving a little bit of one's land from the bulldozer's teeth. In addition to the construction delays and the adjustments in the wall's path that nonviolent action has managed to affect, however, there is a longer-term reason for hope, even if this hope might at times appear faint. Over the past few months, Israelis, at the invitation of Palestinian communities, have been joining with Palestinians in nonviolent attempts to stop the uprooting of trees, to halt the wall's seemingly inexorable path of destruction. In addition to whatever short-term successes these Israelis and Palestinians chalk up, I would suggest that, in their shared work for justice, they offer signs of hope for the future. Perhaps Israel's iron separation wall will be quickly dismantled, and a two-state solution based on a withdrawal to the Green Line will still be possible; the United States' blessing of Sharon's disengagement plan, however, makes this exceedingly unlikely. Determined not to resolve the conflict, Israel looks to manage it through iron walls, and one fears that with its military might and American backing, it will succeed in the medium term. (Five years? Ten years? Longer?) The walls and fences and the apartheid-style reservations they create will not, however, succeed in the long term. The question is what will replace them. The shared struggle of Palestinians and Israeli Jews against injustice and dispossession in the present embodies the Ephesian vision of the breaking down of the dividing walls of hostility, and thus offers a sign of hope for a shared, binational future in Palestine/Israel. May such signs increase.[12]

---

[12] While Israeli Jewish and Palestinian supporters of the one, binational state solution remain minorities in their respective communities, their numbers are growing. Israeli historian Ilan Pappe poignantly suggests that the future lies not with those who would suggest yet another partition, but with those who look for coexistence in one state. Pappe puts the matter bluntly: "The tragedy of Palestine is that the next peace plan, whenever it appears, will also be based on the false assumption that peace means an Israeli withdrawal to its 1967 borders and the establishment of a Palestinian state next to it." Ilan Pappe, *A History of Modern Palestine: One Land, Two Peoples* (Cambridge: Cambridge University Press, 2004), 267-268. In addition to the many writings of the late Edward Said, see the following for defenses of the one, binational state future: Mazin B. Qumsiyeh, *Sharing the Land of Canaan: Human Rights and the Israeli-Palestinian Struggle* (London: Pluto Press, 2004); Meron Benvenisti, "Which Kind of Binational State?", *Haaretz,* 20 November 2003; Tony Judt, "Israel: The Alternative," *The New York Review of Books* 50/16 (23 October 2003).

NON-VIOLENCE AS A STRATEGY FOR STRUGGLE AND METHOD FOR PEACE-MAKING

Zoughbi Elias Zoughbi

Allow me to share with you the following story entitled "The Smarting Dervish":

> A dervish was sitting peacefully by a river, when a passerby saw the bare back of his neck and yielded to the temptation to give it a resounding whack. He was full of wonder at the sound his hand had made on the fleshy neck, but the dervish, smarting with pain, got up to hit him back.
>
> "Wait a minute," said the aggressor. "You can hit me if you wish. But first answer this question: Was the sound of the whack produced by my hand or by the back of your neck?"
>
> Said the dervish, "Answer that yourself. My pain won't allow me to theorize. You can afford to do so, because you don't feel what I feel." [1]

It seems that we are the Smarting Dervishes. We have no time to theorize since we are trying to survive and always should be on the alert. Yet I highly appreciate the invitation to give a paper so I have time to reflect. As much as there should be time for action, there should be time for reflection.

Many Palestinians have conducted a non-violent campaign against the Israeli occupation, on the personal, NGO, political party, community, and country levels. According to Gene Sharp, the director of the program on non-violent sanctions at Harvard University's Center for International Affairs, there are three classes of methods in conducting non-violence:

---

[1] Anthony De Mello, *The Song of The Bird*, Image Books, Double Day 1982, p. 35.

1) Symbolic forms of non-violent protest
2) Non cooperation
3) Intervention

Palestinian non-violence drew on the first two methods and on the third through international diplomacy, governmental as well as citizen's diplomacy.

There are two major aspects of non-violence in the Palestinian struggle. First, there is the non-violence of the Palestinians in Occupied Palestine and in the Diaspora, and second, there are the political routes and diplomatic channels. Non-violence is a commonly misunderstood term. By non-violence, I do not mean passiveness, weakness, or surrender. Rather, it is an empowerment and an ongoing struggle that requires inner strength and perseverance.

In my view, it is the most effective way of ending the occupation. I can summarize my bias towards non-violence in the following points:

First, as a Palestinian, I believe violence dehumanizes human beings. Therefore, through non-violent struggle, we find the common ground among Judaism, Christianity, and Islam in their belief that human beings are created in the image of God.

There are currently four types of violence influencing the lives of the peoples of this land. The most talked about is insurgent violence, carried out by nationalists and others who have opted to revolt against the occupation, siege, and oppression inflicted upon them for more than 37 years.

But the Israeli government and settlers are carrying out the other three forms of violence against the Palestinians. Structural violence, environmental violence, and state sponsored violence are all part of the system being used to continue to subjugate the Palestinians to the *de facto* apartheid that is currently in place.

Second, through non-violence we not only seek the liberation of our nation but also seek the liberation of our enemy by alleviating Israeli fears of an inevitable Palestinian state. As the educator Paulo Freire says, "Only power that springs from the oppressed will be sufficiently strong to free both." When we consider the dehumanizing acts the Israeli government has asked its army to perform, such as beating, maiming, killing, terrorizing, and torturing, we must think of the repercussions these sanctioned actions will have on the future of Israeli society. What kind of citizens will this generation of soldiers make? And, if this policy continues, how many subsequent generations will learn to be racist and to deal with fear and anger through violence?

We are like sitting ducks in a shooting gallery. I can only affirm what the Dutch Father Henri Nouwen, says: "Our great task is to prevent our fears from boxing our fellow human beings into characterizations and to see them as persons."

Third, given Israel's nuclear arsenal, at least 300 nuclear warheads and a very complicated defense strategy, there is little hope of defeating Israel by war. The second *Intifada* shows the futility of using arms, especially when the Israeli reaction is more brutal and conducted in a more damaging fashion. However, with the Palestinian commitment to non-violent struggle, there is no way that Israel can maintain the status quo and obliterate the Palestinian national identity. Israelis must eventually accept the inevitability of change. Non-violence should address these facts in order to pave the way for coexistence, whether in a two-state solution or a bi-national democratic state. Let me draw your attention to the appeal signed by 70 Palestinian intellectuals and officials that was published in the local Palestinian newspaper, *Al-Ayyam*. It calls upon our people to take the initiative and rise again in a wide-ranging peaceful and popular *intifadah* with clear aims and sound speech. Such initiatives are increasing as they are adopted and acted upon by many persons, NGOs and some political parties.

Fourth, in the first uprising, non-violence achieved what violence has not been able to achieve. Palestinians have gained world sympathy for their cause, recognition that occupation is no longer viable, and affirmation from more than one hundred nation-states recognizing the right of Palestinians to have their own state. Some might argue that the armed struggle of the first decade (1964-1974) of the Palestinian revolution put the Palestinians on the world map. One cannot deny that historical background, but being on the world political map is not enough. We need to foster our existence on the geographical map. Will the Second *Intifada* echo the gains of the First *Intifada*? That is the question that poses itself persistently.

Fifth, based on the experience of previous and present popular struggles, I believe that non-violence will foster our relations with peace-loving people who can be mobilized to support the unarmed oppressed in the light of the atrocities and brutalities of the oppressor. This simply illustrates our vision of a new world order based on peace, economic growth, social justice and ecological balance. Although the situation of the world community is bleak, we are cautiously hopeful: "We have an incurable malady called hope!"

Sixth, non-violent strategy can help us address Israeli society by working with those who cannot tolerate the unjust acts of their government. Hundreds of signatories are already on the Ometz LeSarev (Courage to Refuse) declaration. There are different groups who activate themselves, like IDF widows, Yesh Gvul, Gush Shalom, the Israeli Committee against House Demolitions, Ta'yush and others.

According to a brochure circulated in North America by the Refuser Solidarity Network, there are more than 1200 objectors including 27 Israeli air force pilots and 13 reservists in the Sayeret Matkal Commando Unit. Let me salute the five young men, Noam Bahat, Adam Maor, Haggai Matar, Matan Kaminer and Shimr Zameret, who have refused to take part in military action in the Occupied Territories. As a matter of fact, in January 2004, they were sentenced to one year in prison in addition to the year they have already spent.

Palestinians can raise the awareness of Israelis and break down stereotypes, but only Israelis themselves can change the policy of their government. Therefore, I agree with Amos Givrtz, an Israeli peace activist, that Israeli people are advised to become more active in preventative non-violence. In the midst of rising extremism among the Israeli right wing, Israeli peace activists need to be more affirmative and assertive in their struggle to rid themselves of the burden of being occupiers. Because of the Palestinians' unique position, they can liberate Israeli society from dehumanizing, abusing and degrading itself.

Seventh, we see ourselves as members of the world community and are aware of the international impact of the Israel-Palestine conflict. We also realize the need for international support. Opting for non-violence requires the support of others across the world to exert pressure to fulfill our aims. This support would complement local strategies. We need to expose the Israeli government's atrocities. The world community needs to act and respond more efficiently. Indeed, the apartheid regime in South Africa would not have been dismantled nor would East Timor have its independence without *collective responsibility* in taking action.

Eighth, we should not be dragged into the swamp of violence into which Israel is trying to place us. As Nelson Mandela put it, "It is always the oppressor, not the oppressed who dictates the form of struggle." Despite this fact, Palestinians should heed the words of Napoleon: "Never do what your enemy wants you to do, if only because he wants you to do it." Through its daily provocations, Israel tries to push us to use greater violence, precisely because the Israeli government is well equipped to deal with violence. It seems that the Israeli government is threatened more by thoughts of peace and non-violence than by war. Their whole system is trained for war; they are not well equipped to face peace.

Ninth, an honest broker, an objective arbitrator, an even handed mediator, a third party is essential. We need a jump-start to move away from the deadlock of the peace process. This requires three dimensions of joint non-violent struggle: the Palestinians need to continue their proactive struggle to get rid of the Israeli occupation; the Israelis need to affirm and enhance their preventive struggle to rid themselves of being occupiers; the third-party pro-justice groups need to raise awareness among their constituencies to gain leverage over those in power so that they succumb to the international will by resolving conflicts through the channels of government, citizen diplomacy and UN resolutions.

Let us not postpone the inevitable. I strongly believe that war, violence and negative diplomacy are combinations of actions that delay the inevitable. Inevitability says that we can live together either in two states or one bi-national democratic state. This could be a model solution that renders justice, restores hope, alleviates fear, heals trauma, and increases potency for co-existence and economic growth. This inevitability will not occur without radical changes from within our societies and a resounding wake-up call.

The strategy of waging peace should replace once and for all the strategy of waging war. Yes, we opt for non-violence. Nevertheless let me share with you some of the challenges that might impede our march towards non-violence:

How can people as a whole be convinced to adopt non-violence as a way of life and a strategy taking into consideration the following realities?

1. the intransigence of the Israeli Government
2. the appalling imbalance of power
3. the media bias toward Israel
4. the lack of direction of the Arab and Muslim governments and societies
5. the politics of Uncle Sam which speak and act upon the equation of "might makes right."
6. Hizbullah's resistance, which has sped up the Israeli withdrawal from South Lebanon.

We must also consider the following realities:

—UN bodies, which could act as a better broker and more objective mediator than one country alone, have been marginalized and alienated. Europe also looks impotent in creating a more understanding, effective policy in the Middle East.

—The West is still held hostage to feeling guilty. Therefore, perpetuating the Israeli mentality of victimhood and enhancing the guilt feeling of the West are very dubious approaches which are used to silence prophetic voices and actions against the Israeli occupation. Will the West ever be liberated from such manipulative burdens?

—Efforts are required to strengthen global networking to fight against injustice. The challenge is how to build globalization at the grassroots level since, "Any injustice anywhere is injustice everywhere." Can the forces striving for change, peace, justice and transformation empower each other and work together so that they ultimately will emerge as the parallel power to multinational corporations and capitalism?

—We are not expecting or even asking the world to bring

Israel to its knees, even if we find no sincere efforts to bring the Israeli government to its senses.

—We are looking for a new spirituality which deals with the etiology of hate and finds a suitable remedy for it. I am looking for a spirituality of transformation on the personal level, community level and cross-cultural level. Such spirituality satisfies the needs of all parties concerned. We need to address the issues of fear, psychology, history, and education in a more daring way by emphasizing constructive approaches to dialogue. Arms of Dialogue should replace Dialogue of Arms. This kind of spirituality requires from us a shift from blame, guilt, and victimhood to collective responsibility.

In conclusion, allow me to share with you a story illustrating true spirituality:

The master was asked, "What is spirituality?"

He said, "Spirituality is that which succeeds in bringing one to inner transformation."

"But if I apply the traditional methods handed down by the masters, is that not spirituality?"

"It is not spirituality if it does not perform its function for you. A blanket is no longer a blanket if does not keep you warm."

"So spirituality does change?"

"People change and needs change. So what was spirituality once is spirituality no more. What generally goes under the name of spirituality is merely the record of past methods."

THE AFRICAN-AMERICAN EXPERIENCE

Damu Smith

Well—Amen!

First of all, let me tell you what I am not. I am not a biblical scholar. I am in training in the Congregational Church to do ministry. I am already in ministry and have been in ministry for many years, doing the work that I do for justice and peace. Last night it was difficult for me to sleep, thinking about yet another act of violence, on top of all the violence that people in this Holy Land are currently experiencing. And I kept saying to myself over and over again, "What shall I say, what shall I say today, to God's people?" And I think what I wanted to say from the outset is that we really must have a sense of urgency about what we are called to do. We *must* have a sense of urgency. And part of spiritual leadership is to properly define the moment we are in so that we comprehend and understand what we must do in the present situation, for every generation is called to determine what to do in its time, even as we borrow from and connect to history to comprehend lessons to help us move forward.

I am looking at where we live in the world house that Dr. Martin Luther King talked about, this world house, and then I look at one of the rooms in the world house—there are lots of rooms. Every room represents a nation in the world house. There is a big room that I live in, that those of us from the United States live in. That's the room of the house currently under the domination officially, of George Bush, with all of his minions, all of this evil, with all of this danger that comes with all of the evil that his policies represent. This is the most dangerous regime ever to ascend to power in the history of United States of America. It is dangerous because they want war, they want to bully people to make war; they want to bully nations. They do not want to listen to people, not even to their own allies. They proceed with arrogance, unilateralism, domination, an attitude of "I'm bigger than you, I'm more powerful than you so I'm going to stomp on you; I want to do whatever I want to do no matter what anyone else says." This is the mindset of this administration, and it is dangerous.

So what do the people of God do when one member of the house, and in fact, the whole house, is being pushed around by one of the other members of the house, this big superpower in the world? Before I address this question and the response of the people of God in this period, I want to go back to the historical context and experience out of which I come as an African American, as an African-descended person, because we African-descended people come from a global community of African people who have experienced racism, who have experienced colonization, who have experienced race-based apartheid in South Africa, in Zimbabwe. We come from a people who have experienced the transatlantic, genocidal slave trade, the murders and brutal institution of slavery in the Americas, the lynchings and violence and terror from white supremacists in the United States, church burnings and church bombings and murders at the hands of racist organizations. We know something about the quest for justice. And we—except for Condoleezza Rice and Colin Powell—we tend to see things a little differently. Not because of any genetic predisposition, but because of our historical and current experiences. When we see the Palestinian people, we see people who have been oppressed as we have been oppressed. We see people who have been dispossessed; we understand dispossession. Not only have we been dispossessed, but we witnessed the genocide against the indigenous peoples at the hands of the colonizers who came to America.

Why am I cantering on this history? Because I think it is important for me and for all of us to connect spiritually to those who had to make that difficult voyage and who laid the basis for what we must do today. Coming out of that African-American experience, we developed a theology of liberation born of our experience. One of our gifts to the world is the African-American and Negro spiritual, "Steal Away, Steal Away". When we were singing songs to Jesus, they had a double meaning in the middle of the night because we were trying to come out of slavery. We were trying to escape white domination. So the black preachers crafted a theology of liberation, coming out of the whip and the lash and the sting of slavery and all the brutality and pain that it represented.

We did not understand God in the same way that the slave master understood God. The slave master wanted us to worship God and remain slaves. Our people said, "No, no, no. Our God is a God of righteousness, a God of liberation, a God of truth, a God of freedom." So we developed a theology, a language and music, our gift to the world, to move us out of slavery, and we used that to take us into the next period of Reconstruction, through the period of lynchings and Jim Crow and the development of our non-violent movement.

And we have the prophetic voice of Dr Martin Luther King, a Nobel Peace Prize Winner, one of the most incredible theologians the world has ever produced. Howard Thurman, Nat Turner, Sojourner Truth, and Harriet Tubman—all of these names are names of African-Americans who resisted slavery and racism but held on to the Biblical Scripture to keep the faith and the vision for a new reality and a new society. It was an African-American question. The question of what to do with African-Americans was the reason the US Civil War was fought. It was a critical issue that wise thinkers like Fredrick Douglass and others brought to Lincoln, who said, "If I can abolish slavery and keep the Union together, I'll do that. If I can keep slavery and keep the Union together, I'll do that—whatever it takes." Lincoln wasn't passionately against slavery. He was passionate about keeping the Union together. He was a politician. Black people were saying, "Wait a minute! Don't you know who we are? We can help you maintain the union, but without slavery!"

Many people going to school today in America do not understand the contributions that African-descended people have made to what vestiges of democracy we do have in America. We have been collectively criminalized as a people, which is why we understand the collective criminalization of the Palestinian people by the Israeli government. We have been there—we have been profiled, we have been stereotyped. As a black man in the United States, no matter how I dress, on any day if I am driving a car, a police officer will pull me over quicker than a white man because of the badge of my skin. I cannot take it off. So my colour has become my designation. For Palestinians their Arab-ness has become their designation. This is a racist society in which we find ourselves. Christians need to say that boldly and without fear. We need some truth telling. "Ye shall seek the truth, and the truth shall set you free." We cannot be shy about truth telling. Truth telling paints the picture, truth telling illustrates, truth telling puts it together so we can understand what we are looking at, and whether we want to buy the picture or not.

I am saddened by what I've been hearing and seeing here in Israel. People here are being suffocated in a most despicable way. And the world still does not know the truth the way it ought to. What must we do under those conditions? Go tell it on the mountain. Go tell it! Shout out what Israel is and what it is not; don't be afraid! I'm telling you, I'm leaving here, and I'm better prepared, I don't know about you, but I'm going up to the mountain. And I'm telling it, and I'm shouting it. The Palestinian people need their liberation now. Not gradually, not tomorrow, not whenever Bush and Sharon decide they ought to have it but when they want it and they want it now. We must say it.

Sometimes we can be so pathetically shy about truth telling, because we're afraid to offend. But in this equation, it is always, "We do not want to offend the Jews." But wait! Palestinians exist, too. We offend the Palestinians when we shy away from truth telling. We offend the dignity of people who are already humiliated, disenfranchised, dispossessed, living under colonialism, living under official state terror. Yes, it is state terror. Every day.

I detest the tactics of Hamas. But, if we contextualize the actions of Hamas, we do not detest them in the same way Bush and Sharon detest them. There are different ways of detesting, because you have to understand what drives people to do what they do. Any form of injustice is like a serious cancer in the precious spiritual body of the human family. Like medically diagnosed cancer, injustice throughout the world is a treacherous disease on the body politic and morality of God's people, requiring urgent and radical action and attention in order to heal the human family. Injustice must not only be arrested, but it must also be prevented. MLK said injustice anywhere is a threat to justice everywhere. So as Christians, we must do battle against injustice wherever we see it, wherever we find it, wherever it rears its ugly head. We must go after it, root it out.

Now as Christians on this side of the faith, we have got to work for justice with a new attitude, a new disposition, a new vigour and spirit of the faith because justice is an urgent question. It is not something to be passive about. You have to be pro-active about justice. You have to be excited about justice; you have to feel it in your bones, in your feet, in your blood, in your hands. Clap for justice! You know the people on the other side, these people whom we call zealots? Well, they are zealous about what they believe in! When are we going to get zealous about what we believe in? I am excited about the possibility of experiencing justice, so every day I wake up in the morning with my mind stayed on freedom, as the Negro spiritual says. It is in me; I want to live my day for justice. Justice in my personal life, in my personal relations with people, justice between me and my little daughter, justice with my friends and family, justice in terms of how institutions should be.

Isaiah 61: 8 says, "For I the Lord love justice." It doesn't say, "I like it." I love it! "I hate robbery and iniquity." I hate robbery. It doesn't say I hate the person who is doing it. I hate robbery! That is passion. Verse 10 of the same chapter goes on to say, "I delight greatly in the Lord. My soul rejoices in my God, for he has clothed me with garments of salvation, and arrayed me in a robe of righteousness." I delight greatly in the Lord, the Lord of righteousness, the Lord of freedom, the Lord of justice, liberation, truth, revolution in many instances. "The Spirit of the Lord," the Bible says, "is upon me, because he has anointed me to preach good news to the poor." Really listen to that statement. "The Spirit of the Lord"—the Spirit that Jesus was carrying around this land—calls us to preach good news.

When you read the four gospels of the Bible, it is like reading an action flick. Jesus was everywhere, healing people, feeding people, trying to clothe people. Jesus was doing all these things. It was an exciting time in Jesus' ministry to the poor and oppressed. Hence, "The Spirit of the Lord is upon me, because he has anointed me—anointed *us* -to preach good news"—the news of liberation, truth, justice, freedom. No slavery. No occupation. None of that! That is good news we are anointed to carry to the poor: "He has sent me to bind up the broken-hearted." I have a mission here. I have been sent to bind up the broken-hearted. I have been sent to proclaim. You do not proclaim stuff by being passive. You proclaim things by proclaiming. Proclaim! Proclaim! Proclaim "freedom for the captives and release from the darkness for the prisoners. Proclaim the year of the Lord's favour." That's insane stuff! So when you read that next time, do not whisper in a low, bored voice, "The Spirit of the Lord is upon me."

I watch these electronic preachers. They are preaching! These televangelists come at it with passion. They have schools. Not just any kind of school. I read an article in the *New York Times* about Jerry Falwell and how he trains his students to debate on television. They research issues, all the issues that they care about and they learn about them. They have debating contests. They go around the country competing in debating contests. Where are our debaters being trained in that way? They are happy about what they believe in. But this is what we are up against. That is why I think we need to challenge ourselves about what we have to do. I have learned so much and am so eternally enriched by the presentations at this conference and am just so happy that we are here. But, faith without works is dead. The papers and statements do not mean a lot unless we get the Spirit of the Lord anointing us.

Psalm 101 says, "I will sing of your love and justice." Singing refers to really singing! "To you, O Lord, I will sing praise." When we sing about the Lord, we are singing to the Lord of justice, not just any God. Psalm 103 declares, "The Lord works righteousness and justice for the oppressed." That's what the Lord does. So when we say we are singing of God's love and justice, we are singing to the Lord, we are singing praise, we are singing of the Lord's righteousness and the justice he has for all people, oppressed people. Psalm 140 too says, "I know that the Lord secures justice for the poor and upholds the cause of the needy. Surely the righteous will praise your name and the upright will live before you." You know Micah 6:8: "He has shown you, O man, what is good, and what does the Lord require of you?" He doesn't say, "What does the Lord suggest to you?" "What does the Lord *REQUIRE? To act justly and to love mercy and to walk humbly with your God.*"

Now, we have another problem within our own community. Too many Christians and too many Christian pastors and preachers focus almost exclusively on the phenomenon of individual sin. Now, let me be clear. We must do that. We have to clean ourselves up on the inside so that we can better function on the outside. I am very clear that we must have a passion and emphasis on dealing with individual and personal sin. But this is where the problem comes in. Even those of us in the progressive Christian church have this problem. Very little is said on Sunday morning about societal and institutional sin. You know it is true. The reason why I know it is true is because I travel extensively around the United States, around the country. I go to churches all the time. I am in there listening. People talk about, "He is worthy to be praised." Why is he worthy to be praised? Why should we sing, "He is worthy to be praised"? He is worthy to be praised for what is described in the four gospels and not just for the love parts of the Bible that we might want to select so we can encourage people to accept their condition and stay the way they are so they can come back to us, and we can feel their pain and have consultations and counselling sessions with them but they are still in pain. A lot of the pain is caused because they are unemployed, they do not have money, they are poor, they are homeless. They are coming to us for counselling, but our counselling is not going to bind their wounds if societal and institutional sin—that is, the corporate murderers and the government institutions that enact the evil, unjust, oppressive policies that put them in the condition that they are complaining to us about—are not addressed. Radically addressed.

It is not enough for Christian churches to have soup kitchens. That is good. It feels good, but we do not want people to come to our soup kitchens. Some preachers do for other reasons that I will not go into right now. I am very serious about this. We have to challenge ourselves on what the role of the church is. The nearly exclusive focus on individual, personal sin disarms and bifurcates Christians and Christian theology. It neutralizes our ability to focus on the need to serve as Jesus served in the context of conducting a justice ministry that genuinely and effectively serves the masses of oppressed people. The exclusive focus on individual sin neutralizes our ability to focus on the grand injustices that help give rise to so much of the individual sin that we see. The things that aid and abet individual sin are things like the occupation of Palestine, colonization of peoples around the world, slavery, rape as a weapon of war, mass violent genocide, sexism, racism, apartheid, war, militarism, corporate and economic exploitation of workers, the use of nuclear weapons, the creation of nuclear weapons—all of these things are instances of societal sin. Can the preacher talk about them?

Is it not interesting that the kinds of policies which create massive conditions of poverty, hunger, death, disease, environmental destruction, suffering and misery get so little attention on Sunday morning in our churches and throughout the rest of the week? I will never forget a young woman I saw in a restaurant. I was giving her a flier about coming to a peace rally and after she had completed her dinner, she angrily gave it back to me and said, "I don't want that. That's political." My goodness, sister, did you read the Bible today? Jesus was about peace and about justice. But this is the problem, you see, because churches do not want to think that peace is political. Peace is spiritual. No, peace is about life. Under such conditions of oppression, oppressed people often act out. They rob. They steal. They do whatever is necessary to survive. And that is why it is the poor and oppressed people of the world who languish in the prisons of all the nations. None of the poor and oppressed who overflow the prisons of nations possess or wield the kind of economic, political or military power which creates or sustains the wretched conditions under which they live. Yet they are the ones who are branded as dangerous, dysfunctional, lazy, irresponsible, stupid. They are the people who are stereotyped, marginalized and disenfranchised. Not the rich who plunder the world. Not the rich who wage war. Not the rich who pay workers less than a minimum wage and force conditions of slavery on people around the world—workers in the most unsafe, unsanitary conditions throughout the world. But my friends, if you have read the Bible carefully, you know that these are the people Jesus spent most of his time with. These are the people, Jesus reminded his disciples, who were to take priority in their lives.

So theology has been used to disarm, but Christian theology has also been used to justify racism, slavery and oppression. That is why historically, sadly, tragically, in many instances Christians and the Christian church have been partners in the oppression of people; the residual effects of that history still remain. The colonizers came to Africa with a Bible in one hand and a gun in the other telling Black people, "You must submit to me. You must be a slave. You must be oppressed." We rejected that as part of our struggle. So what must Christians and people of God do in this time of crisis? Especially what must people of God be doing in these times of crisis when empire building, military threats, occupation, bully-ism, extremist ideology, arrogance, and targeted assassinations are all part of the world today. What must we do?

Certainly, we must engage in strategies of non-violence. It is easy for people outside of Palestine—and I am not going to mention any names, but someone from my community came over here some few months ago and told Palestinians, "You would do better to use non-violence in your struggle." I am not saying that was bad advice at all, but here is my caution. It is easy for those of us who live outside to tell people inside to be non-violent. Now, I want to be clear—I am for the non-violent struggle. But Israel's policies do not make it easy to be non-violent in Palestine. So, if we want the Palestinians who desire to be non-violent to be non-violent, and if we want to encourage them, then internationally we have to organize politically for their protection. Because we cannot depend on the IDF. We cannot depend on Sharon, the mass-murderer and butcher of the Middle East. We cannot depend on Bush, who is leading mass-murder around the world. It is up to us. The non-violent movement cannot grow inside Palestine unless there is an international movement of solidarity at the level and of the kind that was produced for the people of South Africa at the height of the anti-apartheid struggle. It was through the international solidarity that was developed around the apartheid struggle that the United Democratic Front and other organizations under the leadership of the Most Revd Desmond Tutu and Revd Allan Boesak and others were able to grow and flourish. In large measure they flourished because the global anti-apartheid movement provided them with political protection.

But that is not enough. We can come here. We can stand in front of bulldozers. Important! We can come here and we can be at the checkpoints as international observers. Important! But in the United States it is our job, in Britain it is our job, in France it is our job to organize a solidarity movement that pro-actively, aggressively stands in solidarity with the just struggle of the Palestinian people against racism and occupation and not be afraid to cry it out.

Dr. Martin Luther King took Matthew 4 and 5 and Isaiah 61:1-3 and transformed them into a strategy of non-violent action by African Americans against Jim Crow racism and segregation. Read Matthew 4 and 5. What we see there are lessons for how the non-violent movement must act, but also we have to understand that in every situation, it cannot be exactly the same. Dr. King used the Beatitudes, and the non-violent movement used the Beatitudes to give Black people self-esteem. You know, when you are living under racist oppression, you do not always feel self-esteem. "Blessed are the poor in Spirit, for theirs is the Kingdom of Heaven. Blessed are those who mourn, for they will be comforted. Blessed are the meek, for they will inherit the earth. Blessed are those who hunger and thirst for righteousness, for they will be filled." All these things were used in the non-violent training sessions to prepare us when we were going to face those dogs, and those billy-clubs and those hoses and those rifles of the Klan.

And then we were given strength by the saying, "You are the salt of the earth. You are the light of the world." So, Black people, oppressed people, understand what is wrong. "You are the light of the world" no matter how many times they put you down. "For I tell you, that unless your righteousness surpasses that of the Pharisees and the teachers of the law, you will certainly not enter the Kingdom of Heaven." Do not stoop to their level. Do not curse them back. Do not be mean and mean-spirited like they are. Do not strike back. Love your enemies so that you do not debase yourself. Do not fall into temptation and sell out. Jesus did not sell out when he was in the wilderness. He did not compromise his principles when the Devil came to him. That is what I want Colin and Condoleezza to understand.

So, my brothers and sisters, we must leave here, come out of this city with a new attitude, this city which represents so much of what the struggle is about. Isaiah says, "For Jerusalem's sake, I will not remain silent. For Jerusalem's sake, I will not remain silent until her righteousness shines out like the dawn, her salvation like a blazing torch." (Isaiah 62: 6). "I have posted watchmen on her walls, O Jerusalem. They will never be silent, day or night. You who call on the Lord, give yourselves no rest." Let me repeat that, "You who call on the Lord, give yourselves no rest." Do not get sleepy. "Give him no rest until he establishes Jerusalem and makes her the praise of the earth." If we are going to make Jerusalem and Palestine, this part of the world, the praise of the earth, we must be the watchmen. We must never be silent. We must not rest from doing what God requires, and from serving as Jesus served.

We must go out today saying we are going to build a new house, a new world out there, beautiful and lovely. It is going to be the beloved community. And it is only going to be that community if we are warriors for justice, if we are true Christian soldiers, not soldiers who want to kill and maim, but soldiers who want to heal and tell the truth. In the process, we must do what the former head of the Christian right, Ralph Reed suggested: "We're going to go and find every Bush supporter. We're going to go to their house. We're going to put them in a van and we're going to take them to the polls." That is the attitude. We are not going to win, those of us from the United States—we are not going to defeat the politics of Bush, and get Bush out of the office, unless we understand just one more thing.

This is my last, final point. We have to understand what these polls mean when we see them. Why is it that 95 percent of African American voters in the United States are against Bush, 75 percent of Latinos are against Bush, 95 percent of Native Americans are against Bush, and when you poll white people, they are divided? Is it because white people are somehow genetically problematic? No, but white people have issues. I am generalizing and I say this in love. In the United States, the reason why so many white people wrap themselves unconditionally and uncritically around the red, white, and blue is because of the racism that blinds them from seeing the world the way that they ought to see it, so Bush can collectively criminalize Palestinians, collectively criminalize Iraqis, and racist people will go and rally around the flag. That is wrong. We must struggle against racism. I want my white brothers and sisters in America and all around the world to understand. We cannot defeat the politics of Bush unless we also confront the politics of racism and the attitude of racism. So let us go to all four corners of the earth, preaching the good news, preaching the gospel with zealousness, with enthusiasm, with energy and with love. God bless you.

NONVIOLENCE AS A LEGITIMATE MEANS TOWARD PEACE

Mubarak Awad

Nations that use armed struggle inherit dictatorships.
Nations that use nonviolence inherit democracy.

After a long exile enforced by the Israelis, coming back home to a conference in Jerusalem produces in me very special feelings as well as an opportunity to see old friends, to learn, and to share with internationals our efforts to use nonviolence in our struggle to end occupation. These efforts are continuing in the present by a younger generation who are educated to take us to a better future. It is gratifying that the nonviolent methods that we have been using for more than 20 years in the struggle for justice and peace in Palestine are catching on.

Now, we continue our dialogue about the challenges of Christian Zionism. The work of Naim Ateek and Sabeel in developing a theology of liberation for the tiny number of Christian Palestinians who have remained steadfast in the Holy Land and who have a goal of promoting harmony between Jews, Muslims, and Christians deserves attention and gratitude.

Even in the worst times of brutal military occupation by the Israelis, the thing which has kept us going is our spirit of resistance, an overwhelming spirit of endurance. You have heard our grief and you have seen our pain and felt our sorrow; we want you also to see our joy. Nonviolent action has not been a casualty of the conflict but is becoming stronger, spreading to towns and villages throughout the entire region. To my delight, nonviolent struggle has also become the talk of the Palestinian Authority.

Religious fundamentalists, Christian Zionists, even Muslim Zionists—oh, yes, we have them—may be very different from one another in many regards. However, they have the same mentality of using religion for their political, financial and personal aspirations and using the name of God to do the hurting and the killing for which generations to come will suffer.

The term nonviolence has been used in many ways. It has been used to describe pacifism, a lifestyle, a set of beliefs, an instrument of power, a strategy for liberation, and even a method of achieving economic empowerment. Here, we refer to nonviolence as a means of effecting lasting change and resolving conflict. Nonviolence motivates people to act justly and ethically and to demand just and ethical action, particularly by those in power, without resort to causing physical harm. The first premise of nonviolence is never to participate in anything that is immoral, and from that position to speak truth to those who would wield power.

Plato sets forth this principle in *The Republic,* as exemplified by Socrates' refusal to take part in unjust action. There is an injunction to act morally and not to be silent in the face of injustice. Each of us must develop our own morality from within, even though all of us have a duty to assist others and the community at large in the development of a collective reality by sharing and discussing our own views. Nonviolence is action based upon principle that is undertaken in a tactical way so as to make the moral point effectively. It is not based on religion, yet it requires a religious zeal and self-discipline to be successful. Many have been attracted to nonviolence in the name of religion. For example, consider the Quakers, Mennonite and Brethren churches, as well as Sufism in Islam.

Nonviolence as proposed by Henry Thoreau and Ralph Waldo Emerson and as used by Mahatma Gandhi asserts that violence is always wrong and should never be undertaken for any purpose. Just what constitutes violence is a complex question. Clearly, killing people or inflicting serious injury is violent. Other physical, social, political, economic or psychological actions may also be deemed violent, depending upon their intent and effect. The ultimate aim of nonviolence is to achieve justice and moral interaction among people without doing violence. Ideally, all human interactions should be built upon a basis of mutual respect and understanding in which all parties see themselves as members of a community soul or mind, regardless of whether they are members of the exact same community as defined in the usual political and sociological sense.

The relationship between the principle and the practice of nonviolent action is always intended to have an effect. Occasionally, the action itself may directly or indirectly cause the desired end, as when a demonstration convinces Israeli political leaders to change their course of action. Most often, nonviolent action is a catalyst in building moral and political support for changing social and political policy. Socrates made his moral point effectively by his willingness to die for his principles. Gandhi's march in an attempt to take over the salt monopoly of the British peacefully finalized the end of the British occupation of India.

Tactically, nonviolent action is often provocative. It puts the Israeli military in a double bind. If the nonviolent act is allowed, it makes its point, and the movement gains strength. If the Israelis resist, particularly where they resort to violent means, the relative justice of the actors and injustice of their opponents is magnified, bringing considerable political gain to the activists.

Many factors are involved in the effect to be produced by any action in Palestine, but perhaps the biggest factor is how open Palestinians are to a particular action and to the general principle or movement to which it relates. How will an action be perceived? One needs to consider carefully where Palestinian people are now and what affect a given course of action may have. From that essential standpoint, it is not enough just to act on principle. The greatest concern in the long run is what impact an act may eventually have in moving consciousness forward.

The history of nonviolence in Palestine has yielded seven principles of nonviolent struggle:

1. An education process is needed to bring attention to the history of nonviolence in the lives of Palestinians, Muslims and Arabs in general, such as the six month strike in 1936 that even Gandhi spoke about. During the Egyptian nonviolent movement to quickly dethrone their monarch, King Farouq, not a single Egyptian died. Abdul Gaffar Khan, a Muslim from the Pathan province in India, joined Gandhi in believing that Islam is a nonviolent religion and he wanted all the Muslims to join the Gandhi movement. His life story was translated into Arabic and distributed in Palestine and the Arab and Muslim world.

2. Nonviolent methods and practice are not an imported concept from the West or the East. Their use is practical for each and every person who is willing to work for justice without the use of arms or any means of killing.

3. Symbolic forms of nonviolent protests such as vigils, marches, and flying of the Palestinian flags are important.

4. The ideas of this movement must be brought to Palestinians in every village and every refugee camp so that young people know they have a choice in developing strategies and using nonviolence as part of their operation. Also, the concepts of nonviolence can be spread by giving seminars to the leadership of the PLO and by continuous sharing of certain methods that can be implemented in order to reach peace.

5. Non-co-operation must be employed, including social boycotts, economic boycotts, labor strikes, and many forms of political non-co-operation, ranging from civil disobedience and refusal to pay taxes to campaigns to promote eating Palestinian products and the use of Palestinian goods, even cigarettes.

6. Contact must be made with Israeli groups who are interested in peace, and partnerships should be formed with them so that both sides can see the humanity and fear of the other as well as the suffering.

7. Nonviolent interventions, ranging from hunger strikes to the establishment of self-reliant institutions, nonviolent occupations and blockades, and even the establishment of a rival parallel government, should be used. During the first *Intifada*, Palestinians, without the Palestinian Authority or any government, established NGO committees that joyfully took care of the needs of many Palestinian people and helped establish a common feeling that all persons have to meet their responsibilities in order for each community to take care of its own needs.

Nonviolent strategy has a long history with varying degrees of success. Success sometimes has come through changing the minds and attitudes of the opponents, but that is rare. More often, partial success has been achieved through accommodation (gaining and giving up part of one's objectives). Nonviolent strategy has also demonstrated its capacity to produce nonviolent coercion of the opponent so that no alternative remains but to capitulate. At times, the opponent's regime has even disintegrated in the face of massive repudiation and paralyzing non-co-operation, as was the case in the "animal March", in which protestors requested permission from the Israelis to include animals in a march to protest the Israeli confiscation of sheep, goats, and other animals from their owners because they were feeding on land taken for Israeli target practice.

Nonviolence strategy has been waged in recent years in many parts of the world including Mexico, Chile, Korea, South Africa, Palestine, Israel, Sudan, and various parts of the former Soviet Union, Poland, Hungary, Burma, Brazil, and China. Historically, nonviolent strategy has wielded significant power in conflicts when applied skillfully and has often been met with serious repression by the opponents. That response is recognition of its power. In fact, the brutalities of repression against nonviolent resisters trigger a process of "political jiu-jitsu" which increases the resistance, sows problems in the opponents' own camp, and mobilizes third parties in favor of the nonviolent resisters.

A dear friend of mine, Afif Safieh, who is the Palestinian General Delegate to the United Kingdom and to the Holy See wrote a letter to the Pope on March 30th, 2004, which begins:

> I am writing to you because of my belief we should not allow the situation in the Middle East to further deteriorate and I wish to appeal to you, Holy Father, to hopefully intervene. President Yasser Arafat has been immobilized for about 3 years incapable of moving out of what remains of his compound in Ramallah. Besides the humiliation it constitutes to the entire Palestinian people to see their democratically elected President so besieged, this Israeli policy has deprived the Palestinian National Movement of the person who has been its locomotion for so many years. At a moment when a healthy debate is taking place within Palestinian society about a possible reorientation of the Palestinian struggle towards popular non-violence, we all are, more than ever before, in need of President Arafat to regain his freedom of movement."

My point for a long time has been that a strategy of nonviolence needs to be endorsed from top to bottom. If Arafat had adopted nonviolence and if all Fatah groups were to follow now, we could have a higher moral aspiration and belief in the result. We can accomplish a great deal by our full, unrelenting commitment to non-violence. Other tenets we must embrace:

1. We must support the Palestinian people to continue the struggle to get rid of the occupation because no people should be under another people's control. Even as high as the price of freedom can be, economically, physically, psychologically, we as Palestinians should continue to fight the Israeli occupation and not let the Iraq issue take a priority over our struggle. We should condemn the occupation of Iraq and show the Iraqis the power of nonviolence that we are engaged in.

2. We need to increase the numbers of delegations. First, we must have a delegation with noteworthy people like Mandela and Jimmy Carter or with 5 to 10 Nobel Peace Prize laureates to meet with Palestinians and Israelis together to promote peace rather than to prolong the conflict and to bring the conflict back to the media's attention. Second, a delegation of seasoned nonviolent activists must meet with leaders of the Palestinian Authority to promote the use of nonviolence as part of the struggle from both sides as well as from the top and from the bottom. Third, a broad-based delegation should meet with Palestinians as a reminder that we are not forgotten, that people around the world stand with us. We need to combat our feelings of hopelessness. This third delegation should meet with people in the refugee camps, business people, professors and workers.

3. We need to work on the media and public relations. At this time the Israelis are able to control and black out information. We need to suggest and request that Arab leaders regularly visit American, European and other international political leaders, officially and unofficially, while co-ordinating with us.

4. We need to have the church leadership once again assume the moral responsibility of communicating to their congregations about what is happening to the Palestinians and emphasizing that we are paying the price for their own bad deeds against the Jews. We have been doing it for more than fifty years and we will suffer more for you; just do not forsake us.

5. We need action on several levels, on the international level, on the Palestinian level and on the Israeli-Palestinian level. For example, let us have a monthly march to demand that the Israelis lift one blockade in

any place and then have a march of victory when they have done it.

6. We need to eliminate the divisions within the Palestinian community. We have divisions between Palestinians who came from Tunis, Palestinians inside the 1967 line, Palestinians who are in refugee camps as well as those who are in Gaza. We do not need the Israelis to dictate to us who we are.

7. We have to stop the divisions between the larger Arab world and Palestinians and keep uppermost in our minds that the biggest division is between the Israeli and Palestinian peoples.

8. We need to have local town meetings for Palestinians to express themselves and choose the kind of struggle they want, to discuss the consequences of that struggle and their expectations of the outcome of that struggle, and to define their goals and objectives. It seems that there is no leadership to lead the Palestinians into thoughtful decision-making. Unfortunately, it seems this has been true for the Palestinian Authority as well as the general leadership.

9. We need funds; nonviolence can't continue to be the activity of the poor. To make changes in lives of people and bring a just peace, funds have to be given in significant amounts to make a difference. If we had had funds in the first Intifada to implement all our strategies, we would have had a normal peace between us and the Israelis long before this time.

10. We all have different approaches as human beings about how to resolve the problems we face and some suggestions may be unique. Let me share some ideas that can change the thinking of everyone so that all can see the power of nonviolence. For example, here are some radical suggestions:

> —Let us burn all our belongings and commit ourselves to walk to the River Jordan, not looking back until we cross to the Promised Land which is ours. The refugees simply cannot wait for another fifty years and continue to endure their current suffering and degradation. Thousands and hundreds of thousands

of Palestinians from Jordan, Lebanon and Syria will be supported by Palestinians inside Israel as well as the Palestinians in other countries. Palestinian families with homes and resources can adopt an entire family so that they can survive and regain control of their lives. This is a huge commitment that needs a strategy: divide the miles of the Jordan River into many sectors so that each segment has sponsorship from churches, countries and individuals.

—Members of the Palestinian Authority should resign, all of them, and give everything back to the Israelis. The occupying forces will have to pay for our schools, hospitals and civil service jobs. The Israelis need to pay and know that occupation costs a lot of money. We will not lose and it will make things very simple. An Authority without authority is like a nightmare.

—The commitment to nonviolence requires the support of all Arabs. We need to export this commitment to nonviolence to the Arab masses and bring changes in Arab regimes everywhere.

—The Arab world and its leaders must realize how much of an influence and impact they can have on the Palestinian struggle. It is in the best interest of the Arabs to create flexible funding mechanisms. Funds can be used to wage a massive media campaign locally within Israel and Palestine as well as regionally and internationally. The campaign should highlight the life struggles of ordinary Palestinians and illustrate the relationships that can and must be forged between Israelis and Palestinians so that neither will once again mourn another son, a daughter, a brother, a sister, a father, or a mother lost to violence. Areas in Palestine that are the most affected should be the focal point for media campaigns.

—Another aspect of this campaign is for Palestinians to host more international conferences that welcome women, various religious organizations, academics, and students from across the globe. The relationships formed will reach across oceans and lands and create waves of support for Palestinians suffering and struggling on the ground. These international guests can also act as international observers as they see and hear for themselves the life experiences of Palestinians without the distortion of media censors. These people-to-people networks will unite us in peace and forge a psychological, political, and spiritual bond that no bullet, missile, bomb, or stone can replace.

—Palestinians should call for an *International Day of Solidarity* every Monday with supporters fasting for one meal that day and contributing the cost of the meal to the cause. The Palestinian struggle is an Arab struggle so let us not make it seem to be only a Muslim struggle. Places of worship would organize prayers on this day for the Palestinians. Teach-ins would be organized on campuses in the region and internationally.

—This struggle should also be the people's choice. Leaders in the legislature and Palestinian community should embrace this nonviolent campaign. This effort would encourage the Palestinian leaders to produce a "declaration" of what the people themselves want.

—The support of the civil society organizations at this juncture is of utmost importance. Local and international NGOs should continue their struggle to promote nonviolent means of bringing a real change in life and society for Palestinians and Israelis. This also means that the various NGOs themselves must act morally and ethically.
NGOs supporting the Palestinian struggle have confronted Israelis about the injustices done against Palestinians; however, when Palestinians inflict violence on other Palestinians, NGOs have remained quiet. For the sake of justice, NGOs cannot afford to be selective. Injustice is injustice no matter who the perpetrator is.

—Fortunately, nonviolent activities have been on the rise in recent months as Palestinians and supporters of their struggle, both locally and internationally, have protested, making their voices heard in a variety of nonviolent actions. These efforts can be complemented beautifully when open communication between Israeli and Palestinian is established. This is where real leadership begins. Palestinians must take the lead in opening channels of communication with Israelis. Palestinians should welcome Israelis who are speaking against and are calling for the end of the occupation. Trust building is of utmost importance here. Palestinians must take the chance to build trust. To succeed, Israel must reciprocate with good will.

Great satisfaction arose for Palestinians when elections took place to choose the Palestinian legislature and president; however, the rejoicing was short lived when the re-election dates passed by and the people lost their opportunity to participate in a democratic practice that makes a nation strong. Elections are sacred and so are election dates. The government should not make excuses to avoid these historic moments in time. These acts of avoidance were a betrayal by the Palestinian leadership. It was a sad moment in our struggle that destroyed pride and effort to work to end occupation. [*Editor's note:* Elections have since been held for both the presidency and for local governing bodies, with the election of the national legislature scheduled for early 2006.]

Elected officials and election organizers must respect the outcomes of elections. Even though they as individuals might have different viewpoints or preferences, elections should be sacred. Palestinian elections should also be free of pressure from the US and Israel. This means that tremendous trust should be given to the process. The process will bring about what people really and truly want.

We recognize that many people have lost their lives in this long struggle. We are confident that these sacrifices were not wasted. These lost lives have pushed the PLO into the occupied territories. The second *Intifada* opens the door to the establishment of an independent Palestinian state. But now, as we continue, this *Intifada* must be nonviolent. A moratorium on violence must be accepted and embraced by all parties involved.

As we look ahead, Israel should realize that there can be no real peace without Palestinian rights. For Israel to live in peace with the Arab world they must commit to the rights of Palestinians being respected and consistently implemented. We do feel that this land should not be treated by one group as if it is a gift from God to them and only them. Until the great majority of the Israeli public recognizes and accepts the rights of Palestinians to live in their homeland as equals, there will be no final solution to this conflict.

We should also remember that our struggle is not the only struggle. Some struggles have used arms and violence and some have been nonviolent in nature. As we look at history for guidance, we can learn from the tremendous successes of nonviolent struggles. There are many events in history that have used nonviolence as a legitimate means to alter the relations of power. We, as Palestinians, would be proud to count ourselves as the next victors of a nonviolent struggle. We want peace and we want our children to have a better life and a peaceful world; we must rise above hatred, fear or religious fundamentalism. We need not wait for the other side to stretch out their hands to us. We can create our future and make a new beginning. It can be done. Let us do it together.

RELIGION: PROBLEM OR POTENTIAL FOR TRANSFORMATION

Jean Zaru

I have struggled most of my adult life with issues of theology and liberation. And it has been life experience, rather than a library, that has served as my source of inspiration. My life experience has taken me to all five continents, where, over the years, I have been enormously enriched by contact with activists and theologians engaged in various struggles of liberation. Moreover, my life experience is deeply rooted in my identity as a Palestinian Christian woman.

As I have struggled on my journeys to affirm the presence of over twelve million Arab Christians in the Middle East and of the Palestinian people struggling for justice and freedom, new obstacles and pressures continuously reveal themselves. For liberal Christians, influenced by Holocaust theology, European history and guilt, I am, as a Palestinian Christian, NOT a part of their agenda. My very existence disturbs the balance, as if there were such a thing as balance in a situation of conflict and oppression. For fundamentalists, I am not among the chosen; rather, I am one of the cursed. As a Palestinian, I stand in the way of their understanding of the fulfillment of the prophecy of God. I cannot win! For it seems I am not a part of the theology of quite a few of my Christian brothers and sisters.

Nevertheless, my entire life has been affected, even encompassed by biblical teachings and interpretations. As a Christian, a Palestinian, a woman, an Arab and a Quaker, the teachings of western churches have influenced me personally, and my people collectively, in very specific ways. The use and abuse of the Bible in reflecting on the legitimacy, policies, and conduct of the state of Israel have become common, especially, but by no means exclusively, among conservative American Christians. They see a firm link between biblical and modern Israel. The history of condoning evil in the name of alleged biblical justification is, of course, a long one. Discrimination, oppression, dispossession, and war are often justified by references to biblical texts. In recent times, David Ben-Gurion referred to the Bible as a sacrosanct title-deed to Palestine for the Jewish people. In Jerusalem today, the so-called International Christian Embassy is a most overtly political supporter of Israel. Its publications proclaim that God gave the land to the Jewish people and, therefore, God will bless or curse nations in accordance with the treatment of the "chosen" people of Israel.

Zionism is responsible for the last 56 years of dispossession, dispersion and humiliation of the Arab population of Palestine. Palestinians now living in Israel, the West Bank and Gaza, as well as in the Diaspora, are well aware of their devastation, loss and expulsion. We experience daily the loss of our land and homes, and we continue to be denied our basic rights, especially that of self-determination. The Zionist dream has become our nightmare. In many international Christian circles anyone who opposes Zionism is considered to be either anti-Semitic or to be in opposition to God or God's plan—at least as they understand it.

Now let us focus on religion. In both its progressive and reactionary forms, religion has entered into and shaped almost every major conflict and crisis in the world today. On the progressive side, there are movements toward the radical alliance of the churches and other groups with the poor and oppressed. There are activist, feminist, reform and peace movements. On the reactionary side, there is narrowness and chauvinism, and patriarchy in every religious tradition. This easily allies itself with narrow and chauvinistic national and economic interests. When people speak about fundamentalists, some people speak of fanatic Muslims, forgetting that right wing religionists exist everywhere, not least in Palestine and Israel.

Religion is both a problem—or rather, *the* problem where its structures of dominance have oppressed us as Palestinians and as women—and also a solution where its vision of liberation and equality has generated powerful social and political movements for progressive change. The same religious tradition may be both a problem and a solution. It can be both a positive and a negative force. Let us just remind ourselves of the masses of participants in peace movements who demonstrated against the invasion of Iraq, and the mass movements working to end the Israeli occupation. Motivation for many derives from their faith, which is a spirituality that energizes the soul to provide what the world lacks. Spirituality plunges us into life rather than withdrawing from it. The greatest contemplatives were often our most active people. Dorothy Day, Martin Luther King, and Mahatma Gandhi were simultaneously visionary and contemplative.

Religion is one of the major sources of human rights. However, we must acknowledge from the outset that anti-human forces have also paraded under the banner of religion, claiming religious authority as a justification for all manner of inhumane actions. Water at its source may be pure, but it can get exceedingly muddied along the way. Let me begin by stating that I personally cannot take the Bible literally. It is my understanding that the stories in the Bible reveal people's perceptions of God but not the full reality of God. There are many narratives that are problematic, containing texts of unsurpassed violence. There are many passages that encourage ethnic cleansing, subordination of women and slaves, and some other very exclusive verses. My faith tradition, ethics and the religious value of equality contradict such texts. This understanding of religion is significant, both for me as a woman and for the processes of social and political change. Insight into religious issues is foundational if we want to rely on religion as a power for transformation rather than as a power for oppression.

For example, the religious exclusivists claim that their community, their tradition, their understanding of reality, their encounter with God is the one and only truth excluding all others. The inclusivists' response would be that there are indeed many communities, traditions and truths, but that their way of seeing things is superior to that of others. And when they include others, they include them on their own terms. The most ideal understanding of our religious traditions, if we are to provide peace and understanding in our world and our country is the pluralistic response. Truth is not the exclusive or inclusive possession of any tradition or community. These three attitudes, streams or ways of thinking are also social and political responses to diversity.

The exclusiveness of the rightwing religionists is reflected in marginalizing others who are different. The outcome of this is racism, sexism and violence to say the least. We see this exclusiveness in the practices of Israel, such as when they deny equal rights to those who are not Jewish. To accomplish the grand designs of Apartheid, we are imprisoned in our own towns and villages. Palestinian life is being undermined, not accidentally but by deliberate Israeli government policy. The adherents of all faiths should not be silent in the face of injustice, oppression, suffering or poverty. If they remain silent, then they themselves are disobedient to the imperatives of their faith.

My sisters and brothers, evil is evil no matter who is the perpetrator. If people of faith are to uphold the integrity of their religious teachings, then we must consistently condemn injustice, exploitation and oppression, arbitrary arrest, house demolitions, and the extrajudicial killings of activists and their leaders. Palestinians have been pushed to the periphery, outside the corridors of power. They have no one to champion their cause except the adherents of the different religions who understand their religion as a source of transformation, and other peace and justice activists who respond out of a sense of our common humanity. We must stand up. We must speak on behalf of the hungry, the homeless, the oppressed, and the captives. This was the mission of Jesus. If we fail to stand, if we fail to speak, if we fail to act, then our faith becomes irrelevant and devoid of purpose.

I am committed to the message of the First Coming rather than certain interpretations of the Second Coming. Allow me to explain. Once, in Kansas in the United States someone accused me of not accepting the theology of the Second Coming because I am Palestinian. I smiled and stated that exactly the opposite was true. That is, it would be easy as a Palestinian Christian to go home, put my feet up and say God will take care of it all. And yet, that would be contrary to my understanding of the reality of God. Such a theology does not respect Judaism, and it views Islam as a demonic, satanic faith. Christians who disagree with this theology are merely considered to be in the way. To champion the cause of the weak may bring the wrath of the powerful on those who act, but we should not let that deter us.

The way of transformation calls us face to face with the forces of death and evil, both within us and around us. Examples are not far from reach: war, threats of war, annihilation, famine, poverty, racism, sexism, global warming, deforestation and the despoiling of the earth. We have become aware that these have, to a great extent, sinful human causes as well as roots and legitimization in some of theological and cultural presuppositions of the modern world. These destructive causes and effects are interrelated.

The one word that describes best the complexity and relatedness of the world is "interdependent". Problems cannot be isolated one from the other and neither can be the people who hope to solve them.

Interdependence describes not only the relatedness of nations and economies, but that of people, religious traditions and cultures. People of faith can work together and form coalitions with secular activists to bring about conditions for the implementation and protection of human rights. For it is not only meaningless if we try to do it alone; it is unattainable. Simply, we need each other. Moreover, the formation of such networks is especially urgent today as we watch how anti-human forces have falsely paraded under the banner of religion, claiming religious authority as justification for all types of inhumane action.

If the divine glory is to be found today, it can surely be seen in the humanity and wisdom of those talented men and women whose experience of oppression and the ways by which they survive and even overcome such circumstances may inspire and embolden us all. There are countless ordinary people who rise out of grave constraints, out of unimaginable oppression and humiliation, to witness, through the living of their lives and the lifting of their voices, to the power of truth in their every day living. Our road to renewal is to be truth-tellers, not to cover-up. Cover-up is the tool of our contemporary culture; indeed, half truths and lies fill government halls, institutions and the media.

As Jeremiah declared, "They all deceive their neighbors and nobody speaks the truth; they have taught their tongues to speak lies" (Jeremiah 9:5). It is our duty to tell the truth, to uncover even our own scars and wounds. This requires great courage, yet it is the way by which we disarm the principalities and powers whose lies and deceit are fed by our silent cooperation.

I walk alongside many others in my journey of struggle and carry with me hope to move from oppressive and destructive power to liberating life-enhancing power. We should cease to seek, as women and as Palestinians, to simply transfer power from men to women or from the Israelis to the Palestinians. What we should struggle for is the transformation of our communities from:

> —Militarist, coercive power to the power of mutual trust;
> —From ethnic and religious exclusiveness to the celebration of diversity in mutual justice;
> —From racist and sexist discrimination to the protection of human rights and the humanity of all;
> —From neutrality and objectivity to compassion and ethically based priorities;

—From exploitation of nature to gentle cooperation with nature;
—From God above and power over to God within and power together;
—From death and destruction to resurrection and life.

Power would then signify the very positive relationship between God, human beings and the whole community of creation. Power is not a cake which diminishes the more it is shared. Power, when shared, is a relationship that enriches everyone. The great rift is not between God, human beings and the whole community of life. We all belong together. Rather, the great rift is between care and carelessness, justice and injustice, mercy and mercilessness, compassion and indifference. What divides us is not our differences but sin, oppression and injustice. Difference does not destroy creation; rather it is our sins of allowing oppression and injustice to be perpetrated.

To create a culture of life, we need more than psychology, spirituality and community. We need economics, sustainable agriculture, and a politics of liberation capable of healing our world and restoring the earth to life.

Many of you in church and human rights communities have inspired me personally in my journey of resistance and renewal. Let us continue to be steadfast in our work together, forming communities of hope in practice. Words rarely speak louder than actions and genuine commitments.

Throughout the ages, people have engaged in a universal search for meaning in life but have turned this search into a struggle for a particular ideology, religion or nation. Our age of unparalleled advancement in education, science and technology has been an age of enormous violence. Meanwhile, the need for imaginative understanding, simple trust and creative cooperation was never more urgent. Maybe the time has come when we should unite in common affirmations of life and these might be:

—A pledge of honor and respect for every race, culture, religion and individual;
—Recognition of the claim of every individual upon the resources of the earth for the necessities of human survival, and the moral obligation of the more fortunate to share with the less fortunate;

—The right and responsibility of every individual to use their talents, energies and resources for the benefit of the community;
—Commitment to the search for universal values, however differently expressed, in hopes that these values may enable both the individual and the community to overcome greed, power and self-seeking;
—Affirmation of the "presence", the presence of a spirit of hope and compassion available to all by which our lives may be more whole, more creative, and more harmonious as we draw directly upon that power around us, and within us and within all life.

We cannot live a day without saying "yes" or "no" for death or for life, for war or for peace. The choice is ours. There is no compromise on the matter. To postpone or evade decision is to decide. To compromise is to decide. There is no escape and this is our challenge and charge as true disciples of the prince of peace. Let us pray for the coming of the Holy Spirit to empower men and women for community from Jerusalem to the ends of the earth.

Lord, make us instruments of your justice. Make us instruments of your peace. Make us instruments for the renewal of your creation.

Thy kingdom come, thy will be done.

I would like to end with these words by Elizabeth Gray Vining:

> *The realization that there is a spark of the divine in every human soul draws together people of all races, all creeds, all nations, all classes. That is why war is evil and social injustice unendurable, why religion is incomplete without service.*

FEAR NO MORE

Abuna Elias Chacour

"Christ is risen!" "He is risen, indeed!"

While driving from the Galilee to Jerusalem, I asked myself, "What the hell are you going to do in Jerusalem? Haven't you had enough of going up there and being disappointed?" In fact we have never forgotten the experience of when our man from Galilee came to Jerusalem. We have never forgotten how he ended, in prison, tortured, crucified. We have never stopped talking about what happened to him afterwards, despite the will of all the authorities, despite all their wicked plans. Three days later he was raised, and it is for that reason that I come to Jerusalem to remember that we have something absolutely unique. We have an empty tomb, and we have a risen man. On one side it is our joy and on the other side, it is our pride, but it is mainly our responsibility to spread the news all over and to tell everyone that since he is risen, we have some good news to share that can be summed up with the following: for those in him there is no more privilege for Jew against Gentile. I wish that many Christians who are in love with a certain abstract idea of Zionism had stood up sixty years ago and said publicly, "There is no privilege for German against Jew." Where were they? And today we invite them to cry out: "There is no privilege for Jew against Palestinian," and "There is no more privilege for man against woman, lord against slave." Do you know why? Because we are all called to become adopted children of God, even you people who come to attend the Sabeel conference!

It is a very unique opportunity to have you receiving the message of local Christianity, of Palestinian Christianity, to listen to what we think, how we live our faith in that Lord, my compatriot, the man from Galilee. It has never been easy to witness for what happened in Jerusalem, but it seems it is increasingly more complicated, more difficult, to witness and speak about the risen lord. It is becoming even more difficult because of the immensely dangerous threat to the lives and the existence of the small Christian Palestinian community in the Holy Land, Israel-Palestine. What remains of the Christian community is the small remnant that represents approximately 25 percent of Palestinian Christianity. The rest, 75 percent, are in the refugee camps, in exile or self-exile. The 25 percent that remain in the Holy Land are disappearing day after day because they don't see any hope in the future and because they very often fall between the chairs of two fundamentalist groups who reject our language, who reject our lexicon. We cannot endorse violence. We cannot endorse home demolitions. We cannot endorse oppression. We cannot agree with terror, whether it is done by resistance or by state terror. It is only producing more horrible terror, and we are witnessing this ongoing procession of funerals on both sides, Israelis and Palestinians. If we ask the martyrs on both sides that are considered terrorists by the other side, "What do you want to say to us jointly?" they would say, "No more martyrs. It's enough."

In the past I was very puzzled about Christianity and proclaiming faith in Christ. I was confused to read the Sermon on the Mount. How could I go to Gaza and read "Blessed are you because you are hungry and thirsty for justice?" How could I go to Nablus and read, "Blessed are you because you want to become peace makers?" They would have no ears for me because they are convinced that they are not blessed. They have been cursed to be reduced to refugees, to be reduced to marginal people, to be reduced to something that every other person would reject. We inherited the label which has hidden the real face of our Jewish brothers and sisters before and during the Second World War. They were named "dirty Jew". Very few stood up courageously and said, "It cannot be true that children in Auschwitz are dirty." The dirt was somewhere else; it was in the Third Reich's doctrines. It is the same thing we Palestinians are hearing, that we are the "dirty Palestinians, the dirty Arabs, '*Aravi meluchlach*.'" We are the "Palestinian terrorists".

I don't need to convince people that we Palestinians are born with empty hands waiting for society to put something in those hands. I myself am confused about who I am. I am a Palestinian, a proud Palestinian. I have nothing to be ashamed of by being a Palestinian. I am a Palestinian Arab. (Many of you think that speaking Arabic is impossible, but Arabic is a very easy language to learn. Don't you believe me? Come with me to the school and you will see 4000 children.

They all speak Arabic. If they can, why can't you? Because you don't feel the need. I felt the need to learn English and I tried my best. A language is never difficult to learn. You need to be motivated. You need to feel the need to communicate and you will do it.) I'm also a Christian, as you might guess, and I have to say that I am also a citizen of the State of Israel. All these facets of my identity are very often in contradiction. I cannot forget that I was born in Biram, a village that was destroyed by the Israeli army. I cannot forget that I yearn to return to my village and to rebuild my father's house. That is my right. That is where I was born. That is where my family has had roots since the middle of the 16th century.

Once I had the pleasure of welcoming Shimon Peres at my school, Mar Elias Educational Institutions. I reminded him of the refugees from Biram who are waiting to return and that I am one of them. He spontaneously responded, "Father Chacour, when you left Biram you were eight years old. That was 50 years ago. Isn't that enough for you to forget that Biram is your home land?" I said, "Shimon, you left Palestine 2000 years ago, and you are back here to make our lives hell. When are you going to forget that Palestine is also your homeland?" He was modest enough to say, "I deserve such a reaction for my speedy reply."

As a Palestinian Arab Christian living in Israel, I wanted to organize some priority within the facets of my identity. As you might guess, I could not be first of all an Israeli citizen. I had a problem, at least one problem, with Israel. Israel is an entity of 56 years old. It did not exist before that. I am 64 years old. I'm older than Israel. I did not immigrate into Israel. It is Israel that immigrated into my country and reduced the larger part of my country, Palestine, into present day Israel. I wish Israel a long life. It is not the existence of Israel that is making problems for me and for my Palestinian brothers and sisters. Inside Israel the problem is the quality of that existence, my socio-political status within the Jewish state. Is it a Jewish state for the Jews, or is it a Jewish state for all its citizens? What we are working for is to convince our Jewish brothers and sisters that they are unable today to provide any sign of hope for humanity. They are unable to provide any sign of trust for the humanity that is waiting for that. Without the Palestinians inside Israel (and how many more in the occupied territories) the handicap will be worsening more and more. It is only together, Palestinians and Israeli Jews, that we can join hands together, not around a cup of coffee, but with equal rights on the same land. It is only then that we can say to President Bush, that we can say to Tony Blair and to many political leaders, that their theory of fear, mistrust, and terrorism is creating what they fear. They are creating the very monster they fear. It is time that you internationals listen to us; we bring you good news. We are together, Israeli and Palestinian. We want to live together. We want to share this land together. We want to be masters of our home together, and we want to serve together.

Today the international community is looking for some sign of hope. Political leaders have failed lamentably, whether in many of your countries or in our country. They have no word of hope, and we are urging them to listen again to the very small town of Beit Sahour, near Bethlehem, where the very important message came out to the world, "Fear no more. I bring you good tidings." Since we Christians are living after the resurrection, we know that the first message of Christ is, "Fear no more, peace be unto you, I give you peace." I am really eager not to speak to you, but to speak to the Christian brothers and sisters in the Bible Belt and to tell them that the Jews are very happy to have your money and to have your political support, but that they hate your guts when you speak to them about wanting to convert them to Christianity.

I wish I could speak to all of these people. My message to them would be that if they really and truly love the Jews (and I hope all Christians love them), the first thing they should do is to get in touch with the local Palestinian Christians, and to prove to the Jews that among Christians there is genuine love. The Christian Zionists refuse to be in touch with us. They're afraid to be in touch with us because we shall not speak about money; we shall not speak about power. We shall speak about man and woman being created in the image and with the likeness of God. Our Christianity can not be continually enslaved by political leaders. I wish I could speak to all these Bible Belt Christians who have created their own god. If we want to do anything today, if we want to declare war against those gods, if we want to declare war against self-made images of god, I wish that you would be our ambassadors and that you would speak courageously. We need to let God, the true one God, free from our own human categories and fantasies.

Don't give up. Sabeel is the way. Sabeel is an inspiration; Sabeel brought you here because you brought Sabeel to what it is. Don't give up. I think that the Lord is not so simple and so naïve. Don't you know that he will not judge us on how accurately we guess his return? He will not judge us on how many times we went to church on Sunday. He will not ask us how much we contributed to our church community. He will ask us a simple question, "I was hungry, naked, sick, a prisoner ... What did you do for me?" The Third World is going to judge us in front of God on human rights. I am afraid whenever I read what comes after the 8th beatitude, when the Lord says, "You are the salt of the earth." What does that mean? Are we trying to turn all the earth into a plate of salt that nobody can eat? Are we ready to disappear in order to give flavour to the food we give to others? "You are the light of the world." When I see five thousand Christian Zionists come to Jerusalem to dance on the streets while despising the situation of their Palestinian Christian brothers and sisters, I imagine they believe they are the light of the world. Palestinian Christians would tell them, "For God's sake, we know your power. Turn down your projectors. You're blinding us with your light."

I wish to tell everybody, and for those among you who are still not sure what is going on, that we have a serious problem in Israel. A baby is going to be born. The mother is pregnant. The name of the mother is Israel. The baby is Palestine. Israel is pregnant with Palestine, and we can feel how uncomfortable that pregnancy is for many Jewish leaders, including Prime Minister Sharon. They know that they are pregnant with Palestine. They wish they were not, but wishful thinking is not reality. So what do we do? Either we kill the baby and destroy the health of the mother, or we mistreat the baby and he will be born handicapped and will always be a burden on the shoulders of the mother, or we care for the mother and care for the baby so that he can be born healthy and love his mother and grow to be independent. We are going towards this experience of the birth of Palestine.

I hope that our Christian brothers and sisters understand that our small Palestinian Christian minority inside the Holy Land needs a smile of hope, needs an act of solidarity, needs you to come and visit and knock on the door (wherever there is still a door) and come in. Don't come with cookies. We don't need that. Don't come with pencils and pens to distribute to our children. We don't want them to become beggars. Come with something from your heart, a smile of friendship. Come and share with us what we have. And please convey to all your friends what we do to sustain life and the Christian presence in the Holy Land. We who are here are not a perfect community. We still need much prayer to be united among ourselves though not in denominations; we are all part of the Christ. Rather, we are looking for ways to express ourselves in a genuine way, and we do that in many places. If I have good news to announce to you, it is that on 21 October 2003 I was privileged to announce the opening of the first ever Arab Christian Israeli University. It is running now. No one will be able to kill it, but many are required to help its growth.

I would like to express a very special appreciation to Naim Ateek, a man of God who has always seen beyond his denominational affiliation. I want to express my friendship, my admiration, and surely my prayers for Naim, who has always been an example of a man of God who knows when to keep silent and when to speak out no matter what the consequences are. God bless all at *Sabeel*.

FAITH AS THE SOLUTION

Edmond Lee Browning

We were to have gathered in Bethlehem, the place where nearby the angels sang for joy, "Glory to God in the Highest and peace to God's people on earth." Although closed out of Bethlehem by military closure following the targeted assassination of Ahmed Rantisi, political spokesperson for Hamas, we gather seeking that peace. We are called to be peacemakers.

I greet you also in the name of the God of Abraham and Sarah, the God claimed by the three great religions: Islam, Judaism and Christianity. To give honor to God, these three faiths must be the solution, not the obstacle, to peace on earth. Need I say more? I needn't, but I'm a preacher, so I'll build a little on that basic message.

The depth of discussion and the commitment to justice in the Holy Land that has marked the proceedings of this conference make it an important marker on the road to peace. We are grateful to the Reverend Naim Ateek for the vision he has shown over these many years and for his faithful work through *Sabeel*, which has been such a blessing and sign of hope to thousands of people in different parts of the world as well as to the local community here. And we appreciate the efforts of the incredible team that organized and tended to the myriad details for the gathering.

Now we come together to offer thanks and praise to the God of the three faith traditions even though our worship is imperfect because of divisions among God's peoples. Clearly, the Christian community is divided between two views. One view would see God's plan being enacted through the return of the Jewish people to Israel, to be followed by Armageddon and the second coming of Christ. The other holds up a vision of this land based not on one interpretation of Scripture but on a God of justice as revealed in the totality of the Scriptures. How we will resolve this division among us is unclear, but the voice for justice must be proclaimed from our pulpits and shouted among the lands over all the earth because any vision that says God would bring about deliverance for one group of people at the expense of suffering and injustice to another group of people is just simply not acceptable Christian theology. It is, indeed, not of God.

We need to remember that Jesus was not born in Bethlehem so that he could start a new Church. He came to usher in the Reign of God for the whole world. And God's reign will not take root until we recognize that every human being is made in the image of God. We stand together to proclaim good news for all the people of this land. Not one must be left out.

For most Palestinians, there is rage and frustration beyond measure. None of us who are visitors in this land can begin to imagine the incredible suffering of the Palestinian people who live under such gross injustice every day. I salute their incredible humanity, which is assaulted but never defeated. The world community carries the burden of guilt for their continued oppression, none more so than the government of the United States of America. President Bush's letter of April 2004 giving away Palestinian land to Prime Minister Sharon underscores the US role as co-oppressor of the Palestinian people. None of us can escape responsibility for God's ultimate judgment. The so-called "Wall of Separation" is only one more travesty of justice added to the draconian measures that define the Occupation.

I was deeply pained to hear of the senseless death of George Khoury, a 19 year old Palestinian Christian whose family has close ties to *Sabeel*. He was shot by Palestinian militants while jogging in a Jewish neighborhood because they thought he was a settler. George was a wonderful young man who counted Jews among his friends and who was a sign of hope for a new day when Jews and Palestinians would find a life of harmony together to live as neighbors should live, even as sisters and brothers. This is a distant and hard vision for both the oppressor and the oppressed. But we have to remember it is the vision of God. The death of George Khoury encapsulates in many ways the foolish lack of vision of both the occupiers and those who think revenge is a solution.

Our challenge is to honor young George Khoury by a determination to bring about peace with justice in this land. His life must be redeemed by the peacemakers. We simply cannot allow either the Israeli or Palestinian people to be lost in a sea of violence driven by fanaticism that threatens to engulf the very souls of both peoples who lay claim to this land. Both the oppressor and the oppressed suffer damage to the soul. Both must seek the vision of God that sees a future built on justice, repentance, restoration, forgiveness and reconciliation.

George's death is but one more example that violence is not the answer—ever. It is a tool of evil. Violence is crippling the journey to peace. The extremists on both sides are driving events. There is, of course, a simple way to end the violence: End the Occupation! The Occupation itself is violence. And the Occupation is the root cause of all the violence today, including George Khoury's death.

There appear to be so many forces of evil arrayed against justice in this land that we must ask what the mission now is for Sabeel, for the Christian remnant in the Holy Land, indeed for the Christian community worldwide, for Jews and for Muslims, and for all the peoples of the earth. Everyone is called to a time of action in our respective homes. Those from overseas are challenged to meet with their government representatives to tell them that violence and hatred can only be defeated in this part of world by seeking justice for the Palestinian people. Seeking every opportunity to tell the story of the injustice encountered here is crucial to ending the tragic conflict.

Jesus says these very difficult words in Luke 6: 27: "I tell you who hear me. Love your enemies, do good to those who curse you, and pray for those who mistreat you. If anyone slaps you on one cheek, let him slap the other one too." It is in this context that Jesus says, "You will then have a great reward." This passage convicts much of the world as we know it today because violence against perceived enemies is destroying nations and peoples on every continent. Jesus himself eventually suffered death, the victim of a dreadful act of violence. Because my own country, the United States, relies on violence, terrible violence, it has impugned its own moral authority.

Violence cannot be co-opted by any of the Abrahamic faiths, not by Muslims to seek vengeance, not by Jews in pursuit of other people's land, not by Christians to seek fulfillment of some Scriptural apocalypse.

Some people would say that those of us who espouse nonviolence are a moderate voice in the midst of the Israeli/Palestinian conflict. I don't think we are the moderate voice at all. The compelling presentations in this conference make clear that nonviolence is the most radical challenge to oppression and injustice that we have at our disposal. Our nonviolence is a threat to the oppressors, who don't know what to do with us and who live in fear of us. Nonviolence is born from God's love for humanity and is a threat to all perpetrators of violence.

The nonviolence of Gandhi drove the British out of India; the nonviolence of Martin Luther King defeated segregation in the United States; the nonviolence of the anti-apartheid movement brought down the evil of apartheid. And the nonviolence of Jesus overcame death itself. I prophesy that nonviolence will usher in God's justice for all the people of this land because that is the inevitable will of God.

Our prayers at all times must also be for Israeli Jews as well. Isaiah 58:9 speaks directly to the Jewish community: "If you put an end to oppression, to every gesture of contempt, and to every evil word; if you give food to the hungry and satisfy those who are in need, then the darkness around you will turn to the brightness of noon."

In these words are both a caution and a hope. We know that for many Jewish people, there is a sense of darkness, a fear of enemies all around who wish them harm. They lose innocent lives in acts of dreadful violence. The caution in this verse of scripture speaks of contempt and evil words. There is too much contempt and there are too many evil words—and evil deeds—emanating from some of the Jewish leadership, both in government and in some segments of the Jewish religious community.

However, the hope for our Jewish sisters and brothers lies in these words: "Put an end to oppression ... Then the darkness around you will turn to the brightness of noon." There is no light of day to be found in policies of targeted assassinations, which only assure the continued cycle of violence and revenge, as do dozens of other policies that deny Palestinians their dignity and their human rights.

We of the Christian nonviolent tradition hold a vision that is an open invitation to all people. It is not limited to one group or to one race or even to one religion. God's reign includes us all. As Jews, Muslims, and Christians, as Israelis and Palestinians, as citizens from many lands, we cannot let extremism prevail, whatever the source.

I exhort you to hold on to the prophecy that Jesus himself fulfilled when he read from Isaiah: "He has sent me to proclaim liberty to the captives...to set free the oppressed, and to announce that the time has come when the Lord will save his people."

We remember George Khoury and all those who have been the innocent victims of this long and tragic conflict. We give thanks for them, and we draw our strength from them, not only in this dark night but in the dawn to come.

A MAORI PERSPECTIVE

Jenny Plane Te Paa

E te whanau a te Ariki tena koutou katoa. Tena hoki koutou e pae nei I runga I te aroha me nga manaakitanga a to tatou Matua Nui I te Rangi. Mana tatou e arahi, mana tatou e atawhai I nga wa katoa. No reira tena koutou, tena koutou, tena koutou katoa.

Warm and sincere greetings to my family in God. Greetings in the name of the love and the blessings we know are from God alone. May our God of peace and justice continue to guide and protect us for all the days of our lives. Therefore, my sisters and brothers, I greet you once, twice, three times with inestimable love.

I greet you first in the language of my ancestors and secondly in the language of our colonizers. I hesitate to use the word 'oppressors,' because as painful and unjust as so much of our history has been, in many critical respects it bears no comparison to that of yours, my indigenous sisters and brothers of Palestine. Today the hearts and the hands of my people reach out in solidarity and with love to you who are still and have been for too many years, irrefutably, unjustly and brutally oppressed here in your own and your only 'home' land.

My people, known as Maori, are a minority in the only land we will ever call "home". We are currently around 15 percent of the total population of just 4 million people. Our experience of colonization began in the early-to-mid 1800s. It was swift, devastating and destructive of much our people's language, traditions, art and aspirations. It was decisive and utterly dishonest in its removal of the title and ownership of millions of acres of our land. It was catalytic in sharpening the intellect (especially among those chosen to lead the inevitable resistance movements). It was singularly responsible for raising extraordinary levels of moral and political outrage among those victimized. There were wars and diseases, there was death and there was greatly changed life.

In the midst of the social chaos of colonization were the missionaries. It was the Church Missionary Society that exacted the first and most enduring ecclesial franchise over Maori souls. The Anglican Church continues to be the most numerically significant of the "mainstream" institutional churches in Aotearoa, New Zealand, and it is probably still the one to which the majority of practicing Maori Christians belong. The CMS legacy of a somewhat conservative evangelical social reformist theology is what has tended to inform and influence Maori Christian activism and leadership right from the time of colonization through until the present time. While not "spotless" in its dealings with Maori since the earliest times, the Anglican Church has certainly worked very hard over the past 20 years to redeem its past practice of cultural and ecclesial imperialism. Today Maori Anglicans in New Zealand know that cultural oppression can no longer be exerted by those still numerically dominant within the Church, and certainly not over those of our indigenous practices and beliefs which are considered to be in accord with best Gospel practices and beliefs.

Any Church is, however, morally obligated to serve primarily within the secular society, to name and expose injustice, to care for those who suffer, to feed the hungry, to fight oppression, to be a prophetic witness within the public square. In the secular realm over the past century, subsequent governments have employed a variety of legal instruments to justify their imperial right to rule over all New Zealanders, thus apparently subsuming any indigenous rights which Maori people have always believed exist. Historically this has in turn led to ongoing bitter, and at times seemingly irresolvable, tensions between the state and Maori people. British colonization has been pervasive in its socio-political and economic after-effects, especially those which statistically reveal that disproportionate and often heartbreaking disadvantage accrue to Maori on virtually every social indicator—education, housing, employment, health, justice.

In spite of all of this, Maori have proven to be one of the most resilient, determined, well-organized, inventive and irrepressible of all previously colonized indigenous peoples in the world. Many of us have maintained unflagging commitment to the Christian churches planted all those years ago by well meaning, well intended evangelical missionaries; and mercifully, many of these same originally monocultural, monolingual, somewhat racist and invariably sexist, classist and homophobic institutions have now begun to transform themselves in response to years and years of relentless Maori activism.

For our pioneering initiatives across a range of secular institutional settings, including health, education, justice, media and business, contemporary Maori are looked to by many of our international indigenous sisters and brothers for our models of resistance, reconciliation and of ongoing development.

Today in Aotearoa, New Zealand, we co-exist not only with the descendants of the original British colonizers but also with our near sisters and brothers drawn from throughout the South Pacific Islands of Tonga, Fiji, Samoa, Cook Islands, Niue, Tokelau and Tahiti, together with an increasingly diverse new migrant and refugee constituency. We have had to maintain very high levels of political activism in order to avoid being set aside as irrelevant relics of a bygone era. Our status as *tangata whenua* or people of the land is one we cherish dearly and will relinquish *never*. We believe our political status to be that of equal partner with those who came to colonize, and we premise this belief on the document we believe to be foundational to our nation state. This document is known as the Treaty of Waitangi. It provided the template or framework for the mutually agreed "settlement" of Aotearoa, New Zealand, in 1840 and thus it enshrined the covenantal promises which were intended to ensure peaceful and just co-existence between British settlers and indigenous Maori. As *tangata whenua*, or, first people of the land, the responsibility we undertook to maintain and uphold was to ensure the protection and nurture of God's created environment and to ensure the provision of hospitality and shelter for those who came wishing to share the land with us.

In return, we anticipated benefiting from introduced systems of governance, law and technology. I do not need to tell anyone what can happen with Treaties or indeed with covenants between human beings. Dishonour and greed and state sanctioned violence served to characterize the outcome for Maori within a few short years of the signing of our Treaty. From the beginning of the Crown's dishonouring of the agreement, extremely dynamic and courageous protest movements have always been a feature of the socio-political landscape in New Zealand. Traditionally right-wing conservative governments have tended to adopt a patronizing, reactionary response to Maori grievance, whereas left-wing governments tended toward similarly patronizing, but somewhat more 'accommodating,' social policies. Up until the last 30 years no government was prepared to concede that proven historical grievance/ injustices inflicted by the Crown upon Maori people pointed unequivocally to the need for a sustained and sincere redemptive justice project.

However, more recent, primarily left wing, Labour-led governments have been far more conciliatory and demonstrably prepared to begin, advance and attempt to conclude, the extraordinarily complex and challenging process of addressing, and then redressing, historical grievances. Although far from content with our overall political position, it would be fair to say that in 2004, compared to virtually all other previously colonized indigenous peoples throughout the world, Maori are 'relatively' advantaged. This contemporary reality I believe obligates us to speak words of encouragement and of hope to those of our indigenous sisters and brothers far less fortunate.

While in the overall scheme of things this paper may appear to be somewhat inconsistent with others presented, I want above all else to first give honour to the indigenous people of this land of Palestine. I want to respectfully acknowledge those whose abundant hospitality embraces and nurtures us all. I then want to link that contextual reality to my own indigenous situation as I address the ideology of Christian Zionism and, in particular consider its impact upon indigenous peoples. Ironically, in so doing I realize that it *is* my own indigenous tradition *and* our associated relentless struggles for justice which have been and continue being, profoundly strategic in preventing the growth and development of a strong Christian Zionist organization in my country. I will return to this extremely important 'irony' later in this paper.

Now I know there are some who will argue my apparently uncritical or even generalized use of the word indigenous. Then there will be others who will challenge me on how I could possibly know whether or if being indigenous in the South Pacific has anything to do with being indigenous in Palestine. First, I simply reject this kind of pedantic intellectual arrogance masquerading as genuine enquiry. As minority and thus marginalized peoples, we already suffer enough from self-doubt, powerlessness and impoverishment. These perverse 'enquiries' about our definitions of ourselves (which are always framed within supposedly benign questions) are actually hopelessly insensitive to the very core of who we know and believe ourselves to be. The possibility arises that such questions are deliberately intended to destabilize our sense of individual and collective identity and our sense of connectedness to one another as globally unique indigenous peoples.

From my own considerable experience of being indigenous and of working with indigenous people and issues at an international level, I would actually claim that the most authentic basis of our knowing one another as indigenous peoples remains in the realm of the mysterious—it is in the instinctive moment of spiritual connectedness transcendent to the particularities of language and look that we know we belong to one another. It is on that basis of spiritual connectedness that I stand today, and always, in solidarity with you, my Palestinian sisters and brothers, in your struggle for freedom from oppression, in your struggle for justice, in your heartbreaking struggles for peace.

When I read Samia Khoury's beautiful introductory piece in the Winter 2003 edition of *Cornerstone* I felt I was listening to my own elders speaking. Samia's words were these: "as a lay Palestinian Christian, I share with Jesus the same homeland. I can relate to his parables and to every step he took because it is part of our landscape and our heritage. I can sit on the shores of Lake Galilee and understand the power of faith that enabled Christ to heal so many." Resonating with Samia's words, I feel my heart being moved by the profound sense of connectedness all indigenous peoples have with the lands to which we belong—the land which in many of our languages is, literally, our mother earth—our birth mother, our nurturer and sustainer, our refuge in death. We indigenous peoples are our land and our land, literally, is us. All of us have in our traditions stories, mythologies, art, poetry, carving, songs and dances which tell and retell of our oneness with our land.

So what has any of this to do with Christian Zionism? Some with whom I have consulted tried to tell me that the claims to the land between Christian Zionists and indigenous Palestinians are exactly the same except that one is supported by Scripture and the other is not, and therefore it follows that the former claim is far more authoritative! So I began to think about why I felt so uneasy about accepting this assertion—I began to think about what characterizes indigenous attitudes toward land. I began to think about the words I would use to describe the attitude of my people toward our land. I recalled the words my First Nations sisters and brothers use, I recalled the yearning of those dispossessed of their indigenous lands, and I heard in all of these words the same sentiments as those which Samia has articulated.

Sentiments like sacred, protection, nurture, trusteeship, legacy, spirituality, organic, embodied, sustainer of life, being "at one" with the land, surfaced immediately—of course the indigenous words for all of these things are far more poetic and visually evocative.

Then I thought about what appears to me to characterize the Christian Zionist claim to the same land. I tried to identify the sentiments and the attitudes behind the words that I read and hear in respect to the Christian Zionist claim toward the land of Israel—words like ordained ownership, restoration, dominion, Holy, defense, sovereignty, control, reclaiming, Armaggedon. It occurs to me that there is an entirely different set of values and attitudes indicated here. One has to do with establishing and maintaining mutually beneficial and interdependent relationships characterized by being at one with God's creation; the latter has to do with being at one with God alone in the complex and always dynamic process of ordering creation. Dare I say it—one is an attitude of humility and gratitude, the other, an attitude of arrogance and assumption. As an outsider to this land nowhere is this juxtaposition of attitudes and actions illustrated more starkly than in the comparison between beautiful, enduring, life-giving olive trees and ugly, reactionary, dehumanizing concrete walls.

My dear friend and colleague Revd Dr. George Armstrong explains the difference in far more precise theological terms. He reminded me that in our homeland as in most 'First World' countries, Christian Zionists read Hebrew Scriptures through a Western Christian evangelical lens. This means that the issue of land is seen as secondary to the issue of history, and the issue of creation is secondary to redemption. Thus, salvation history is a matter of objective history and is transmitted through an actual limited single "Jewish" people or nation. The rest of history or humanity is secondary to this single people understood in terms of Western historiography or pseudo-historiography. Land in this sense is seen and experienced as being 'owned' by people, rather than people being 'owned' by land. Indigenous spiritual communion with land, George claims, is an incongruous if not inconceivable logic for Western patriarchal spirituality to reconcile itself with. As one acutely conscious of the indigenous attitude toward land, George proffers the following comment on Genesis 2:7, "Then the Lord God formed man from the dust of the ground, and breathed into his nostrils the breath of life, and the man became a living being." There is nowhere else in the Bible a more dramatic symbolism of divinely imbued indigenous intimacy. The created human is divinely crafted, upright, "walking earth". Is it possible that the Hebrew scriptures themselves are being popularly interpreted in ways which subvert this profoundly important Hebrew indigenous intimacy of humans with land to the more dramatic notion of divinely decreed human domination over land? This domination involves 'ownership' of the land in the material sense and therefore eventually in the spiritual sense also.

All of this he sees as indicative of the manifest evil of Christian Zionism as a Western phenomenon distinct from any form of Jewish Zionism itself. Christian Zionism's Western fundamentalism, often finding its "Muslim" fundamentalist counterpart as the root of all evil, shares this same condemnation that it, itself, delivers. To its literalistic distortion or reversal of biblical material, it adds all the typical aberrations of Western cultural preoccupations: social Darwinism, historicism, Enlightenment scientism and bourgeois property rights.

When I was asked to comment on the presence of Christian Zionism in the South Pacific and in Aotearoa, New Zealand, specifically, the initial request took me by surprise because from where I sit, within a reasonably small group of church leaders, I have never really been conscious of a strong Christian Zionist presence in my land. So my first thought was of real concern. Had I been less vigilant than I should? Had I been distracted by other ecclesial politics from seeing such an insidious presence? Had I been naïve in my indigenous preoccupation with the struggle for justice (particularly within theological education) for my own people?

Preparing this paper has provided me the timely incentive to resurvey my own context and thus to assess the extent to which Christian Zionism is or could still be a danger. My considered assessment is this. Christian Zionism is not yet a significant, well-organized, well-funded dangerous presence within our ecclesial landscape, but it is certainly a significant reactionary force surfacing from time to time in response to specific public controversies to do with perceived anti-Semitism.

The latest example of this involves the response to the sacking of one of New Zealand's top political cartoonists over his alleged anti-Semitic messages. Examples of his work indicate the profound level of political analysis readily evident in my country and the unequivocal support there is for justice to prevail for those currently denied even the most fundamental of human rights.

I am particularly grateful to those friends and colleagues who have provided superb academic papers to do with Christian Zionism. I have learned so much myself from listening, reading, thinking and talking on the subject. I would want, however, to pose a challenge to the well meaning, but necessarily limited, Western and predominantly North Atlantic academic preoccupation with discerning and articulating an essentially white, middle class refutation of Christian Zionism. Please do not inadvertently bypass or dismiss indigenous reality. We may not possess the socio-political nor economic advantages so many of you so easily take for granted, but we are here present just as we always have been, and we do have something to say, and we do have something of worth to contribute to the ongoing struggle for justice for all of God's peoples.

It is ironic that the indigenous struggle in my own homeland may well have been utterly strategic in preventing the establishment (to date) of a well-organized and well-positioned Christian Zionist movement. Maintaining the highest levels of political consciousness around indigenous rights to the land has clearly been a most crucial factor in inhibiting the emergence of a strong Christian Zionist presence. Vigilance however is essential and it may well be that this conference has served as a timely reminder to those of us not yet "infiltrated" to be extra cautious now as opposed to finding ourselves being forced into a reactionary position in the years ahead.

Our caution, however, ought never inhibit our pride and our confidence in the embodied goodness, the spiritual simplicity and the intellectual profundity of indigenous understandings. I want to urge my indigenous sisters and brothers to continue, as Samia has so eloquently done, to tell and to endlessly retell the simple stories of who the ancestors are and of how this beautiful ancient land of the olive trees has actually always been known as Palestine—blessed homeland of the Palestinian people.

Thank you, Ramallah, for the abundance of your hospitality, for your inexorable courage and hope. Thank you, Sabeel, for the privilege of belonging. Thank you Naim, Maha and your entire family for the precious gift of your friendship and for the gentle and abiding graciousness of your prophetic witness among us all.

THE THIRD KINGDOM

Mitri Raheb

Those concerned with the effects of Christian Zionism must first of all understand its ideology, for Christian Zionism is, indeed, an ideology. Only by understanding it from within can we challenge its assumptions. An important link is to think about the relationship between history and theology. Goran Gunner's article gives a wide angle perspective of biblical texts which are important for Christian Zionists. Now, we will take one Biblical text frequently cited by Christian Zionists and offer an alternative reading of it, not providing their ideological interpretation as they must do that themselves. Acts Chapter 1, verses 6-11 provides a good case study.

> "So, when they met together, they asked him, 'Lord, are you at this time going to restore the kingdom to Israel?' He said to them: 'It is not for you to know the times or dates the Father has set by his own authority. But you will receive power when the Holy Spirit comes on you; and you will be my witnesses in Jerusalem, and in all Judea and Samaria, and to the ends of the earth.' After he said this, he was taken up before their very eyes, and a cloud hid him from their sight. They were looking intently up into the sky as he was going, when suddenly two men dressed in white stood beside them. 'Men of Galilee,' they said, 'why do you stand here looking into the sky? This same Jesus, who has been taken from you into heaven, will come back in the same way you have seen him go into heaven'" (Act 1:6-11 NIV).

It must have been around the time of the Jewish Pesach feast after the resurrection of Jesus in this very city of Jerusalem that this conversation of Jesus with his disciples took place. The question of the disciples is something unbelievable. *"Lord, are you at this time going to restore the kingdom to Israel?"* It seems that even after the cross and the resurrection, the disciples did not yet get it. Today we might call people who ask such questions Christian Zionists, and Christian Zionists themselves would love to claim the disciples of Christ in their movement. But the truth is that not everyone who asks such a question is to be labelled a Christian Zionist. The disciples, I think, were pre-programmed to ask such questions. Their religious and social upbringing, their education, and their environment were all pointing in that direction.

There are today millions of grassroots Christians throughout the world who are asking such questions. Our role is not to condemn them but first to educate ourselves and then to educate them because they really need an answer. Condemnation is not the thing we best do as mainline Christians. These grassroots Christians, often labelled Evangelicals, have questions that are relevant to them. Their leaders are of a totally different category. I do not think we can educate them; I do not think we can even enter into dialogue with them, but we must speak to the broad evangelical movement. They need help; they need an answer; we should not leave them to the false prophets and Christian Zionist agencies to answer their questions. And who says that people with such questions are a hopeless case? In fact, maybe 25 percent of those gathered at this conference on Challenging Christian Zionism consider themselves former Christian Zionists. The battle is not lost at all. This is why we have to come up with some good education.

First, we have to understand this ideology. We do not necessarily need more research on their theology. Theological analysis is important, and I am glad that many people are doing it, but Christian theologians, politicians, or economists also need to look into their economy and books because much of this ideology is a business and we have to analyse it as such and to uncover it as such. We should not focus too much on theology or react too much to their Biblical references because someone from the outside would not find as many biblical quotations as one would expect. Sometimes watching the 700 Club doesn't reveal any theology. Often, it is a business person who is trying to sell something and to do some fundraising. We really need to address these issues. We really need to address their politics.

We must also address Islam because in fact, Islam is one of their enemies. Their biggest enemy used to be communism and all of these ten scenarios which they are now trying to put on Al-Qa'ida, they were attributing to the communists, to the Soviet Union in the past. We should uncover all of their political prophecies about enemies which did not materialise and remind them of some of their sayings. We need to look closely at their politics to understand what is going on, and we need also to do more analysis of this relationship between the Israeli lobby, the United States and this movement because they share the same bed, but out of selfish reasons. In fact, they don't love each other as many of us would think; they hate each other, but for selfish reasons they want to satisfy some of their "natural needs", if I might use some of their words. So we need to understand them to understand their questions and then to look at the rest of these issues.

It is interesting that the disciples in the passage from Acts were really anxious to see the kingdom of Israel restored. Their vision was one of a Jewish state—a strong, mighty and powerful state which they thought to be a very ambitious vision. They thought they were thinking big by dreaming of such a state, but, in fact, they were very narrow-minded. If it had been up to these disciples, our forefathers—our forefathers as Palestinian Christians also—there would not be Palestinian Christians and Christians of so many different countries here today. In retrospect, we have to say that what they thought was a very ambitious goal was but a very nationalistic and narrow-minded goal. In retrospect, we can clearly see how blinded they were. They were eager for Jesus to restore what I call the "first kingdom". They wanted to reproduce history, to restore a lost kingdom.

In a Christian Zionist video, a woman talks about history repeating itself, as if history really does reproduce itself exactly, as if the story and history of this ancient and lost kingdom was something to be proud of. This woman speaks about Joshua as if the ethnic cleansing after the Exodus was something to be proud of. However, wasn't the whole project called "Israel" nothing but a chain of fatal failures? I am not speaking according to myself as a Palestinian, but according to the Bible itself. The expectation of a future with both the north and the south kingdoms was an eschatological interpretation of the monarchy. This is why the king was replaced with the Messiah. But it seems that our fathers were so blinded they couldn't read history any more. They were living too much in the past and they glorified this past. In their imagination this past was transformed into something different; they forgot all about the failures of this lost kingdom and slowly it felt as if it were the lost paradise.

I have a friend like this; he always lives in the past. Everything which took place in his childhood and youth is seen as something that was so good. The past gets a life of its own, but it is a life only in his brain. It was never, never the reality. In fact by fantasizing about the past, my friend is escaping reality and the present. Our forefathers were living in the past, in that the best they could think of was to restore a lost kingdom, a kingdom that never functioned, a kingdom defined by nationalistic ambitions and desires. In fact, it was a kingdom that was limited to a few square miles. Or maybe because the past was such a disaster, they were longing for a kingdom that would function differently from the kingdom of the past. Because they were living so much in the past, they were not able to see what God in Christ was preparing them for.

The second point is that Christian Zionists are eager to restore this first kingdom. They haven't learned much from the Old or even from the New Testament. From Balfour to Bush there has been a deep desire to restore this first kingdom, Israel. This desire, and this is important, almost always coincides with another desire to restore a greater kingdom or let us call it by its name, an empire—something which might come in a French, a British or an American version. Is not the idea today behind the "new American century" nothing but another attempt to restore an earthly first kingdom? The danger is that the kingdom of Israel was most of the time but a frontier of this other French, British or American empire. I think this larger picture is something always to keep in mind.

The third point is that another important feature of this text is that it talks about Jesus' return. *"Men of Galilee," they said, "why do you stand here looking into the sky? This same Jesus, who has been taken from you into heaven, will come back in the same way you have seen him go into heaven."* The second coming is the hermeneutical key for Christian Zionists. The interesting question is how these Christian Zionists, who know this first kingdom was a total failure, think they transform this idea of restoring the kingdom. They can only do it because they link it to the second coming of Christ. And by putting the kingdom, the restored kingdom, in the light of the second coming of Christ, this first kingdom gets a totally different color as a "second kingdom" through the second coming of Christ. We think they are very pessimistic about history, for they are anxious for Armageddon. They love to see all of this unfolding. What we think to be very depressing, very pessimistic and very frightening is for them just a source of joy. The Christian

Zionist woman who spoke of the end times seemed to be an angel proclaiming good news to people for whom all of this is good news. And this is only because they put it in this light of the second kingdom so that an earthly state gets an eschatological quality.

The fourth point is that Christ in his answer was really trying to move his disciples from thinking about the historical first kingdom and from just standing there looking into the sky as spectators, waiting for the second coming, into another alternative which I call the 'third kingdom'. In fact, we see that Luke is saying that Jesus from his first day of teaching until the days after his resurrection was teaching about just one subject, the kingdom of God, which I call the "third kingdom". This third kingdom was for our forefathers, the disciples, something new, never heard of before, something outrageous, never thought of. "You will be my witnesses," Jesus' answered, "in Jerusalem, Judea, and Samaria until the ends of the earth." Let's look more deeply into this third option, into this third way and kingdom Jesus was proclaiming. Here are some of the characteristics of this third kingdom, which we read, but usually do not think about.

First of all, the idea behind this kingdom is really big. It encompasses the whole world; it aims at reaching every corner of this world; nothing should be left out or overlooked. This is very important, for this kingdom includes concrete countries and reality. It even takes the divisions of this world seriously. It takes into consideration that Palestine, for example, at the time of Christ was divided into Judea and Samaria. There is nothing about a state of Israel, not even Jesus' teaching about something old or something expected or desired. Often as Palestinian Christians, and as people who are involved in seeking peace and justice, we give away these words, Judea and Samaria, because they have been claimed by these Zionist Christians. But, in fact, we have to remind them that by just saying these words they are already saying that the land is divided into two political entities, which they do not want to recognize.

Not only is this kingdom really big, but its second characteristic is that it acknowledges these divisions but does not stop at their boundaries. Although those called as disciples were Jewish, this kingdom is challenging them to reach out to Samaria, something unthinkable, untouchable. But Jesus wants us to think of the unthinkable. There are no lands hostile per se to this kingdom, no axis of evil, if you will. The citizens of this kingdom keep crossing boundaries, all kinds of political, social, economical and ideological boundaries. They are always on the way, always hitting the road, constantly discovering that new territories are God's territories. Maybe you noticed that one characteristic of Christian Zionists is that they love to look for enemies. They search everywhere: "Where can we find enemies?" Having enemies is very important for them; they cannot live without finding enemies. The enemy might be Communism, it might be Islam, it might be the Pope or the Catholic Church. It might be whatever they think of, but they always need an enemy to define who they are. They cannot imagine crossing borders. In fact, the 700 Club once talked about building a wall around the United States for protection; they love to find enemies.

The third characteristic of the kingdom is that these missionaries or disciples are crossing boundaries not as soldiers sent to occupy new territories but as witnesses. In all of the Christian Zionists' teachings, even on the covers of their books, there are many descriptions of missiles and tanks. They need invasion. In fact, one of the books even has "invasion" as the title. They love to see soldiers, invasions. However, in their crossing over, the disciples of the third kingdom seek only to witness. By crossing borders not as soldiers but as witnesses, they are stating that they are not living for and by themselves. By doing that, they witness to a kingdom that knows no boundaries, where the king is a servant, the suffering servant, and is, in fact, a victim of religious and national ideology.

The fourth characteristic is that, contrary to the end time vision of the prophets, the movement of this third kingdom is not outwards-inwards, meaning from the ends of the earth to Jerusalem. The whole movement of Christian Zionist theology comes from outside into Jerusalem. Jerusalem is the goal. This is why it is very important for the Christian Zionists to bring the Jews from the Soviet Union and from Ethiopia to Jerusalem. But, in fact, in Jesus' teaching it is exactly the contrary. It starts in Jerusalem and goes from there out into the world. So, the whole philosophy of bringing those exiles back to Jerusalem is not seen by Christ as a goal at all.

The fifth characteristic is embodied in the lines, "And you will be my witnesses in Jerusalem, Judea and Samaria." Usually when we quote this passage, we think about the ends of the earth and we forget that it is very important to have witnesses in Jerusalem, in the northern part of the West Bank, in the southern part of the West Bank and in the

Gaza strip. Unfortunately for the Christian Zionist, the Christian witnesses in this country are a stumbling block, because we make their lives a little bit more difficult. Without us as witnesses to Christ in Judea and Samaria, their image of a war between Islam and Judaism, or the Judeo-Christian world and Islam would be more easily fulfilled. However, we are here as a stumbling block, a stumbling block that was created by Christ himself, "my witnesses" witnessing to the crucified Lord. In fact, the theology of Christian Zionists is a theology of glory, not the theology of the cross. They don't care for minorities because minorities are powerless. These people are interested in power; it is a theology of the glory. This is why you cannot tell them about the suffering Palestinians; suffering does not sell. They really want the American dream of success; it is very important to their theology. This is why you see that they were flourishing after the victories in '48, '67 '82, even in '91 after the collapse of the Soviet Union, after the first Iraq war. They need all these military victories to survive. They are not witnessing to the suffering Christ because the suffering Christ is a loser, and who wants to be on a losing end? They want to win wars, not to be witnesses of the suffering Christ. I think this is why the theology of the cross is the most important thing we have to teach over and over again, because the whole issue of justice is always related to the suffering of Christ.

Yet, we have to give more attention to how we witness if we really want to reach the ends of the earth; this is the real challenge we face. The Christian Zionists are utilizing media very effectively. They use media to take their message all over the world. Thus, we cannot challenge them just by doing research and preaching even though both are very important. We have to think more and more about how to challenge them. First, we have to utilize the media. They should not claim the Bible for themselves; we know the Bible much better than they do. And they should not claim the media for themselves. We should develop ways to work with the media. We are still in the beginning on that; they are ahead of us.

Secondly, it is very important that we witness in new styles. The Zionists are using lots of art in attracting people, and we cannot just counter them with 19th-century European-style conferences. We must use dancing, music, art, new approaches.

Third, finally yet importantly, we should encounter and challenge these people in a new way. Many people have said that they were transformed after meeting Christians from the Middle East. We should bring Christians from the Middle East into more contact with these Evangelicals. We should try not only to preach to the choir but also to find ways to reach into their own communities. We have to find ways to infiltrate into their congregations, and we have to bring many Palestinian Christians and Middle Eastern Christians there as well as to bring many of them here to meet with local Christians.

This is how we can proclaim a "third kingdom".

THE PROMISE OF A NEW JERUSALEM: RAPTURE IN REVERSE

Barbara Rossing

How do we read the Bible today in light of ongoing agreements between President Bush and Prime Minister Sharon to legitimize the settlements? As an American I feel a deep sense of betrayal. I am ashamed of my country's policies and I apologize. I am horrified by the occupation. The question then becomes "How do we read the Bible in this context, with the eyes of liberation? How do we read the Book of Revelation today?"

What does the Book of Revelation say in light of the ongoing occupations of Palestine by Israel and of Iraq by the most powerful nation on earth? Now obviously these are highly contested questions, and that is why we are meeting here today, looking at the Book of Revelation.

Different Christian voices in the world claim this biblical text from their own perspectives, and I seek to try to reclaim this wonderful text, the Book of Revelation, to help interpret our situation today, to help see what God is doing in our world today, to help reclaim God's message of hope in our time. Even when we look around ourselves in the world today, we see superpowers engaging in terrible, escalating violence. What is the message of hope today?

I want to argue that the Book of Revelation can help us. But first, we have to figure out what it says, and indeed, what it doesn't say. Is the Book of Revelation a recipe for Armageddon as many claim? Is it a chronology for the end times, charting a countdown of events of ever escalating violence, including occupation, seizure of land, even of the Haram al-Sharif for the building of a third temple? Does it culminate in Jesus' return as an avenging warrior on a white horse to do battle with his enemies after three quarters of the world's population has been killed? Some claim that is what the Book of Revelation says, but it does not. That is not the heart of the message of this book of the Bible, and we need to say that. What God wants us to hear in the Book of Revelation is a different message, and it is an important one.

The Book of Revelation was written in a time of occupation also. Some people say that this is the book that most helps us to live in a context of empire—to diagnose the problem of unjust empire and occupation that God wants us to address—to help us see God's presence even more deeply in that context. The Book of Revelation was written about 20 years after Rome had reconquered this land of Palestine and had crushed an act of resistance on the part of the Jewish people. The Book of Revelation, I would argue, is indeed a highly political book but it's also a deeply spiritual book. The visions of contrasting cities at the end of the book are the place to focus.

The Greek word for city is *polis*, from which we get the English word political, so it is indeed a political book and helps us to see empires differently. The author of Revelation, John, looked around in the 1st century in a context of occupation and hopelessness in this land. Perhaps he was a refugee himself, which may be what compelled him to write Revelation. He was living in Turkey at that time, on the island of Patmos. The author looked deeply into the world's situation and addressed the issue of injustice by writing an apocalypse. The word apocalypse means *unveiling*—it means pulling back a curtain to expose something. *Apo* is the Greek word *from*, and *clypse* is the *pyric* helping us to see more deeply into the world, into the heart of the structures that make up our world. That is why we need it, precisely because it is an apocalypse, because it gives us eyes to see.

One little picture I carry around with me all the time has become a little frayed now. It is a picture that on a flat surface seems like blue and turquoise shapes, one of those magic eye things. What happens when you blur your eyes is you begin to see beneath the outermost images into the deeper image. Similarly, if we continue to fix our vision only on the surface appearance of the Book of Revelation, we will never see the deeper image that God wants us to see.

The Book of Revelation is not meant to be read literally—you cannot just look at the surface and understand it purely literally. Even the Christian Zionists know this. For example, taken literally Jesus is portrayed as a lamb—obviously Jesus is not actually a sheep! What this book invites us to do is look deeper into the imagery. The lamb is meant to be the absolute contrast to the lion. We are introduced suddenly to the lamb in chapter 5, as the author says not to worry when no one is found worthy to open the seals on the scrolls but an angel proclaims, "The lion of the tribe of Judah, the Root of David, has conquered, so he can open the scroll and its seven seals."Therefore, we are expecting a lion. What we get instead, however, is Jesus pictured as a lamb—a lamb who is slain, yet standing, who replaces the expected violent lion.

Therefore, what the apocalypse asks us to do is to see more deeply into the picture of our situation as we look around us. We feel betrayed by the political events around us, and yet we have hope in Revelation as God invites us to look more deeply at our world, centered on the image of this non-violent lamb that teaches us to follow peace, not the violent conquering lion. That is what the Book of Revelation is about.

The author of Revelation wrote one of the most daring critiques of empire that we have anywhere in the New Testament. More and more biblical scholars today are looking at the New Testament in the context of empire, especially Rome's imperial claims. The author of Revelation looks straight into the face of Roman claims to eternal empire, and says, "No, God is going to conquer."

It is also an important vision of healing. That's why I entitled this presentation "Rapture in Reverse". Contrary to what fundamentalists want to claim, that there is a message in the Bible of rapture, less than 200 years ago, British pastor John Nelson Darby took the second coming of Christ, and split it into two parts:

> —First Jesus would come to rapture people off the earth, snatch them to heaven, and then there would be a seven year period of tribulation in which God would inflict terrible disasters on the earth.
> —Then Jesus would come again, a second "second" time to establish his reign on earth.

This fiction invented by Darby is very interesting for our time because it has an escapist slant in which true-blue born-again Christians are snatched up to heaven, thus avoiding the period of tribulation, while they watch God inflict disasters on earth.

This is terrible theology. This is not what the Bible is about. Rather, in the Gospels Jesus clearly says that God is with us. This is also the message of Revelation, most clearly in Chapters 21 and 22, in the final vision of New Jerusalem—but fundamentalists never get to this point. They stop at chapter 19 with Armageddon and never get to the heart of this book—the vision of God's new world, of the 11 cities descending from heaven. The core vision of the book is not of people being raptured away to heaven but rather of God being raptured down to earth with us in a renewed, beloved, paradisiacal community.

This is the vision that helps us understand our political situation today. In chapter 22, John envisions a river of life, flowing through the city of God from his throne. On either side of the river is the Tree of Life, whose leaves are for healing of the nations. This is the key image. The leaves of the Tree of Life force us to ask ourselves, "Where is the healing, and how can we participate in that?" Our world is ill. We all feel that. It is a sickness, this war mongering and the conflict in the Holy Land. God comes with a message of hope, to lay the leaves of the tree of life on these our wounds, to help heal and reconcile the brokenness of our world. How can we understand this vision as hurtful?

The ideas for understanding the Book of Revelation go exactly in the opposite direction of the fundamentalists' view and offer some courage to go back into our contexts, to counter the destructive rhetoric that is so harming our world today.

First, the book is prophetic. What this means is not that it predicts future events, but rather that it is an urgent wake-up call for God's people on earth. Prophesy means prediction, as seen throughout the Old Testament. Jonah for example, the reluctant prophet, went to Nineveh with a prediction warning the people that the city would be destroyed in 40 days. The people, however, repented, turned to God and God did not carry out his threat of destruction. Jonah was upset, having hoped that prediction meant fact, but God showed Jonah that destruction is not the point of biblical prophesy. It is about warning, about calling the people to live in God's light.

In addition, the book is an apocalypse. As noted, this means unveiling, but apocalypses do not mean chronologies of destruction. John takes us with his on a series of journeys of his visions, such as in Dickens' *A Christmas Carol.* The miserly old man is taken into the past, present and future, and seeing his own grave in the future, he says, "No, this cannot be." This vision is not a future fact, but a warning. The Book of Revelation takes us on a series of journeys full of colourful, amazing, terrifying images, including talking animals, talking altars, symbolic numbers—this is typical of apocalypses. It is part of the transforming purposes of apocalypses, which function as wake-up calls. After seeing in Chapters 4 and 5 the vision of God's presence in the throne room, we are changed. We come back from the vision as different people. The Book of Revelation presents a wonderful, life-changing vision, not a literal chronology of events.

The question is, "What does Revelation unveil for us today?" In the 1st century, it was a critique of Rome's empire as demonic. Since Rome has long since fallen, what does it mean today? I would recommend that you listen to voices around the world from people reading Revelation in their own contexts. Pablo Richard, for example, in his book *Apocalypse* writes about Latin views on the Apocalypse, describing the *pax romana*—empire through peace, compared to *pax Americana*. This is a key comparison we should look at. We need to look at John's diagnosis in the 1st century and compare this with our present situation.

The most important image in Revelation is in the final vision of God's New Jerusalem. These chapters bring us on a kind of Exodus out of empire, into God's kingdom. The entire Book of Revelation is saturated with Old Testament images—from Isaiah, from Daniel. However, the story of Exodus is the most relevant Old Testament comparison to Revelation. Jesus is exactly like the Moses who leads the people out of the plagues. However, the plagues of the past are now the political crises of the present. What Revelation wants us to do is to get through the middle chapters and see at the end the New Jerusalem and the hope therein. This is God's vision for all time, for every time.

In conclusion, I must ask what your wounds are. How can you use the leaves of the Tree of Life as described in Revelation to heal your wounds? How can we be bearers of God's vision of hope in our times? Revelation was written in a time even more violent, even more hopeless than our own. It was written from the underside, giving us a hard-hitting diagnosis of imperial power. It shows us that even if it looks as if Caesar, Bush or Sharon hold ultimate power in our world today, that is not where the true power is. Rather, in Revelation we are promised that the one who will conquer is a non-violent lamb, a lamb that has been slain, yet still stands. I invite you to try each day to see how that lamb is beside you—wherever things seem most hopeless, know that there is a slain and standing lamb beside you. Even in the darkest times of deep despair, there is hope.

THE PROMISE OF THE FATHER

Bishara Awad

As a person committed to the Lordship of Jesus Christ, my risen Lord and Savior, I always seek and look for the truth. My commitment to Christ must take priority over my feelings, as a Palestinian, as one who has been oppressed, became a refugee and is still suffering.

The celebration of Easter always reminds us of one of the greatest stories ever told. God the Almighty, sending His begotten son, loved the world so much that He allowed His son to die on the cross. Humanity now has a redeemer, a savior. We, then, humbly give Him all adoration, worship and glory.

This Savior, Jesus Christ, has a great plan for humanity. This plan has been set since The Fall, when Adam and Eve sinned. The plan was completed in Jesus Christ our Lord, when on the cross He said, "It is finished" (John 19: 30).

All human history came to a point of no return and in the "fullness of time" Jesus became the pivot point for the destiny of every human being. All history revolves around this person, Jesus Christ. In Ephesians 1: 13, we read, "And you also were included in Christ when you heard the word of truth, the gospel of your salvation. Having believed, you were marked in him with a seal, the promised Holy Spirit." We are thus sealed with that Holy Spirit of promise.

The text of Acts 1: 1-8 is important:

> "In the first account I composed, Theophilus, I wrote about all that Jesus began to do and teach until the day when He was taken up, after He had by the Holy Spirit given orders to the apostles whom He had chosen. To these He also presented Himself alive, after His suffering, by many convincing proofs, appearing to them over a period of forty days, and speaking of the things concerning the kingdom of God. And gathering

> them together, He commanded them not to leave Jerusalem, but to wait for what the Father had promised, 'which,' He said, 'you heard of from Me; for John baptized with water, but you shall be baptized with the Holy Spirit not many days from now.'
>
> And so when they had come together, they were asking Him, saying, 'Lord, is it at this time you are restoring the kingdom to Israel?'
>
> He said to them, 'It is not for you to know times or epochs which the Father has fixed by His own authority; but you shall receive power when the Holy Spirit has come upon you; and you shall be my witnesses both in Jerusalem, and in all Judea and Samaria, and even to the remotest part of the earth.'"

The Bible tells us that "every good and perfect gift is from above, coming down from the Father of the heavenly lights, who does not change like shifting shadows" (James 1: 17).

Thus, God's plan for humanity is good. As Timothy 2: 4 states, the Lord wants the best for us and "wants all men to be saved and to come to a knowledge of the truth." The apostle Paul said in Philippians 4: 4-7: "Rejoice in the Lord always. I will say it again: Rejoice! Let your gentleness be evident to all. The Lord is near. Do not be anxious about anything, but in everything, by prayer and petition, with thanksgiving, present your requests to God. And the peace of God, which transcends all understanding, will guard your hearts and your minds in Christ Jesus."

Philippians 4: 8-9 continues: "Finally, brothers, whatever is true, whatever is noble, whatever is right, whatever is pure, whatever is lovely, whatever is admirable—if anything is excellent or praiseworthy think about such things."

Jesus certainly cares for us and he wants the best for us. He wants us to enjoy life and live it to its fullest. The Lord admonishes us to live by the fruits of the spirit, which are recorded in Galatians: 5: 22-23: "But the fruit of the Spirit is love, joy, peace, patience, kindness, goodness, faithfulness, gentleness and self-control. Against such things there is no law." The Lord is so good and He loved us so much that he even died for us. But God's goodness is always opposed by the wickedness of mankind and mankind's sinful and selfish nature.

In the verses cited in Acts, the disciples saw the resurrected Lord Jesus, witnessed the mighty power of the resurrection. They saw him, touched him and then believed that He is the true Messiah, the Son of God. They had a very important question for Jesus, a question that had been in the heart of every Jew for hundreds of years. All the political and religious leaders had been waiting for the restoration of the kingdom of Israel. Only the Messiah could bring to them liberation, freedom and an end to the occupation. Now that the disciples were convinced that He is the Messiah, they reminded him of his responsibility. "Lord, are you at this time going to restore the kingdom to Israel?" (Acts 1:6). This appeared to be the day they had been waiting for and they knew from the Scripture that only the Messiah would give them political freedom, and they expected that He would be their king. They were anticipating the coming of the Messiah.

In the book of Daniel there are many references to the coming of the "Son of Man" or "the Anointed One." To the Jews he is the Messiah that will set up the Kingdom which will never be destroyed. (See Daniel 7: 13-14.)

At one point, when Jesus fed the five thousand, they thought that he was the anticipated one and they wanted to make him King. Even the sign on the cross said, "This is the King of the Jews" (Matthew 27: 37). What they really wanted was a liberator, a great and mighty king, to set up the Kingdom of Israel, defeat all their enemies and make a great Jewish nation. This claim was certainly supported by the scriptures.

This was their dream, and this was the moment they had been waiting for. Now they wanted to manipulate Jesus to act and do something about it. This was their agenda, their understanding of how things should end. I am sure they were prepared to bring out verses from the books of the Old Testament to prove their point. Books like Isaiah, Ezekiel, Psalms and Daniel are full of Messianic expectations.

The response of Jesus to the disciples' question was amazing. Jesus was so gentle with them. In reality, he should have gotten very angry and should have told them, "What is wrong with you? You have it all wrong. Yes, I am the Messiah, but I did not come to set up an earthy political kingdom. My kingdom is not of this world. As far as establishing the Kingdom of Israel, 'It is not for you to know the times and the seasons which the Father has put in His own authority.'" (Acts 1: 7)

Jesus, in effect, was telling his disciples that the subject they were concerned about was not important. He had better things for them to think about. He had better plans. The plans of Jesus do not affect one particular nation but the whole world. The plan of Jesus had been thought of for thousands of years. It is a plan of redemption, of love, care and compassion.

The Father set the plan and it is called "The promise of the Father". The promise of the Father is for everyone, including the Jews. Jesus told the disciples, "Do not leave Jerusalem, but wait for what the Father has promised, which you have heard from me" (Luke 24: 49). Here is a summary of the promises:

1. You will receive power when the Holy Spirit has come upon you.
2. You shall be baptized with the Holy Spirit.
3. You shall be my witnesses both in Jerusalem, Judea, Samaria and the remotest parts of the earth, for the promise is for you and your children and to all who are afar, as many as the Lord our God will call .

Our days are not different from the days of Jesus. People are still confused and have no conception of the will of God. Many of the things we do may be in conflict with what the Lord really intended. Many believe they are right and everyone else is wrong. The disciples themselves were confused. Jesus told them on more than one occasion that the Kingdom of God

—is near you (Luke 10: 9)
—is for the little children (Mark 10: 14)
— is for those who produce good fruits (Mathew 21: 43)
—is for the poor (Luke 6: 20)
—is like a mustard seed (Matthew 13: 21)
—is for those of faith in Jesus (John 3: 3)

And the list continues, always explaining the intention of God and that all promises were fulfilled in Jesus.

Jesus was emphasizing the Kingdom of God and not the kingdom of Israel. This is the good news—the promise of the Father to us is to be empowered with the Holy Spirit and preach the Gospel, the good news, to all nations. The Kingdom of God is not political. It does not include a piece of land. The Kingdom of God is not to be expanded by wars, weapons, destruction of lives and property, but by love, righteousness, justice, compassion and having faith in Him, who suffered enough on the cross. In other words Jesus was telling His disciples: don't think of the idea of restoring the kingdom of Israel. More important is the Kingdom of God. The Kingdom of God is to be established in Jerusalem, Judea, Samaria, and all the parts of the world.

The book entitled *The Heavenly Man, the remarkable story of Chinese brother Yun* is so encouraging because from it we learn that today there are millions of Chinese believers who love the Lord and are now partakers of the promise of the Father. They are people of hope even in the midst of persecution. The book ends with the call "Back to Jerusalem." These Chinese Christians wanted to preach the Gospel starting from China all the way to Jerusalem. Watch out, Jerusalem! The Chinese are coming with the Gospel of Jesus Christ. When I read this, I said to myself, "Thank God they did not say: next year in Jerusalem." They are not warriors and conquerors but carriers of good news. It is very unfortunate that the Israeli came to destroy, to kill, to occupy, to steal, to deny people their basic human rights. This is not the will of God for the Palestinians. The will of God is good.

The Gospel has reached not only China, but Africa and all the continents. And the work continues as the nations are accepting the message of the good news and are empowered by the Holy Spirit. These are the people of God. These are the elected ones. They are the people of faith and the promises are for them alone.

On the other hand the promises and the blessings can be forfeited through unbelief and disobedience. The prophet Jeremiah gives the following warning:

> "Then you will call upon me and come and pray to me, and I will listen to you. You will seek me and find me when you seek me with all your heart. I will be found by you," declares the LORD, "and will bring you back from captivity. I will gather you from all the nations and places where I have banished you," declares the LORD, "and will bring you back to the place from which I carried you into exile." (Jeremiah 29: 12-14)

The physical restoration of Israel did take place at the time of Ezra and Nehemiah. The Jews returned to Jerusalem and the Temple was rebuilt.

The real restoration as far as our Lord Jesus is concerned, however, is the work of the Holy Spirit. The Holy Spirit came upon the disciples at Pentecost and thousands of Jews came to faith. They became partakers of the promise of the father.

The work of this restoration continues even today as the Gospel is being preached. Every Jew and every gentile who finds Christ partakes of that restoration promise. God fulfilled His word to Abraham, Abraham's seed (the people of faith) have ascended to the throne of glory, and all the families of the earth find blessing and salvation in Him.

It is sad that 20th-century western Christians think that the prophets were addressing their personal wishes and desires and their own interpretation of scripture. They get it all wrong when they think that Israel today, a nation that does not believe in Jesus, is a fulfillment of the Father's promise.

In an interview on Cairo Television, Pope Shnuda, the Pope of the Coptic Church, made it very clear that the land belongs to the people of faith. He also said that the return of the Jews had already been fulfilled at the time of their return from the Babylonian exile which King Cyrus made possible. They did return and the temple was rebuilt and was dedicated in the year 516 BC. Restoration to the land in the Old Testament, however, is conditional. Since the people of Israel disobeyed God, they forfeited any right of return or the blessings of promises

As we enjoy the promise of the Father, we need to be very careful when we come to the subject of prophecies and end times. Jesus is telling us today also that "It is not for you to know times or seasons which the Father has put in His authority" (Acts 1: 7).

For example many have ignored the words of the Lord and have falsely predicted the time of the return of our Lord Jesus. They have deceived many Christians. The Jupiter effect, for instance, came and went without the return of Jesus. 1988 came and there was no return. The year 2000 came and nothing happened. Forty years of Israel came and no return. The Bible is very clear: "that day and hour no one knows, not even the angels of heaven, but my Father only" (Matthew 24: 36).

Right now, a lady named Mary is staying at the Alexander Hotel in Bethlehem. She believes that the Lord is going to return to the Church of the Nativity and she is waiting for Him. We will see after her three month visa has expired if the Lord has returned to Bethlehem. But what is the difference between this lady and all those others who think they know everything and have adopted this modern Israel to be the Israel of God. Let us stop playing at being gods.

At the end of the year 2000, many such Christians got the notion that the Lord would be returning at the Mount of Olives. They sold everything and waited. They caused so many problems to the State of Israel that finally Israel deported them. Some of them wanted to see a war like the one of Armageddon because they believe it will take something that dramatic for the return of our Lord. These and many other people need help, and they need to take another look at the Bible. They are being deceived and are deceiving others.

The Zionist Christians are part of this great deception. To them 1948 was a triumph of God''s purpose, a fulfillment of the promise made by God to Abraham. Another year of fulfillment was 1967. Every action that Israel has taken against the Palestinians, whether ethnic cleansing, killings, house demolitions, building settlements, building a separation wall, dragging natives to jail by the hundreds, is blessed by these Christians. Palestinians are considered the enemy of God.

The promise of the Father does not include a kingdom of Israel nor a return of the Jews, nor the rebuilding of the temple. Any Christian that promotes these things is out of line with New Testament teachings and needs to repent. These persons have missed the real will of the Father. The promise of the Father is not the restoration of one particular nation (Israel) but is for all the nations to live in hope and to come to the full knowledge of the Messiah. The promise of the Father is building God's Kingdom and this Kingdom is to be built on love, righteousness, justice, goodness, kindness and so on. Look at these verses from Isaiah 42 quoted in Mathew 12: 18-21:

> Here is my servant whom I have chosen,
> the one I love, in whom I delight.
> I will put my Spirit on him
> and he will proclaim justice to the nations.
> He will not quarrel or cry aloud.
> No one will hear his voice in the streets.
> A bruised reed he will not break
> and a smoldering wick he will not snuff out
> Till he leads justice to victory.
> In his name the nations will put their hope.

The promise of the Father is certainly for the Jews, not to have a political state but to have a spiritual awakening and to accept their Messiah, Jesus, who is a Jew, and who wants every Jew to be saved and live for Him.

In the meantime let us stay away from fanciful interpretations of scripture. We are to go and preach the Gospel to all the nations (Matthew 28: 19). We are to exalt the Lordship of Jesus so that we all can function in love, grace, justice and, most of all, in faith.

Ephesians 4: 12 admonishes us to prepare God's people for works of service, so that the body of Christ may be built up until we all reach unity in the faith and in the knowledge of the Son of God and become mature, attaining to the whole measure of the fullness of Christ.

At one point Jesus and the Jews had a great misunderstanding:

> "Jesus answered them, 'Destroy this temple, and I will raise it again in three days.'
> The Jews replied, 'It has taken forty-six years to build this temple, and you are going to raise it in three days?' But the temple he had spoken of was his body. After he was raised from the dead, his disciples recalled what he had said. Then they believed the Scripture and the words that Jesus had spoken." (John 2: 19-22)

Which interpretation is correct? Certainly the Jewish leaders were wrong since Jesus was talking about His body.

If the temple is rebuilt, it will not be part of God's plan. God will not dwell in it and no sacrifice will be accepted by God for the remission of sin. The spirit of the Lord stopped dwelling in the temple when Jesus died on the cross and the veil of the temple was torn from top to bottom. (Mathew 28: 51).

Paul, in Acts17: 24, puts it beautifully: "The God who made the world and everything in it is the Lord of heaven and earth and does not live in temples built by hands."

Hebrews 10: 12-14 tells us very clearly that Jesus was the last sacrifice for sin:

> "But when this priest had offered for all time one sacrifice for sins, he sat down at the right hand of God. Since that time he waits for his enemies to be made his footstool, because by one

> sacrifice he has made perfect forever those who are being made holy."

In conclusion, let me emphasize that great and beautiful things are awaiting all those who take Jesus as Lord and Savior. The promises of all the blessings are theirs. Let us not be concerned with the fulfillment of promises. Leave them to God who will fulfill them in His own time. In the meantime let us hold on to the commandment of Jesus to be witnesses for Him. We are thus people of hope; we are part of the Kingdom of God. It is now. It is a real kingdom with living souls from all over the globe.

THE PROMISE OF THE LAND (GENESIS 12:1-3)

Peter de Brul, SJ

"The promise of the land." This paper is not about the "promised land," but about the *promising* of the land, about the question of fulfillment or keeping of promises, about the nature of a certain "beyond" that is inherent in every down-to-earth promise.

I have been asked to comment on the words from Genesis 12:1-3 in which God first calls Abram to leave his basic situation for another. I promised the organizers of the Sabeel Conference to reflect on this passage, and I am hereby keeping that promise even though the keeping of the promise is not quite what I expected. Even you may be surprised!

> "Now the Lord said to Abram:
> 'Go from your country and your kindred and your father's house to the land that I will show you. And I will make of you a great nation, and I will bless you, and make your name great, so that you will be a blessing. I will bless those who bless you, and him who curses you I will curse; and by you all the families of the earth shall bless themselves.'"

We will first look at these words from a rhetorical point of view, and then from a more philosophical or spiritual point of view. This may help us to see their possible relevance to the situation in which we find ourselves together, yet sometimes deeply apart.

Rhetorical Stages

There are three stages to the discourse and three terms are to be found in each stage.

1) In a first stage we hear the order to go from three *relationships* to three other relationships: to go *from* your country, your kindred, and your father's

house, *to* another land to become a great nation with an effect on all the families of the earth.
2) In a second stage we notice the three *persons*: an "I" who speaks to a "you" about "them". The "I" is especially present: "the land that I will show you...I will make of you a great nation ... I will bless you ... I will bless those who bless you, and him who curses you I will curse ..."
We may also notice at this stage the triple development of the *blessings*: "And I will make of you a great nation ... and I will bless you, and I will make your name great, and you will be a blessing ... and by you all the families of the earth will bless themselves." The blessing passes from God to Abram to all the families of the earth.
3) In a third stage we notice the three *times*: the past where you were, the present where you are now in this listening relationship, the future where you are commanded to go.

Deeper levels: three axes

This surface level leads to a deeper level that we may call by various names, be it more analytic, more synthetic, more philosophical or spiritual, in the sense of getting at the heart of a thing, in the sense of wising up. Now the name no longer matters.

1) We notice the passage from one to all: from God to Abram to a great nation to all the families of the earth.
2) We also notice the distinction between, indeed, the separation of those who bless and those who curse. Here the axis or polarity of positivity and negativity, affirmation and negation, emerges, and reveals a situation that recalls the blessings and curses found in the stories of creation. We recall God's blessing of the birds and fishes of the fifth day, and the man and woman of the sixth day, telling them to increase and multiply and fill the earth. We recall that God cursed the serpent, Eve and finally Adam. Yet he promised that one of her children would bruise the head of the serpent, at the price of the bruising of his own heel. And God covered their nakedness with garments of skins before sending them from the garden onto the road where we ourselves still walk, run, loiter, live and die with one another.
3) We also notice the imperative: Go *from* ... and (go) *to*. Thus, it is a statement that expects a response: an act of trust and an act of going.

In these few lines, therefore, we find singularity and universality, blessing and curse, and an order to act on an external level that implies an internal trust. This inner aspect of Abram's response will be explicitly articulated in God's fourth discourse with Abram, when he makes his first covenant with him: "And he believed the Lord; and he reckoned it to him as righteousness" (Gen. 15:6). These three axes will underlie the whole development of the relationship between Abram and God, as they indeed underlie the development of the whole book of Genesis, the whole Bible, right down to the end of Revelation.

The Relevance of Symbol for our Situation

But what is their relevance with regard to our subject of Christian Zionism and Abram? I would claim that their relevance is the relevance of passage from one situation to another, from one state to another. And this is the passage from an image to a symbol.

1) We might first approach this passage by an example from the history of what is called "art". In his fine book entitled *The Nude*, Sir Kenneth Clark distinguishes between the state of nakedness and the state of nudity; the stage and state of a certain shamefulness, negativity, and anxiety before oneself and others, and the stage and state of a certain forgetfulness, affirmation, and relaxation before oneself and others. He illustrates in sculpture and painting this development and passage through various countries in the West. The distinction may be no less true in sports, bath-houses, and physical examinations. But the point is that there is a change in the relationship, in the level of one's "being". It may seem strange for me to call this a symbolic level, for the body is all too real, but it has a way of being "otherwise", of being even more real. And this is the level of nudity. And this is the level I would claim for my discourse here with you, and for God's discourse with Abram. I see it as one of the doors that is essential for our passage, indeed our escape, from the murderous and deceitful situation in which we find ourselves. Without the distinction between the three terms—the image, the symbol, the real—we are confined in a bipolar world, in a bipolar prison, in a bipolar mind-set, where one tends to see only an axis of good and an axis of evil. Captain Ahab rides again the back of the

deadly white whale, Moby Dick! And he takes his whole ship and crew down with him.

This distinction and passage from the naked to the nude might also be found in the passage from space to land, from chronological time to charismatic time, from what is old to what is new. What is as important as the terms is the passage from one term to another, a passage which does not destroy the preceding term, but permits the revelation of a third term which is the very passage.

2) Another approach to this passage can be illustrated by relations of power, force, and attraction. This is no less physical, but also powerfully, forcefully, attractively otherwise.

One cannot force this passage. It is not a question of pushing or pulling, of proving, but of attracting. What is good and true attracts, especially when it is willing to run the risk of its own extinction for the sake of another. There is a certain emptiness, a vacuum, an incapacity, a weakness, an impossibility that lies before us, and it sort of sweeps us into it, calling us to risk.

For at the heart of symbol is an absence. There cannot be a symbol without this absence. For it is belief in the symbol that constitutes the thing as a symbol. The symbol exists in a relationship of trust, where one person has one half of the ticket or shard or ritual or story, and another person has the other half. This absence can be the very death of another, but these deaths can be so numerous and so deep that one forgets or loses the relationship in which they occur.

This is one of our major obstacles to life here in the Holy Land, and to the fulfilling of the promise. There is too much DEATH. If it is not the Holocaust, it is Sabra and Shatilla, Jenin, Rafah. There is no time for the mourning to reach its conclusion before further deaths occur, not only extending in chronological time, but compounding, impacting, until the pressure is unbearable, exacerbating, and dehumanizing. There is such a compacting of levels, of speech and deed and thought and feeling, that one cannot find the words to say it, the time to let it be spoken and listened to, the time to unwind and be unwound. The pressures are horizontal and vertical: horizontal in the borders, the check-points, the Wall which is Llaw spelled backwards; vertical in the water being pumped out from under our feet to the impersonal drone which circles, whines and surveys from the sky. This pressure can lead to breakdown, but it can also lead to grace. Grace under pressure. Coal under pressure becomes diamond. "Immortal diamond," as the English poet Gerard Manley Hopkins wrote in his poem on the Resurrection. *Allahu akbar* is another way of saying it—of finding that when one cannot go out, one can go in; that when one cannot go on alone, one has to go on together, go in together; to draw on as yet undiscovered resources in our relationships. The deaths seem to compound this, to be an obstacle to this. Words come to my lips: I want to say: "LIVE! and f*** the dead!" Here I start to talk like so many people in the TV gangster dramas. Jesus put it more modestly: "Let the dead bury the dead." He had another task at hand, other nails on his mind, in his hands and feet. And death did not stop him, on the assumption that he found someone to believe in him. Someone to pick up the symbol and live on with it, really, but not forgetting that the map is not the territory, the land is not just space, the other person is not just "somebody".

3) A final approach toward the sense of symbol is this: it can bring about the reconciliation and the blessing here, remove the curse, end the mourning, release grace. This effective and communicative sense of symbol was once described as one of the four traditional levels of meaning. The first and literal level was to determine what was said. The second or allegorical level was to determine what was meant. The third or moral level was to determine what was to be done. The fourth or anagogical, mystagogical, or symbolic level was to determine where it was all going: what was its end or purpose. It is the symbolic level of meaning of the drama revealed through the conflicting issues of Christian Zionism and Christian Anti-Zionism that I would bring to your attention, consideration, judgment, decision, and action. We must beware of falling into the bipolar mindset and language and action/reaction.

We have to go up the road, the *sabeel*, to the spring, the *sabeel*; we must discover the play on words, the work of word and realize that this discovery reveals our own capacity to see that difference, that play and work as stemming from a third position which is a real person, a real group of persons, who recognize where they are, where they were, where they are going, singly and together.

We speak of Christian Zionism, and its historical and scriptural roots. We can speak similarly of the historical secular and scriptural roots of Jewish Zionism. We might even speak of a Muslim Zionism, if we mean to say that al-Aqsa Mosque, the Dome of the Rock, the *Mi'raj*, and the Ka'ba sanctuary where the Night Journey to Jerusalem began, can become the focus of a symbolic and eschatological affirmation, requiring a negation, affirming universality, requiring action now. In my view here today I would claim that all of us, some of us, each of us, can get stuck on an image, make it into a symbol, forget it is a symbol, and then try to bring it into reality, and do the world and ourselves extensive and even definitive damage. We can forget that the map is not the territory. We can forget that land is not just space; Time is not just time. For there are two words for time: "chronos" which is diachronic time, second after second. And "kairos" which is synchronic, even panchronic time, where an unrepeatable grace and opportunity is here and now. This "charismatic" space and time is real, on a level of reality that needs to be respected, but it cannot be possessed. It can only be expressed by symbols, and Abram—in all the stages of his life—is such a symbol. The symbol is there where the three axes previously mentioned cross one another and, in the shadow or penumbra of one another, reveal what is symbolized and what is not to be mistaken for an image.

Irrelevant Conclusions

I have no hope that anyone here will be affected in the least way by anything I can say in this conference. But who am "I" to despair of this? Is not this "I" the very one who has to "go"? Who *is* "I"? Who *are* "you"? Who *are* we? We should all be higher, deeper, better, truer, realer than we think or imagine ourselves to be. And further expressions come to the lips: What in heaven are we doing to one another? What on earth...what in the hell...what in the devil, what in God's name—*bi hiyat Allah*—are we doing?

From what level in myself am I speaking? To what level in you am I trying to address "myself," that other who trusts enough to "go"? Death keeps pressing us away from such a level of communication and exchange. To a certain degree, we do not know where we are going, and this ignorance can be sanctifying, liberating, in that it provides a space in which people can exchange. We may recall the lines of John Donne in his poem *Negative Love*:

> May I miss, whene'er I crave,
> If I know yet, what I would have.

Such missing knowledge, such ignorance provides space for a market, for a fair, for passage, for possible meeting from various sides of ourselves, especially those sides of ourselves that we are somewhat ashamed to show. We are ashamed there where we are vulnerable or wounded. We need to trust the other to take the "beam" from our own eye so we might be trusted to take the "straw" from the other's eye.

Such an act of bold trust is found at the beginning of Luke's Gospel, when Mary answers the angel Gabriel at the Annunciation: "Behold the handmaiden of the Lord. Be it done to me according to your word." In John's Gospel, she made a similar bold act at Cana, when she did not take her Son's refusal as a final answer. He demurred to step in to solve the problem of the lack of wine, but she simply turned to the servants and told them to do whatever he told them. She put him to the task, whether he liked it or not. She could count on him. In the same Gospel, in the scene of the Last Supper, Jesus tells Judas to get on with it. "Go, and do what you have to do. And do it quickly." In another context, in Mark Twain's *Adventures of Huckleberry Finn*, the boy Huck makes up his mind. Huck realized that he had broken all the rules of his racist society by sheltering Jim, the black runaway slave who had helped him flee down the Mississippi River. Fearing hellfire, he began to compose a letter confessing his crime, but then he stopped and thought about all that Jim had done for him. He held his breath, finally decided, and said to himself: "All right then, I'll *go* to hell"—and tore it up. And so the adventures took a quantum leap into new and unexplored territory.

In this situation, under these pressures, we are at the edge of new and unexplored territory. This talk is intended to be a Bible study on the promise of the land to Abraham and his children. It is not just a study, but a meditation on those words, a contemplation, to the point of realizing that they are addressed to the believer. The promise is just words unless one believes in the promise; and the promise is not kept unless the believer holds on until the end. Without such faith, the promise and the land can become a fetish, a deadly toy, a refuge from the truth which is not just a position, but a way, and a way of life: a *sabeel*, if we may play on words. The three themes that emerge on the rhetorical surface, and the three polarities that underlie the promise have led us to several approaches to the relevance of those words for us, for the various levels of ourselves, and especially for that anagogic or final level, which aims at a mysterious unknown, a symbolic goal, that helps us to recognize the difference between our images, our realities, and our symbols.

The land is real, but its reality is not exhausted by being bought and sold, being taxed and expropriated, being walled and confiscated, being measured and named, being watched and drilled and even promised. All those verbs are in the past tense; the present tense of what God is still promising depends on the deeper shared levels of ourselves, who came from dust and know that to dust we will return. What do we do with our handful of dust in the meantime, in this mean time, but wait for that Spirit, that Breath or Wind, of which Jesus spoke to Nicodemus: "The wind blows where it wills, and you hear the sound of it, but you do not know whence it comes or whither it goes; so it is with every one who is born of the Spirit" (John 3: 8). It is this wind or breath with which the words of the promise are formed and spoken and realized. We are still far from the end of listening and responding to those words spoken and written long ago. I hope that these words of mine have increased your desire and willingness to respond to the words of Genesis on which I have promised to speak. To a degree, to an anagogic degree, I have kept my promise.

As a final encouragement, I would invite you to listen—one day in the future—to a short piece of music entitled *Harmonium*. It lasts barely a half-hour: a poem by John Donne and two poems by Emily Dickenson set to music by a contemporary composer, John Adams. The poems and the music are affirmations of the call to go out together into the unknown. As Dickenson writes:

> Futile the Winds—
> To a Heart in Port—
> Done with the Compass—
> Done with the Chart!
>
> Rowing in Eden—
> Ah, the Sea!
> Might I but moor—Tonight
> In Thee!

HOLY LAND AND HOLY PEOPLE

Rowan Williams, Archbishop of Canterbury

Editor's Note: Seven months before the *Sabeel* International Conference entitled Challenging Christian Zionism, the Archbishop of Canterbury agreed to give the keynote address. However, approximately three weeks prior to the Conference of April 2004, the Archbishop sent his apologies and asked his Secretary for Ecumenism, the Revd Jonathan Gough, to deliver the following message. Because of the strong reaction to the Archbishop's message, three critiques of his remarks are included directly after his address. See also "Christian Zionism and Main Line Western Christian Churches" by Rosemary Radford Ruether in this volume.

The subject of this conference is one that goes deeper than simply the critique of a deeply eccentric form of Christian theology; and it should take us further than yet another analysis of the cyclical patterns of violence and injustice in the conflicts of the region. It should also be an opportunity for us to clarify something of what as Christians we can say about Israel, as one dimension of a "liberation theology" that will carry the good news to all in the Holy Land and more widely. The two extreme positions we are wearily familiar with fail to carry such good news. At one end of the spectrum, there is the view that argues for unconditional support of any decision made by an Israeli government that furthers maximal claims for territory and security on the grounds of an apocalyptic myth whose relation to both Hebrew and Christian Scripture is tenuous (to put it mildly). At the other end is the view that there is essentially nothing to be said about the Jewish people and the state of Israel from the standpoint of Christian theology, a view which runs up against the complexities of much of Christian Scripture, not least Paul's great and tormented meditation in Romans 9 to 11.

In other words, I am not at all sure that we best respond to distorted theologies of Israel by denying that there could be a good theology of Israel. But what does "Israel" mean? In these remarks, I shall address two distinct but overlapping realities: "Israel under God", the Jewish people considered as bearers of the covenant and witnesses to God's revealed justice, and the State of Israel, a contemporary and secular political reality which is also seen as the homeland for "Israel under God", the sole place in the world where the Jewish people have guaranteed place. Jewish-Christian dialogue has been trying for decades to find a way of talking about all this without colluding with uncritical attitudes towards Israeli government policy; and part of this discussion has naturally focused upon the theology of covenant, the heart of any account of "Israel under God". "I am not saying that the promise of God has failed", says Paul in Romans 9.6, as he seeks to explain the sense in which the primordial alliance between God and the Hebrew people is fulfilled and extended in the work of Jesus. What is the role of this promise that does not fail? If it is simply a matter of a covenant with Israel being overtaken or replaced by something else, we do not do justice to Paul's argument; but no more do we do justice if we suppose that the covenant with Israel exists sealed off from what has happened in God's dealings with the rest of humanity in Jesus.

It helps to ask what the covenantal promise is thought to be *for* in the Hebrew Scriptures. And the answer, given in various forms in parts of Leviticus, in many strands of the prophetic tradition, especially the Second Isaiah, in aspects of the Wisdom literature, might be summarised by saying that Israel is called to be the *paradigm nation*, the example held up to all nations of how a people lives in obedience to God and justice with one another. This is how a nation is meant to be: living by law, united by a worship that enjoins justice and reverence for all, exercising hospitality, with a special concern for those who have fallen outside the safety of the family unit (the widow and orphan) and those who fall outside the tribal identities of the people (the resident alien, the "stranger within the gates"). What is more, as Deuteronomy insists (4. 5-6, 32-34, 7. 7-8), this is a people, a community, that exists solely because of God's loving choice; they have been called out of another nation specifically to live as a community whose task is to show God's wisdom in the world. Already there is the hint of what becomes a powerful theme in some later Wisdom literature, that this is a people in whom divine wisdom has chosen to be at home—which in turn foreshadows the later speculations about how the *Shekhinah*, the divine glory, is present in people and temple and land, when the people are living by law and wisdom.

It is because this is a people called to embody wisdom in the form of justice that the covenant is also the principle of the most severe critiques in scripture of the prevailing habits and structures of power in the ancient Hebrew kingdoms. The prophecy of Amos is perhaps the most sustained expression of such critique. Of course, God has chosen and worked with other peoples; but this people alone has been given the explicit vocation to justice, has been known and recognised by God and allowed to know God's purpose in a specific way. Therefore, this people is *accountable* in unique measure. The visions of Ezekiel dramatise this by showing divine presence and glory departing from a temple and a territory where idolatry and injustice prevail.

A biblical theology of Israel under God has to begin here. Gary Burge, in an important study of the situation from an evangelical point of view (*Whose Land? Whose Promise? What Christians Are Not Being Told About Israel and the Palestinians*), stresses the fact that if biblical arguments are used to defend the State of Israel, biblical principles must be used in defining what makes the people itself distinctive and in assessing the common life of this people, instead of moving seamlessly from biblical Israel to the modern state and bracketing out the prophetic challenge to biblical Israel. The Israel of Scripture is a community whose identity is bound up with a calling to show wisdom and justice, a calling which successive modes of government for the people fulfil in very varying degrees; the land of Israel is not a gift given in the abstract to the Hebrew tribes: it is a territory given as the necessary backdrop of stability for a law-governed community to flourish. It is, so to speak, "leased" to the people for their use (Lev. 25); God remains the true owner of the land. The prohibition against selling off or diminishing the land inherited in any family is not in the least meant to be a reinforcement of absolute possession; it is rather a warning against using God's land, into which the people are invited, as a means to build up private wealth, instead of using it as the means to secure just provision for all for whom God has made you responsible. It is extraordinary that such texts can be deployed as they sometimes are by self-styled conservative Christians in arguments about land exchange and settlement patterns with such total disregard for their actual wording and purpose.

The implications of the theology of covenant in Hebrew Scripture include two salient points for our task of finding an appropriate liberation theology. First, the identity of Israel under God is 'missionary': it is to manifest not God's supreme and arbitrary power in choosing and shaping a nation, but God's wisdom and justice as the pattern for human society. In Deuteronomic terms, God chooses a small and oppressed people to demonstrate this, lest his justice be confused with the interests of a powerful and successful nation. Take away this vocation, and the history makes no sense. A 'chosen people' that has become not only powerful but oppressive in its practice has made nonsense of God's calling to them. But secondly, if the land is to be understood in and only in this context, as a condition for stable, hospitable law-governed life together, anything that makes the land a cause of radical instability undermines the basic point. That is, if the land has to be defended by ceaseless struggle which distorts the very fabric of the common life, it ceases to be a "sacramental" mark of God's calling. There is a well-known *halakhic* argument that the defence of land does not *of itself* justify the taking of life; and this is, understandably, a point much argued in Israeli religious controversy in the last two decades, as people seek to define what constitutes an ethic of self-defence.

A biblical theology of covenant, then, begins to define something of what a liberation theology for Israel would mean. The modern political reality of Israel is not biblical Israel; but it is ideally one of the conditions for biblical Israel's message and witness to be alive in the world today—a context in which God's people can manifest God's justice. The community of faithful Jewish people committed to justice and wisdom in the world today, as a community consciously living before God, has its rationale in the calling to embody justice and wisdom; to have a homeland in which to exercise the political virtue this involves is an intelligible requirement, especially in the light of a history in which this liberty has been systematically denied for so many centuries by Western Christians. To be hospitable, you must have a home. But what if a point comes at which the location of Israel under God in a national home becomes bound up with policies which undermine the possibilities for others of a stable homeland, the kind of setting which alone makes political virtue possible? I am not here discussing the rights and wrongs of binational or unitary solutions to the tormenting problems of the region, but simply raising the question of how the conditions under which God's people can exercise their calling are to be held together with the rights and liberties of other peoples, especially neighbouring peoples, to their own integrity. Without stable and agreed borders, neither internal stability nor the universal service of external witness to justice can be sustained. The land becomes a prison, not a gift. The State of Israel has had to sustain its existence against enemies who would not grant its right to exist. But the problem increasingly lies less with aggressive neighbours than with a failure to tackle the underlying issues about regional stability. This is why so many Israeli commentators will say that life in Israel today threatens to become just such a prison, as the spiral of overwhelming violent reaction to the indiscriminate violence of suicide bombings and the consequent desperate anxiety over security creates more and more barriers and walls.

The theology we need, in other words, will reinforce the insistence that security for Israel and security for its neighbours in the contemporary setting are absolutely inseparable: good news for one is good news for the other. There can be no more important matter to insist upon at present; which is why—apart from the simple human awfulness of these acts for their direct victims—every suicide bomb in Israel is an appalling injury to the Palestinian people, and every demolition of a house, every collateral death of a bystander or child in the Palestinian territories, is a wound to Israel in the long run. There is no good news for Palestinians in the proclamation of a programme to humiliate and destroy Israel; there is no good news for Israelis in a 'security' that sets in stone the impotent anger and resentment of Palestinians.

So a biblical theology of Israel, simply on the basis of how the Law and the Prophets conceive Israel's identity and destiny, cannot support an uncritical approach to extreme policies about territory and security; quite the contrary. But we need to add a further point to avoid misunderstanding. Scripture presents us with many texts about how God chastises his people through the intervention of other nations. Yet it is always clear in the prophets that others should beware of assuming a divine right to chastise on God's behalf. Attacks on the existence and liberty of the Jewish people as such are likely to arise from aggression and hatred. God can use this evil, but does not create it. Thus, in the scriptural context, any attempt in the non-Jewish world to set oneself up as the judge and punisher of God's people is, like any act of self-righteous aggression, to be condemned. More significant is the tradition in the

Bible of acts and histories which involve non-Jewish people reflecting back to Israel its own true vocation—the records of righteous Gentiles like Ruth and Job, the ready repentance of the Ninevites in Jonah compared with the rebelliousness of the Prophet himself. What the Gentile can do under God is not to undertake aggressive or punitive violence against the Jewish people as such, but to offer back to Israel-under-God its own gift of the ideal of wisdom and justice, and, in proper solidarity and love, refuse to collude if Israel settles for less than its own deepest wisdom. It is the point made by a good many serious Jewish thinkers—that Jewishness itself becomes altered and diminished when bound to political priorities and strategies that are never challenged. Thus to question the political reality that is the state of Israel in the name of the calling of Israel-under-God is not an assault on that state's rights or integrity, but a witness to the fact that part of the very rationale of that state is to be a home for that different kind of political reality which is the Jewish people as called by God to manifest his justice.

Fear and instability erode law; which is why indiscriminate slaughter, the suicide bombs, are so terrible for the soul of Israel (as well as the soul of Palestine), pushing it further towards a defensiveness that sits light to national and international law and inexorably undermines "wisdom" in its policy and polity. The question for both Israeli and Palestinian must be how each encourages lawfulness and stability in the other. It is meant to be Israel's gift under God to the nations; other nations aware of that have the responsibility to reflect this back and to hold Israel accountable to itself and its God; and engagement with the concrete difficulties of the policies of the state of Israel is part of that, as is the whole enterprise of continuing Christian dialogue in solidarity with the Jewish people.

Practically speaking, the implications of what I have been saying are that the existence of a homeland for the Jewish people remains a theologically positive matter if we agree that the existence of the Jews as a people is a theologically positive matter. The horror of the 20th-century history of European Jewry is, of course, pertinent here. One of the things that might be said theologically about this is that when the Jewish people have an identity only as dispersed minorities, the witness of a nation existing solely because of God's call to wisdom and justice is weakened; and sooner or later the nations around will begin to lose awareness of their moral accountability. At its highest level, the decision about the creation of a Jewish state was a recognition that its very existence would be a warning against the nightmarish extinction of political morality in modern totalitarianism—not because the modern state of Israel is in some way the heir of biblical promise in a literal way, but because it is the condition for Jewish people of faith and conscience to be able to exercise their historic calling. Israel's existence as a state ought to be a mark of the recognition that God's justice stands in judgement over all secular and self-interested political and nationalist systems. It would be the bitterest irony if the state of Israel were simply encouraged to subvert its own moral essence in order to survive, encouraged and enabled to become not a paradigm for the nations but a nation deeply caught in the same traps of violence and self-interest that affect us all. But if this is not to happen, we need far greater political will in engaging Israel in the most searching and critical reflection on its practice, and involving those, Jewish and Palestinian, who acknowledge what their responsibility in faith and conscience is for the creation of peace. I have no doubt about defending the right of the state of Israel to exist, and the right of that state to protect its identity as a place statutorily safe for Jews. But so few inside or outside Israel have helped it work out how to sustain its existence in partnership with it neighbours and in accountability to the wider community of nations. Hence, I attempt here to argue for the essential place of accountability in a biblical theology of the identity and meaning of Israel under God.

Thus I am suggesting that we cannot properly confront distortions about the theology of Israel without trying to understand why in biblical terms Israel's being as a people is still, and in spite of all, a gift to the community of nations; and also that we cannot do this without taking seriously the question of how the state of Israel as a concrete political agent is to be engaged with—not because it should not exist but because, in the light of the biblical vision of justice, it should. This is more and more the theme of the best critical minds in the internal Jewish debates; it should be more and more the theme of Christian discussion of this question.

But this raises issues about the whole theology of Jewish-Christian relations, and I need to add some thoughts on this. The alternatives are often seen—as I suggested earlier—as either an uncritical affirmation of Israel's abiding unique status in a way that raises real questions about the work of Christ, or the classical "supersessionist" or "replacement" approach, in which there is no positive assessment at all of the special role of the Jewish people and a simple affirmation of the Church as the 'new' people of God. Once again, the biblical picture denies us these simplifications. If we read Paul in Romans 9-11 carefully, it seems that what he is saying is something like this: Israel has not responded to its vocation as it could and should; only in connection with Jesus can Israel fully be itself, becoming a transforming and inviting sign of God's justice and ultimately extending the realm of justice and wisdom to all peoples of the earth, so that all may be incorporated into God's people. The paradigm nation becomes the kernel of a renewed community without ethnic boundaries, united by God's justice; and for Paul, that justice is made possible only by the gift of God *creating* justice through the death and resurrection of Jesus, in whom Israel's calling is perfectly realised. What is contested between Jew and Christian is whether this dramatic divine intervention in Jesus of Nazareth to bring Israel's calling to its climax is essential to the story of God's people or not—and so whether that calling is or is not extended beyond the ethnic limits of Israel to the enlarged 'nation' that is the Church.

If the answer to that is Yes, as it has to be for the Christian, this does not imply that Israel-under-God loses significance; it remains the core of the whole story, the primary sign of God's free election and God's gift of wisdom and justice. The Church cannot say to the Jewish people either, "You must abandon Jewish identity, which has now been overtaken by the new people of God," or "You are forever absolutely unique and isolated, accountable to no-one because chosen by God." It is rather that Jew and Christian share a conviction that they have one calling—to be the place where wisdom and justice make their home in history, on earth; in the light of that, they have the freedom to call each other to account, despite their differences. Something of this enters in also to the relation of Jew and Muslim, to the extent that they too partially share some common history of covenant and prophecy; but I cannot do anything like justice to this matter in a short reflection here. When they are able to do this, it is a mark of maturity in the relationship, of the acknowledgement that we are not talking about a God who abandons his people and changes his self-definition with the passage of time.

In our present Western historical context, the right of the Jew to call the Christian to account has, understandably, been uppermost in the minds of most thoughtful Christians. The Church's claim to be the extension or universalisation of the Jewish calling is profoundly challenged by the unspeakable betrayals of wisdom and justice that have so often prevailed in the Church, especially in its history in respect of the Jews. For a European approaching the question of Israel, this is simply an irremovable fact; I am aware that for the non-Western Christian, or indeed the Muslim, this is felt differently; but I have to say that the Jew is entitled to call these groups to account also, to the extent that lying and hateful attitudes have sometimes been allowed in to their talk about Jews and Judaism, even if this has not involved the depth of betrayal the westerner recognises in the Holocaust. And whatever deliberately feeds the mentality that produces suicide bombings must be confronted in the name of justice and humanity; as so many have repeated, this is a nightmare distortion of another great religious tradition and its commitment to divine law and divine compassion. The demand for Jewish honesty requires honesty from all of us too.

The difficult moment comes when the Christian, western or eastern, or for that matter the Muslim, has to call the Jew to account. But it is essentially a matter of treating Jewish people as adults who are responsible for how they act out the calling they proclaim—not as perpetually damaged people who are too weak to be challenged, too wounded to be responsible. What could be more patronising and oppressive than this mythological attitude to a people who have, out of indescribable suffering, created a society that is in so many ways immensely powerful? But no-one disputes that the critic has to earn the right to be heard; a criticism that does not recognise the full and complex reality of the other and is not prepared to stand in solidarity with the other will never earn that right.

Part of wisdom and justice as God gives them is the ability to stand with the other and understand something of the depth of their suffering. The Israeli who senses something of the outrage of Deir Yassin, for example, and the Arab (Palestinian or non-Palestinian) who is prepared to be honest about the Holocaust and about the demonisation of Jews in some Arab media are the people who are capable of making a difference. When my colleague and friend Bishop Riah suggests that the mothers of children killed on both sides of the conflict exchange photographs of their children across the security fence, he is giving intensely dramatic expression to the challenge of solidarity. If such an exchange happened, those making it would be showing what might be needed for the two communities to grow into the right to call each other to account, in justice and mercy.

Anyone trying to reflect on the present situation is bound to do so with some of that mental anguish that St. Paul describes in his meditation on Israel; we are caught in the profoundest tensions. I find it inconceivable as a Christian that the freedom of Israel as a people under God to be a people with a home should be challenged in the name of a Christian universalism that tries to dispense with the specifics of the history of revelation. I cannot understand any attitude that assumes the calling of the Jewish people is not still a calling to be special, by God's gift and grace. Hence the distress felt by many of us who share such a conviction when we see what looks like a refusal in the State of Israel to think around and beyond policies of control and containment to justice for all and mutual reinforcement of welfare and safety and dignity. I have no patience with those who speak as though the *fact* of the state of Israel is the source of anti-Semitism, as though Israel's extinction would spell the end of anti-Semitism. It is important to hear and to understand what such language sounds like to those who listen from within the Jewish community across the world. Nor do I think we can ever helpfully suggest that the legitimacy of the state of Israel's political existence depends on her meeting specifications imposed from outside. The tragedy that threatens, as many within Israel see it, is that this state's welfare and stability are undermined not simply by pressure from outside, but by its own inner tensions and its inability to face the imperatives of shared security. That is why a proper theology of liberation in the region is something that is necessary for Israel's life as well as Palestine's.

It is because I believe all this that I want to pursue the question of how Israeli policy is called to account in a way that is spiritually as well as politically sensitive and constructive; that is why I think we have to develop a good alternative to bad and collusive theologies of Israel, as part of the liberation theology we all need. We all need: that is to say, we in the Church need it also. We need liberation from uncritical triumphalist attitudes, of which anti-Semitism is always a sign. Thomas Merton, forty years ago, noted in his journal that Western Christendom was always most anti-Jewish when it most identified *itself* with the militant and irresponsible episodes in Old Testament history, when it became most aggressively confident of itself as the new chosen people, without any of the critical nuance of the prophetic tradition. The real agenda for our work is how we come to regard each other as sufficiently adult for critical exchange to take place. That depends on trust; and trust depends on tangible signs of commitment to each other.

Any theology of liberation is a challenge about how trust is created by commitment- by taking risks for each other in a way that decisively breaks down barriers because it demonstrates a solidarity of welfare and vision and hope. In the 17th century, the ninth guru of the new Sikh faith was executed by a fanatical Indian ruler seeking to impose Islam on all his subjects; but he was martyred not for professing Sikhism but for defending the rights of Hindus. That is commitment; that is the liberated conscience at work. If we repudiate an attitude to Israel that is unwilling to confront its own darker and more fear-driven elements, we need to ask how we can show a commitment to it that will cost something; as we need also to ask Israel for signs of its commitment to the security of its neighbours—signs both positive and negative, positive in investing in stability and good government in Palestine, negative in recognising the dangers of fundamentalist obsession about unsustainable boundaries and the unjust practices that they involve.

Throughout this brief essay, I have been asking what it is that liberates Israel as a community under God to give the gift God has called it to give; and this is to ask how the modern political reality that is the state of Israel nurtures and honours the historical and theological Jewish identity that is dedicated to manifesting wisdom and justice for the sake of the whole human community. Bad and unscriptural Christian theologies become part of the problem, theologies that collude with the violence of either side. We can do better; and if we succeed, we shall have learned practically how we exhibit mutual commitment and common belonging in and with God's just and compassionate project for all his human creation. If only Jerusalem could be, in the full biblical sense, a sign lifted up among the nations, not of nationalist rivalry but of common belonging! It seems almost unimaginable; but our job is to imagine, day by day, and to pray and work and risk for that end and for all that goes with it. May that prophetic imagination prosper.

AN OPEN LETTER TO ARCHBISHOP ROWAN WILLIAMS FROM JONATHAN KUTTAB

The Most Reverend Rowan Williams
Archbishop of Canterbury
Lambeth Palace
London
SE7 1JU

9 September2004

Dear Archbishop,

I am writing belatedly in response to the paper you sent as a contribution to the International *Sabeel* Conference on Challenging Christian Zionism that was held in Jerusalem in April 2004.

I regret to say that Palestinian Christians attending the Sabeel Conference listened with profound disappointment to the message you sent to the Conference. Palestinian Christians have suffered much at the hand of theologies and interpretations of scripture that provide a mantle of divine legitimisation to the ideology of Zionism and the political movement that worked for their displacement from their homeland and built a Jewish state on the basis of their exile and oppression. One of our constant complaints has been that Christian Zionism ignores our national rights and indeed our very existence. The creation of the State of Israel was done on our land, and the ingathering of Jews from all the world came at the price of exiling and scattering our people throughout the world. All this was supported by Christian theologies that ignored or delegitimized us as a people, claiming a divine imperative based on scripture for the creation of the state of Israel.

Such views generally side-stepped or totally ignored the Palestinian people on whose land the state was created. While the Jewish people were seen to hold a divinely mandated right to peoplehood, and even chosenness, as well as a promise to ownership of the land by its creator and ultimate sovereign, the Palestinian people had only individual and transient rights, at best, as "strangers in the midst" of God's people. These issues were not of passing theological or academic interest to us, but had direct tangible consequences for us of life and death, as well as of faith.

It was therefore most distressing to us to hear these same views echoed in your keynote address when you also asserted a theological imperative to recognize a special "Jewish peoplehood" which needed to be exercised in political statehood in a concrete land inhabited by others whose peoplehood is NOT recognized. There were several references in your lecture to the "neighbours" of such a state, presumably Jordan, Syria, Lebanon, and Egypt, but none to the indigenous people of Palestine who had necessarily to be displaced and marginalized to make room for the exercise of Jewish nationhood. It was unclear where the "good news" lay in this for the Palestinians or indeed for the Arab neighbours of the new Jewish state.

To be sure, you did not give unqualified support to the Jewish state, and affirmed that it is required to act with "law and intelligence", but one gets the impression that such a requirement is viewed solely from the perspective of the dominant Jews themselves, as if Palestinians have no value in and of themselves in the sight of God, and that the most they can get is the crumbs of the state of Israel's willingness to live up to the requirements of "justice and intelligence".

However, if Israel fails to live up to those requirements of "justice and intelligence", then the tragedies, suffering, torture, and displacement suffered would be regrettable, not because of what the Palestinian victims are suffering, but more for what this does to Jews—that is, because of their failure to live up to their role as God's people.

Your lecture did not support eschatological or prophecy-driven interpretations, yet you affirmed, theologically, the need for a Jewish state as a necessary paradigm to the world of a community living "under God". You even lamented that we did not have the benefit of such a living example for almost 2000 years. As you seem to see it, Israel, in biblical terms, is still a gift to the community of nations.

In taking this view, you not only bracketed out 2000 years of history, but also the entire teachings of Jesus and the New Testament with respect to the Kingdom of God, the removal of the barriers of distinction between Jews and Gentiles, and Jesus' emphatic separation between Church and State ("My kingdom is not of this world"), which is the basis for the Christians' critical attitude towards politics, states and nationalism in the modern world. The concrete challenges with which Jesus responded to those zealots who yearned for an earthly kingdom and the restoration of power to the Jews by pointing repeatedly to His Kingdom, which is open to all and not just to the "children of Abraham, according to the flesh", are also side-stepped as we are brought back to the Old Testament covenant of tribal possession and conquest of the Land.

By utilizing the "tormented meditation in Romans 9 -11" and rejecting the Supercessionist or replacement approach, you appear to be left with the Old Testament model of the covenant, tempered perhaps by the requirements for justice towards the "alien in your midst" but nothing more. Unfortunately, you were not present to explain to us what happens to the indigenous population when such a model state is established on their land:

> —What rights, if any, would such indigenous non-Jews (Christian or Muslim) have in a professedly Jewish state?
>
> —Is discrimination against them (necessary in both theory and practice if one sets out to create a Jewish state) legitimate, and divinely mandated?
>
> —Is Palestinian nationalism and peoplehood dangerous or even evil because it resists elimination and marginalization within the divine scheme of creating the 'paradigm state'?
>
> —Are Palestinians the Amaleks to be exterminated or Canaanites to be reduced simply to 'hewers of wood, and drawers of water'?
>
> —Is their resistance to this scheme legitimate self-defence, or sinful rebellion against God's plan that must be harshly repressed?
>
> —Are they (or at least the Christians among them) required to graciously vacate their homes, fields, shops, and villages in favour of Jews to whom God is granting this land to be their home, since it is obvious that "to be hospitable, you must have a home"?

I would welcome the opportunity to discuss these questions with you in person whenever you are in Palestine again, or if it is possible for me to visit you in London. On behalf of the indigenous Palestinian Christian community, I would urge you to lead in challenging the heresy of Christian Zionism, which dares to justify in God's name an apartheid regime that will, if unchecked, lead within 20 years to a Holy Land devoid of local Christians.

Yours in His Grace,
Jonathan Kuttab

ON KNOWING ONE'S PLACE: A LIBERATIONIST CRITIQUE OF ROWAN WILLIAMS' 'HOLY LAND AND HOLY PEOPLE'

Robert B Tobin

"Holy Land and Holy People", the message which the Archbishop of Canterbury sent to the 2004 *Sabeel* International Conference is remarkable for its failure to make more than passing reference either to the subject of Western Christian Zionism or to the contemporary situation of Palestinian Christians. Instead, it is devoted almost entirely to placing the concept of liberation theology into an exclusively Jewish context. That this was the real purpose of Dr Williams's address was not, it must be said, immediately apparent to many of those who had gathered to hear it, but this confusion had less to do with their acuity as listeners than with the opacity of the text itself. Dr Williams has been criticized elsewhere for his seeming inability to speak clearly and concisely on certain key issues. In the case of "Holy Land and Holy People", he has produced a document which invokes the language of liberation and progressivism but which in fact carries a message deeply discouraging to those Christians who seek and need these things, as a close reading of the text reveals.

A discussion of Christian Zionism, suggests Dr Williams in his opening lines, ought not merely to serve as an exercise in critique but "should also be an opportunity for us to clarify something of what as Christians we can say about Israel, as one dimension of a 'liberation theology' that will carry good news to all in the Holy Land and more widely." Having thus promised to speak about Israel within the context of liberation theology as a vehicle for the Good News in this particular time and place, it would seem reasonable for the Archbishop at least to acknowledge the current struggles of Palestinian Christians, the primary and indigenous witnesses to the Good News in modern Israel/Palestine, as key to the development of a liberationist discourse. But this he does not do. Rather, he goes on to address the concept of Israel exclusively in terms of 'two distinct but overlapping realities', the first of which he defines as the biblical entity of 'Israel under God', and the second as the contemporary entity known as the state of Israel, "the sole place in the world where Jewish people have guaranteed place." In discussing attitudes towards the former, Dr Williams rightly points out how incomplete within the context of the Jewish tradition itself are arguments which cite Hebrew scriptural sources to justify unconditional support for contemporary Israeli domination. While Jewish and Christian literalists alike may be content to understand God's covenant with the Hebrews primarily in terms of a land grant, Dr Williams insists that the divinely-sanctioned claim of physical space by the ancient Israelites must always be read as only one aspect of their larger responsibility to constitute a "paradigm nation". From Deuteronomy to Isaiah to Amos, the Archbishop illustrates that the scripture constantly reminds the Jews that with their unique blessing has come a unique obligation to create a just and compassionate society. "A biblical theology of Israel under God has to begin here," he asserts, concluding that "if biblical arguments are used to defend the State of Israel, biblical principles must be used in defining what makes the people itself distinctive and assessing the common life of this people, instead of moving seamlessly from biblical Israel to the modern state and bracketing out the prophetic challenge to biblical Israel." This is an important sentence, because in it Dr Williams is actually confirming the legitimacy of employing biblical arguments to defend the state of Israel, even as he seeks to distance himself from those who do so in a manner he deems inadequate. In other words, his aim here is to qualify and improve the basis for such arguments, not to challenge their inherent validity. But why should modern Christians feel obliged to acquiesce in *any* biblical arguments used to defend the state of Israel, even those in which the Jewish prophetic tradition is fully included? It would seem Dr Williams himself regards as self-evident some type of scripturally-based continuity between "Israel under God" and the modern State of Israel, an assumption that leaves the Archbishop open to the charge that he, too, is a kind of Christian Zionist.

In fairness to Dr Williams, he later states explicitly that "the modern political reality of Israel is not biblical Israel." No sooner has he made this assertion, however, than he adds a series of qualifying statements that function to undermine his original point. Even if the modern state is not the same as biblical Israel, he writes,

> it is ideally one of the conditions for biblical Israel's message and witness to be alive in the world today—a context in which

> God's people can manifest God's justice. The community of faithful Jewish people committed to justice and wisdom in the world today, as a community consciously living before God, has its rationale in the calling to embody justice and wisdom; to have a homeland in which to exercise the political virtue this involves is an intelligible requirement, especially in the light of a history in which this liberty has been systematically denied for so many centuries by Western Christians. To be hospitable, you must have a home.

Certainly no Christian could wish to inhibit biblical Israel's "message and witness" being "alive in the world today", nor could any Christian seek to oppose "faithful Jewish people committed to justice and wisdom … as a community consciously living before God." Affirming that these things (among others) might find their expression within the context of the modern state of Israel does not necessarily lead, though, to acceptance of the Archbishop's next claim, that "to have a homeland in which to exercise the political virtue this involves is an intelligible requirement." An intelligible requirement from what source exactly? The ancient Hebrew covenant? As if realizing that he is about to commit himself overtly to the premise that the modern state does indeed take its primary justification from the biblical legacy, Dr Williams suddenly shifts his ground and suggests that the need for a Jewish homeland gains additional impetus from the long history of Western Christian persecution. Deprived by non-Jews over the centuries of the opportunity to fulfil their destiny as the chosen people of God, Jews are now owed the contemporary political reality of a homeland to demonstrate what the 'paradigm nation' is supposed to look like: "To be hospitable," pronounces the Archbishop, "you must have a home." Having thus sidestepped the literal equation of biblical Israel with the modern state, Dr Williams nonetheless encourages a general endorsement of Zionist aspiration, both as a way of compensating for the legacy of anti-Semitism and as a means of facilitating the Jews' divinely-mandated expression of 'political virtue'.

What also cannot be overlooked at this stage in the Archbishop's address is that, having introduced his discussion of "Israel under God" in terms that take Jewishness as normative, he then continues his analysis of modern Israel from the same perspective. "[W]hat if a point comes," he asks, "at which the location of Israel under God in a national home becomes bound up with policies which undermine the possibilities for others of a stable homeland, the kind of setting which alone makes political virtue possible?" This is certainly a good question, and one which justice-loving Jewish people have been asking ever since the state of Israel came into existence. Yet Dr Williams, speaking in his capacity as a Christian teacher and leader, phrases the question in such a way that his own co-religionists are relegated to the anonymous status of 'others'. One need not be an expert in social linguistic theory (only to have read Genesis 1:19-20) to appreciate that there is a power that comes with the ability to name things, as well as an enhanced status that comes with having been recognized and named. Conversely, to refuse or to neglect to name something or someone functions as a form of belittlement. Thus to speak as Dr Williams does here of all Palestinians as the "others" in the region is automatically to demean them, just as to introduce their claim to a homeland as a mitigating factor in the Jewish realization of political virtue is to deny the Palestinian claim an integrity in its own right. Why the man sitting in St Augustine's Chair should approach the problem of contemporary rival claims to the Holy Land in such a lopsided manner demands explanation. He tries to reclaim the mantle of objectivity by insisting that "I am not here discussing the rights and wrongs of binational or unitary solutions to the tormenting problems of the region," but it is difficult to imagine the Archbishop would ever be a serious proponent of the one-state, pluralist solution, given the exclusively Israeli Jewish outlook and language he employs in his approach.

If this attention to Dr Williams's word-choice seems unduly pedantic, note that he does not actually mention the Palestinians by name until the eighth paragraph of his address, and then in direct reference to suicide bombing: "apart from the simple human awfulness of these acts for their direct victims, every suicide bomb in Israel is an appalling injury to the Palestinian people." Again, what the Archbishop says is less worrisome than he says it and what he omits. He is absolutely correct that these bombings are both awful for their immediate victims and deeply harmful to the wellbeing of the community in which they have their source. But why is it not until he has alluded to this wicked behaviour by a handful of individuals that the Palestinians as a whole finally gain an explicit identity in his remarks?

Having named the Palestinians as a people capable of inflicting suffering upon their Israeli neighbours, Dr Williams also indicates they are a people who endure suffering at the hands of those neighbours, and by identifying this cruel reciprocity he would at last seem prepared to grant that moral equivalency between the two exists. However, after timidly reiterating that "a biblical theology of Israel ... cannot support an uncritical approach to extreme politics about territory and security," he promptly retreats to his one-sided discourse based upon the Old Testament. His footing restored to this familiar ground, the Archbishop warns that "any attempt in the non-Jewish world to set oneself up as the judge and punisher of God's people is, like any act of self-righteous aggression, to be condemned."

Having just discussed the present-day reality in which Palestinians and Israelis alike do terrible things to each other, it is troubling that he should then make a biblical argument for why the 'non-Jewish world' (presumably both Palestinians and the rest of us) should not presume to react negatively to Jewish wrongdoing, lest it offend God as a form of "self-righteous aggression". In contrast to this hubristic posture, he holds up the example of such righteous non-Jews of old as Ruth, Job and the Ninevites. In following their lead, "what the Gentile can do under God is not to undertake aggressive or punitive violence against the Jewish people as such, but offer back to Israel-under-God its own gift of the ideal of wisdom and justice, and, in proper solidarity and love, refuse to collude if Israel settles for less than its own deepest wisdom."

Presumably when translated into more immediate terms, this means God-fearing Palestinians should espouse non-violence and forgiveness amidst the oppression they are suffering at the hands of the Israeli state. That Dr Williams as a Christian leader should advocate such a stance is hardly surprising, given Jesus' teachings. What is harder to fathom, however, is that the Archbishop should counsel these behaviours not because they are Christian, nor even because they will ultimately show the Palestinians to be a blessed people in their own right, but because they are behaviours which are quintessentially Jewish. Apparently it is not enough that Palestinians should suffer and strive to be moral amidst such suffering; they must also accept that if they succeed in being moral, it is only in emulation of the truer nature of those who oppress them. Such logic is plainly insulting to the human dignity of the Palestinian people.

All of which inevitably leads to the question, whether Dr Williams chooses to acknowledge it or not, of how much responsibility the state of Israel, of which Israel-under-God constitutes an integral if unquantifiable part, must shoulder for the ongoing cycle of violence that exists between Palestinians and Israelis. Undoubtedly, on the Palestinian side of the equation, the resort to suicide bombing has not only devastated many innocent people but also greatly exacerbated the bitterness and mistrust that Israelis generally feel towards their neighbours. Recognition of this fact leads the Archbishop to remark that "fear and instability erode law; which is why indiscriminate slaughter, the suicide bombs, are so terrible for the soul of Israel (as well as the soul of Palestine), pushing it further towards a defensiveness that sits light to national and international law and inexorably undermines 'wisdom' in its policy and polity."

If one were not already wary of Dr Williams's manipulation of words by this point in his message, now would be a good time to develop a healthy scepticism. His statement that "fear and instability erode the law" is, as a generic proposition, reasonable enough; the objection must arise with his selective application of this premise to the matter at hand. Citing the terrible arbitrariness of its impact, the Archbishop again singles out suicide bombing as a particularly reprehensible practice, not only evil in itself but also the chief cause of the Israelis' increasing lawlessness and hysteria. Yet without in any way wishing to excuse the moral depravity of suicide bombing, it is necessary to insist that this phenomenon is only one among many causes for the deterioration of lawfulness in the Holy Land, and arguably not even a primary cause. From the Palestinian perspective, fear and instability have their roots in the foundation of Israel itself and the increasing recourse to terror by certain groups is viewed as a reaction to longstanding illegalities, and not, as Dr Williams suggests, a source of them. If one is willing to entertain, even for a moment, the Palestinians' view of themselves as a people who have been systematically deprived of their land and liberty over the last five-and-a-half decades by an aggressive military state, there is something perverse in the Archbishop's conclusion that "the question for both Israeli and Palestinian must be how each encourages lawfulness and stability in the other." Largely powerless to protect themselves and their families from ongoing harassment and displacement, Palestinians might be forgiven for asking how they should "encourage" lawfulness and stability in their overlords. Perhaps he believes they should do this by assiduously obeying all the regulations put in place to restrict their movements, hinder their livelihoods and upset their domesticity. Why Dr Williams believes Palestinians should frame their own struggle for survival in terms of encouraging lawfulness and stability among Israelis is by now familiar territory; it is because such qualities are "meant to be Israel's gift under God to the nations; other nations aware of that have the responsibility to reflect this back and to hold Israel accountable to itself and its God." Once again, Gentiles must both literally and metaphorically know their place, which would appear to be wherever God and the Israeli Defence Force decide is most beneficial at any given moment.

It is only after he has so firmly located the Palestinians within a theological matrix of Jewish supremacy that the Archbishop turns his attention to the rest of us. Here, too, he proves willing to concede very little to his fellow Westerners on the question of Zionist aspiration: "Practically speaking, the implications of what I have been saying are that the existence of a homeland for the Jewish people remains a theologically positive matter if we agree that the existence of the Jews as a people is a theologically positive matter." Here again Dr Williams propels his argument by yoking a debatable assertion to an entirely benign one. In this case, affirming the existence of *any* people as a "theologically positive matter" should go without saying for the Christian believer, and so it should regarding the existence of the Jews. This need not mean, however, that all Christians are required to join Dr Williams in assuming that the Jews' right to exist as a people automatically leads to a corresponding theological affirmation of contemporary Zionism.

Nor will it do, as the Archbishop does here, simply to invoke the Holocaust as the ultimate evidence of what happens when this correlation is questioned or resisted. As unspeakable as the extermination of the Jews in 20th-century Europe was, this cataclysm cannot be used indefinitely to rationalize the political and military hegemony of a Jewish state in the Middle East in the 21st century. Yet Dr Williams appears to be making just such a rationalization by following his allusion to the Holocaust with the warning that "when the Jewish people have an identity only as dispersed minorities, the witness of a nation existing solely because of God's call to wisdom and justice is weakened; and sooner or later the nations around will begin to lose awareness of their moral accountability."

This is a truly astonishing assertion for the Archbishop of Canterbury to make. It would seem that unless the nations of the world acquiesce in the theological arguments supporting the modern Zionist project, they themselves are destined to go astray, incapable as they are in his estimation of generating a sustained moral vision from within.

Does Dr Williams detect no challenge to the integrity of his own Christian witness in such a statement? However shameful the history of Christian anti-Semitism through the ages and unconscionable the churches' failure to defend European Jewry from destruction during the Second World War, it is remarkable indeed that he should display so little confidence in Christianity's ongoing potential to serve as an autonomous conduit of God's wisdom and justice in the post-1945 world. Perhaps, however, such pessimism is only the socio-political corollary to a theology which regards Christian salvation as contingent upon Jewish fulfilment. From this position of moral deference, Dr Williams therefore proceeds to reason that "Israel's existence as a state ought to be a mark of the recognition that God's justice stands in judgment over all secular and self-interested political and nationalist systems." It is deeply regrettable that since 1948 the Israelis have succeeded in creating a state which is every bit as self-interested and chauvinistic as other nations, but it should not be surprising, given that they are human beings like the rest of us. What is surprising is the way certain Christians like the Archbishop continue to cling so blindly to an idealized conception of the State of Israel, when plainly the reality is now something far sadder and more complex.

Throughout his address Dr Williams alludes to the necessity of speaking the truth forcefully about modern Israel and its policies, but there is little or no evidence that he is prepared to do so himself. When he does finally broach the matter of Israel's culpability in Middle Eastern conflict, he presents it not as a fact to be confronted but merely a possibility to be guarded against, one whereby Israel might be driven to betray its values by unnamed agents dedicated to its corruption. So he posits that "it would be the bitterest irony if the state of Israel were simply encouraged to subvert its own moral essence in order to survive, encouraged and enabled to become not a paradigm for the nations but a nation deeply caught in the same traps of violence and self-interest that affect us all." While it would be illuminating to know who in this supposedly hypothetical situation Dr Williams thinks would thus encourage Israel's worst impulses, it is clear he will not consider the question of Israeli moral responsibility without also affirming Israel's role as perpetual victim. Despite reiterating the need to engage Israel frankly in the matter of its troubling practices, he laments that "few inside or outside Israel have helped it work out how to sustain its existence in partnership with its neighbours and in accountability to the wider community of nations."

Besides blithely overlooking the efforts of thousands of Israelis, Palestinians and internationals who have worked tirelessly to help Israel find lasting peace and stability, this statement reveals the advanced degree to which the Archbishop has embraced the concept of Jewish victimhood. He further contends that despite the necessity of calling Israel to account, neither Christians nor Muslims can do so without feeling compromised by the anti-Semitic legacy of their own creedal histories. It is obvious to Dr Williams why Jews should freely call others to account; however, "the difficult moment comes when the Christian, western or eastern, or for that matter the Muslim, has to call the Jew to account."

As is the case repeatedly in "Holy Land and Holy People", the Archbishop advances a controversial line of reasoning here, only to contradict it in the next sentence. Having just explained to non-Jews why they must take care in confronting Israel morally, he then warns against treating Jews "as perpetually damaged people who are too weak to be challenged, too wounded to be responsible." Given the very narrow passage he is navigating as to what constitutes an acceptable critical approach to Israel, Dr Williams's audience might be excused for not knowing how he would have the rest of us follow him. Perhaps providing such leadership is not the point of the exercise. "[N]o-one disputes that the critic has to earn the right to be heard," he argues, adding "criticism that does not recognise the full and complex reality of the other and is not prepared to stand in solidarity with the other will never earn that right." Has the Archbishop chosen to use this public occasion to build up his own credibility with Israeli Jews as a trustworthy critic and sympathetic theologian?

The remainder of the lecture would seem to confirm this suspicion, devoted as it is to reaffirming the essential chosenness of the Jews, past and present. Dr Williams finally lays his cards on the table, asserting that

> I find it inconceivable as a Christian that the freedom of Israel as a people under God to be a people with a home should be challenged in the name of a Christian universalism that tries to dispense with the specifics of the history of revelation. I cannot understand any attitude that assumes the calling of the Jewish people is not still a calling to be special, by God's gift and grace.

The Archbishop must learn to understand this attitude better if he is half as interested in contemporary 'bridge building' in Israel/Palestine as he purports to be. For indeed, there are many Christian believers, Palestinian and otherwise, who can scarcely be accused of dispensing with 'the specifics of the history of revelation' by affirming that such history is ongoing and that God's promise of freedom to Israel has not so much been superseded by Christian universalism as fulfilled by it. Moreover, such people are neither so inscrutable nor peculiar as Dr Williams implies simply because they prefer the radical inclusiveness of their own theology to the tribal exclusiveness of someone else's. Whatever the nuances and equivocations of his arguments, then, the Archbishop cannot finally escape this basic distinction between Christian and Jewish conceptions of covenant and belonging.

One of the points Rowan Williams makes most effectively in "Holy Land and Holy People" is that Judaism has always contained within it a powerful sense of justice and compassion. The present critique of Dr Williams's address will have failed if it serves in any way to contradict or obscure this basic truth. And as those who have spent any time at all in the Holy Land can testify, the Jewish moral conscience in both its religious and secular forms is alive and well in modern Israel and continues to mount some of the most effective resistance to the state's inhumane policies and practices. Even in the largely Christian context of the *Sabeel* conference, there were several Jewish speakers who by their very presence bore eloquent witness to the growing diversity of Jewish opinion. Had he attended the conference, Dr Williams might have recognized this fact and adjusted his own remarks accordingly. As it was, there was something strange indeed about the Archbishop counselling Palestinian Christians to appreciate the complexity of a situation whose complexities they have been forced to live and breathe all their lives. Even if he judged it necessary to say certain contentious things in order to stimulate debate among his co-religionists, his failure to do so in person and to participate in the ensuing conversation must nullify whatever benign intentions one might wish to attribute to him. Ultimately, one must conclude that the Archbishop of Canterbury simply abdicated his responsibility to stand with his fellow Christians in the midst of their very real and present crisis. Not only that, but he had the temerity to use the platform these Christians offered him as an opportunity to build up his own credibility among those they perceive as their oppressors. He signally failed to address their need for an evolving theology of liberation in the midst their suffering. In short, he did not bring them a message of Good News, and neither, alas, did the many and contradictory words he chose to send in his stead.

A RESPONSE TO ROWAN WILLIAMS' MESSAGE TO THE SABEEL CONFERENCE

Helen Lewis

Rowan Williams' lecture to the *Sabeel* Conference on Challenging Christian Zionism sets particular challenges to those of us who witness from afar the troubles in Palestine, and who may, despite our best endeavours, take sides unfairly in the present conflict. It offers a lucid and concise summary of the Old Testament texts dealing with the theology of the covenant and challenges us to think harder and more deeply about how we can contribute positively to genuine peace-making in the Middle East. So why did it cause such disappointment and even outrage?

In his lecture Dr Williams aimed to explore whether anything theologically positive could be said about the state of Israel, and in the course of that, "How the modern political reality that is the state of Israel nurtures and honours the historical and theological Jewish *identity* that is dedicated to manifesting wisdom and justice for the whole community."

The first part of the lecture explores the meaning of the covenant, summarised as follows: "*Israel is called to be a paradigm nation, the example held up to all nations of how a people lives in obedience to God and justice with one another,*" and he illustrates what this might mean. Over and over again the theme of justice occurs in the context, for instance, of the treatment of all members of the community, not simply the tribal group, and of the ownership and use of the land. With the covenant and with the requirement for justice comes accountability, and the argument is a familiar one: that if biblical principles are used to justify the actions of the State of Israel, biblical principles can equally be used to challenge unjust policies. Dr Williams is clear that some policies *are* unjust, even though the criticism of Israel may seem oblique: "*A 'chosen people' that has become not only powerful but oppressive in its practice has made a nonsense of God's calling to them.*"

But Dr Williams goes further than exploring the implications of the covenant for Israel. He is concerned with "two distinct but overlapping realities: Israel under God, the Jewish people ... as bearers of the covenant ... and the state of Israel," and the complex relationship between the two. The State of Israel is, he says, "ideally one of the conditions for Biblical Israel's message and witness to be alive in the world today." The adverb is made to carry a good deal of nuance here; I take it that he means that the State of Israel is not an *actual* condition for "Israel under God" to realise its calling, but that *ideally* it *could* be. However, three pages further on, the qualification has disappeared, and the modern state of Israel has now become "the condition for Jewish people of faith and conscience to exercise their historic calling," a hugely contentious statement, not least because it appears so dismissive of the contribution made to human civilisation by Jewish communities in the diaspora.

Dr Williams seems at this point to have embarked on a kind of theological justification of the actual state of Israel. There cannot be serious disagreement about his judgement that "Israel's being as a people is ... a gift to the nations;" the debt owed to Judaism by Western societies at least is incalculable. But when we are told that the State of Israel "as a concrete political agent" should exist "in the light of the Biblical vision of justice," we might well pause, not least because the point simply isn't clear. It might well be read as a reference to the injustice that has characterised much Western treatment of European Jews, but I *think* he means that it should exist because it can be a home for "that different kind of political reality which is the Jewish people as called by God to manifest his justice," or, in other words the home for the "paradigm nation" that Israel is called to be.

It is essential here to distinguish between recognition of the State of Israel within its 1948 boundaries endorsed by the United Nations, together with the right of its citizens to live in peace and safety, and theological justification of that state on the grounds of what it might potentially become. The former is one to which anyone working for peace in the Middle East must subscribe. The latter is fraught with difficulties.

Briefly, he argues that the State of Israel is the condition for Jewish people of faith and conscience to exercise their calling as a "paradigm nation". He is not merely talking about a homeland for Jews, but the actual State of Israel in which Jews may exercise "political virtue". But there are two questionable assumptions here: first, that this is the universally held view of observant Jews, and second, that a nation state created on the 19th century model can be reconciled with his vision of a "people living under God".

First, although since the Holocaust and the political success of Israel, it has become a *commonly-held* view that the State of Israel is a necessary expression of Judaism, it is by no means universal. Jacob Neusner states in "The Doctrine of Israel" (*Blackwell Companion to Judaism*):

> In every Judaic religious system "Israel stands for the holy people whom God has called into being..., to whom the prophetic promises were made , and with whom the covenants were entered. In every Judaism "Israel" is a theological category, not a fact of society or ethnic culture or secular politics. The "Israel " of every Judaism forms a supernatural social entity, "chosen", "holy", subject to God's special love and concern. *That Israel is not to be confused with the Jewish people, an ethnic group, the people of Israel in this-worldly framework, let alone the State of Israel, a modern nation state* (my italics).[1]

The interdependence which Dr Williams perceives between the "two overlapping realities" of a "people under God and the State of Israel" is here explicitly denied. Before the establishment of the State of Israel, both British and American Jews opposed the concept of a Jewish homeland on the grounds that the Jews no longer constituted a nation, but a religious community. The potential discordance between ethical Judaism and the *realpolitik* required of any nation state is the subject of continuing controversy within Judaism, yet it is not really explored. There are many Jewish voices who would find Dr Williams' assertion that the State of Israel is "the condition for Jewish people of faith and conscience to exercise their calling" wholly bewildering. Roberta Strauss Feuerlicht, for example, comments:

> Judaism as an ideal is infinite, Judaism as a state is finite. Judaism survived centuries of persecution without a state; it must now learn how to survive despite a state.[2]

While it would be presumptuous for any non-Jew to argue *against*

---

[1] Jacob Neusner (ed.), *The Blackwell Companion to Judaism,* Blackwell 2003, p. 230.
[2] Quoted in Marc Ellis, *Toward a Jewish Theology of Liberation,* SCM Press, 1987, p. 44.

the connection of Judaism with the Holy Land, other traditions of Judaism should surely not be ignored.

Could the State of Israel become the kind of paradigm nation that Dr Williams envisages? A major problem here is that the nation state that is Israel has a history and reality of its own independent of theological propositions and systems. The agenda of Zionism's founding fathers, such as Herzl, Pinzer, Weizmann, and Ben Gurion, was overwhelmingly secular. They had no aspirations for Israel to be a "paradigm nation"; neither did they see Israel as "a community of faithful Jewish people ... consciously living before God". On the contrary, Israel was explicitly intended as a Western nation state like Britain or France, and its identity was to be ethnic, not religious or ethical. It was never part of the "rationale" of the *actual* Israeli state to be "a home for that different kind of political reality which is the Jewish people as called by God to manifest his justice."

Indeed, ironically, the early Jewish voices warning against the setting up of a Jewish nation state came from those who shared Dr Williams' vision of a "people living under God". "Spiritual Zionists" such as Ahad Ha'Am and Martin Buber feared that a Jewish state might frustrate or destroy those very spiritual values which Dr Williams appears to think need a state in order to exist. Buber was in favour of settling only as many Jews in Palestine as were needed for Jewish life to flourish and held that sovereignty would need to be shared with the Palestinian Arabs on an equal basis. Ahad Ha'Am condemned early settlers' sacrifice of "the great ethical principles ... for the sake of which alone it is worthwhile to return and become a people in the land of our fathers"[3] as early as 1922, while Einstein suggested that

> The very nature of Judaism resists the idea of a Jewish State ... I am afraid of the inner damage Judaism will sustain ... We are no longer the Jews of the Maccabean period. A return to a nation in the political sense of the word would be equivalent to turning away from the spiritualization of our community which we owe to the genius of our prophets.[4]

Dr Williams talks of the danger of Israel *becoming* "a nation caught in the same traps of violence and self interest that afflict us all," but

---

[3] Quoted in Colin Chapman, *Whose Promised Land,* Lion 1983, p. 92.

[4] Quoted in Chapman, p. 93.

historians like Norman Finkelstein and Avi Shlaim have demonstrated that military force has always been part of Israel's *modus vivendi*, not something subsequently forced upon it.

The fundamental problem, of course, is that the homeland for those Jews who choose to become Israelis is founded on the dispossession of 750,000 Palestinian refugees who were displaced *as a matter of policy* by the State of Israel in 1948, and who are nowhere even mentioned by Dr Williams. Far from demonstrating any kind of hospitality to non- Jews, it was the explicit intention of the political Zionists from the beginning to expel them. As Tom Segev has shown, "the notion of population transfer was deeply rooted in Zionist ideology"[5] and Benny Morris has exposed the whole sorry story in *Correcting a Mistake- Jews and Arabs in Palestine/ Israel, 1936-1956.* Theodore Herzl himself notoriously claimed that

> We shall have to spirit the penniless population across the border ... Both the process of expropriation and the removal of the poor must be carried out discreetly and circumspectly,[6]

Ben Gurion was even blunter: "We will say to the Arabs: 'Move over'; if they resist, we will push them by force." Josef Weitz also advocated the "transfer" of the entire Palestinian population. The Zionist Committee on Population Transfer was founded in the 1930s, and by 1947 Ben Gurion was planning "the destruction of homes and the expulsion of the population." Forty years before "ethnic cleansing" entered common parlance, it was part of the vocabulary of Zionism; again and again Yigal Allon, for example, referred to "cleaning" Arab areas to the point where Chaim Weizmann could exult: "It was a miraculous clearing of the land: the miraculous simplification of Israel's task."[7]

Audeh Rantisi has described the cruelty and human misery that lay behind this robbery and murder of refugees, their deaths from exhaustion and thirst.[8] Dr Williams' concept of Israel's "moral essence" was subverted from the very beginning. Even Moshe Dayan acknowledged that, "There is not one single place built in this country which did not have a former

---

5 Tom Segev, *One Palestine Complete,* Abacus, 2000.

6 Quoted in Gary Burge, *Whose Land? Whose Promise?,* Paternoster, 2003, p. 37.

7 All quotes from Chapman, *op. cit.*

8 Audeh and Pat Rantisi, *Blessed are the Peacemakers: The Story of a Palestinian Christian,* Eagle Publishing Company, 2003.

Arab population,"[9] yet it is only *Jewish* homes that form the subject of Dr Williams' theological reflections. Why? It surely goes without saying that any theological justification of a Jewish *homeland* should examine the implications for the people who were made *homeless.* Many Jews would agree as, for example, Rabbi Benjamin, former editor of *Ner,* who stated: "We had no right to build a settlement and then to realise the ideal of Zionism with other people's property. To do this is robbery."[10]

Yet, despite the fact that population transfer remains part of the Israeli political discourse, and forms the ideology behind both house demolitions and the restrictions on Palestinian building, the exiled Palestinians appear to have been cleansed as effectively from this lecture as they have from the State of Israel.

The attempt to justify theologically political and historical events raises extraordinary difficulties, which are not in any sense addressed. Once theology embarks on consideration of particular episodes in history, it cannot pick and choose the bits of history that suit its agenda. So while one may sympathise with Dr Williams' impatience with Christians who wish to "dispense with the specifics of revelation", attempts to dispense with the specifics of history are equally doomed to failure.

For if we consider what Israel would need to do in order to become a "paradigm nation" in the way described, we can see what a gulf opens up between the theological concept and the political and historical reality. If the State of Israel were to demonstrate an "*explicit vocation to justice",* it would need to allow the Palestinian refugees to return, or compensate them justly; either withdraw from the West Bank, or open up the settlements to Palestinian as well as Jewish occupation; compensate justly those whose land has been confiscated, including the villages who have lost common land, or whose houses have been destroyed; abolish all discriminatory practices; ensure a fair distribution of natural resources; abolish child poverty and malnutrition; award full civil rights to those living in territory controlled by Israel. I doubt if Dr Williams would agree to those requirements because the result would almost certainly be the loss of a specifically Jewish state. The Biblical ideals of which he writes cannot be fulfilled without the loss of what he sees as the very condition needed to sustain it.

---

[9] Quoted in Feuerlicht, *The Fate of the Jews: A People Torn between Israeli Power and Jewish Ethics,* 1983 (Internet).

[10] Quoted in Chapman, p. 93.

This is really where the theological proposition breaks down. There is simply too wide a gulf between the theological *concept* and the historical *reality*. The one cannot become the other without losing its identity. This perhaps accounts for the reluctance to explore "how the modern political reality that is the State of Israel nurtures and honours the historical and theological Jewish identity that is dedicated to manifesting wisdom and justice for the whole community". The portrayal of the conflict between Israel and the Palestinians hardly addresses the fundamental issues. On the contrary, the language used almost turns history on its head.

His language suggests that the Palestinians are the active party in the violent confrontations that we all deplore, and that Israel's actions are in response to these: while Palestinians commit acts of "indiscriminate violence" and "indiscriminate slaughter", Israel is motivated by "defensiveness" and a "desperate anxiety over security" which lead it to "overwhelmingly violent reactions". No-one would guess from this the innate violence of the occupation of the West Bank or the active oppression of the inhabitants for at least the past 20 years: the unprovoked destruction of communities and of livelihoods; the denial of basics like water to the inhabitants; the theft of land.

It is in this context that Dr Williams almost appears to lose his moral focus. While suicide bombers slaughter "indiscriminately" (true), the manslaughter and murder of Palestinians are described as "collateral deaths". Dr Williams is a poet and a skilled user of language; he is well aware of linguistic connotations, and we must assume that he uses the word *collateral* with intent. In the period 1987-1998 (i.e. even before the current *intifada*), 1463 Palestinians were killed, as against 178 Israelis; 300 Palestinian children as against 4 Israeli children. Between 2001 and 2003, 2,400 Palestinians were killed, 85 percent of them civilians and 280 under age 15. Are we to understand that this is not *indiscriminate slaughter*? Anyone reading World Vision's report on the deaths of children in Israel and Palestine must be struck by the number of times Palestinian children are killed by shots to the head and chest. *Collateral* deaths? The Israeli public relations machine could not have done better.

Then Dr Williams utters one of his most breathtaking comments about non-Western Christians and Muslims: "Lying and hateful attitudes have sometimes been allowed into their talk about Jews and Judaism, even if this has not involved the depth of betrayal the westerner recognises in the Holocaust." There is no dispute about the first statement here, but to link by implication Arab demonisation of Israel and/or the Jews with the Holocaust is extraordinary—particularly when one considers who "betrayed" whom. For nowhere in Dr Williams' lecture is there any reference whatsoever to the *Nakba*. Palestinians must acknowledge the Holocaust, but the evils visited on *Palestinian* society by the *Israelis* must remain unspoken. It seems to amount to a refusal to acknowledge, as Edward Said has pointed out, that "what binds us together is a common history of persecution, which must be shown not to be the exclusive possession of the Jewish people".[11]

The "lying and hateful attitudes", like all racist propaganda, should be both confronted and condemned, but such faults do not all lie on one side. Racism is evil, however expressed, but why does Dr Williams not similarly confront those Jewish communities where, according to Marc Ellis, "Images of the unwashed, the ignorant and the terrorist are repeated *ad nauseam*"?[12]

Where does Dr Williams confront the extremist Jewish Israeli attitudes which lead to the equating of the Palestinians with the Amalekites, or the kind of mentality which leads to Israeli soldiers and settlers' children treating Palestinians as *untermenschen;* to the looting and destruction of Arab-owned homes and businesses; to the smearing of excrement on Palestinian possessions; to the graffiti proclaiming "Death to the Arabs", or the behaviour of those Israelis who, after the Arab Mayor of Nablus lost both legs in an assassination attempt by Jewish Israeli terrorists, roasted cats and offered their meat to passers by as "shish kebab from the legs of the Arab mayor"? Why does Dr Williams not comment on the deliberate refusal to issue gas masks to Palestinians during the Gulf War? Rabbi Ginsberg's assertion (1985) that "a Jew and a goy are not the same"[13] is reflected in the persistent failure to prosecute Jewish Israeli crimes against Palestinians, but one looks in vain in the Archbishop's remarks for any awareness of the racist interpretations of the Pentateuch and the Talmud voiced by some Orthodox Jews within and outside Israel.

But it is with the reference to the supposed "programme to humiliate and destroy Israel" that we enter Looking Glass World. In what

---

[11] Quoted in Chapman, p. 114.

[12] Quoted in Shahak, *Jewish, History, Jewish Religion,* Pluto Press, 1994, p. 112.

[13] C.f. Shahak, *op. cit.*

way has Israel ever been "humiliated" by Palestinians, and how can such a militarily powerful nation, supported almost unconditionally by the one Superpower, be destroyed? On the other hand, Dr Williams ignores the *daily* humiliation of Palestinians within Israel and the West Bank; the degrading treatment meted out to Palestinians at checkpoints and Tel Aviv airport; the insults and violent physical abuse meted out to Palestinian parents in front of their children - this in a society which has traditionally honoured elders. Settlers are allowed to harass and attack Palestinians with impunity, all too frequently with the support of the army. He fails to mention the deliberate destruction of the agricultural basis of Palestinian communities and of the ways that this is leading not only to disastrous poverty, but also to moral and cultural disintegration. Young men cannot marry because they have no means of supporting their families; children, on whose behalf Dr Williams is so eloquent in the West, are traumatised and have their childhoods destroyed. What prevents Dr Williams from bearing witness to the *actual* destruction of a society?

His reluctance to confront Jewish and Israeli racism and aggression contrasts starkly with the courage of the Christian Peacemakers Team. Arthur G. Gish, while living by the principles of non-violence, is willing to confront the racism, oppression and dehumanisation that he has seen in Hebron and call it by its proper name: evil. He provides one of the most moving illustrations of the theme of hospitality it is possible to imagine: a Palestinian family in Hebron bringing coffee for the Israeli soldiers under whom they have suffered.[14]

Rosemary Radford Ruether comments in *A Tale of two Books* that "Western Christians who want to stay in official 'ecumenical' relations with Jews avoid talking about Palestinians, indeed even avoid learning anything about them, lest they transgress the boundaries of this dialogue and even be marginalized and vilified".[15] While this is not true of Dr Williams (His comments on the Wall led to his being vilified by at least one prominent British Jewish writer.), his avoidance of Palestinian issues in this lecture does beg the question of how much he really wants to know, or how afraid he is of breaking what Marc Ellis calls "the ecumenical deal".[16] Or is it that Dr Williams' commitment to his own theological

---

[14] Arthur G. Gish, *Hebron Journal*, Herald Press, 2001.

[15] Rosemary Radford Ruether, *A Tale of Two Books* in *They Came and They Saw*, ed. Michael Prior, Melisende, 2000, p. 73.

[16] C.f. Ellis, *Out of the Ashes*, Pluto Press, 2002.

schema is so great that he cannot explore the historical and political realities that might modify or even fracture it?

The "ruthless intellectual honesty which will break every barrier of emotionalism, sentiment, tradition and nationality,"[17] which, as Denys Baly notes, is often frustratingly missing on both sides of this conflict, is not to be found in a theology which is so selective in its frame of reference. In contrast, both Gary Burge and Naim Ateek are far more rigorous in their examination of the implications of the Biblical texts for Israel today. Dr Williams' apparent fear of calling Israel to account leads to the omission of some startlingly obvious points: the ownership of the land, for example. It is, as he says "'leased' to the people for their use (Lev. 25)", but then ignores the wholly different interpretation of "ownership" promulgated by the majority of Orthodox rabbis in Israel, an interpretation which has led, as Naim Ateek[18] has pointed out, to the story of Naboth's Vineyard being repeated thousands of times in the modern state and the West Bank. Significantly, Naboth's Vineyard is one of the stories omitted from this lecture.

Dr Williams asks how we can show a commitment to Israel that will "cost" something; it is fair, therefore, to ask Dr Williams and Lambeth Palace for commitments that will "cost". One costly commitment might be more overt support for Palestinian Christians, a marginalized and rapidly declining group, barely recognised as Christians by many visitors to Israel/Palestine, and barely acknowledged in this lecture, which is written almost entirely from a Western standpoint. Secondly, the "cost" of a more rigorous inquiry into the relationship between a theological concept and the actual historical and political reality might be the modification of some dearly held beliefs. No "theology of liberation" for the Holy Land can work unless it takes full account of the Palestinian experience, and it is important to remember that Palestinians have already paid the cost of Westerners' guilt.

---

[17] Quoted in Chapman, p. 198.

[18] Naim Ateek, *Justice and Only Justice,* Orbis, 1989.